NCAER

INDIA
POLICY FORUM

VOLUME 2   2005|06

EDITED BY
Suman Bery
Barry Bosworth
Arvind Panagariya

NATIONAL COUNCIL OF APPLIED
ECONOMIC RESEARCH
New Delhi

BROOKINGS INSTITUTION
Washington, D.C.

SAGE Publications
New Delhi / Thousand Oaks / London

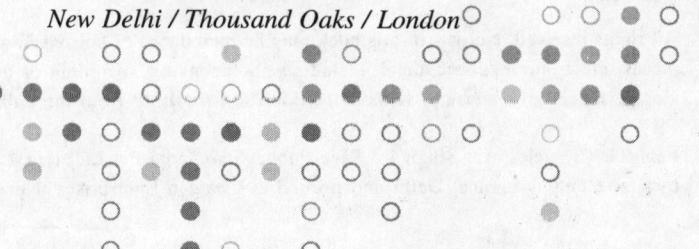

Copyright © 2006
BROOKINGS INSTITUTION
AND
NATIONAL COUNCIL OF APPLIED ECONOMIC RESEARCH

First published in 2006 by

 Sage Publications India Pvt Ltd
B1 / I1, Mohan Cooperative Industrial Area
Mathura Road
New Delhi 110 044
www.indiasage.com

Sage Publications Inc
2455 Teller Road
Thousand Oaks, California 91320

Sage Publications Ltd
1 Oliver's Yard, 55 City Road
London EC1Y 1SP

Second Printing 2007

Library of Congress Serial Publication Data applied for

ISSN: 0973-4805
ISBN: 10: 0-7619-3540-1 (PB)   10: 81-7829-706-X (India-PB)
      13: 978-0-7619-3540-7 (PB)   13: 978-81-7829-706-4 (India-PB)

Published by Tejeshwar Singh for Sage Publications India Pvt Ltd, typeset in 10.5/13 Times by Star Compugraphics, Delhi and printed at Chaman Enterprises, New Delhi.

INDIA POLICY FORUM 2005|06

VOLUME 2

PURPOSE

India Policy Forum 2005–06 comprises papers and highlights of the discussions from the second India Policy Forum (IPF) conference, held July 25–26, 2005, in New Delhi. IPF is a joint venture of the Brookings Institution and the National Council of Applied Economic Research (NCAER) that examines India's reforms and economic transition using policy relevant empirical research. The Editors acknowledge the generous support of the State Bank of India, Tata Sons, Citigroup, and HDFC Ltd.

The objective of the IPF is to generate theoretically rigorous, empirically informed research on important current and unfolding issues of Indian economic policy. A panel of established researchers has agreed to support this initiative for an initial period of three years. Overall guidance is being provided by a distinguished international advisory panel.

Papers appear in this publication after presentation and discussion at a yearly conference in New Delhi. During discussions at the conference, the authors obtain helpful comments and criticism about various aspects of their papers. These comments are reflected in the journal as discussants' comments. The papers, however, are finally the authors' products and do not imply any agreement by those attending the conference or providing financial support. Nor do any materials in this journal necessarily represent the views of the staff members or officers of the NCAER and the Brookings Institution.

CORRESPONDENCE

Correspondence regarding papers in this issue should be addressed to the authors. Manuscripts are not accepted for review because this journal is devoted exclusively to invited contributions.

Editors' Summary

This is the second volume of the *India Policy Forum*. The journal is jointly promoted by the National Council for Applied Economic Research (NCAER) in New Delhi and the Brookings Institution in Washington, D.C., with the objective of presenting high-quality empirical research on the major economic policy issues that confront contemporary India. The forum is supported by a distinguished advisory panel and a group of active researchers who participate in the review and discussion process and offer suggestions to the editors and the authors. Our objective is to make the policy discussion accessible to a broad nonspecialist audience inside and outside India. We also hope that it will assist in the development of a global network of scholars interested in India's economic transformation.

The five individual papers included in this volume were selected by the editors and presented at a conference in Delhi on July 25–26, 2005. In addition to the working sessions, John Williamson, a member of the advisory panel, gave a public address on the topic "What Follows the Era of the USA as the World's Growth Engine?" The papers focus on several issues of great relevance to India's current economic situation. The first three papers involve issues of government fiscal and monetary policy: the implications of a large and sustained fiscal budget deficit, India's experience with tax reform, and the relevance of the inflation-targeting framework for Indian monetary policy. The fourth paper provides a detailed review of developments in labor markets and the distribution of income since the initiation of large-scale economic reforms in 1991. The last paper provides a critical assessment of policies aimed at promoting universal access to telecommunications services.

In their paper, Willem Buiter and Urjit Patel explore the mechanisms by which India's continuing high fiscal deficits (at both the federal and state levels) affect the sustainable growth of the economy. In their view, the abuse of a financial system heavily dominated by the government represents a key channel by which the fiscal position influences economic growth and vulnerability; accordingly, their paper also extends to an examination of the financial system.

Following a crisis in 1991, India has witnessed a turnaround on many indicators of macroeconomic performance. It has transited from an onerous trade regime to a market-friendly system encompassing both trade and current payments. The sum of external current payments and receipts as a ratio to gross domestic product (GDP) has doubled from about 19 percent in 1990–91 to around 40 percent currently. There has also been some liberalization of cross-border capital account transactions, although significant constraints remain in place on cross-border intertemporal trade and risk trading.

Although average annual real GDP growth over the postreform period has been only modestly higher than in the previous decade (6.2 percent from 1992–93 to 2004–05 compared with 5.7 percent from 1981–82 to 1990–91), India continues to be one of the fastest-growing economies in the world. India's balance of payments has been strong and inflation has been moderate.

After a sharp initial adjustment in the early 1990s, India's net public debt has risen steadily as a share of GDP, although at about 70 percent of GDP, it remains below the levels recorded at the time of the 1991 crisis. Following custom, Buiter and Patel consolidate the central bank into these estimates, but not the publicly owned commercial banks, on the grounds that to do so would be to assume that the (implicit) guarantee of liabilities in such banks is certain to be called. In addition to public debt of this magnitude, recognized and explicit guarantees in 2003 amounted to a further 11.3 percent of GDP.

By the standard of most emerging markets, including several that have experienced crisis, India's public and publicly guaranteed debt is very high. The composition of this debt has changed significantly in the fifteen years since the crisis of 1991. Net external debt has declined sharply, shifting the burden of public debt onto the domestic market. This domestic debt is rupee-denominated. In addition, India continues to maintain selective (discretionary) capital controls, particularly those that keep arbitrage-type flows (external borrowing by domestic financial intermediaries, investment by foreign institutional investors in fixed-income securities, and short-term borrowing by practically anyone) in check. While India faced a combined internal (fiscal) and external (foreign exchange) transfer problem during the years leading up to the crisis of 1991, the weakening of the fiscal position since the late 1990s represents an exclusively internal resource transfer problem.

Given repeated and costly crises in several emerging markets associated with possible public debt default, Buiter and Patel first conduct formal fiscal sustainability tests, revisiting an analysis they undertook a decade earlier. Although their fiscal sustainability tests are not conclusive, they find that government solvency may not be a pressing issue at this juncture. The reason India has been able to remain solvent despite the sustained fiscal deficits of the past twenty years is the combination of fast GDP growth and financial repression.

They note that globally, the level of risk-free interest rates at all maturities and credit-risk spreads are extraordinarily low at present. Continuation of the pattern of recent years—a steady increase in the debt–GDP ratio—will sooner or later raise the public debt to unsustainable levels. Political pressure to enhance government expenditure on social sectors and improve public (infrastructure or utility) services has increased in the aftermath of the 2004 general election.

Buiter and Patel then examine two potential channels for the impact of the government on the quantity and quality of capital formation in India. The first is financial crowding out—the negative effect of public borrowing on aggregate (private and public) saving. The second is the effect of government institutions, policies, actions, and interventions, including public ownership, regulation, taxes, subsidies, and other forms of public influence on private savers, private investors, and the financial markets and institutions that intermediate between them. A simple growth accounting framework is constructed to compare India's investment efficiency with that of selected large countries. They find Indian investment inefficiency to be relatively high, China's to be even higher.

Across the world, from the European Union's (ill-fated) Stability and Growth Pact to the United Kingdom's Golden Rule and Sustainable Investment Rule, there have been attempts to bind governments to fiscal rectitude through formal legal or constitutional devices. In September 1994 an agreement was reached between the Reserve Bank of India and the Central Exchequer to phase out ad hoc treasury bills, which hitherto facilitated automatic monetization of the budget deficit. The Indian Parliament, in August 2003, voted for the Fiscal Responsibility and Budget Management Act (FRBMA), which required that the central government's fiscal deficit not exceed 3 percent of GDP and that the deficit on the revenue (current) account be eliminated.

The fiscal rules that India has embraced—perhaps in recognition of the serious systemic inefficiency that the fiscal stance has engendered—are evaluated. The requirement that the revenue budget be in balance or surplus is very likely to be the binding constraint on the central government. Even if the gross investment version of the golden rule (limiting debt issues to capital financing) is the operative one, the Indian central government's gross capital formation program amounted to no more than 1.5 percent of GDP in 2003–04. Net central government capital formation is even less than that and may well be negative in years that economic depreciation is high. The authors judge that a great deal of current expenditure will be reclassified as capital expenditure if the golden rule were ever to be enforced seriously. Regarding the likelihood of the rules being enforced, they point to the absence of any features of the FRBMA that compel governments to act counter-cyclically during periods of above-normal economic activity or (as in India during these past three to four years) exceptionally low interest rates. Furthermore, the fiscal rules under the FRBMA do not address the key distortions imposed by the Indian state on the private sector through financial repression, misguided regulations, and inefficient ownership and incentive structures.

Tax reform has been a major component of the economic reform agenda in India during the last twenty years. In their contribution on this subject, Govinda Rao and Kavita Rao offer a comprehensive treatment of the evolution of the direct and indirect taxes in India, their shortcomings relative to an ideal tax system, the reforms undertaken so far, and their future course. They note that according to the theory of optimal taxation, revenue-raising taxes should consist exclusively of consumption taxes with the rates of taxation being dependent on various demand elasticities. In turn, the ideal consumption tax can be mimicked by a value-added tax (VAT) that taxes output at the desired rate but rebates the tax paid on the inputs, thereby only taxing the extra value added at each stage of production. In practice, the information on the demand elasticities required to implement the optimal VAT is rarely available. Moreover, its variegated structure is administratively complex, gives rise to tax disputes and tax evasion, and results in lobbying pressures becoming the main determinants of the tax structure. Therefore, a system characterized by greater uniformity in tax rates has gained popularity with policy analysts and policymakers in recent years.

Since the 1950s, India has relied on both direct and indirect taxes to raise revenue. Direct taxes include both the personal income tax and corporate profit tax. Indirect taxes include domestic commodity taxation and custom duties. Domestic commodity taxation initially took the form of excise duties that taxed output up to the manufacturing stage with no tax rebates on inputs and the sales tax by the states. In recent years, a modified value added tax (MODVAT) that rebates the tax paid on inputs at each stage of production up to the manufacturing stage has progressively replaced the excise tax. Custom duty revenues have principally been a by-product of import protection, and their share in total revenue increased especially rapidly in the 1980s when the government decided to replace the previous system of import quotas with enhanced input tariff rates. With the decline in protection after 1990, the importance of this source of revenue has been declining.

The reforms during the last two decades have focused on both the design as well as the administration of taxes. Marginal tax rates on personal income, which had reached near 100 percent levels in the early 1970s, have now been brought down to around 30 percent (with occasional surcharges). Simultaneously, the number of tax slabs has been reduced to three, and some progress has also been made toward eliminating numerous ad hoc exemptions. Similar steps have been taken in the area of corporate taxation.

The big push in the area of domestic commodity taxation has been toward the development of a genuine VAT and unification of the tax rates. Considerable success has been achieved in both tasks. Custom duties have been brought down substantially, and their dispersion has been considerably reduced. Improvement in tax administration has been more pronounced in direct than indirect taxation.

Rao and Rao observe that the ratio of personal income tax to GDP has increased from 2.1 percent in 1985–86 to 4.3 percent in 2004–05. Reductions in indirect tax revenues as a proportion of GDP have more than offset this gain, however. Central government domestic indirect tax collection declined by 1.6 percentage points and the custom duty collection by 1.8 percentage points over the same period.

It is tempting to argue that the increase in the income tax–GDP ratio represents the operation of the so-called Laffer curve whereby reduced rates by themselves lead to increased revenue. Rao and Rao offer evidence to the contrary, however, and argue that the increase in the revenues from the personal income tax resulted from a more rapid growth of the organized industrial sector that is covered by the tax net; deepening of the financial sector, which makes transactions easier to track; and administrative measures including the spread of tax deduction at source.

Rao and Rao also find that contrary to suggestions in some of the recent literature, personal income tax reform has resulted in increased equity. Granted, the reduction in the dispersion of effective tax rates has led to the richest individuals being subject to lower tax rates. But the reform has also brought into the tax net many relatively rich individuals who previously did not pay taxes. This is reflected in a significant increase in the number of income tax payers and the doubling of revenues from the personal income tax.

Despite substantial rationalization of various components of the tax system, indirect tax revenues remain highly concentrated in terms of commodities. Just five groups of commodities—petroleum products, chemicals, basic metals, transport vehicles, and electrical and electronic goods—contribute 75 percent of the total central domestic commodity tax revenue.

Petroleum products alone, which have tripled their share over a thirteen-year period, contribute over 40 percent. Almost 60 percent of custom duty is collected from just three commodity groups: machinery (26.6 percent), petroleum products (21 percent), and chemicals (11 percent). This concentration exceeds the concentration of output or of imports across commodities.

Rao and Rao recommend further rationalization of central taxes through a reduction in the number of tax rates and the elimination of exemptions. In the area of corporation tax, they argue in favor of reducing the depreciation allowance to more realistic levels. They also point to a need for aligning the corporate profit tax rate with the highest marginal tax rate on personal income tax. With regard to import duties, the authors recommend a minimum tariff of 5 percent on all imports as a step toward harmonizing duty rates across commodities.

In the area of domestic commodity taxation, the goal must be a single, unified goods and services tax. The achievement of this goal has several components. All specific duties must be converted into ad valorem rates and the tax on services must be widened substantially. The sales tax must be harmonized across states and, for collection purposes, integrated with the central VAT, which should eventually cover all goods and services. This unification will also allow the adoption of the destination-based sales tax on all interstate trade. Keeping in view revenue needs, Rao and Rao recommend that the total burden of taxation on goods and services should be 20 percent. Of this, 8 percent should be borne by the center and 12 percent by the states.

The state of tax administration, resulting partially from the virtual absence of data on both direct and indirect taxes, has been a major reason for low levels and high costs of compliance. The absence of information has also led to the evolution of a compliance system in which tax payments are negotiated between the payer and the government. The recent initiatives for administrative reform that include the development of a computerized information system and procedural changes such as expanded coverage of tax deduction at source and systematized audit procedures have alleviated this problem to some degree. Within direct taxes, efforts include outsourcing of issue of permanent account numbers, a tax information network established by the National Securities Depository Limited with special focus on tax deductions at the source; and the Online Tax Accounting System. Within indirect taxes, a few examples of new information systems are the customs e-commerce gateway, known as ICEGATE, and the Customs Electronic Data Interchange system. Further initiatives are under way, including a systematic approach to compiling relevant data from a variety of relevant sources. Rao and Rao believe that, as a part of this initiative, it is critical that mechanisms be set up for data sharing between direct and indirect tax authorities, as well as between central and state tax authorities.

Inflation targeting has emerged as one of the most significant developments in the theory and practice of monetary policy. Disenchantment with the outcomes of the activist monetary policies of the 1970s and 1980s led many economists and policymakers to advocate a simplified and more rules-based approach to monetary policy, one in which attaining and sustaining price stability is given a clear priority. Many countries, however, have experienced difficulties in attempting to use the growth in monetary aggregates or the exchange rate as a guide to such a policy. An inflation-targeting framework (ITF), which consists of setting an inflation target and aligning monetary policy to ensure its attainment in a transparent and accountable manner, is increasingly advocated as a best-practice approach to controlling inflation.

In the long run, the inflation rate is the only outcome that monetary policy can influence. However, because there is a short-run cost of disinflation, a trade-off between inflation and unemployment, the optimum path of future inflation implies a gradual return to the desired rate. At the heart of the ITF is a specific view of the inflation-generating process as a largely demand-determined phenomenon, a conviction that the most efficient way of dealing with inflation is through an interest rate rule, and the belief that the public's inflation expectations can be managed. From this follows the prescription that the central bank, as the custodian of interest-rate policy, should play a dedicated and dominant role in promoting the inflation objective. Initially, inflation targeting was adopted by several industrial countries, but it has recently spread to some emerging markets. At present, much of the focus on monetary policy is on credit growth, not interest rates. Is the ITF practical in the absence of a large role for market-determined interest rates?

In their paper, Sheetal Chand and Kanhaiya Singh ask whether such a framework might be applicable to developing economies. In particular, is the ITF suitable for guiding the monetary policy of India? Earlier discussions focused on the difficulties that developing countries would have in adopting a policy rule that assigns absolute priority to the control of inflation. They often have less-developed financial institutions (requiring a more nurturing approach by the central bank), an aversion to large exchange rate fluctuations, or a need to be accommodative of some changes in fiscal policy. Widespread public knowledge of these constraints implies that a policy based on inflation targeting would lack credibility.

Chand and Singh examine the issue from a different perspective, however, arguing that the inflation process in India differs in significant respects from that commonly assumed to hold for the industrial economies. The paper first tests a standard formulation of the ITF, relying on a paper by Lars Svensson. This formulation explicitly incorporates a short-run trade-off between inflation and the deviation of output from full employment (a Phillips-curve type relationship). In their tests of the Indian experience from 1970–71 to 2002–03, Chand and Singh find that the output gap is not a significant determinant of inflation. Thus, they argue that Svensson's derivation of the optimal policy rule is not satisfactory in the Indian context.

However, this does not necessarily imply that demand factors have negligible effects on inflation. The authors develop an alternative specification that defines excess demand as the difference between the nominal GDP growth rate and the growth rate of potential output valued at the preceding year's rate of inflation. They find that this alternative version accords better with conditions in India. However, the demand-side effects are supplemented by a substantial role for variations in input prices. In the final model, the coefficients on the measures of demand conditions indicate some effect, but the dominant role is that of supply-side factors.

The authors interpret the large role for supply-side shocks in the generation of inflation as arguing against reliance on the ITF approach. In addition, the nominal interest rate appears to be a less powerful instrument with which to influence the inflation rate. They are also concerned about the potential for undesirable side effects that might result from large variations in interest rates, such as large and persistent swings in exchange rates or asset values.

Chand and Singh favor a more balanced approach that employs both monetary and fiscal policy as instruments to control inflation and that is reflective of supply-side phenomenon. The more active role for fiscal policy is justified by their finding of a shorter transmission lag between an expenditure stimulus and the inflation rate than is typical for the advanced countries. However, they agree that more research is needed to establish fully the role that fiscal policy should play.

Within the monetary policy sphere, they advocate the use of multiple instruments rather than relying solely on interest rates. Examples would be adjustments in liquidity requirements to regulate the supply of credit that finances investment expenditures and direct controls on capital inflows. They perceive these measures as having fewer adverse effects on asset valuations. With regard to interest rate policy, the Reserve Bank of India might seek to maintain a desired real interest rate, with the nominal interest rate being adjusted whenever the underlying inflation rate deviates from target. From time to time, shifts in liquidity preference will result in asset transactions that push interest rates above or below the target long-term level.

Accommodating liquidity preference shifts through appropriate open market operations would help keep interest rates stable. All this implies that it may be more prudent and welfare enhancing for India to pursue a strategy other than the standard ITF to control inflation.

The performance of the Indian economy following the initiation of an economic reform program in 1991 has been a subject of intense intellectual debate. There are sharp differences of view on whether the economic situation of Indian workers improved in the postreform years. Some commentators characterize the postreform period as a largely jobless expansion with a marked slowing of real wage growth, particularly in rural areas.

Surjit Bhalla and Tirthatanmoy Das undertake a detailed review of the available survey data on employment, unemployment, agricultural wages, and income inequality over the past thirty years to examine several of these controversial propositions. Much of the evaluation of the effects of the economic reforms is confounded by the low frequency of detailed survey data on the economic situation of Indian workers. The discussion has centered on the results from large-scale quinquennial surveys of their employment status conducted in 1983, 1987–88, 1993–94, and 1999–2000. Bhalla and Das construct a more expansive time series of available data by including two surveys from the 1970s and twelve smaller annual surveys from the 1980s and 1990s. The major advantage of the additional data is that it allows a better alignment of the data on labor market conditions with the initiation of the reforms in 1991. Because 1991 was also a year of economic crisis in India, the precise dating of the end of the prereform period and the beginning of the reform era plays a crucial role.

On the employment front, Bhalla and Das conclude that employment growth slowed between 1991 and 2003 to 1.7 percent a year, compared with a 2.6 percent rate in the 1983–91 period. They attribute a large portion of the slowdown during the 1990s to a slower rate of growth of the population of labor force age and to a decline in the labor force participation rate related in part to a rise in the proportion of persons who remained out of the labor force while enrolled in educational institutions. They argue that the slow employment growth of the 1990s is not therefore a reflection of weak labor market conditions.

Labor market surveys in India produce three alternative measures of employment status. First, usual status classifies individuals among employed, unemployed, and not in the workforce on the basis of the principal activity status of the individuals over the prior 365 days. Current weekly status follows international conventions of classifying those who worked at least one hour in the prior week as employed, and distinguishing between unemployed and out of the workforce on the basis of whether they were available for work in the prior week. A third concept of "current daily status" is also determined in the quinquennial surveys. Individuals are asked to report their activities over a seven-day period and to distinguish half days in determining the activity status. Those who work four or more hours are considered employed for the full day, and one to four hours is considered a half day. Similarly, persons who did not work but were available for four or more hours are considered to be unemployed for the full day, and those who were available for one to four hours are reported as unemployed for half a day.

Bhalla and Das point to a general perception that unemployment has increased in the postreform years as the primary rationale for a new government program aimed at providing job guarantees for rural families. They argue, however, that the measures of unemployment based on usual and weekly status show significantly lower rates of unemployment in the years after 1991 relative to the experience of the 1970s and 1980s. This conclusion also accords with their earlier interpretation that the slowing of employment growth in the 1990s was not indicative of a weak labor market. They also point out that the educational level of the unemployed is high; this is consistent with a view that much of the unemployment is the result of the more skilled members of the workforce spending longer in search of better job matches.

Third, the authors examine the patterns of real wage change in the postreform era. That analysis is faced with a severe shortage of high frequency surveys of wage developments. The quinquennial surveys provide the only information on economywide wages, and annual measures are available only for agricultural wages. The quinquennial surveys do suggest an acceleration of real wage growth after 1993, from an annual rate of 2.5 percent between 1983 and 1993–94 to 4.5 percent in the period of 1993–93 to 1999–2000. That pattern is apparent in the wage data for both urban and rural workers.

Bhalla and Das undertake a more detailed analysis of the annual data on agricultural worker wages, a subgroup of the rural workforce. This is also the group for which wage growth is alleged to have slowed sharply after the introduction of economic reforms in 1991. They compare two basic measures: the Survey of Agricultural Wages in India (AWI), and wage data from a lesser-used Survey on the Cost of Cultivation (CoC) of major crops. The AWI survey was terminated after 1999–2000 and the last available year for the CoC is 2000–01. They use a new survey to extend the other wage measures through 2004–05. The measures of real wage growth do grow at different rates over some subperiods and the year-to-year changes are erratic; but neither the AWI not the CoC measure supports the notion of significant deceleration of real wage growth after 1991.

Finally, the trend in income inequality during the 1990s is a subject that has generated great controversy among the group of researchers who have written on the subject. The analysis is largely limited to a comparison of data from the quinquennial surveys, and it is complicated by some changes in the survey methodology. Bhalla and Das believe that there may have been some increase in inequality after 1993–94 but that the change is small and largely limited to a widening of inequality at the very top of the distribution. It is also difficult to match the timing of the change with the introduction of economic reforms. In summary, Bhalla and Das maintain that the frequent assertion that the economic reforms have not helped Indian workers is not supported by the data.

Though telecommunications reform in India began in the 1980s, it achieved at best limited success in the initial decade. Beginning in the early 1990s, technological change and new government policies exhibited greater promise, with dramatic gains made in the quality of service as well as its availability in the new millennium. Telecommunications reforms represent a major success of the economic reforms in India in the last decade. Unsurprisingly, however, telecommunications access has increased more rapidly for wealthy and urban consumers than for poor and rural consumers. To address this gap, India has adopted so-called "universal service" policies, especially targeting rural villages. The philosophy behind the desire to spread the service to all is that certain services, such as electricity, water, and telecommunications, should be available to all.

In their paper, Roger Noll and Scott Wallsten remind us that universal service policies are typically justified on three grounds. First, the presence of economies of scale may lead to the underprovision of the service. At best, the firm will price the service at the average cost, which is higher than the marginal cost when scale economies are present. If, in addition, the market turns imperfectly competitive due to a single supplier or a handful of suppliers, the service may be further undersupplied. Second, the government may view some services as "merit goods" that everyone should have, regardless of their willingness to pay. Finally, politics or regional development goals may induce government to transfer resources to rural or low-income constituents.

The "merit good" argument is easier to justify for universal access to some types of infrastructure than to others. Water and sewerage, for example, involve large health externalities, and bringing these services to everyone can yield large social benefits. The provision of universal telecommunications service is more difficult to justify along these lines. Given the presence of a large proportion of the poor in the population, it can be argued that the government revenues are better spent on direct poverty alleviation programs. The issue of economies of scale points to the need for regulatory measures rather than universal service. It is true that the scale economy may take the form of an externality in the sense that the addition of new customers may lower the cost of supplying the service to the existing customers. But the firms, which are capable of figuring cost at various levels of supply, can readily internalize such externalities. Nevertheless, perhaps because of its political appeal, most countries in the world pursue the goal of universal access to telecommunications services in some form.

Noll and Wallsten also argue that the case for subsidizing the incumbent wire-line carrier, whether privatized or state-owned, to achieve the universal service objective is weak since it offers relatively little service in the poor areas in the initial equilibrium. In the era of state-owned monopolies, the telecom provider had little incentive to invest in telecommunications services in general, as witnessed by the long waiting period to obtain connections and the poor quality of service following installation. Telephone penetration and usage were low, even considering developing countries' low incomes, with service to poor and rural areas virtually absent.

India's first official universal service program was introduced as a part of the 1994 National Telecom Policy. That policy set the goal of providing certain "basic telecom services at affordable and reasonable prices" to all citizens. This policy was revised under the New Telecom Policy of 1999, which made the provision of telecom services in remote rural areas a higher priority and set certain specific goals to be achieved by 2002. When those goals were not met, the Department of Telecommunications adopted two objectives: providing public telephones in villages and providing household telephones in rural areas. The first objective was given higher priority.

A universal service fund was created based on the implicit assumption that competition among private providers would not generate adequate service in rural areas. The government also took the view that it could minimize the magnitude of the subsidy necessary to provide universal service by opting for only one firm in any given area. The government finances the subsidy through two taxes. The first, the universal service levy, which goes into the Universal Service Fund (USF), is a tax of 5 percent of adjusted gross revenues on all telecommunications providers except "pure value added service providers" such as Internet service providers. The second includes access deficit charges (ADCs), which are incorporated into interconnection charges and are paid directly to the incumbent state-owned enterprise Bharat Sanchar Nigam Limited (BSNL) to compensate it for providing below-cost service in rural areas.

The USF is intended to reimburse the net cost (total cost minus revenues) of providing rural telecom service. Telecommunications firms bid for subsidies to be received in return for providing service in rural areas in an auction. The firm bidding the lowest subsidy, subject to the bid being no higher than a benchmark established by information from the incumbent wire-line monopoly, is eligible to be reimbursed that amount from the fund. Any firm with a license to provide basic or cellular service in the relevant service area is eligible to bid. The winner receives a subsidy for seven years, subject to review after three years.

In nearly all service areas, only one firm bid: the incumbent BSNL. Not surprisingly, the BSNL bid exactly the benchmark amount, which was the maximum subsidy the government was prepared to provide. The failure to create genuine competition for rural public service arose from three problems.

First, the benchmark subsidy was based on data provided by BSNL, whose accounts are aggregated in a way that makes it impossible to separate costs of its various operations. Second, BSNL receives nearly all of the ADC cross-subsidies. The incumbent has potential gains from manipulating how cost information is aggregated across service categories and across high-cost and low-cost areas, because these data not only determine the benchmark subsidy, but also the magnitude of the net deficit for all local access service. Allocating some ambiguous cost elements to subsidized areas can increase both the public telephone subsidy and the ADC subsidy. Third, the auction allowed only basic service operators already providing rural service in the area to bid. Given the existing service was in any case quite limited, there was no advantage to choosing the provider from among the existing operators. Therefore, the exclusion of the firms not already present had detrimental effect on new entry into rural services commensurate advantage of choosing an existing operator.

ADCs, the second major source of universal service, are paid by private entrants to the incumbent based on the premise that basic access providers face unprofitable social service obligations and should therefore be compensated for them by entrants who are free to seek out profitable customers. The assumption underlying the expectation of these losses is that regulated price ceilings on basic monthly access service charges applying to a large number of customers are below the cost of service.

The ADC fee structure is highly inefficient for two reasons. First, the price elasticity of demand is much greater for usage than for access. Hence, taxing usage to finance access substantially distorts the former for the relatively small gain in the latter. Second, applying the tax to only some calls creates another distortion. The regulatory authority had intended to impose ADC charges for five years and has recently reduced the fee so that it now represents about 10 percent of the sector's revenue rather than 30 percent when it was first introduced

Noll and Wallsten argue that India's universal service policies may unfortunately have had the unintended consequences of deterring investment in precisely the areas they had hoped to target. The subsidies discourage competition, and the most efficient operators are taxed to support the least efficient operator. Fortunately, most of the telecommunications market in India is sufficiently competitive and dynamic that growth may not been hampered significantly by these inefficient policies. Nonetheless, because telecommunications is such an important industry, it is crucial to minimize inefficiencies. Noll and Wallsten conclude that India's best approach for achieving universal service is to ensure that its policies promote competition and do not favor any single firm over another.

WILLEM H. BUITER
European Institute,
London School of Economics and Political Science

URJIT R. PATEL
Infrastructure Development Finance Company Limited

Excessive Budget Deficits, a Government-Abused Financial System, and Fiscal Rules

C apital formation is a key driver of the growth of potential output. With India's continuing widespread capital controls and persistently small inward foreign direct investment, the volume of capital formation in the country is constrained by domestic saving. Depressed by the continuing large public sector deficits, the national saving rate in India (the sum of the saving rates of households, enterprises and the state) is much below China's saving rate of nearly 40 percent of gross domestic product (GDP). Even the extant Indian saving rate should be able to support a higher growth rate than has been achieved thus far. An important reason it does not is that the intermediation of savings, by the formal financial system, into domestic capital formation is inefficient.

Since its external crisis of the early 1990s, India has witnessed a turn-around on most indicators of macroeconomic performance. The process of economic reform, including widespread general liberalization and reduction in protectionism, launched in 1991 and steadily pursued thereafter, has yielded positive results by eliminating some longstanding structural rigidities and has thus created potential for higher growth. During that period India made the transition from an onerous trade regime to a market-friendly system encompassing both trade and current payments—IMF Article 8 compliance was at last achieved. There also was some liberalization of cross-border

We would like to thank Suman Bery for detailed and comprehensive comments on an earlier version of this paper. We are also indebted to Abhijit Banerjee, Barry Bosworth, Kenneth Kletzer, Robert Lawrence, and Indira Rajaraman. The views expressed in the paper are those of the authors and not necessarily of the institutions with which they are affiliated.

1

capital account transactions, although significant constraints remain in place on cross-border intertemporal trade and cross-border risk trading.

Average annual real growth in GDP since the 1991 crisis has been only modestly higher than in the previous decade (6.2 percent over 1992–93 to 2004–05 compared with 5.7 percent over 1981–82 to 1990–91). Yet India continues to be one of the fastest growing economies in the world. The most far-reaching change has been its integration with the global market place after four decades of inward-looking policies; the sum of external current payments and receipts as a ratio to GDP has doubled from about 19 percent in 1990–91 to around 40 percent currently.

After improving moderately during the five years immediately following the crisis, fiscal fundamentals have deteriorated again, as exemplified by rising ratios of public sector debt and financial deficit to GDP. This buildup of aggregate public debt has been accompanied by a sharp reduction in external indebtedness by the public sector. Although the private sector's foreign currency indebtedness has increased, it is still very small (less than 3 percent of GDP). Vulnerability to external financial shocks consequently has eased to the point that an external financial crisis is not considered much of a possibility by politicians, in policy circles, or, even among academic economists. Official foreign exchange reserves are more than adequate to cover (official and private) external debt. In addition, India continues to maintain selective (discretionary) capital controls, particularly those that keep in check arbitrage-type flows—for instance, external borrowing by domestic financial intermediaries, investment by foreign institutional investors in fixed income securities, or borrowing of a short-term nature by practically anyone. It is therefore fair to say that while India faced a combined internal (fiscal) and external transfer problem during the years leading up to the crisis of 1991, the weakening of the fiscal position in recent years represents an exclusively internal resource transfer problem.

After peaking at 11.2 percent of GDP in 1986–87, public sector investment (gross domestic capital formation) declined, to 9.5 percent in 1989–90, to 7.7 percent in 1995–96, and to about 6 percent currently. It is not a straightforward exercise to make inferences about the volume of investment in the provision of public goods and services on the basis of the behavior of the share of public sector gross domestic capital formation in GDP. On the one hand, the public sector investment figures include the behavior of a wide range of public sector enterprises (PSEs) that produce private (rival and excludable) goods and services. On the other hand, there has been growing investment by private entities in the provision of certain public goods and services (especially in telecommunications and ports). That notwithstanding, it is no exaggeration to say that public investment in infrastructure, along with associated capital maintenance expenditures, has been cut to the bone, and the state of services (drinking water and sewerage, roads, power supplies, and the like) are testimony to the lopsided fiscal "adjustment." [1]

This infrastructure-unfriendly fiscal "correction" cannot be "seen" in overall fiscal deficit numbers; to a large extent, committed and "sacred cow" expenditures, comprising interest payments, defense spending, and salaries and pensions, combined with declining indirect tax revenue, have to a large extent offset cuts in public investment. In fact the overall public sector financial deficit as a share of GDP was about the same in 2003–04 as it was in the crisis year of 1990–91; furthermore, the revenue (current) deficit is substantially higher than it was.

Across the world, from the European Union's (ill-fated) Stability and Growth Pact to the United Kingdom's Golden Rule and Sustainable Investment Rule, there have been attempts to bind governments to fiscal rectitude through formal legal or even constitutional devices. India too in the last decade has enacted such mechanisms. In September 1994 an agreement was reached between the Reserve Bank of India (RBI) and the Central Exchequer to phase out by 1997–98 the ad hoc treasury bills which hitherto facilitated automatic monetization of the budget deficit (the borrowing gap after all other financing instruments have been exhausted). This, in itself, did not preclude the RBI from participating in primary issues of central government securities or operating in the secondary markets for central government debt, but it left these decisions to the RBI's discretion. The Indian Parliament, in August 2003, passed the Fiscal Responsibility and Budget Management Act (FRBMA), which requires that the fiscal deficit of the central government should not exceed 3 percent of GDP by 2007–08 and that the deficit on the revenue account would be eliminated by the same date. The specified annual reductions in the two measures are 0.5 percentage point of GDP (or more) for the revenue deficit and 0.3 percentage point of GDP (or more) for the fiscal deficit. The FRBMA was amended in July 2004 to shift the terminal date for achieving the numerical targets pertaining to fiscal indicators by one year to 2008–09. The act also barred the RBI from subscribing to government paper after March 31, 2006. Nevertheless, borrowing from the RBI to cover "temporary excess of cash disbursement over cash receipts during any financial year"—essentially ways and means advances—is permitted. In February 2004 the government constituted a task force to

---

1. One must, of course, consider the growth aspect of infrastructure provision. These "network industries" are considered to be "accelerators" for total factor productivity.

devise a strategy for implementing the FRBMA; the task force analysis and recommendations were made public in July 2004. The critical recommendations were on the revenue side of the deficit equation and included measures to enhance direct taxes by 2 percentage points of GDP and to shift the revenue base of indirect taxes to include a greater share of services.

Under India's federal political structure, states are highly autonomous. Extending the framework of the FRBMA to the states therefore requires independent legislative action by the states. In addition to the government of India, several states have passed fiscal responsibility acts; the first six to do so (accounting for 45 percent of GDP) include Karnataka (which acted as early as August 2002), Kerala, Punjab, Tamil Nadu, Uttar Pradesh, and Maharashtra. The common features include imposition of quantitative and time-bound targets for fiscal consolidation, multiyear fiscal plans, and regular reporting to respective legislatures of progress toward annual targets.

India's overflowing foreign exchange coffers have created a set of political economy consequences different from those that were faced during most of the post-independence period. Specifically, the foreign exchange reserves have eased pressures to rectify India's fiscal mismanagement. In the past, when external reserves were much more modest and external debt much higher, India's policymakers were quite aware that large fiscal deficits sustained over a long time period would either spill over into higher levels of inflation (if the deficit was monetized) or a balance of payment crisis (if the government relied increasingly on external borrowing). Since both outcomes had harsh political repercussions, policymakers were forced to act with due caution—most of the time. Now with high levels of reserves and low external debt, politicians are much less worried about either concern. Market-based liberalization has eased (but not eliminated) supply-side weaknesses, and monetization has not yet been seriously resorted to, thereby attenuating inflationary pressures. Indeed, the increasing disjuncture between large internal fiscal imbalances on the one hand and improving external balances on the other is analytically relatively unexplored territory in India.[2]

The following observations broadly identify the picture that emerges:

—The country has no history of default or even restructuring on external (or internal) debt servicing.[3]

2. Kapur and Patel (2003). A lively debate on the analytical specifications of the Indian macroeconomy in the context of liberalized trade and capital flows is under way, with notable contributions by Lal, Bery, and Pant (2003), Sen (2004), and Singh and Srinivasan (2004).

3. The country does have a long history of forcing domestic banks to absorb public debt at rates well below commercial levels.

—The likelihood of an external payments crisis is universally considered to be remote. The current configuration of the relevant fundamentals (large international reserves, low external debt, and remaining capital controls) supports this confidence.

—Nevertheless, complacency is not warranted. There is underlying disquiet: a public sector financial deficit that is very high, and a (gross) public-debt-to-GDP ratio of 90 percent. Commentaries that accompany regular reviews of international credit-rating agencies almost invariably make a song and dance about the fiscal stance, cautioning the government against fiscal misadventures (exhorting it to "hold the line," in a manner of speaking).

—Large past, present, and anticipated future government budget deficits have not given rise to monetary growth (actual or anticipated) of a sufficient magnitude to threaten price stability. At some point, however, excessive deficits would lead either to growing default risk or to unpleasant, Sargent-Wallace-type monetarist arithmetic and rising inflationary pressures. Even without the support of an explicit inflation target, the inflation aversion of the Indian polity has produced a form of implicit inflation targeting, where the monetary authorities tighten policy whenever inflation exceeds a fairly modest tolerance level. It would seem that Indian monetary policy uses the exchange rate as its main instrument, probably in part because financial repression and other financial distortions make for a relatively weak interest rate transmission channel.

—Political pressure to enhance government expenditure on social sectors and improve public (infrastructure and utility) services has increased in the aftermath of the May 2004 general election. An employment guarantee scheme is being implemented; its (estimated) cost to the exchequer when fully executed could be as high as 1 percent of GDP. Governments at the federal level since 1996 have had to rely on coalitions of up to a dozen parties to stay in power with attendant (reported) instances of fiscal for-bearance; the support of communist parties is critical for the longevity of the Congress-led coalition comprising a clutch of regional parties.

The remainder of the paper is organized as follows. In the next section we update our earlier work on the fiscal-financial sustainability of the Indian government by reviewing the evolution of public debt and reporting the results of some formal solvency tests. Sustainability (feasibility) is necessary but not sufficient for optimality. There are bound to be many sustainable fiscal-financial programs, most of which may well produce undesirable outcomes. An extreme example is Ceausescu's policy during the 1980s to pay off the Romanian external debt in its entirety by starving the people of Romania. Nevertheless, a diagnosis of unsustainability would doom a fiscal-financial rule, so our investigation is of some modest interest.

Our conclusion is that government solvency is not today the pressing concern it was in the early 1990s. This leaves two potential areas of interest and concern about the impact of the government on the quantity and quality of capital formation in India. The first is financial crowding out—the negative effect of public borrowing on aggregate (private and public) saving. The second is the effect of government institutions, policies, actions, and interventions (including public ownership, regulation, taxes, subsidies, and other forms of public influence) on private savers, private investors, and the financial markets and institutions that intermediate between them. After reviewing these two areas, we make a brief comparison, deploying a growth accounting framework, of India's investment efficiency (as it is affected by financial sector characteristics, among other things) with that of China. The next section looks at key aspects of the financial sector to convey that the sector remains "by, of, and for the Indian state." We argue that India is paying an especially heavy price for its fiscal excesses because the standard financial crowding out of interest-sensitive private spending by government borrowing is intensified through deep-seated government-created distortions in the financial system. Next we evaluate the fiscal rules that India has embraced, perhaps in recognition of the serious systemic inefficiency that the fiscal stance has engendered. We embed the rules in the basic budgetary arithmetic, and the operational outcomes that are envisaged in the FRBMA are brought out formally. Then we reflect on the likelihood of the rules being enforced, and on the scope for the FRBMA to create a mechanism that enhances macroeconomic volatility and promotes a procyclical fiscal policy—a fate that befell the EU's Stability and Growth Pact. We conclude that without a vocal and influential domestic constituency in favor of fiscal responsibility and restraint, the adoption of a formal set of fiscal-financial rules in India is likely to prove as ineffective in India as the Stability and Growth Pact has been in the EU for the twelve countries that have achieved membership in the European Monetary Union or for those countries, like the United Kingdom, that are not interested in achieving it.

Our paper does not focus on the macroeconomic stabilization roles of fiscal and monetary policy. We do not believe that the nominal wage and price rigidities that make monetary and fiscal policy potentially important tools for macroeconomic stabilization policy are an important feature of the Indian macroeconomic transmission mechanism. Neither old nor new Keynesian specifications of the wage-price mechanism capture the reality of India's labor and product markets. We view output as constrained by supply rather than by effective demand. The supply constraint binds, however, at far too low a level because of real rigidities and distortions in labor, product, and financial markets. Financial crowding out therefore matters from our perspective not because of what it does to short-run aggregate demand and employment, but because of what it does to the level and composition of "full employment" saving and investment.

Evolution of Public Debt and Solvency Tests

India pursued fiscal consolidation, albeit relatively briefly, in the aftermath of the 1991 balance of payments crisis. Reflecting this, the ratio of net public total debt (NTD) to GDP declined sharply—from a peak of about 80 percent of GDP in 1991–92 to about 60 percent in 1996–97. Since then, the ratio has crept back up to over 70 percent of GDP (figure 1).[4]

FIGURE 1.   NTD–GDP, 1970–71 to 2003–04

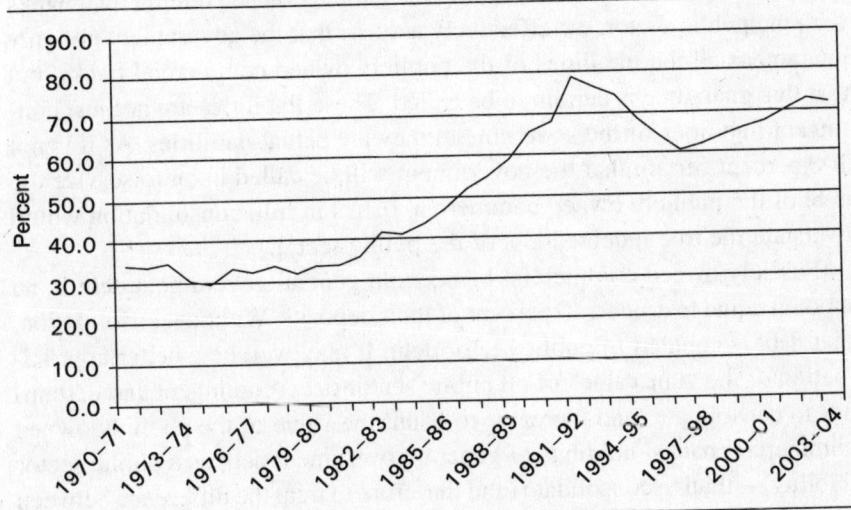

Source: See table A-1 for data and definitions.

4. Although recognized and explicit guarantees outstanding of central and state governments have stabilized in recent years, in 2003 they still amounted to 11.2 percent of GDP.

The composition of the public debt, however, has undergone substantial change. While public and publicly guaranteed external debt continues to decline in both gross and net terms (as a ratio to GDP), internal indebtedness of the government (that is, debt denominated in domestic currency) has shot up to 75 percent of GDP (table A-1). In effect, Indian policymakers have swapped creditors—replacing a potent pressure group of foreigners with hapless future generations of Indian citizens. At least one major international rating agency recognizes this shift by evaluating India's foreign currency rating as investment grade but classifying the long-term domestic currency rating as below investment grade. Within the internal debt aggregate, relative shares have shifted slightly. In an indication of continuing fiscal stress on state governments, the proportion of state government debt in total domestic debt has inched up to about one-fifth. On the external side, official foreign exchange reserves now exceed public debt denominated in foreign currency (indeed, RBI reserves exceed all external debt liabilities, both public *and* private).

Our definition of the public sector includes public enterprises as well as central, state, and local governments, and the central bank. We do not include the publicly owned commercial banks. That was a judgment call. Our reasoning was as follows. By consolidating the publicly owned commercial banks with the public sector, we effectively assume that the government not only guarantees all the liabilities of the publicly owned commercial banks, but that this guarantee is certain to be called. These liabilities are not just contingent liabilities of the government, they are actual liabilities. As it is not 100 percent certain that the government will be called upon to service the debt of the publicly owned commercial banks in full, consolidation would overstate the true indebtedness of the public sector.

Publicly owned commercial banks hold general government debt in an amount equal to around 40 percent of their deposits. Without consolidation, that debt is counted as public sector debt. It may well be a better approximation of the "fair value" of all public sector debt (contingent and certain) not to consolidate (and therefore to count the value of the publicly owned commercial banks' holdings of general government debt as a public sector liability)—than to consolidate (and therefore to treat the difference between the liabilities of the publicly owned commercial banks and their holdings of general government debt as a certain liability of the public sector).

The analysis of the debt sustainability of the public sector does not turn on whether the publicly owned commercial banks act commercially or emulate the bureaucratic behavior of a general government department. A country can act noncommercially in many ways that do not involve "soft budget constraints." Ceausescu's Romania was an example of ultra-hard budget constraints and utter economic irrationality.

As in our previous work on Indian public finance, we conduct formal solvency tests on the debt series.[5] The formal definition of the discounted debt (strictly speaking, the period t debt discounted to period 0) is given in equation 1:

$$(1) \qquad \text{PDV}(B_t) = \prod_{j=0}^{t-t_0} \left(\frac{1}{1+i_{t+j}} \right) B_t$$

Here B_t is the "notional" value of the national debt at time t measured in rupees. For variable-rate debt, the notional value at time t is the face value at time t. For fixed-rate debt, it is the present value, at time t, of all current and future contractual debt payments, discounted at default risk-free nominal discount factors; i_{t+j} is the default risk-free nominal interest rate in period $t + j$. A statistically testable implication of the solvency constraint is that the unconditional expectation of the discounted public debt should be zero (or nonpositive). Since we have not put forward a formal structural political-economic model to explain the evolution of debt and deficits, we are restricted to a mechanical description of the time series properties of the debt stock in terms of reduced form data-generating processes. The statistical tests endeavor to shed light on two aspects: whether the data-generating process describing the discounted public debt is stable in the sense of parameter constancy, that is, whether there are structural breaks in the process; and, conditional on an invariant structure having been identified, whether the discounted debt process is covariance stationary or not.

A discounted debt process that is not stationary need not be taken as evidence that the government will default; it only means that if extant fiscal policies continue, then the exchequer will go bankrupt. Covariance stationarity of the data-generating process implies that its unconditional mean will be zero if the univariate representation of the stochastic process governing it is strictly indeterministic. If the process is covariance stationary but has a deterministic component, its unconditional mean may of course be nonzero.

5. Buiter and Patel (1997). A recent contribution to the literature on Indian fiscal deficits and government debt is Rangarajan and Srivastava (2005).

We deploy two methods to test for stationarity. The process describing PDV(B_t) can be assumed to be represented by a multivariate, autoregressive, integrated, moving average process:

(2) $$[1 - \rho(L)][(1 - L)^d X_t - \alpha_0] = [1 - \theta(L)]\varepsilon_t$$

where $\rho(L)$ is a ρth-order polynomial, $\theta(L)$ is a qth-order polynomial, X_t is a random vector the first element of which is PDV(B_t), α_0 is a vector of constants, and ε_t is a vector white-noise process. $(1 - L)^d X_t$ is a covariance stationary series, that is, the series X_t is integrated of order d. It is assumed that both $[1 - \rho(L)]$ and $[1 - \theta(L)]$ have their roots outside the unit circle; under this assumption equation 2 has the autoregressive representation

(3) $$\eta(L)[(1 - L)^d X_t - \alpha_0] = \varepsilon_t$$

where

(4) $$\eta(L) = \sum_{i=0}^{\infty} \eta_i L_i = [1 - \theta(L)]^{-1}[1 - \rho(L)].$$

The univariate special case of equation 3 is implemented:

(5) $$PDV(B_t) = \alpha_0 + \alpha_1 t + \beta(L)PDV(B_{t-1}) + u_t$$

where $\{u_t\}_0^{\infty}$ is an infinite sequence of weakly stationary random variables, to test whether the discounted Indian public debt is covariance stationary or not. Eventual insolvency will occur if at least one of the following conditions holds:

1. The roots of $1 - \beta(L)$ do not all lie outside the unit circle.
2. $\alpha_1 > 0$, that is, there is a positive deterministic time trend.
3. $\alpha_0 > 0$, that is even though the PDV(B_t) process is stationary, its unconditional expectation is positive.

To allow for a wide class of error structures, the Phillips-Perron test statistics, $Z(\beta)$, $Z(t_\beta)$, and $Z(\phi_3)$ can be used to test for the null hypothesis that $\beta = 1$ and $\alpha_1 = 0$ within a maintained hypothesis that permits a nonzero drift α_0.

It is now widely appreciated that standard unit root tests (for example, Dickey-Fuller and Phillips-Perron) are not very powerful against relevant alternatives such as trend stationarity (linear or nonlinear), fractionally integrated processes, and even level stationarity. This is important because the manner in which classical statistical hypothesis testing is conducted results in the null hypothesis being accepted unless there is strong evidence against it. The null in case of the standard unit root tests is one of nonstationarity, that is, a unit root is present. Although it is possible that the vast majority of aggregate economic time series do not have a unit root, it is probably preferable to formulate a statistical procedure that has stationarity as the null. This is especially relevant given the relatively small sample size available to us using annual data for India. Kwiatkowski and others are useful here.[6] Using a parameterization that provides a reasonable representation of both stationary and nonstationary variables, they have derived a test that has stationarity as the null hypothesis. The series under consideration X, is assumed to have the following decomposition:

$$X_t = \xi t + \Gamma_t + \varepsilon_t \text{ where}$$

(6) $$\Gamma_t = \Gamma_{t-1} + u_t; \, u_t \sim \text{i.i.d.}(0, \sigma_u^2)$$

X_t is modeled as the sum of a deterministic trend, a random walk, and a stationary error, ε_t; the initial value of Γ_t is treated as fixed and serves the role of an intercept. The null hypothesis of trend stationarity can be stated in two equivalent ways: $\sigma_u^2 = 0$, or $\sigma_\Gamma^2 = 0$.

The disturbances ε_t being stationary, X_t is also trend-stationary under the null hypothesis, and the test statistic is thus based on the estimated residuals. The distribution of the test statistic is derived under assumptions about the regression residuals, e_t, that allow for many weakly dependent and heterogeneously distributed time series, including a wide class of data-generating mechanisms such as finite order, autoregressive, moving-average models, under very general conditions.[7] The statistic for testing trend stationarity is derived from the residuals of a regression of X_t on intercept and trend and takes the form:

(7) $$\hat{\eta}_t = T^{-2} \sum_{t=1}^{T} \frac{S_t^2}{s^2(k)}$$

where

$$s^2(k) = T^{-1} \sum_{t=1}^{T} e_t^2 + 2T^{-1} \sum_{s=1}^{k} \left(1 - \frac{s}{(k+1)}\right) \sum_{t=s+k}^{T} e_t e_{t-s}$$

6. Kwiatkowski and others (1992).
7. Phillips and Perron (1988).

s is the partial sum process of the regression residuals, e_t, and $1 - [s/(k + 1]$ is an optional Bartlett spectral window to allow for residual correlations. To test for *level* stationarity instead of *trend* stationarity, ξ in equation 6 is set equal to zero and the residuals are from a regression of X on only the intercept. This statistic is denoted by $\hat{\eta}_\mu$.[8]

As tests both under the null hypothesis of a unit root and under the null hypothesis of (trend) stationarity are carried out, the following four outcomes are possible:

1. If the null of (trend) stationarity is accepted and the null of a unit root is rejected, we can conclude that a series is (trend) stationary;
2. If the null of (trend) stationarity is rejected and that of a unit root cannot be rejected, then the series is nonstationary;
3. If both the nulls are accepted, then we cannot be sure whether there is stationarity;
4. If both nulls are rejected, then we cannot reach any conclusion.

Obviously if either of the last two conditions prevails, we would be unable to conclusively interpret the stationarity properties of the time series under consideration, but the first two conditions are categorical.

The first three of the five test statistics given in table 1 are derived in Phillips and Perron for the null that $\beta = 1$ and $\alpha_1 = 0$.[9]

$Z(\beta)$ makes use of the standardized and centered least squares estimates of β. $Z(t_\beta)$ makes use of the t statistic on β, t_β ($\beta = 1$), and $Z(\phi_3)$ is the regression F test of Dickey and Fuller.[10] These three statistics possess, for a very wide class of error processes, the same limiting distributions as the statistics developed by Dickey and Fuller for the case of i.i.d. errors; therefore, the critical values of the three statistics are the same and can be found in Fuller and in Dickey and Fuller.[11] Much, but not all, of the evidence for the null of unit root and the null of stationarity points to nonstationarity of the debt series; the exception is the trend stationarity test, $\hat{\eta}_t$, for B_2^* (debt in foreign currency discounted at the foreign-official-creditors dollar interest rate). The finding of stationarity for B_2^*, the total debt measured in U.S. dollars discounted at the foreign-official-creditors dollar interest rate, but of nonstationarity for B_1^*, the same debt measured in U.S. dollars but using the higher foreign-all-creditors dollar interest rate, is probably

8. Kwiatkowski and others (1992) provide critical values for tests of both level and trend stationarity.
9. Phillips and Perron (1988)
10. Dickey and Fuller (1981).
11. Fuller (1976); Dickey and Fuller (1981).

TABLE 1. Unit Root and Stationarity Tests for Discounted Debt and
NTD–GDP Ratio

	$Z(\beta)$	$Z(t_\beta)$	$Z(\phi_3)$	$\hat{\eta}_\mu$	$\hat{\eta}_t$
B_1	−6.796	−1.923	1.887	1.720	0.192
B_2	−6.064	−1.635	1.435	1.302	0.224
B_1^*	−8.536	−1.807	1.917	1.646	0.206
B_2^*	−9.750	−1.827	2.312	1.714	0.136
NTD–GDP	−7.228	−1.918	1.844	1.556	0.189
Critical values	−18.508	−3.568	7.403	0.463	0.146

Source: Regarding the exercise of discounting net total debt, time series for the two rupee interest rates are from the Reserve Bank of India, *Handbook of Statistics on the Indian Economy (2003–04)*; and time series for the two U.S. dollar interest rates are from the World Bank, *Global Development Finance Report* (various years). Net total debt is from table A-1. We would like to thank Alok Kumar for his help in programming the tests.

Notes: NTD–GDP is the ratio of net total debt to GDP. Tests cover the period 1970–71 to 2003–04. All tests have been run on RATS; the lag lengths for the KPSS tests have been chosen on the basis of the Schwartz method.

B_1 is the debt measured in rupees discounted at the long-term government bond yield.

B_2 is the debt measured in rupees discounted at the average advance rate.

B_1^* is the debt measured in U.S. dollars discounted at the "foreign all creditors" dollar interest rate.

B_2^* is the debt measured in U.S. dollars discounted at the "foreign official creditors" dollar interest rate.

explained by the behavior of B_1^* implying long-run "super-solvency" rather than insolvency (figure 2 profiles the behavior of the discounted debt series).

On balance, our review (both informal and formal) indicates that the overall net public debt burden does not give cause for immediate alarm. There is also the possibility that the Indian sovereign has been helped to some extent by high GDP growth raising the denominator of the public debt (in rupees)-to-(nominal) GDP ratio, (B_t/P_tY_t), rather than the numerator being lowered by fiscal consolidation and restraint. The change in the ratio can be decomposed as follows:

$$(8) \quad \frac{B_t}{P_tY_t} - \frac{B_{t-1}}{P_{t-1}Y_{t-1}} \equiv \frac{B_t - B_{t-1}}{P_tY_t} - \frac{B_{t-1}}{P_{t-1}Y_t}\left[\frac{Y_t - Y_{t-1}}{Y_{t-1}}\right] - \frac{B_{t-1}}{P_tY_t}\left[\frac{P_t - P_{t-1}}{P_{t-1}}\right]$$

The decomposition of changes since 1990–91 in the net total debt–GDP ratio is given in figure 3.[12] Negative growth surprises, whether for cyclical

12. Inflation and positive real growth would help to reduce the nominal-debt-to-nominal-GDP ratio for a given nominal debt; conversely, deflation and negative growth shocks would increase the ratio. Obviously, in practice, changes in all three variables contribute to the (aggregate) temporal variation in the NTD–GDP ratio (of table A.1), hence the four bars for each year in figure 3.

FIGURE 2.   Discounted NTD Series (1970–71 to 2003–04)

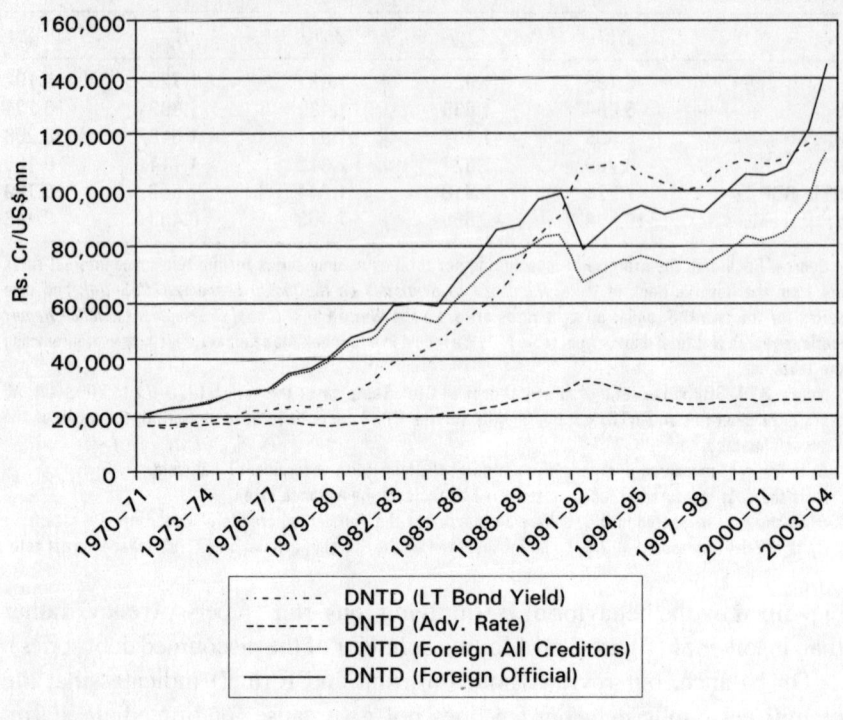

Source: See table A-1 for data and definitions.

or structural reasons, could cause the recent increases in the debt-to-GDP ratio to become explosive. There can be no rest for the wicked.

The reasons India has remained fundamentally solvent despite the sustained fiscal deficits of the past twenty years are fast nominal GDP growth and financial repression. The rate of change of the debt-to-GDP ratio, b, can in continuous time be written in the following two equivalent ways:

$$(9) \qquad \dot{b} = d - (\pi + n)b$$
$$(10) \qquad \dot{b} = -s + (r - n)b$$

where

$$(11) \qquad d = -s + ib$$

and

$$(12) \qquad i = r + \pi$$

FIGURE 3. Decomposition of Changes in the NTD–GDP Ratio (1990–91 to 2003–04)

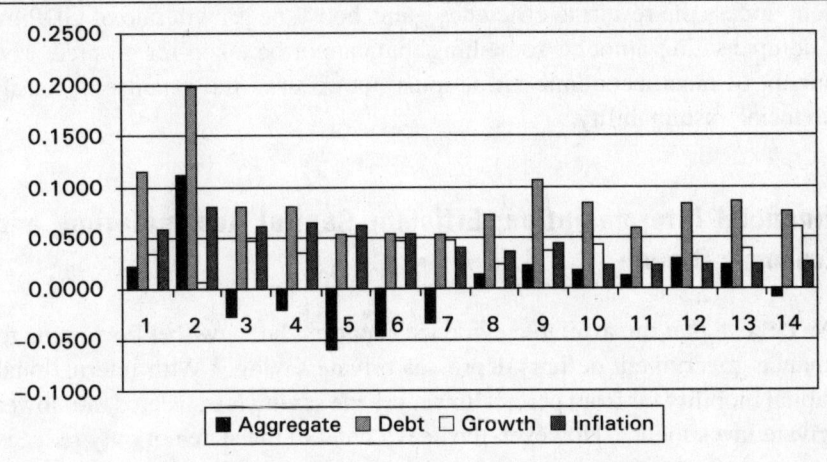

Source: See table A-1; also see footnote 12.

Here d is the conventional public sector financial deficit as a fraction of GDP, s is the public sector primary (noninterest) surplus as a fraction of GDP, π is the rate of inflation, n is the growth rate of real GDP, i is the short nominal interest rate, and r is the short real interest rate. Equations 9 and 10 assume that Indian public debt is rupee-denominated.

Equation 9 shows that with an annual growth rate of 12 percent in nominal GDP ($\pi + n = 0.12$) and with the stock of public debt equal to 80 percent of annual GDP ($b = 0.80$), India's debt-to-GDP ratio will be constant (fall) if the deficit is equal to (less than) 9.6 percent of GDP [$d = (<)0.096$]. Financial repression means that both the nominal and the real interest rates on the public debt are kept artificially low. From equation 11, this means that for any given primary surplus s, the conventionally measured deficit d will be lower because the cost of debt servicing is lower than it would have been had market interest rates prevailed, and the debt dynamics will be more benign. The difference between the actual interest rate bill, ib and the interest bill at market interest rates, i^*b, is a (quasi-fiscal) tax on the holders of the public debt, with $(i - i^*)b < 0$. In terms of equation 10, financial repression reduces the intrinsic growth rate of the debt-to-GDP ratio, $r - n$. The debt–GDP ratio stabilizing value of the primary surplus falls by 0.8 percent of GDP for every 100 basis points increase in financial repression. Elimination of the market distortions that produce the gap between i and i^* will have adverse effects on the sustainability of the government's fiscal-financial program because the elimination will raise the interest bill on the public debt, unless the resulting efficiency gains boost the growth rate of GDP by a compensating amount, something that cannot be taken for granted. The pursuit of macroeconomic virtue must not occur at the expense of fiscal-financial sustainability.

Financial Intermediation, Efficient Capital Accumulation, and Economic Growth

We believe that the available evidence supports the view that borrowing to finance government deficits depresses private saving.[13] With international capital mobility far from perfect, lower private saving is translated into lower private investment.[14] However, the heavy hand of the state not only reduces the amount of private investment, it also reduces the efficiency of both private and public investment.

Although it is not easy to reach a conclusion about the magnitude of the cost of inefficient financial intermediation in terms of forgone GDP growth, there is not much doubt that India is inefficient in transforming its domestic savings into productive capital investment.

Let $Y \geq 0$ denote real GDP, $K \geq 0$ the stock of physical capital, i real gross investment as a share of GDP, and $\delta > 0$ the proportional rate of depreciation; $v \equiv \dfrac{\partial K}{\partial Y}$ is the ICOR, or incremental capital-output ratio. It follows that the proportional growth rate of real output, $n \equiv \dfrac{\dot{Y}}{Y}$ can be written as follows:

$$(13) \qquad n = v^{-1}\left(i - \delta \frac{K}{Y} \right)$$

Assume the aggregate production function takes the Cobb-Douglas form $Y = AK^{\alpha}$; $A, \alpha > 0$. Here A stands for everything other than the physical capital stock that influences potential output (labor and land inputs, technical and managerial efficiency, and the like). It follows that $v^{-1}\dfrac{K}{Y} = \alpha$, so equation 13 can be written as:

$$(14) \qquad n = v^{-1}i - \delta\alpha$$

13. See Federal Reserve Bank of Boston (2006), especially the chapters by Cotis and Friedman.
14. See, for example, Shah and Patnaik (2004).

While α is always the elasticity of output with respect to the capital stock, it will equal the share of net capital income in GDP only in a competitive constant returns to scale economy.

Financial intermediation and financial development can, using the framework of equation 14, influence the growth of output, either by changing the investment rate, i, or by changing the ICOR, v.

Let s be the national saving rate (private plus public) as a share of GDP and ca the current account surplus on the balance of payments as a share of GDP. Since $i \equiv s - ca$, the growth equation can be written as

$$(15) \qquad n = v^{-1}(s - ca) - \delta\alpha$$

Thus, assuming that δ and α are independent of the stage of development of the financial sector, financial development raises the growth rate of potential output either by raising the national saving rate or by permitting a larger volume of net capital inflows, or by lowering the ICOR, that is, by increasing the marginal product of economy wide capital in terms of aggregate GDP.

Net capital inflows are the sum of net inflows of foreign direct investment, FDI, net portfolio inflows, ΔP, net external commercial borrowing, ECB, minus the net increase in official international reserves, ΔR, that is,[15]

$$(16) \qquad -ca \equiv \text{FDI} + \Delta P + \text{ECB} - \Delta R$$

We can therefore rewrite equation 14 as

$$(17) \qquad n = v^{-1}(s + \text{FDI} + \Delta P + \text{ECB} - \Delta R) - \delta\alpha$$

Can enhanced domestic financial intermediation raise the domestic saving rate, s? More effective intermediation reduces borrowing spreads on lending, raising the rate of return for lenders while reducing the cost of borrowing. The evidence on the sensitivity of the aggregate saving rate to changes in the return to saving is mixed at best. The greater-than-unitary elasticity of intertemporal substitution assumed in much of the theoretical and numerical calibration literature cannot be easily extracted from the available empirical evidence. Opening up the capital account allows the domestic investment decision to be decoupled from the domestic saving decision. By running a current account deficit, a nation can invest more than it saves. A fair number of transition countries have taken advantage of this opportunity since the mid-1990s and continue to do so today. Russia, in contrast, has run current

15. All flows are expressed as fractions of GDP.

account surpluses every year since the collapse of the Soviet Union. Ukraine, too, has frequently run sizable current account surpluses.

Domestic financial development can be expected to reduce the nation's ICOR or to raise the marginal efficiency of investment. It does so by ensuring that funds owned by domestic households or domestic enterprises with poor investment prospects are transferred to domestic enterprises with better investment prospects. Opening up the capital account may also reduce the ICOR. Foreign direct investment not only brings additional funds to domestic residents, it tends to come bundled with technology, know-how, and managerial skills that are superior to those available domestically.

The simple growth accounting framework of equation 14 hides a lot of important institutional, technological, and behavioral features of the economy behind the four parameters v, s, δ, and α. The great virtue of its simplicity is that it does not require the availability of data on the stock of capital or the stocks of other productive inputs that are required for a Solow-style growth accounting exercise.[16] And despite its simplicity, equation 14 permits some interesting observations.

First, for any reasonable values of $\delta\alpha$, India's ICOR these past two decades has been much lower than China's. With India's ICOR as one's benchmark, the obvious question about China's recent economic performance must be: "Given its spectacular saving and investment rates, why has China's growth rate been so low these past two decades?" The only really surprising feature of the Chinese economic miracle is the sustained high levels of domestic saving and domestic capital formation. Chinese growth has been and continues to be, woefully inefficient, indeed more inefficient than India's.

Consider the following illustrative stylized facts for China: $n = 0.09$, $i = 0.45$, $\alpha = 0.25$, and $\delta = 0.08$. It follows that China's ICOR is high ($v \approx 4.1$) or, equivalently, that on average China uses its investment very inefficiently. The 5–6 percent of GDP that comes into China as foreign direct investment is probably used efficiently, but the bulk of investment by state enterprises and of infrastructure investment is inefficient and unproductive.

For India, for the past ten years, the following stylized facts apply: $n = 0.062$ and $i = 0.25$; with an appeal to the principle of insufficient reason, we assume the same values for the capital elasticity of output and the depreciation rate as was assumed for China ($\alpha = 0.25$ and $\delta = 0.08$). If follows that India's ICOR, with $v \approx 3.0$, is significantly lower than China's.

---

16. While we would like to be able to back out estimates of total factor productivity growth, we lack the data to make accurate measurements of *all* relevant factor inputs—labor, capital, land, and imported primary and intermediate inputs.

Of course, China, a model of inefficient growth, does not set a tough standard to beat. Nevertheless, we believe that the inefficient intermediation of domestic savings into domestic capital formation is likely to be an important part of the explanation of the high ICOR of India and the extremely high ICOR of China.

Aspects of the Financial Sector

... The public sector continues to dominate the financial system through public sector banks and financial institutions... [which has] important consequences for the allocative efficiency of the financial system and for corporate governance....

The Economic Survey, 2001–02[17]

"With the gradual disappearance of development banks..., a gap in credit availability is emerging. There is some concern that adequate long-term finance is not available to the medium and more particularly small industries."

Prime Minister
Manmohan Singh, June 2005[18]

The financial sector in India, which includes commercial banks, mutual funds, and insurance companies among other institutions, changed during the reform period of the 1990s. Although many changes were supposedly effected, these have been relatively narrow in scope. The strategy (introduced as a cornerstone of safety) has been ratio-centric, underpinned by loosely interconnected strands of a Basle regulatory framework, encompassing capital adequacy and other "hard" parameters; these are only a subset of wide-ranging institutional changes essential for "effective" reform and market discipline. The outcomes of these actions thus far have not been as far-reaching as required; while the financial sector is probably more robust than it was before the reforms, it is still characterized by substantial inefficiencies born of the blunted incentives (underlined by stylized facts and anecdotal evidence) associated with large public sector presence in the sector.[19]

17. Annual publication of the Economic Division, Ministry of Finance, Government of India.

18. Address at the State Bank of India's bicentennial celebrations in Mumbai (reported in *The Hindu* of June 5, 2005).

19. In September 2003, Standard and Poor's revised its outlook on the Indian banking sector upward, from negative to stable, and Fitch Ratings assessed that economic reforms have considerably "strengthened" financial sector fundamentals.

Involvement of the government in India's financial sector remains high; for most of India's post-independence period, the government has used intermediaries to direct and allocate financial resources to favored recipients in both the public and private sectors. Until 1992, in practically all areas of nonagricultural economic activity, the state's involvement in the financial sector included the implicit assumption of counterparty risks. Currently, 70 percent of the financial sector's assets are held by government-owned or sponsored entities (table 2 gives a summary for key segments). In fact this figure is higher (around 73 percent) once institutions like the Employees Provident Fund Organization (for contractual and pension savings) and the National Small Savings Scheme (post office savings plans used to finance the government deficit), both operating essentially from within the government with not even a semblance of arms-length relationship, are factored in. Within the Indian financial sector, banks are the dominant intermediaries accounting for about 63 percent of assets. (The extent of government ownership of banks in India is quite high compared with international levels.) Moreover, the Reserve Bank of India has majority ownership in the State Bank of India (SBI), the largest public sector bank.[20]

TABLE 2. **Share of Public Sector Institutions in Specific Segments of the Financial Sector (March 31, 2004)**

Institution type	Public sector (percent)	Private (percent)	Total (Rs. billion)
Scheduled commercial banks (SCBs)	71.9	28.1	20,457
Mutual funds (MFs)	24.8	75.2	1,396
Life insurance	99.5	0.5	3,231

Source: Reserve Bank of India, *Report on Currency and Finance (2003–04)*; *Insurance Regulatory and Development Authority Annual Report (2003–04)*.
Note: SCBs include total assets; private banks include foreign banks; MFs include total assets of domestic schemes of MFs (public sector includes Unit Trust of India); life insurance includes policy liabilities (public sector insurance includes Life Insurance Corporation and SBI Life).

Experience suggests that the government as owner typically lacks both the incentive and the means to ensure an adequate return on its investment.[21] As a result, the pursuit of adequate rates of return is compromised, with political considerations often dominating hard-nosed, risk-return trade-offs in determining resource allocation. Also, besides the standard problems that result from information asymmetry and "agency" issues, moral hazard

20. Parts of the rest of this section draw heavily on Bhattacharya and Patel (2005).
21. La Porta, Lopez-de-Silanes, and Shleifer (2002).

might be *aggravated* because both depositors and lenders count on explicit and implicit government guarantees.[22] Across the world, such pathological forms of government involvement in the financial sector, far from ensuring greater stability, have led to greater fragility of the sector, with macroeconomic turbulence often not too far behind.

The government's involvement in India is more extensive (and deeper) than mere ownership numbers can express.[23] The scope ranges across appointment of management, regulation, mobilization of resources, and provision of "comfort and support" to depositors; moreover, the government influences lending practices of all intermediaries and the investment incentives of private corporations. The government deploys an array of formal and informal instruments, including treating banks as quasi-fiscal instruments (including instances of de facto sovereign borrowing from these banks), preempting resources through statutory requirements, directed lending and bailouts, encouraging imprudent practices such as cross-holding of capital between intermediaries (so called "double-gearing"), and allowing unjustifiable levels of government-controlled and -guaranteed deposit insurance. A multiplicity of regulators (with varying degrees of independence) covering the full financial spectrum is in place, but enforcement of directives has been patchy.[24]

The implications, in India, of a government-dominated financial system are well known. A proximate outcome is the unwarranted, intrusive, and onerous oversight by a multitude of government inspection and (criminal) investigative agencies—such as Parliament, the comptroller and auditor general, the central bureau of investigation, the central vigilance commission, and the enforcement directorate—in audits of decisions made by bank managers, thereby undermining "normal" risk taking intrinsic to lending.[25] This

22. See Bhattacharya and Patel (2002), and Patel and Bhattacharya (2003). Note that *aggravated* is distinct from *enhanced*. The former may be considered as a parametric shift of the underlying variables as opposed to a functional dependence in the case of the latter. More explicitly, increasing moral hazard enhances the incentives of banks to accumulate riskier portfolios, whereas an aggravated moral hazard results in a failure to initiate corrective steps to mitigate the enhanced hazard, such as increasing requirements of capital, proper risk weighting or project monitoring. India's decision not to provide deposit insurance after the fact to nonbank financial intermediaries was commendable in this context.

23. Patel (2004).

24. For instance, cooperative banks were lax in implementing RBI notifications on lending to brokers.

25. Banerjee, Cole, and Duflo (2004). Acts of commission can come under the scrutiny of enforcement agencies, but acts of omission are ignored (regardless of whether they result in profit or loss).

sort of intrusion is compounded by institutional rigidities that include weak foreclosure systems, deficient legal recourse for recovering bad debts, and ineffective exit procedures for firms. Furthermore, during difficult times, relief for fiscal stress is sought through regulatory forbearance; there are demands for (and occasionally instances of) lax enforcement (or dilution) of income recognition and asset classification norms (box 1). The conjunction of these characteristics contributes toward giving financial intermediaries incentives to, among other things, roll over existing substandard debt, usually by swapping substandard debt for equity (an example of the reportedly widespread practice of "ever-greening" assets), thereby building up the riskiness of their asset portfolio and further diluting equity-debt norms.

BOX 1. **Regulatory Forbearance in the Indian Financial Sector**

—Loopholes in the treatment of distressed assets persist. Projects deemed to be "under implementation" may not be classified as nonperforming assets despite interest and principal repayments remaining overdue for more than 90 or even 180 days. An independent group constituted in 2002 to look into such projects and establish deemed completion dates, estimated that intermediaries had already disbursed about Rs. 360 billion to twenty-six such nonperforming projects with a total cost of Rs. 560 billion (including a debt component of Rs. 390 billion).
—As domestic interest rates hardened in the second half of 2004, commercial banks' holding of government securities that should have been marked-to-market (downward) were allowed (by the Reserve Bank of India) to be redesignated as held-to-maturity (rather than as "available-for-sale") to insulate them from rate rises; this happened after banks booked huge gains in immediately preceding years during a period of falling interest rates, thereby imparting a (what may turn out to be temporary) sheen to their financial health.

Distortions in intermediaries' cost of borrowing and lending structures persist because of continuing restrictions on interest rates. Floors on banks' short-term deposits and high administered rates on bank deposit—like small savings instruments and provident funds contribute to artificially raising the cost of funds (table A-2). On the lending side, constraints apply to various prime lending rate-related guidelines for small-scale industries and other priority sector lending. In recent years an environment of declining interest rates combined with the structural factors discussed above has made treasury operations an important activity in improving banks' profitability.[26] The

---

26. Declining interest rates increased trading profits (in securities) of public sector banks in 2001–02 more than two and a half times that of the previous year and accounted for 28 percent of operating profits. While growth of trading profit subsided in the following

consequence of this environment is "lazy banking."[27] It is felt that banks in India have curtailed their credit creation role and have, if anything, intensified their role of predominantly being passive conduits for resources rather than active risk management intermediaries that offer appropriately priced capital to firms. (Box 2 gives anecdotal evidence on this subject from the perspective of entrepreneurs in the textile industry.)

BOX 2. Anecdotal Evidence on Financial Intermediation in the Textile Industry

India is likely to miss the opportunity offered by the demise of the WTO Agreement on Textiles and Clothing at the end of 2004. To achieve scale economies, consolidation and investment are essential. However, banks, the main source of institutional finance, have been disinclined to support the necessary evolution in the textile sector because loans made to textile companies during past export booms turned sour; habit-based risk aversion has been substituted for prudent risk management. Should he wish to issue equity instead, a textile manufacturer looking for risk capital is highly likely to be frustrated and constrained; if he attempts to raise more than five times his pre-issue net worth, he has to find qualified institutional buyers (which include the same Mumbai-headquartered commercial banks, life insurance companies, and nonbank financial companies) for 60 percent of the issue amount. For many entrepreneurs this is a hard sell.

Source: Ashok Desai, "Textiles Will Fail Us—and Why," *Business World*, October 18, 2004.

Because of these many distortions, government borrowing imposes costs on the private sector over and above the financial crowding out of private agents that occurs even in well-functioning, undistorted financial markets. In addition to direct government borrowing, the government, for example, is also facilitating (or distorting) economy wide lending and borrowing activity through credit enhancements and guarantees. Although policymakers are cognizant of the inherent dangers regarding contingent liabilities that could come home to roost, outstanding government guarantees exceeded 11 percent of GDP in 2002–03; furthermore, the 2005–06 Union budget has new proposals for adding to these guarantees through an off-budget financial vehicle.

Commercial bank holdings of government securities are much higher than the mandatory minimum levels. As figure 4 and table 3 show, a large fraction of bank deposits (estimated at 43.2 percent as of March 2005) are being deployed for holding government (and other approved) securities, (mis-)perceived to be free of default risk (and indeed of market risk). Despite

---

two years, its share in operating profit had increased to 39 percent by 2003–04. See Reserve Bank of India (various years).

27. A term attributed to a deputy governor of the RBI.

a strong economic rebound, the statutory liquidity ratio (on a flow basis) was higher than the regulatory requirement (25 percent) even during 2003–04 (59 percent) and 2004–05 (30 percent)—the peak of the current business cycle—when average annual GDP growth was in excess of 7.5 percent. The government, it would seem, has somehow (inadvertently, to give the benefit of doubt) managed to extend its makeover of weak banks into "narrow" banks to the banking sector as a whole; the banks have even exceeded the statutory 38.5 percent preemptions of the pre-reform days.

FIGURE 4. Ratio of Investment in SLR Eligible Securities to Deposits

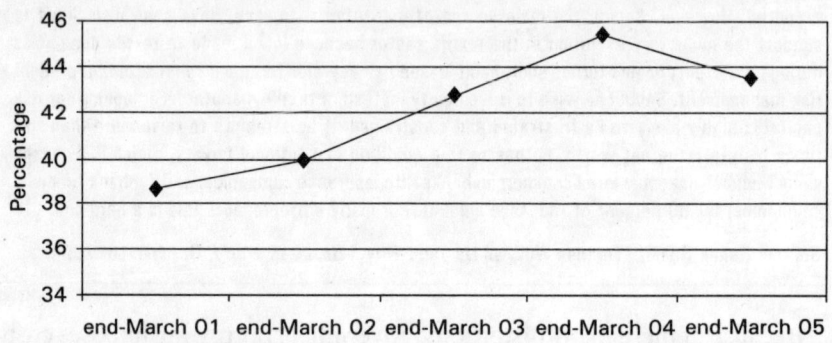

Source: Reserve Bank of India, *Weekly Statistical Bulletin.*

TABLE 3. Portfolio Allocation of Lendable Resources of Commercial Banks
Percent of deposits

Period	Balances with RBI	Nonfood credit	Investments in government securities
1980s	12.6	60.3	24.2
1990s	11.6	52.6	30.6
2000–04	5.3	51.1	41.5
2005[a]	5.1	61.1	43.2

Source: Reserve Bank of India, *Report on Currency and Finance* (various years) and *Report on Trend and Progress of Banking in India* (various years).
a. Through March 2005; decadal figures are annual averages.

These actions also have implications for the financial health of public sector banks. It has to be recognized that the only sustainable method of ensuring capital adequacy in the long run is through improvement in earnings profiles, not government capitalization or even mobilization of private capital from the market (for given profits, both these options only dilute the return on equity). Conceptually, a bank can sustain its capital adequacy at the existing level (or improve upon it) if it can generate retained earnings sufficient for its capital base to grow at the same rate (or higher) as its risk-weighted asset base. While capital adequacy ratios of most public sector banks are in excess of the minimum 9 percent, fresh capital will be necessary to cover new regulatory obligations and for funding credit expansion. [28] It is estimated that new regulations under the Basle 2 accord will shave off about 2 percentage points from current capital adequacy ratios for public sector banks; that means a fair amount of capital will be needed, going forward, to support existing balance sheets. Given the government's explicit (and oft-repeated) policy of not reducing its shareholding below 50 percent and the fact that the fiscal situation is not conducive to the government subscribing fresh equity, the authorities may revert to the deceptive practice of forcing banks to subscribe to each other's Tier 2 capital, similar to the "double gearing" that took place in 1999–2000 (a la Japanese banks); alternatively, nonvoting preference shares may be issued.

On the capital markets side, the share of the public sector in resources raised has increased over the last decade; the average share over the last three years has been in excess of 60 percent (table 4). Not surprisingly, on the face of it, there is little evidence that public issues of capital market instruments (equity and debt) have supported growth of *nongovernment* public limited companies; in fact, both the number of companies and the amount raised in the market have declined since the mid-1990s (figure 5).

Financial crowding out of productive private expenditure (especially private investment) by government borrowing *is* a clear and present problem. The costs may be higher than is prima facie evident because distorted incentives caused by the public ownership of a significant share of India's financial sector and unnecessary constraints on lending and borrowing rates amount to a covert form of "financial repression" of the private sector. The capacity of the financial sector to intermediate resources efficiently for private investment is impaired since, for practical purposes, even after a decade of reforms, many distortions persist that allow banks to avoid taking "prudent risks" and sidestep desirable regulatory norms at the same time.

Furthermore, the moral hazard in the sector is palpable. There is a conviction among depositors and investors alike that there is no downside and that the system is insulated from market risk and default crises. A sense of confidence has permeated both depositors and intermediaries because of the government's deep involvement, thus making deposit runs unlikely,

---

28. The additional "charges" on capital are for operational risk and for market risk. The latter, based on the duration of bond holdings, captures mainly the interest rate risk on the bond portfolio designated for trading or available for sale.

T A B L E   4.   Resource Mobilization through Capital Markets

Rupees in billion

	1993–94	1994–95	1995–96	1996–97	1997–98	1998–99	1999–2000	2000–01	2001–02	2002–03	2003–04	2004–05
Public issues of debt and equity	296.5	307.8	206.4	154.2	46.2	93.6	77.0	63.6	71.1	48.7	78.0	218.9
Private sector	195.0	264.4	161.7	104.2	31.4	50.1	51.5	48.9	56.9	18.8	36.8	134.8
Public sector	101.5	43.4	44.7	50.0	14.8	43.5	25.5	14.7	14.2	29.9	41.2	84.1
Public issues of equity by private corporations and banks	99.6	174.1	118.8	61.0	11.6	25.6	27.5	26.1	8.6	4.6	24.7	114.5
IPOs	60.1	137.5	85.8	41.7	3.8	3.4	16.6	23.7	8.5	2.1	14.7	83.9
Private placements	n.a.	n.a.	133.6	150.7	301.0	496.8	612.6	678.4	648.8	669.5	639.0	840.5
Private sector	n.a.	n.a.	40.7	24.9	92.0	170.0	194.0	231.1	286.2	250.8	187.6	357.4
Public sector	n.a.	n.a.	92.9	125.7	209.0	326.8	418.6	447.3	362.6	418.7	451.5	483.1
Share of public sector in capital market resources mobilized (percent)	34.2	14.1	40.5	57.6	64.5	62.7	64.4	62.3	52.3	62.5	68.7	53.5

Sources: Reserve Bank of India, *Handbook of Statistics on the Indian Economy (2004–05)*; *Annual Report* (various issues).

Notes: Public sector incudes public sector banks and financial institutions. Public issues are through prospectus and rights.

n.a. Not available.

FIGURE 5.   New Capital Issues by Non-Govt. Public Companies

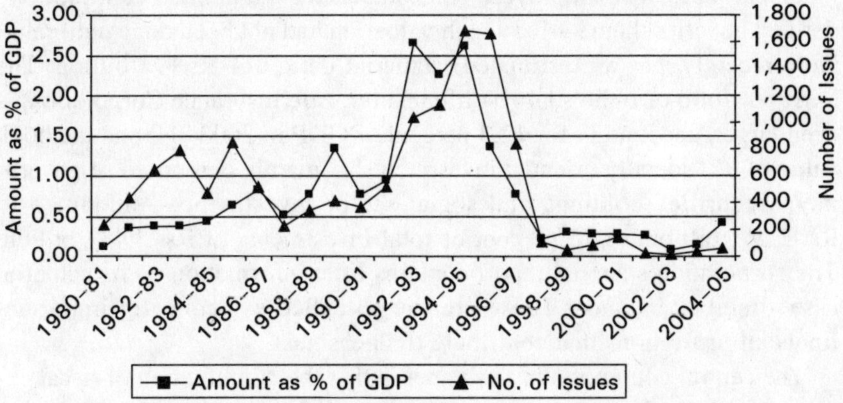

Source: Reserve Bank of India, *Weekly Statistical Bulletin.*

even when insolvency is a possibility. As Bhattacharya and Patel conclude, "In effect," the government has "'signed a social contract' with depositors that substitutes 'support and comfort' to intermediaries in lieu of market discipline in attempting to mitigate systemic risk."[29]

Although the focus of prudential regulations has been the banking sector, other intermediaries have often been the proximate source of serious problems in the Indian financial sector. Even if the current situation does not appear to be precarious, the potential for turbulence is there. The stream of problems that have plagued Indian intermediaries in the recent past has originated in the group of investment and financial institutions. The most well-known of these was Unit Trust of India (UTI), the largest mutual fund in India; others involved to a lesser extent were Industrial Finance Corporation of India and Industrial Development Bank of India. After some dithering UTI's troubles have been contained.

Possible future problems may emanate from other government-owned intermediaries with very large asset portfolios. Total cumulative investments of the three employees provident fund organization (EPFO) schemes are Rs. 1,700 billion (6.1 percent of GDP), with the employees provident fund (EPF) being the largest scheme.[30] A government bailout of the largest fund

29. Bhattacharya and Patel (2005).

30. Three schemes are administered by the employees provident fund organization, which in turn comes under the ambit of the Ministry of Labor; the schemes are the employees provident fund scheme (begun in1952); employees pension scheme (1995); and employees deposit linked insurance scheme (1976).

began in 2005 when Rs.10 billion were paid out of the exchequer to meet members' dues. The employees pension scheme—a defined contribution–defined benefit scheme—for which valuation had not been done until relatively recently, has an (estimated) actuarial deficit of Rs.193 billion. The asset portfolio of India's largest life insurer, Life Insurance Corporation, is even larger, accounting for 12.3 percent of GDP in 2003–04; and the book value of its "socially oriented investments"—mainly composed of government securities holdings and social sector investments—amounted to Rs. 2,561 billion, or 75 percent of total investments of Rs. 3,431 billion. The corporation's annual report contains little information on its actuarial asset–liability balance. These are the so-called systemically important financial institutions that contribute to uneasiness.

The central contention of our paper is that the combination of fiscal excesses (a shift of the saving schedule to the left) with financial repression and distortions in the formal financial system and with poor investment choices by publicly owned financial institutions weakens the quantity and quality of private investment and thus retards growth. An alternative interpretation of the weakness of investment is a shift to the left in the private investment schedule, perhaps reflecting problems in the regulatory environment, for example in infrastructure. While such regulatory problems are indeed present and persistent (and may account for the enduringly low investment rates), it is hard to argue that they have been getting worse since the early 1990s and that they can therefore account for a weakening of investment.

Extant Fiscal Rules

In August 2003, two and a half years after being introduced in Parliament in December 2000, Indian lawmakers approved the Fiscal Responsibility and Budget Management Act, which requires that the central government's fiscal deficit should not exceed 3 percent of GDP by 2007–08 and that the deficit on the revenue account be eliminated by the same date. The stipulated annual reductions in the two measures are 0.5 percentage point of GDP (or more) for the revenue deficit and 0.3 percentage point of GDP (or more) for the fiscal deficit.[31] Increases in guarantees are restricted to 0.5 percent

---

31. The terminal target for the fiscal deficit is stipulated in the rules (framed in July 2004) to the 2003 Act. The target of balance on the revenue account is enshrined in the Act itself.

of GDP a year. Additional liabilities are capped at 9 percent of GDP for 2004–05; the cap is reduced by 1 percentage point of GDP each year thereafter. The law also bars the RBI from subscribing to government paper after March 31, 2006. However, borrowing from the RBI on account of "temporary excess of cash disbursement over cash receipts during any financial year," essentially ways and means advances, are permitted. The RBI may also buy and sell central government securities in the secondary market.

The FRBMA was amended in July 2004. The terminal date for achieving the numerical targets pertaining to fiscal indicators was extended by one year to 2008–09 (the top panel of table 5). Furthermore, in his presentation of the 2005–06 Union budget in February, the finance minister remarked that he was "left with no option but to press the 'pause' button vis-à-vis the FRBM Act." In early June 2004, an update for the 2004–05 fiscal outturn indicates that both the fiscal and revenue deficits are within the targets established in July 2004 (the bottom panel of table 5). However, it is not yet clear whether medium-term targets for subsequent years will be revisited in light of latest numbers for 2004–05.

T A B L E 5 . Central Government's FRBMA-Stipulated (Rolling) Fiscal Indicators as a Percent of GDP

(a) July 2004 (budget)

Indicator	Revenue deficit	Fiscal deficit	Outstanding liabilities
2003–04 (R.E.)	3.6	4.8	67.3
2004–05 (B.E.)	2.5	4.4	68.5
Targets			
2005–06	1.8	4.0	68.2
2006–07	1.1	3.6	67.8
2008–09 (terminal year)	Nil	3.0	...

(b) February 2005 (budget)

	Revenue deficit	Fiscal deficit	Outstanding liabilities
2003–04 (actual)	3.6	4.5	
2004–05 (R.E.) Feb. data	2.7	4.5	68.8
2004–05 (latest est. June data)	2.5	4.1	n.a.
2005–06 (B.E.)	2.7	4.3	68.6
Targets			
2006–07	2.0	3.8	68.2
2007–08	1.1	3.1	67.3
2008–09 (terminal year)	Nil	3.0	...

Source: Medium Term Fiscal Policy Statement, 2004–05 and 2005–06, except for June data.
B.E. Budget estimate   R.E. Revised estimate

Regarding outstanding liabilities, we have two observations. First, government securities held by the RBI are included; these would have to be netted out if the central bank and the government are consolidated. Second, "reserve funds and deposits" are added to the stock of outstanding debt; these liabilities are created by borrowing from statutory funds within the government and therefore are not strictly in the nature of IOUs to entities external to the government.

Fiscal Responsibility Laws in the States

We now briefly review the fiscal responsibility laws of the first six states that have enacted them—Karnataka (the forerunner), Kerala, Maharashtra, Punjab, Tamil Nadu, and Uttar Pradesh. All six states impose quantitative and time-bound targets (four to six years) on revenue and fiscal deficits; specifically they eliminate revenue deficits and reduce fiscal deficits to 3 percent of gross state domestic product (GSDP).[32] (Notably, Kerala has a ceiling of 2 percent of GSDP for the fiscal deficit.) In addition, a couple of states have deployed atypical measures. The Maharashtra legislation, enacted in April 2005, stipulates that "The State Government shall by rules specify the targets for reduction of fiscal deficit," with the fiscal deficit target defined in a somewhat novel manner as a "ratio of expenditure on interest to revenue receipts." Tamil Nadu requires the government to reduce the ratio of revenue deficit to revenue receipts every year by 3–5 percent ("depending on the economic situation in that year") to a level below 5 percent in this ratio by the end of March 2008 (see table A-3 for a summary of the laws and the performance under them). Two states have legislated ceilings for official debt. Karnataka and Punjab have capped their outstanding total liabilities at 25 percent and 40 percent, respectively, of their respective GSDP. In contrast, Tamil Nadu has placed a limit on total outstanding guarantees of 100 percent of total revenue receipts in the preceding year or at 10 percent of GSDP, whichever is lower. It is noteworthy that Karnataka, according to revised estimates for 2004–05, eliminated its revenue deficit and achieved the fiscal deficit target one year ahead of schedule.

A couple of laudable initiatives pertaining to fiscal planning and transparency are embedded in these laws. The acts require some form of a medium-term fiscal policy statement (encompassing three-year rolling targets) that

---

32. See Rajaraman and Majumdar (2005) for implications for states of fiscal responsibility laws in the context of recommendations of the Twelfth Finance Commission.

lays out the time path for attaining the fiscal goals, and they also call for changes in accounting standards, government policies, and practices that are likely to affect the calculation of the fiscal indicators to be disclosed in the respective state assemblies. Although the acts oblige the respective governments to take "appropriate measures" (enhancing revenue, reducing expenditure, or both) in the event of either a shortfall in revenue or excess of expenditure over specified levels for a given year, leeway is allowed for targets going awry because of natural calamities or national security.

Basic Arithmetic of the FRBMA

What difference will the fiscal rules embodied in the FRBMA make in the short- and long-run behavior of the government debt burden? We first consider the implications of the rules on the assumption that they are indeed implemented and enforced. Then we reflect on the likelihood of them being enforced. We define the following further notation: d is the conventional central government financial deficit as a fraction of GDP, i^* is the average effective nominal interest rate on central government debt denominated in foreign currency, g^C is central government consumption spending as a share of GDP (excluding depreciation of the central government capital stock), g^I is gross central government capital formation as a share of GDP, δ is the proportional depreciation rate of the central government capital stock, k is the central government capital stock as a share of GDP, θ is the gross financial rate of return (which can of course be negative) on central government capital, α is the share of foreign currency debt in total central government debt, ε is the proportional rate of nominal depreciation of the rupee, and τ is central government taxes net of transfers as a share of GDP. Note that $d \equiv g^C + g^I + ib + (i^* - i)\alpha b - \theta k - \tau$. It follows that the ratio of central government net debt to GDP evolves over time as follows:

$$(18) \qquad \dot{b} \equiv d + \varepsilon\alpha b - (n + \pi)b$$

or, equivalently,

$$(19) \qquad \dot{b} \equiv (r - n)b + g^C + g^I - \theta k - \tau + (i^* + \varepsilon - i)\alpha b$$

Two key features of the FRBMA are the restriction that the overall central government financial deficit be no more than 3 percent of GDP (a number plucked out of the thin, or at least rarefied, air of the Maastricht Criteria for EMU membership and the EU's Stability and Growth Pact) by 2008–09:

$$(20) \qquad d \leq 0.03$$

and the "golden rule" restriction that the revenue budget be in balance or surplus. It is unclear whether this means that central government borrowing should not exceed gross central government investment (including depreciation) or net central government investment (net of depreciation). In the first case the (gross) golden rule can be written as

(21) $$d \le g^l$$

In the second case, the (net) golden rule can be written as

(22) $$d \le g^l - \delta k$$

If the deficit ceiling (equation 20) is rigorously enforced, the central government will never face a solvency or fiscal-financial sustainability problem. Of course, the rest of the general government sector (states and municipalities) may undo what ever fiscal restraint the central government exercises. Ignoring foreign-currency-denominated debt for simplicity, the consistent application of equation 20 implies that

(23) $$b(t) \equiv b(0)e^{-\int_0^t [n(u)+\pi(u)]ds} + \int_0^t d(s)e^{-\int_s^t [n(u)+\pi(u)]du} ds$$

$$\le b(0)e^{-\int_0^t [n(u)+\pi(u)]ds} + 0.03\int_0^t e^{-\int_s^t [n(u)+\pi(u)]du} ds$$

As long as the long-run average growth rate of nominal GDP, $\bar{n} + \bar{\pi}$ is positive, and $\lim_{t\to\infty} b(0)e^{-\int_0^t [n(u)+\pi(u)]ds} = 0$, the long-run debt-to-GDP ratio will satisfy

(24) $$\lim_{t\to\infty} b(t) \le \frac{0.03}{\bar{n} + \bar{\pi}}$$

Were India to maintain its real, annual GDP growth rate of, say, 6.2 percent ($\bar{n} = 0.0062$) and an average annual inflation rate of, say, 4 percent ($\bar{\pi} = 0.04$), the central government's ratio of long-run debt to annual GDP would be less than 30 percent—a comfortable level.

The requirement that the revenue budget be in balance or surplus is very likely to be the binding constraint on the central government, with the 3 percent ceiling on its overall financial deficit a nonbinding constraint. Even if the gross investment version of the golden rule (equation 21) is the operative one, India's central government's gross capital formation program amounted to no more than 1.5 percent of GDP in 2003–04.[33] Net central government capital formation is even less than that and may well be negative in years that economic depreciation is high. We suspect that a lot of current expenditure will be reclassified as capital expenditure if the golden rule were ever to be enforced seriously.

Any limit on the magnitude of the permissible deficit, regardless of whether it applies to the overall deficit or just to the revenue (current) deficit, will restrict the government's ability to engage in countercyclical deficit financing during economic downturns, unless the government generates sufficiently large surpluses during normal and prosperous times to avoid hitting the deficit ceiling during bad times.

Is there any feature of the FRBMA that encourages or cajoles governments to act countercyclically during periods of above-normal economic activity or (as in India since 2001–02) exceptionally low interest rates? The European Union's Stability and Growth Pact failed precisely because of the absence of "carrots" to run larger surpluses (or smaller deficits) during upswings and because the penalties (including fines) that were, in principle, part of the collective arsenal of pact enforcement were not imposed. The failure to exercise fiscal restraint during the upswing by France, Germany, and Italy was not penalized by the EU's Council of Ministers because the political cost-benefit analysis of naming, shaming, and fining a leading member of the EU militated against collective enforcement of these penalties. How much harder would it be for the Indian government to impose countercyclical discipline *on itself* during good times? What are the arrangements, institutions, laws, rules, regulations, or conventions that make fiscal restraint during periods of high conjuncture incentive-compatible for political decisionmakers with short electoral horizons and severely restricted capacity for credible commitment? Political opportunism calls for the postponement of painful expenditure cuts or tax increases—there is always the chance that the political cost of painful fiscal retrenchment will be borne by the opposition when its turn in office comes around. A tentative picture that we can draw, albeit from a short history, is that noncompliance by governments is unlikely to be politically costly; the electorate, the media, or even opposition parties have paid little attention to the subject matter! In fact it is widely felt that supplementary bills that boost expenditure from budgeted levels are unlikely to be rejected. Against this background, obtaining parliamentary waivers for missed targets should not be too difficult.

33. This excludes central government loans to states. Net lending by the central government to the states is about 0.5 percent of GDP.

Fiscal virtue cannot be legislated. It must be implemented and enforced—it must be incentive-compatible even for myopic and opportunistic governments. Unless India discovers a way of tying its fiscal Ulysses to the mast, the siren song of fiscal retrenchment tomorrow but fiscal expansion today will continue to lead policymakers astray.

As for increasing the efficiency and scope of financial intermediation, the problem is not just public ownership. The poor quality of financial intermediation by the formal financial system also results from the absence of effective competitive threats to inefficient incumbents. The sure, quick, and effective way to address this issue is to open up India's financial sector fully and without discriminatory constraints to foreign competition.

Further liberalization of the capital account could be a part of this additional opening up of India's financial sector to foreign competition, but even without this, much could be achieved by further easing the entry of foreign enterprises into the Indian markets for finance and financial services, as long as the service account of the balance of payments, including the remittance of profits abroad, is unconstrained. Foreign know-how, management, and control, through the cross-border movement of enterprises and other corporate entities, intensify competition and thereby boost efficiency even in markets for nontraded goods and services (such as retailing and the management of public utilities). Foreign competition, a fortiori, will boost productivity in sectors and industries where both local provision by foreign-owned firms and targeted exports by firms located abroad make life uncomfortable for established domestic suppliers. For the supply-side failures that limit and distort domestic intermediation, globalization is an important part of the answer.

APPENDIX

TABLE A-1. **Indian Public Debt as a Percent of GDP**

	CDD	SDD	PEDD	STPEDD*	NTDD	TFD	GTD	R	NTFD	NTD
1970–71	17.4	4.3	0.3	n.a.	22.0	13.7	35.7	1.6	12.1	34.1
1971–72	17.0	4.4	0.3	n.a.	21.6	13.8	35.5	1.8	12.0	33.6
1972–73	17.4	4.2	0.3	n.a.	22.0	14.5	36.5	1.7	12.8	34.8
1973–74	14.7	3.9	0.2	n.a.	18.7	13.1	31.9	1.6	11.5	30.3
1974–75	13.9	3.6	0.5	n.a.	18.1	12.6	30.7	1.4	11.2	29.3
1975–76	16.4	4.0	0.7	n.a.	21.1	14.6	35.7	2.3	12.3	33.5
1976–77	16.7	4.2	1.0	n.a.	21.9	14.0	36.0	3.7	10.3	32.2
1977–78	20.9	4.1	0.9	n.a.	25.9	12.7	38.6	4.9	7.8	33.7
1978–79	19.6	4.4	0.2	n.a.	25.2	12.0	37.2	5.4	6.6	31.8
1979–80	20.8	4.3	1.6	n.a.	26.6	12.0	38.6	4.9	7.0	33.6

(Table A-1 continued)

(Table A-1 continued)

	CDD	SDD	PEDD	STPEDD*	NTDD	TFD	GTD	R	NTFD	NTD
1980–81	20.5	4.0	1.6	n.a.	26.1	11.6	37.7	3.8	7.8	33.9
1981–82	20.0	4.3	1.5	n.a.	25.8	12.1	37.9	2.3	9.7	35.5
1982–83	23.9	4.4	1.9	n.a.	30.2	14.0	44.2	2.5	11.5	41.7
1983–84	22.0	4.6	2.1	n.a.	28.7	15.0	43.7	2.7	12.4	41.0
1984–85	23.0	4.6	2.2	n.a.	29.8	16.5	46.2	2.9	13.6	43.4
1985–86	25.1	5.1	2.3	n.a.	32.6	17.4	50.0	2.9	14.5	47.1
1986–87	27.7	5.1	2.6	n.a.	35.4	19.3	54.7	2.7	16.6	52.0
1987–88	28.6	5.5	3.1	n.a.	37.3	19.8	57.0	2.3	17.5	54.7
1988–89	29.6	5.5	3.9	n.a.	39.0	21.9	60.9	1.6	20.2	59.2
1989–90	30.5	5.8	4.4	n.a.	40.8	26.3	67.0	1.4	24.9	65.7
1990–91	30.7	6.0	4.8	1.6	41.4	28.3	69.7	1.8	26.5	67.9
1991–92	30.9	6.3	5.2	0.9	42.4	40.0	82.4	3.5	36.6	79.0
1992–93	32.0	6.4	4.8	2.3	43.2	37.1	80.3	4.0	33.1	76.3
1993–94	36.0	6.5	5.2	1.9	47.7	33.8	81.4	7.0	26.7	74.4
1994–95	35.5	6.4	4.5	1.6	46.5	29.8	76.3	7.8	22.0	68.5
1995–96	33.9	6.6	4.2	1.6	44.7	25.3	70.0	6.1	19.2	63.9
1996–97	33.8	6.7	4.6	1.9	45.1	22.4	67.5	6.9	15.6	60.7
1997–98	35.9	7.0	4.3	1.9	47.2	21.9	69.2	7.2	14.8	62.0
1998–99	37.2	7.5	5.8	2.5	50.5	21.7	72.2	7.9	13.8	64.3
1999–00	40.0	8.7	5.5	2.5	54.3	20.3	74.6	8.5	11.8	66.1
2000–01	43.0	9.9	4.4	2.8	57.3	19.2	76.5	9.2	10.0	67.3
2001–02	47.6	10.8	4.9	3.0	63.3	18.4	81.7	11.4	7.0	70.3
2002–03	53.0	12.1	4.7	2.6	69.8	17.8	87.6	14.8	3.0	72.7
2003–04	56.6	13.8	4.7	2.6	75.1	15.2	90.4	18.6	–3.4	71.8
2004–05	57.4	14.1	n.a.	n.a.	n.a.	n.a.	n.a.	20.1	n.a.	n.a.

Source: Reserve Bank of India, *Handbook of Statistics on the Indian Economy* (2003–04 and 2004–05); Reserve Bank of India, *Report on Currency and Finance,* volume II (various years); Government of India, *Budget Documents, Statement of Liabilities of the Central Government, Receipts Budget* (2002–03 and 2005–06); Government of India, Bureau of Public Enterprises, *Public Enterprises Survey* (volumes for 1970–71 to 2003–04); Reserve Bank of India, *Weekly Statistical Bulletin*; World Bank, *Global Development Finance Report* (various years). (GDP, used in the denominator for computing the ratios, is at current market prices.)

Definitions

CDD: Internal debt of the central government less net credit outstanding from the Reserve Bank of India; plus liabilities on account of small savings fund and other accounts.

SDD: Rupee denominated market and other loans of state governments (excluding loans and advances from the central government) less net credit outstanding from the Reserve Bank of India; plus provident funds etc.

PEDD: Long-term Rupee denominated debt of public enterprises not held by government.

NTDD: CDD + SDD + PEDD (excluding Rupee short-term public enterprise domestic debt, or STPEDD*, reported above, for which data is unavailable prior to 1990–91).

NTDD: Net total domestic debt.

TFD: Foreign currency public and publicly guaranteed long-term debt plus use of IMF credit plus imputed short-term public debt.

GTD: Gross total debt (NTDD + TFD).

R: Official foreign exchange reserves including gold and special drawing rights.

NTFD: Net total foreign debt (TFD – R).

NTD: Net total debt (NTDD + NTFD).

TABLE A-2. Administered Interest Rates on Savings Instruments

Name of the scheme	Limits of investment	Maturity period (years)			Rate of interest (percent per year)							Deductions under Sec. 80C of Income Tax Act	Amount outstanding at end-March 2005 (Rs billion)
		April 1992	Since Sept. 2 1993	Since Jan. 1 1999	Since April 1992	Since Sept. 2 1993	Since Jan. 1 1999	Since Jan. 15 2000	Since Mar. 1 2001	Since Mar. 1 2002	Since Mar. 1 2003		
1 Employees Provident Fund	12% of base salary by both employee, employer.				12.00	12.00	12.00	11.00 (since July)	9.50	9.50	9.50		1,134 (as of 31-3-04)
2 Commercial Bank Savings Account (akin to checking acct.)	No limit.				5.00 prior to Nov. 94	4.50 since Nov. 94	4.50	4.00 April 2000	4.00	4.00	3.50 (Floor Rate)	No	4,431
3 Post Office Savings Bank Accounts	Minimum Rs. 20 and maximum Rs. 1,00,000 for an individual account (Rs. 2 lakh jointly; No limit on group, institutional or official capacity accounts).				5.50	5.50	4.50	4.50	3.50	3.50	3.50	No	149
4 Public Provident Fund 1968	Minimum Rs. 100 and maximum Rs. 60,000 in a fiscal year.	15	15	15	12.00	12.00	12.00	11.00	9.50	9.00	8.00	Yes	143*
5 Post Office (PO) Time Deposit Account	Minimum Rs. 50 and no maximum limit.	1,2,3 and 5	1,2,3 and 5	1,2,3 and 5	12.00 to 13.50+	10.50 to 12.50-+	9.00 to 11.50+++	8.00 to 10.50**	7.50 to 9.00$	7.25 to 8.50**	6.25 to 7.50***	No	320
6 PO Rec. Dep. Account	Minimum Rs. 10 per month or any amount in multiples of Rs. 5 and no maximum limit.	5	5	5	13.50	12.50	11.50	10.50	9.00	8.50	7.50	No	411

No.	Scheme	Limits											Reinvest.	Amount
7	National Savings Scheme 1992	Minimum Rs. 100 and no maximum limit.	4	4	4	11.00	11.00	10.50	9.00	8.50	...		Yes	7
8	PO Monthly Income Scheme	Minimum Rs. 1,000 and maximum Rs. 3 lakh in single account and Rs. 6 lakh in joint account.	6	6	6	14.00	13.00	12.00	11.00	9.50	9.00	8.00	No	1,510
9	NSC VIII Issue	Minimum Rs. 100 and no maximum limit.	6	6	6	12.00	12.00	11.50	11.00	9.50	9.00	8.00	Yes	551
10	Indira Vikas Patra	No limit.	5	5½	6	14.87@	13.43@	12.25@	–	–	–	–	No	8
11	Kisan Vikas Patra	No limit.	5	5½	6@@	14.87@	13.43@	12.25@	11.25@	10.03@	9.57@	8.41@	No	1,364
12	Deposit scheme for retiring govt.–PSU employees	Minimum Rs. 1,000 and maximum not exceeding the total retirement benefits.	3	3	3	9.00	10.00	9.00	9.00	8.50	8.00	7.00	No	12
13	Senior Citizens Saving Scheme	Minimum Rs. 1,000 and maximum Rs. 15 lakhs	...	...	5^^	...	...	...	...	...	...	9.00^^	No	54

Source: National Savings Organization; Receipts Budget, Government of India; Accountant General, Posts & Telegraph; Government of India press releases; Report of the Advisory Committee to Advise on the Administered Interest Rates; Ministry of Labor; Reserved Bank of India, *Handbook of Statistics on the Indian Economy (2004–05)*.

* Relates to post office transactions only.
– 1 Year –12%, 2 Years –12.5%, 3 Years –13% and 5 Years –13.5%.
+ + 1 Year –10.5%, 2 Years –11%, 3 Years –12% and 5 Years –12.5%.
+ + + 1 Year –9%, 2 Years –10%, 3 Years –11% and 5 Years –11.5%.
** 1 Year –8%, 2 Years – 9%, 3 Years – 10% and 5 Years – 10.5%.
$ 1 Year – 7.5%, 2 Years – 8%, 3 Years – 9% and 5 Years – 9%.
$$ 1 Year – 7.25%, 2 Years – 7.5%, 3 Years – 8.25% and 5 Years – 8.5%.
$$$ 1 Year – 6.25%, 2 Years – 6.5%, 3 Years – 7.25% and 5 Years – 7.5%.
@ Compounded interest rate.
^^ Introduced in August 2004.
@@ Maturity period has been raised to 6½ years with effect from January 15, 2000, 7 years 3 months from March 1, 2001, 7 years 8 months from March 1, 2002 and 8 years 7 months from March 1, 2003.

TABLE A-3. State Fiscal Responsibility Legislation Targets and Performance

State	Karnataka	Kerala	Tamil Nadu	Punjab	Uttar Pradesh	Maharashtra
Effective from	2002–03	2003–04	2002–03	2003–04	2004–05	2005–06
Fiscal deficit (FD) as % of GSDP	Not more than 3% by end-March 2006.	2% by end-March 2007.	Not more than 3% by end-March 2008.	Contain rate of growth of FD to 2% per annum in nominal terms, until brought down to 3% of GSDP.	Not more than 3% by end-March 2009.	Rules to be specified for reduction of fiscal deficit, with the target "interpreted in the form of a ratio of expenditure on interest to revenue receipts."
Revenue deficit (RD)	Nil by end-March 2006.	Nil by end-March 2007.	Ratio of RD to revenue receipts (RR) not to exceed 5% by end-March 2008.	Reduce RD as percentage of RR by at least 5 percentage points each year until revenue balance is achieved.	Nil by end-March 2009.	Revenue surplus from 2009–10 onwards.
Debt as % of GSDP	Total liabilities not to exceed 25% of GSDP by end-March 2015.	…	…	Not to exceed 40% by end-March 2007.	Not to exceed 25% by end-March 2018.	…

As % of GSDP	Karnataka		Kerala		Tamil Nadu		Punjab		Uttar Pradesh		Maharashtra	
	RD	FD	RD	FD	RD	FD	RD	FD	RD	FD	RD	FD
2001–02	3.1	5.6	3.6	4.5	1.9	3.3	5.4	7.1	3.3	5.2	3.1	4.1
2002–03	2.3	4.6	5.1	6.2	3.1	4.4	5.2	6.1	2.5	4.7	3.2	4.9
2003–04	0.6	4.6	4.1	6.3	2.2	4.5	4.5	7.4	n.a.	n.a.	2.7	5.9
2004–05	+0.4	2.8	4.6	5.4	0.9	3.0	n.a.	n.a.	2.4	4.4	2.5	3.8

Sources: Reserve Bank of India, *State Finances—A Study of Budgets (2004–05)*, December 2004; and summary of state budget documents for 2004–05 revised estimates.

n.a. Not available.

Comments and Discussion

Abhijit V. Banerjee: The paper argues that while deficits in India are large, at least in the short run the risk of a deficit-induced crisis is minimal. The main reason to worry about deficits is that they crowd out private investment and give the government reason to want the financial sector to remain inefficient, so that there is less competition for the savings. This, in turn, distorts the allocation of savings within the private sector, discourages entry and exit, and reduces the overall growth of the economy.

Buiter and Patel are not optimistic about the current efforts to rein in the deficit. In particular they believe that the recent efforts to bind the hands of the governments, through the Fiscal Responsibility and Budget Management Act at the center and the fiscal responsibility laws at the state level, will be renegotiated when the crunch comes, because right now, there is no real constituency for shrinking the deficit nor any mechanism for automatically punishing delinquent governments (as there would be, for example, if most of the debt was foreign currency debt).

They seem less pessimistic about improving the performance of the financial markets. Their recipe is to make the financial markets more competitive by permitting more liberal entry by foreign intermediaries into the Indian market. They note in passing that this would also make it harder for the government to borrow and, interestingly, they see this as a two-edged sword: It would of course cost more for the government to be profligate, which would have salutary effects, but if the deficit remains large, the economy could be more prone to crises.

I tend broadly to agree with their conclusions, with one important exception. Let me start however with a few points of clarification. First, while the Fiscal Responsibility and Budget Management Act may not in the end bind, they are very important steps toward enhancing the political salience of the deficit. By announcing a target, the government is setting up to fail in public, whereas before it used to fail in private—the press and the opposition can now attack it for reneging on its explicit promise.

Second, the deficit has remained stubbornly high in the face of improved tax performance by both the state and central governments; this fact suggests that the real problem is the government's inability to resist populist demands.

39

Hence, while a case could be made for further tax effort (one could argue that India is still an undertaxed economy), one worries that any extra tax collection would only feed further profligacy until the discourse of public expenditures is altered. Here I do not yet sense any progress—I do not hear anybody speaking the language of trade-offs. When a new initiative is proposed, we do not hear the government saying: "That was a bad program, all the money was going to the rich; let us get rid of it and replace it by this other better program." Instead, the program being introduced is always portrayed as a new gift from the ever-generous government, even though additional programs are often funded by quietly diverting money from existing programs.

Third, whatever the history, it is not clear that the banking system today is bailing out the government. In fact the reverse seems true: it is the government that is bailing out the banks—the government could easily lower interest rates further if it wanted. The political economy of this is complex. The problem is that most middle-class people in India like to have their savings in safe assets, and they have historically been able to get decent returns by putting their money in bank deposits. At the same time, the banks could always lend to the government, and the government paid generously. This particular cozy arrangement has been unraveling over the last decade, as the government became more and more interested in reducing its interest costs.

Lowering interest rates further and borrowing less would force the banks to cut the rates they pay on deposits, which would be politically unpopular. Moreover given that the banks still have a large amount of high-interest liabilities on their books (fixed deposits and the like), cutting interest rates further might endanger the stability of some of the weaker banks. One can therefore understand why the government may be reluctant to move faster.

Which brings me to the one place where I disagree with Buiter and Patel. They end their piece with a plea for allowing the entry of foreign players into the banking sector as a way of making the sector more competitive and efficient. We now have a bit of evidence on the impact of the foreign banks that have already entered. Gormley shows that in the districts in India where foreign banks entered, the probability of getting a loan went up for the 10 percent most profitable firms, but the average firm was actually 7.6 percent less likely to have a long-term loan of any sort.[1] Gormley interprets this as an effect of "cherry-picking" by the foreign banks. The domestic banks, having lost their most profitable clients to the foreign banks, shrank away from risk taking and cut their lending to the more marginal firms.

1. Gormley (2005).

All the accumulated evidence suggests that smaller firms in India are already underserved by the banking system. Banerjee and Duflo exploit two changes in the definition of the priority sector (it was expanded in 1998 and shrunk in 2000), as a natural experiment on credit access.[2] The results from both experiments are almost identical. They both suggest that for the firms that get more (less) credit in the expansion (contraction)—the medium-sized firms in the organized sector—the marginal product of capital exceeds 80 percent.

The evidence from Gormley suggests that just the fact of entry by foreign banks spoils the climate for the smaller firms. There is reason to suspect that in this respect things would only get worse if, in addition, there were takeovers of domestic banks by foreign banks. The core problem in banking is how to make sure that loan officers are lending responsibly; in smaller banks, the loan officers can be monitored more closely and therefore can be given more discretion. As the bank gets larger and the chain of control becomes longer, more and more rigid lending rules replace discretion. This, as Berger and others show for the United States, means that the smaller and more marginal firms, which are the firms where judgment really plays a role in the lending decisions, tend to get less credit once a small bank is amalgamated with a larger one.[3] It seems very likely that something very similar would happen if an Indian bank were taken over by a foreign bank (we already know that the extant foreign banks do not lend to small firms).

This is not to say that no action should be taken to galvanize the Indian banking system. It is indeed true that the structure of growth in Indian banking under nationalization was not aimed at generating competition. Every district was assigned a lead bank, and it was assumed that the lead bank would dominate lending in that region. Vestiges of this system still persist, and in many districts it is not uncommon to find that the dominant bank is one of the weaker and less dynamic public banks and that the better public banks hardly have a presence.

The natural solution to this problem is consolidation. The government should force the public sector banks to come together into a small number of much bigger banks, each under the leadership of one of the best public banks. It probably pays to involve some of the best "private" banks in this process as well. This will give each of these new "big" banks access to an established network of branches almost everywhere in the country and the

2. Banerjee and Duflo (2004).
3. Berger and others (2002).

ability to tap into the cheapest sources of savings. This will create a situation where multiple dynamic banks compete for clients in every location.

Consolidation is also an advantage from the point of view of selling off some of these banks to private buyers (or even foreign buyers), since there is less risk that the government will end up holding on to the weakest banks just when competition heats up. This is especially important because, as Buiter and Patel note, everybody in the system assumes that the government is liable if any of the banks collapse.

Even with consolidation, however, this assumption of liability remains a major problem for a government that is thinking of selling off the controlling shares in the banks to the private sector (or foreign private sector). The danger is that the Indian state will continue to be liable after control has been sold, because this is what the public expects. This would mean that the gains from risk taking go to the owners of the bank, but that the government would have to foot the bill in the event of a disaster. Let me end with two suggestions about how to deal with this issue: first, the government should hold on to a significant amount of equity in these banks even after the control rights have been transferred, to make sure that it shares in the gains from increased risk taking. Second, the liability should be structured to make sure that a substantial part of the buyer's total assets (and not just the assets of the Indian subsidiary of the foreign company), are backing the purchase. What we want to avoid is an Argentina-like situation where the foreign owners of the failed Argentine banks could walk away with their non-Argentine assets intact.

Robert Lawrence: This informative paper makes three basic points. The first is that while the Indian government has been running large government deficits—and has experienced a rising debt-to-GDP ratio—the situation is not unsustainable. Instead India appears to be on a path in which, with plausible assumptions about growth, inflation, and interest rates, it could settle into a long-term equilibrium with high and steady levels of debt to GDP and sustainable budget deficit levels. Second, the deficits reinforce the dominance of the state in Indian financial markets with adverse consequences for the efficiency of capital allocation. Government financial institutions fail to carry out their role as intermediaries between private sector borrowers and lenders and instead devote large amounts of their portfolios to holding government securities. In addition, incentives in many dimensions of behavior are severely distorted, resulting in moral hazard, regulatory forbearance, and generally poor credit allocation decisions. And third, the

Indian government has officially recognized the desirability of increased fiscal discipline and embarked on a program to achieve it through the Fiscal Responsibility and Budget Management Act. However, this program fails to impose the needed discipline on the national government, fails to address the role of states in generating deficits, and could lead to procyclical fiscal policy.

I found this paper very interesting and I learned a lot from it. In these observations I will discuss each of the major points in turn. The time series analysis on stability is compelling. India is not about to run into an explosive situation. Indeed, despite the reemergence of large internal deficits, there is little evidence of upward pressures on either inflation or interest rates. Apparently, Indian households have raised their saving rates sufficiently to finance the deficit and the increased demand for investment without the need for foreign borrowing. In the United States our deficit syndrome is often called twin deficits. In India's case, however, the government deficit is an orphan— because foreign debt is low and foreign reserves high—in essence low government saving is offset by high net private saving. It is particularly interesting that the analysis suggests that the internal debt situation is sustainable when it looks quite similar to the situation in the early 1990s when there was a crisis. This suggests that the source of the problem at that time was really the external constraint.

Nonetheless it is important not to confuse a situation that is sustainable with one that is desirable. Indeed, as the paper makes clear, it is relatively easier to persuade people to change their behavior when you can show they are heading for disaster than when you have to argue that if they changed things, it would be tougher in the short run but better in the long run. Assuming interest rates remain at current levels and the deficit a constant share of GDP, we know that each year until the debt-to-GDP ratio stabilizes, interest payments will rise as a share of GDP, thereby crowding out other government spending. To be sure, if the money goes to public investments with a high social return, borrowing could be justified. But this is not what is happening. It appears that, on the contrary, government investment has born the brunt of the adjustment. Again, it is interesting to ask about history. What has changed? Why was India able to maintain fiscal discipline until the 1980s, and yet today, even though incomes are rising, the government is apparently less able to resist the pressures for bigger deficits?

The authors also argue that large budget deficits have reduced Indian capital formation and thus Indian growth. They claim that the deficits have a negative impact on private saving, and also reduce the efficiency of the financial system in allocating capital. The authors cite several papers to support their claim that borrowing to finance public debts depresses private saving, but they present no proof that this has actually happened in India, and they offer no discussion of why, in theory, bigger government deficits should be expected to reduce private saving. The more traditional debate, is of course, whether private savings *rise sufficiently* to offset the deficit (as suggested by a Barro-Ricardian framework) and thus whether *national* saving is depressed by government deficits. It would have strengthened the paper if a theoretical explanation for the anticipated negative impact on private saving had been offered.

The second part of the paper is also focused on the distortions in capital allocation that result from extensive state ownership of banks. The need to finance the deficits in part by having banks hold the debt reduces the banks' need to invest in the private sector. One might have hoped that this would at least have meant that banks are highly creditworthy and liquid. But the authors argue that other behavior attributable to government influence, such as regulatory forbearance, actually leads the banks to accumulate substandard debt. The net result is therefore too much debt that is safe and too much that is unsafe. One might have expected nonbank capital markets to flourish under these circumstances, but again the authors present us with evidence that suggests they have not. The authors do offer reasons why incentives are distorted and financial intermediation is inefficient, but they also offer one piece of empirical evidence to support their claim that Indian investment is inefficient that is not very convincing. They make much of the fact that India has a capital–output ratio of three to one. But they also report that the Chinese capital–output ratio is considerably higher, at four to one. While this may indicate that China is even less efficient than India it does not really demonstrate the point they are making about India. Indeed, my sense is that a capital–output ratio of three to one is actually quite typical, suggesting the investment inefficiency problems may not be as great as they imply. Their argument would have been more compelling had they provided evidence that other countries have much lower capital–output ratios.

The third issue raised in the paper relates to efforts to control budget deficits through fiscal rules. The paper describes efforts at both the central and the state level to impose such rules. These reflect good intentions, but it is not clear that beyond helping to focus on the medium-term budget outlook, they will actually achieve their objectives. Indeed, the fact that the finance minister felt compelled to delay implementation of the FRBMA even before it became effective does not exactly inspire confidence in its efficacy. At the end of the day, the authors conclude that unfortunately fiscal virtue cannot simply be legislated. While that may well be the case,

given current institutional arrangements, I do not see why it should automatically be taken as given. In particular, I would have liked some consideration of a constitutional provision that would prohibit state governments
from running deficits. Such a prohibition would avoid the free-rider problem
that currently exists because the states can rely on the central government
to bail them out. Yes, there should be fiscal redistribution from the central
government, but the whole point is that fiscal federalism should force the
states to internalize the costs of their own expenditures. By the way, as I
understand it, a significant amount of the state budget deficits is funded
through small savings—and this suggests another way to impose discipline
on the states: eliminate these programs. Indeed they are probably another
important way in which the government is reducing the effectiveness of the
private sector by inhibiting the development of private intermediaries that
compete for savings deposits.

Indira Rajaraman: My comments on the paper are grouped under three
heads. The first is the fiscal stance in India; the second, blunted incentives
implicit in public ownership of banks; and the third, fiscal rules.

The Fiscal Stance

The title of the paper is somewhat value laden, with the wording prejudging
the issues. The term *excessive budget deficits* suggests that a less excessive
budget deficit is preferable, by definition, regardless of how the correction
is achieved. This was the message beamed at the Indian government at the
start of reform in 1991, and in the mad scramble to bring down the fiscal
deficit, there were huge cuts in public expenditure on capital formation.
The paper acknowledges what it calls "infrastructure-unfriendly cuts" in
public capital expenditure but says that these cuts "cannot be seen" in the
fiscal deficit numbers because of compensating increases in current expenditure. That is factually incorrect. Figure 6 shows the consolidated fiscal and
revenue (current) deficits aggregated across central and state levels of government, over the fifty-year period 1951–2001 as a percent of GDP, along
with the (average) interest rate on public debt. The vertical distance between
the fiscal and revenue deficits measures the budgetary capital expenditure
as a percent of GDP (unless there are substantial privatization receipts,
which was not the case over this period). Capital expenditure fell sharply
between 1991 and 1997, and brought the fiscal deficit down with it, by
3 percentage points of GDP. Only after 1997 was the vertical difference not

FIGURE 6. Fiscal and Revenue Deficits and Interest Rates on Public Debt Consolidated across Central and State Governments, 1951–2001

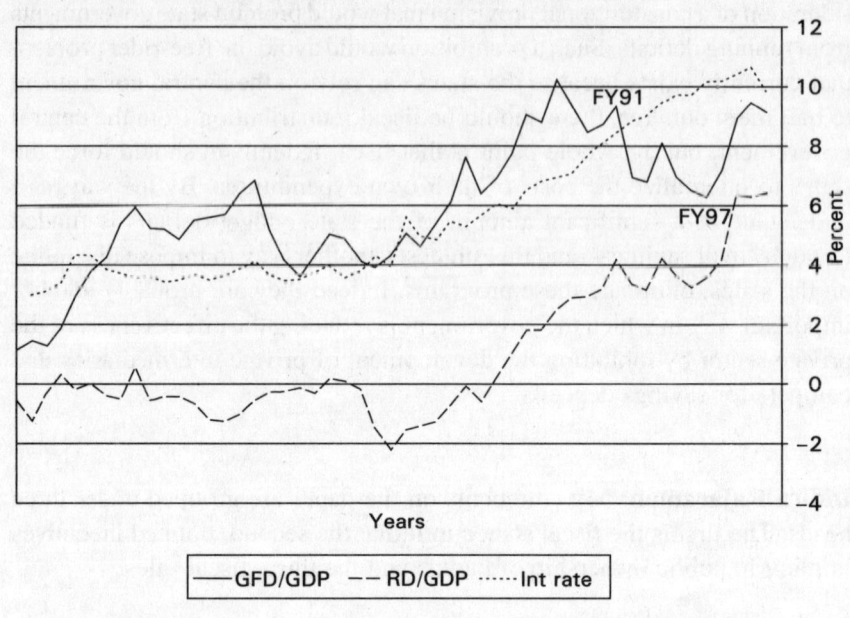

Source: Rajaraman (2006).

reduced any further. The revenue deficit rose after that point, and the fiscal deficit rose with it.

The paper could have made a lasting contribution if it had calibrated the net impact, through a computable general equilibrium model, of fiscal correction achieved through cuts in expenditure on capital formation. In the absence of such estimates, there remains the possibility that during the past fifteen years since the start of reform, the years in which the budget deficit was less excessive through capital expenditure cuts might have inflicted more lasting damage on the growth prospects of the economy than years in which the deficit was more excessive. The introduction of fiscal rules will, it is hoped, put a stop to the capital expenditure route to fiscal correction.

The deficits were clearly driven by the rate of interest on public debt. From 1951 until 1975, when financial suppression kept the interest rate on public debt down at the 4 percent level, the fiscal deficit rarely crossed 6 percent of GDP, and the current deficit (or the revenue deficit, as it is termed in India), was at zero or in surplus. After 1975, when financial suppression was lifted, the interest rate rose steadily and carried the fiscal and revenue deficits up with it until 1991. Interest rates finally turned down only starting in fiscal 2000.

For any responsible evaluation of the fiscal stance over this period, it is clear that the interest rate has to be cleaned out of the fiscal and revenue deficits, to obtain the corresponding primary aggregates. This is shown in figure 7. The primary fiscal deficit shows a stable pattern around a constant trend. The primary revenue deficit was substantially negative during much of the period, which is to say that there was a primary revenue surplus, until post-reform, when it began to hug the zero axis more closely, and finally pushed through into a positive deficit after 1997. The two primary deficits together do not convey a portrait of a fiscally profligate state, at least over the period 1951–97.

FIGURE 7.   Primary Fiscal and Revenue Deficits Consolidated across Central and State Governments, 1951–2001

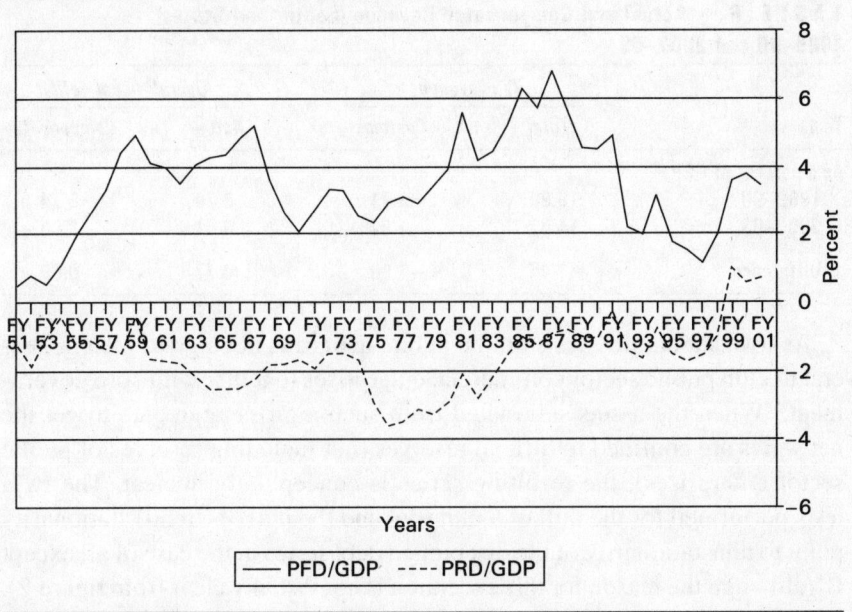

Years

PFD/GDP ---- PRD/GDP

Source: Rajaraman (2006).

The issue of why the primary revenue deficit worsened after the start of reform is an important one. When trade tax reform was initiated in 1991 along with other reforms, revenues from trade taxes declined sharply (table 6). This shortfall was not fully compensated by revenue from other sources. The tax-to-GDP ratio fell from 16 percent (1989–90) to a low of 13.4 percent (1998–99), before rising to 14.5 percent (2002–03), a fall of 1.46 percentage points from its pre-reform high. This fall in overall taxes was lower than that of customs revenue, which fell by 1.89 percentage points. Thus, revenue compensation from other sources totaled 0.43 percent of GDP. The overall fiscal deficit between the two years 1989–90 and 2002–03 shows a rise by 0.77 percent, but the compensated deficit for 2002–03, which subtracts the total revenue decline from the crude deficit, shows a fall of 0.69 percent. What this means is that the fiscal system responded to the fall in the tax-to-GDP ratio by reducing expenditure by 0.69 percent, and allowing the deficit to rise by 0.77 percent, while also compensating for the customs revenue decline from other taxes by 0.43 percent. This fiscal difficulty faced by India as a direct outcome of trade reform is common to many other developing countries.[4]

T A B L E 6 . Actual and Compensated Revenue (Center and States), 1989–90 and 2002–03

Years	Tax revenue		Overall fiscal deficit	
	Total	Customs	Actual	Compensated
As a percent of GDP				
1989–90	15.98	3.71	8.74	8.74
2002–03	14.52	1.82	9.51	8.05
Difference	−1.46	−1.89	0.77	−0.69

As to sustainability tests on the public debt, it is not a good idea in general to club public sector commercial enterprises together with core government.[5] When the assets subtracted from such a gross aggregate to get the net series are confined to official reserves (not including reserves of public sector enterprises), the resulting series is conceptually unclear. The twin tests performed for the null of a unit root and the null of (trend) stationarity point to nonstationarity of the discounted debt series in the case of all except B_2^* (although the reason for this exception is not visually clear from figure 2). Also, the graph of B_1^* does not suggest supersolvency, as the authors suggest.

4. The larger issue, and the failure of the literature to address the issue adequately, is set out in detail in Rajaraman (2004).

5. Rajaraman and Mukhopadhyay (2004).

Blunted Incentives

The section on the financial sector speaks of blunted incentives implicit in public ownership of the commercial banks and other financial institutions. Although publicly owned commercial banks account for 78 percent of total deposits, there are only twenty-eight publicly owned commercial banks (PSU banks) in a field of eighty-eight banks overall.[6]

When going into the ownership issue, theory about blunted incentives should not blind us into not looking at actual outcomes. Although the mean performance of publicly owned banks is lower than that of all other banks, the dispersion within the set of PSU banks is very wide. Regardless of the financial indicator used, whether it is nonperforming assets, or any indicator of operational efficiency, some PSU banks handily outperform other banks, whether foreign or domestic. A panel regression exercise for the twenty-seven PSU banks, over the period 1995–2000, shows fixed, bank-specific effects indicative of systematic differences within the set, although the fixed effects do not say anything about why these differences exist.[7] What the findings do show is that ownership is not destiny, and that it would be more fruitful to focus on the many critical regulatory and other reforms needed in the financial sector, which still remains precariously poised, rather than to focus exclusively on the ownership issue.

The paper mentions the persistence of financial suppression. The lifting of suppression of interest rates in the system, which began in 1975, is now virtually complete, barring a few interest rates on small loans. Rates on small savings continue to be administratively set, the political economy of which is set out in detail elsewhere.[8] This intervention serves to hold up interest rates, rather than hold them down. I am not sure the term *financial suppression* can be applied to such a situation, although I concede that this is a definitional issue.

Fiscal Rules

In the study of the consolidated deficit, which is the source for the figures and table displayed in my comment, the econometric results show evidence that the fiscal deficit in India responds to both the political cycle and the business cycle. There is an inherent tension therefore in the design of fiscal

6. At the end of March 2005, according to the RBI (2005), down from a total of 101 in 2000.

7. Rajaraman and Vasishtha (2002).

8. Rajaraman (2006).

rules for India, whether at national or subnational level, between providing enough flexibility to respond to the business cycle, while constraining pre-election profligacy. The Punjab FRBMA has an explicit provision for barring fiscal profligacy in the six-month period leading up to elections. Clearly this still leaves room for endogenous fixing of election dates so as to subvert the intent of the provision. There is always an enforcement problem, but fiscal rules in India are a start, and a very necessary one, toward requiring that fiscal correction should focus on the current account rather than on capital expenditure.

After the report of the Twelfth Finance Commission (TFC) was made public in March 2005, there is on offer a reward of a substantial reduction by 300 basis points on the interest rate on state debt owed to the national government, for states that enact FRBMAs with five required features. One of the features is elimination of the revenue deficit by 2008–09, with a stated path to that target, and another is reduction of the fiscal deficit to 3 percent (with no stipulated year). States responded immediately to this incentive. As a result, the number of states that had enacted fiscal rules had grown to eighteen by the end of 2005, and is continuing to rise.[9] The TFC has had the salutary effect of making states respond voluntarily to the incentive to enact FRBMAs with a commitment to elimination of revenue deficits by a specific date. The enforcement issue remains.

General Discussion

Ashok Lahiri, as chair, addressed Robert Lawrence's question as to why India's culture of fiscal sobriety had deteriorated after the 1980s. In Lahiri's view, this was in part due to the arrival of coalition politics at the center and the end of the monopoly of the Congress Party. He agreed with Indira Rajaraman that the underlying cause of fiscal stress was less spending profligacy and more the liberalization of interest rates on government debt. While agreeing that even better performance was needed, he observed that India's ICOR as measured by the paper was similar to that of most developed countries, better than India's past performance and better than that of China. On crowding out, he noted that significant demand for government paper remained in the system, as indicated by the Reserve Bank's use of special securities for sterilization operations under the so-called market stabilization

---

9. A detailed discussion of the incentives offered by the TFC, and the problems with them, is in Rajaraman and Majumdar (2005).

scheme (MSS). Lahiri saw the "lazy banking" episode of excessive commercial bank purchases of government debt as largely cyclical and already unwinding. Finally, he felt the paper's critique of the FRBMA was somewhat harsh: the postponement of deadlines was a response to the delay in promulgating the law and announcing the rules; the existence of a law could be useful and was unlikely to do any harm.

T. N. Srinivasan judged that the paper's presentation of crowding out of private investment was too sweeping. His own reading of the experience of the 1990s suggested that there was a break around 1996–97, after which growth rates stopped rising and began fluctuating around an average significantly lower than the 6.8 percent attained during 1992–93 to 1996–97 and private investment weakened. He favored the hypothesis that after the break the private investment schedule had shifted to the left; it appeared now that it was in the process once again of moving back to the right.

On public dissaving crowding out private saving, Srinivasan said the weakness of the Indian private saving data simply did not allow meaningful statements to be made about Ricardian equivalence. He also did not agree that trade liberalization was substantially responsible for fiscal stress and thereby for a collapse of public investment, nor that this reduction had been particularly harmful for economic growth. Public domination of infrastructure had in the past crowded out private investment; as the public sector withdrew, the private sector was expected to step in. Its inability to do so was for a set of regulatory failures (exemplified by the ill-fated power plant at Dabhol) and not for macroeconomic reasons.

The remainder of the discussion focused on the inefficient (or suboptimal) allocation of resources by the financial sector and policy responses to remedy this. Kaushik Basu was troubled by the conclusions reached by Abhijit Banerjee on misallocation of resources by the financial system. He did not consider it inefficient or irrational for banks to lend to cash-rich borrowers. This was an effective marker of a person with the necessary range of contacts needed to realize an entrepreneurial opportunity. Banerjee disagreed: his study suggested that the beneficiaries of bank credit were actually producing very little. Others asked what the penalties were for nonperformance by both borrowers and banks, and the role of the supervisors in enforcing such penalties, particularly where publicly owned banks were concerned.

Action by the regulators in recent cases suggested that 100 percent deposit insurance was in effect irrespective of the ownership of the commercial bank. Ajay Shah noted that where the dominant shareholder was the government, private shareholders were not dispossessed: government was willing to undertake full recapitalization of any capital deficit that might arise. In the case of a so-called "new" private sector bank, however, existing shareholders had indeed lost all their equity. Thus there was the beginning of some incentive by shareholders to monitor bank asset quality, but none as yet by depositors.

The issue was how to change the lending behavior of banks. Shah agreed that privatization of existing public sector banks was extremely unlikely in the current political environment. There was also no reason to be unduly pessimistic; even in the current environment of moral hazard, new private banks had shown themselves to be capable of disciplined, innovative lending. But their expansion continued to be hindered by a range of regulations whose effect, if not intention, was to limit competition. Enhanced freedom of entry was thus important to improve commercial bank performance. Furthermore, at least for major corporations, the capital markets were now providing an alternative source of funding. Banerjee countered that the evidence available from banks that were and were not nationalized in 1980 is that competition per se did not significantly influence bank behavior.

Surjit Bhalla believed that the willingness of the banks to prefer government debt over loans was perfectly rational in an environment of disinflation; he also pointed to the role of high administered interest rates on small savings schemes as an important explanation for high real interest rates and reduced appetite for borrowing. Banerjee believed that there was an important qualitative difference between commercial banks deploying resources in credit operations versus securities, since the former generated valuable information, particularly regarding the opportunities facing new firms. Suman Bery asked whether anybody still believed in the McKinnon-Shaw view of financial repression; in that view, high real interest rates were a positive, not a negative. He also asked if the government had gone overboard in eliminating its recourse to foreign net financing; an optimal debt management strategy would presumably provide some role for foreign debt, reducing the draft on domestic savings. Finally he asked if there was a clear agenda of institutional innovations (such as credit bureaus) that could help improve access to the financial system, as had happened so successfully in the United States over the past fifty years.

References

Banerjee, Abhijit, and Esther Duflo. 2004. "Do Firms Want to Borrow More? Testing Credit Constraints Using a Directed Lending Program." Department of Economics, MIT.

Banerjee, Abhijit, Shawn Cole, and Esther Duflo. 2004. "Banking Reform in India." *India Policy Forum* 1: 277–323.

Berger, Allen N., and others. 2002. "Does Function Follow Organizational Form? Evidence from the Lending Practices of Large and Small Banks." NBER Working Paper 8752. National Bureau of Economic Research, Cambridge, Mass.

Bhattacharya, Saugata, and Urjit Patel. 2002. "Financial Intermediation in India: A Case of Aggravated Moral Hazard?" Working Paper 145, Stanford Center for International Development, July.

————. 2005. "Reform Strategies in the Indian Financial Sector." In *India's and China's Recent Experience with Reform and Growth*, edited by Wanda Tseng and David Cowen. Basingstoke, U.K.: Palgrave Macmillan.

Buiter, Willem, and Urjit Patel. 1997. "Budgetary Aspects of Stabilization and Structural Adjustment in India." In *Macroeconomic Dimensions of Public Finance, Essays in Honour of Vito Tanzi*, editd by Mario Blejer and Teresa Ter-Minassian. London: Routledge.

Dickey, David, and Wayne Fuller. 1981. "Likelihood Ratio Statistics for Autoregressive Time Series with a Unit Root." *Econometrica* 49: 1057–72.

Federal Reserve Bank of Boston. 2006. *The Macroeconomics of Fiscal Policy*. Conference Series 49. MIT Press.

Fuller, Wayne. 1976. *Introduction to Statistical Time Series*. New York: Wiley.

Gormley, Todd. 2005. "Banking Competition in Developing Countries: Does Foreign Bank Entry Improve Credit Access?" Department of Economics, MIT.

Kapur, Devesh, and Urjit Patel. 2003. "Large Foreign Currency Reserves: Insurance for Domestic Weaknesses and External Uncertainties?" *Economic and Political Weekly* 38 (March 15–21): 1047–53.

Kwiatkowski, Denis, Peter Phillips, Peter Schmidt, and Yongcheol Shin. 1992. "Testing the Null Hypothesis of Stationarity against the Alternative of a Unit Root." *Journal of Econometrics* 54: 159–78.

La Porta, Rafael, Florencio Lopez-de-Silanes, and Andrei Shleifer. 2002. "Government Ownership of Banks." *Journal of Finance* 57: 265–301.

Lal, Deepak, Suman Bery, and Devendra Pant. 2003. "The Real Exchange Rate, Fiscal Deficits and Capital Flows: India: 1981–2000." *Economic and Political Weekly* 38 (November 22–28): 4965–76.

Patel, Urjit. 2004. "Role of State-owned Financial Institutions in India: Should the Government 'Do' or 'Lead'?" In *The Future of State-owned Financial Institutions*, edited by Gerard Caprio, Jonathan Fiechter, Robert Litan, and Michael Pomerleano. Washington, D.C., Brookings.

Patel, Urjit, and Saugata Bhattacharya. 2003. "The Financial Leverage Coefficient: Macroeconomic Implications of Government Involvement in Intermediaries." Working Paper 157, Stanford Center for International Development, January.

Phillips, Peter, and Pierre Perron. 1988. "Testing for a Unit Root in Time Series Regression." *Biometrika* 75, no. 2: 335–46.

Rajaraman, Indira. 2004. "Fiscal Restructuring in the Context of Trade Reform." In *The Dynamics of Fiscal Federalism: Challenges Before the Twelfth Finance Commission*, edited by G. C. Srivastava, pp. 201–30. New Delhi: Taxmann.

———. 2006. "Fiscal Developments and Outlook in India." In *Sustainable Fiscal Policy for India: An International Perspective*, edited by Peter Heller and M. G. Rao, pp. 8–43. New Delhi: Oxford University Press.

Rajaraman, Indira, and Abhiroop Mukhopadhyay. 2004. "Univariate Time Series Analysis of Public Debt." *Journal of Quantitative Economics* 2 (New Series) (July): 122–34.

Rajaraman, Indira, and Debdatta Majumdar. 2005. "Equity and Consistency Properties of the Twelfth Finance Commission Recommendations." *Economic and Political Weekly* 40 (July 30): 3413–20.

Rajaraman, Indira, and Garima Vasishtha. 2002. "Non-Performing Loans of PSU Banks: Some Panel Results." *Economic and Political Weekly* 37, no. 5: 429–35.

Rangarajan, Chakravarthy, and Dinesh Srivastava. 2005. "Fiscal Deficits and Government Debt: Implications for Growth and Stabilization." *Economic and Political Weekly* 40 (July 2–8): 2919–34.

Reserve Bank of India. Various years. *Report on Trend and Progress of Banking in India.* Mumbai.

Sen, Partha. 2004. "Modeling Foreign Capital Inflows and Fiscal Deficits." *Economic and Political Weekly* 39 (October 2–8): 4478–80.

Shah, Ajay, and Ila Patnaik. 2004. "India's Experience with Capital Flows: The Elusive Quest for a Sustainable Current Account Deficit," forthcoming in Sebastian Edwards, Ed. *Capital Controls and Capital Flows in Emerging Economies: Policies, Practices and Consequences.* Chicago: University of Chicago Press.

Singh, Nirvikar, and T. N. Srinivasan. 2004. "Foreign Capital Inflows, Inflation, Sterilization, Crowding-Out and Growth: Some Illustrative Models." *Economic and Political Weekly* 39 (June 12–18): 2469–80.

M. GOVINDA RAO
National Institute of Public Finance and Policy

R. KAVITA RAO
National Institute of Public Finance and Policy

Trends and Issues in Tax Policy and Reform in India

Tax systems the world over have undergone significant changes during the last twenty years as many countries across the ideological spectrum and with varying levels of development have undertaken reforms. The wave of tax reforms that began in the mid-1980s and accelerated in the 1990s was motivated by a number of factors. In many developing countries, pressing fiscal imbalance was the driving force. Tax policy was employed as a principal instrument to correct severe budgetary pressures.[1] In others, the transition from a planned economy to a market economy necessitated wide-ranging tax reforms. Besides efficiency considerations, these tax reforms had to address the issues of replacing public enterprise profits with taxes as a principal source of revenue and of aligning tax policy to change in the development strategy. Another motivation was the internationalization of economic activities arising from increasing globalization. On the one hand, globalization entailed significant reduction in tariffs, and replacements had to be found for this important and relatively easily administered revenue source. On the other, globalization emphasized the need to minimize both efficiency and compliance costs of the tax system. The supply-side tax reforms of the Thatcher–Reagan era also had their impact on the tax reforms in developing countries.

The evolution of the Indian tax system was driven by similar concerns and yet, in some ways, it is different and even unique. Unlike most developing countries, which were guided in their tax reforms by multilateral agencies

The authors are grateful to Shankar N. Acharya, Amaresh Bagchi, Raja Chelliah, Arvind Panagariya, T. N. Srinivasan, and Arindam Das-Gupta for detailed comments on the earlier draft of the paper. However, any shortcomings of the paper are the responsibility of the authors.
1. Ahmad and Stern (1991).

55

such as the International Monetary Fund, Indian tax reforms have largely borne a domestic brand. They have been calibrated to changes in the development strategy over time while staying in step with the institutional arrangements in the country.[2] Thus, even when the government sought assistance from multilateral financial institutions, the recommendations of these institutions did not directly translate into an agenda for tax reform. Despite this, the tax system reforms were broadly in conformity with international trends and advice proffered by expert groups and was in tune with international best practices.[3]

Inevitably tax policy in the country has responded to changing development strategy over the years. In the initial years tax policy was guided by a large number of demands placed on the government.[4] These demands can be summarized as the need to increase the level of savings and investment in the economy and hence the need to stimulate growth and ensure a fair distribution of incomes. That in turn meant an effort to raise taxes from those with an ability to pay, with little regard for the efficiency implications of the chosen instruments for the purpose.

The role of history and institutions was also important in shaping India's tax system. Indeed, the nature of the federal polity, the assignment of tax powers, and tax sharing arrangements have influenced the incentives for revenue mobilization and the structure and administration of the taxes in both central and state governments. The overlapping tax systems have made it difficult to enact and implement comprehensive and coordinated tax reforms. Another legacy of the era of planning is selectivity and discretion both in designing the structure and in implementing the tax system. These contributed to erosion of the tax base, created powerful special interest groups, and introduced the concept of "negotiated settlement" into the tax system.[5] In a closed economy, inefficiencies did not matter and relative price distortions and disincentives to work, save, and invest did not warrant much consideration.

2. The important exception to this is the introduction of an expenditure tax on Kaldor's advice in the mid-1950s. See Government of India (1956).

3. Richard Bird (1993, p. 2721), reviewing the three-volume *Report of the Tax Reforms Committee*, states, "The three reports on tax reform in India. . . generally offer clear and sound guidance as to what can and should be done. . . ."

4. Bagchi and Nayak (1994).

5. The *Report of the Task Force on Implementation of the Fiscal Responsibility and Budget Management Act, 2003* (Government of India, 2004b) states, for example: "Indirect tax policy in India tends to be constantly battered by special interest groups that find it to their interest to have the structure cater to their particular benefit."

Because of the size of the country, its multilevel fiscal framework, the unique reform experience, and difficulties in calibrating reforms posed by institutional constraints, the Indian tax reform experience can provide useful lessons for many countries. The reform, by itself, is an important enough reason for a detailed analysis of the tax system in India. Unfortunately, unlike in many developed countries where major tax reform initiatives were followed by detailed analysis of their impact, no serious studies analyzing the economic impact of tax reforms have been conducted in India.[6]

This paper analyzes the Indian tax system. Alternative models of tax system reform are presented with a view to identifying the best-practice approach followed in tax system reforms. Surely, in a democratic polity, it is difficult to achieve the ideal and yet, the framework helps to keep the focus on further reforms. We then analyze the evolution of the Indian tax system and the impact of historical and institutional factors in shaping Indian tax policy. Trends in tax revenue are presented, and these point toward a relative stagnation and deceleration in tax revenues at both the Union, or central, and state levels. An analysis of the reasons for this stagnation is followed by an exploratory discussion on the possible efficiency and equity implications of the tax system. The final section presents directions for further reforms.

Changing Paradigms of Tax Policy and Reform

In the literature on tax design and reform, the thinking on what constitutes the best tax system and an implementation strategy to achieve it have undergone considerable change over the years, mainly because of the changing role of the state in development and internationalization of economic activities.[7] Designing tax policy and reforming an existing tax regime can be two distinctly different exercises, not always generating the same set of results. It is possible to argue that the objective of tax reform should be to chart the course for turning a given tax regime into one that has been "optimally" designed. The history of the existing system, however, as well as political and administrative constraints, could place limits on such a transition path. For instance, a comprehensive consumption tax of the value-added

6. In the United States, for example, there have been several studies analyzing the impact of the Tax Reform Act of 1986. For a detailed review of these studies, see Auerbach and Slemrod (1997).

7. Bird and Oldman (1990); Gillis (1989); Boskin and McLure (1990).

tax (VAT) variety might be best implemented at the national level, to avoid issues relating to treatment of interstate taxation. But the assignment of tax powers in India could make that transition difficult if not impossible. Reform therefore might have to explore other alternatives such as a dual VAT system.

One important school of thought, which focuses on the design of a tax system, is known as the optimal taxation school. It recognizes the difficulties of achieving the first-best solution and emphasizes the need to minimize the deadweight losses in exploring the second-best solutions. Here one can distinguish two key approaches. The first approach, based on the assumption that government is all-powerful, fully informed, benevolent, and driven by efficiency considerations, derives the following result: to minimize the excess burden of raising a given amount of revenue, consumption should be taxed and the optimal rate of tax on individual commodities should be related to the direct and cross-price elasticities of demand. In the special case when the compensated cross-price elasticities are zero, the optimal tax rate is inversely proportional to the direct, compensated price elasticity of demand (Ramsey rule). The lower the compensated price elasticity of demand, the smaller the movement away from the undistorted first-best optimum in response to the tax so that it pays to tax the lower-elasticity goods at higher rates. Since tax structures designed on these principles would involve taxing necessities, the need to address distributional concerns becomes paramount.[8] Incorporating distributional considerations into this paradigm introduces discussions of optimal income tax, applications of which interestingly do not support sharply progressive tax structures.

The second approach recognizes that the government typically lacks the information on elasticities and is subject to lobbying when it is willing to tax different goods at different rates. This approach leans more heavily toward taxing consumption at uniform rates across goods.[9] According to this approach, while efficiency (and distribution weights) is clearly desirable in the design of tax policy, administrative capacity, attention to local institutions and political realities are equally, if not more, important. The principal concern is not to design a system that will be optimal, but to adopt a system that will minimize tax-induced distortions and at the same time, be administratively feasible and politically acceptable. The basic Harberger reform package for developing countries that are price takers in the international market consists, among other things, of uniform tariffs and a broad-based VAT. Panagariya and Rodrik examine the rationale for uniformity in the

8. Stern (1987).
9. This approach is associated with the names of Harberger (1990) and Hatta (1986).

context of import tariffs and argue that while the case for uniform tariffs is not watertight, uniformity minimizes the pressures for favorable (higher) rates on some goods over others.[10] The commitment to a uniform tax rate introduces a free-rider problem for industries to lobby for lower rates for themselves (since such lower rates are then extended to everyone).

While the literature has focused more on the first approach described above, optimal taxation has played only a limited role in the formulation of actual tax policy. The second approach, combined with administrative cost considerations, is a closer approximation of the approach of tax policy practitioners. The thrust of most tax policy advice within this approach is to enhance the ability of the tax system to raise revenue while minimizing relative price distortions. This involves efforts to broaden the tax base, lower the rates, and reduce rate differentiation of both direct and indirect taxes. Adoption of uniform tax rates has been an important feature of practical approaches to tax reform.[11] A broader base requires lower rates to be levied to generate a given amount of revenues. It also helps to ensure horizontal equity, and it is desirable from the political economy viewpoint because elimination of exemptions and concessions reduces administrative costs as well as the influence of special interest groups on tax policy. Lower marginal rates not only reduce disincentives to work, save, and invest, but also help to improve tax compliance. The preference for broad-based and uniform rates of taxation is thus guided by the need to eliminate an arbitrary array of tax differentials determined more by special interest group politics than pursuit of economic efficiency. Further, the limited infrastructure and capacity of tax administrations in developing countries constrain them from effectively administering complicated tax regimes. Broad-based systems of taxation applying uniform rates are a mechanism for providing stability and simplicity to the tax system.

The introduction of a VAT is an important component of recent tax reform packages in many countries, especially in the context of declining emphasis on import tariffs. Keen and Ligthart show that in small open economies, any revenue-neutral tariff cut accompanied by a price-neutral, destination-based VAT will enhance both net revenue and welfare.[12] While this result is contested, especially in the context of developing economies with significant informal sectors, that debate does not extend to cases where a VAT seeks to replace a cascading type of sales tax or broad-based excise duty. In large

10. Panagariya and Rodrik (1991).
11. Rao (1992).
12. Keen and Ligthart (2002).

economies, however, complete replacement of revenue from international trade taxes by a VAT may not be possible since it might be associated with unacceptably high tax rates; even if it were acceptable, the revenue might not accrue to the central government in a federal setup like India where the states have traditionally held the power to levy sales taxes.[13] There may thus be a need to explore all other alternatives.

In many countries, the reason for levying a VAT has as much, if not more, to do with replacing the cascading-type sales taxes, which are often, confined to the manufacturing stage, than to substitute for import duties as a source of revenue. In many cases the expansion of the tax base accompanying the VAT, caused both by extending the tax to the stages following manufacturing and by the self-enforcing nature of the tax, has led to higher revenue productivity. Often, this expansion of the VAT tax base has strengthened the information base for tax administration, resulting in improved compliance for other taxes and thereby enhancing the overall productivity of the tax system.[14] Thus, although a VAT is not necessarily a "money machine," the conventional conclusion holds that a properly administered VAT is the best way to make up for the revenue loss from trade liberalization.[15]

Some recent theoretical explorations have argued that because the VAT is a tax on the formal sector of the economy and is often combined with weak administration, it helps the informal economy to spread, which is not conducive for development.[16] This argument, however, applies to many other taxes levied in developing countries. In fact, most taxes in developing countries are levied on the formal sector. In the context of tariffs, it has been shown that smuggling—the informal sector counterpart in the case of imports—lowers both revenue and welfare.[17] Moreover, the economic agent has to contend with high transaction costs simply because he is in the informal sector. The extent to which a VAT encourages the informal sector also

13. Rajaraman (2004).

14. Rajaraman (2004) cites the estimates of an IMF study (Ebrill and others 2001) to show that countries with higher per capita GDP tended to gain, but poorer countries tended to lose by introducing the VAT. Besides the usual problems with cross-country regression estimates which both papers point out, it must be noted that a properly calibrated VAT with its information on turnovers can improve the income tax. In Thailand for example, the introduction of a VAT replaced the manufacturers' sales tax in 1991 at a uniform rate of 7 percent (which was actually less than the revenue neutral rate of 10 percent), and led to full revenue recovery. What was surprising was that the VAT also increased the income tax by 25 percent. See Government of India (1993).

15. This argument is made by Bird (2005).

16. Emran and Stiglitz (2004, 2005); Hines (2004); Gordon and Wei (2005).

17. Bhagwati and Hansen (1973); Martin and Panagariya (1984).

varies from country to country. This argument against the VAT also overlooks the dynamism created by the formal sector as it opens up avenues to expand businesses.[18]

Another critique of the appropriateness of the VAT in developing countries is based on market structures. Das-Gupta argues that under imperfect competition, since neither the gains from an input tax credit nor the entire tax burden need to be passed on to the consumer, a turnover tax may produce both more revenue and greater welfare than a VAT.[19] This result, however, is based on a static framework. In a dynamic context, the taxpayers in a turnover-based tax system can integrate vertically, thereby avoiding taxes and potentially undermining production efficiency. Further, such a tax regime would perpetuate tax spillovers both across jurisdictions within the country and across international borders. These would undermine the competitiveness of the domestic industry and violate common market principles.

Thus, as stated by Bird, "One may criticise VAT in both theory and practice, and much more such analysis and criticism is not only to be expected but also welcomed. In the end, VAT almost certainly works better both in theory and practice in most countries than any feasible alternative." Again, as Bird states, "the most basic lesson. . . from experience to date with implementing VAT in developing and transitional economies. . . is. . . that doing it right is in most respects a matter more of art than of science. . . the behaviour of the informal sector depends. . . largely on the interaction between formal institutions such as the tax administration and the prevalent norms and customs in a country. . . ."[20]

Apart from concerns of efficiency, tax policy has often been guided by the need to pursue the objective of redistribution. Most policy analysts in the 1950s and 1960s assigned redistribution a central focus in tax policies and considered that an ideal tax system should have a highly progressive personal income tax combined with a high corporate income tax. In fact, in the 1950s and 1960s, the marginal rates of personal income taxes were set at confiscatory levels in many countries. Redistribution was not merely an obsession in countries with interventionist strategies such as India but was fashionable even in countries such as the United States and Britain. In these countries, marginal income tax rates were set above 90 percent

18. According to a report in the *Financial Times* of April 6, 2005, the use of credit cards by foreigners in India increased by 42 percent to $75 million.

19. A turnover tax is one that is fixed as a percentage of total turnover of the tax paying dealer; see Das-Gupta (2004c).

20. Bird (2005).

immediately after the Second World War.[21] That high marginal tax rate persisted in the United States until 1963.

Three important factors led to moderation in the pursuit of redistribution through tax policy. First, experience showed that highly progressive tax systems did little to reduce inequality in developing countries as they were neither progressive nor comprehensive.[22] Empirical studies in the United States and Chile showed that the income redistribution and reduction in inequality achieved by the tax systems were insignificant.[23] Second, a redistributive tax system can impose additional costs on the economy, including administrative costs, compliance costs, economic efficiency costs, and political costs. Third, the focus of equity in fiscal policy itself has shifted from "reducing the incomes of the rich" to "increasing the incomes of the poor" and in this, the alternative approach of using expenditure programs for poverty alleviation has attracted greater attention.[24]

In theory the design of a tax system for developed countries today would rely largely on consumption taxes (VAT) on all goods and services applied at a more or less uniform rate. However, in the presence of large informal sector and constraints in implementing effective expenditure-based redistribution measures, it may be necessary to have a combination of income and consumption taxes, the latter covering all goods and services, at fairly uniform rates. But such an option may not be easily available, with a tax system already in place. The task therefore is to reform the existing tax system so as to minimize the excess burden of taxation within the broad contours of the existing system. This involves reforms of all major taxes at the central, state, and local levels. The direction of reform as guided by the literature on tax reforms in developing countries includes:

—scaling down of and possible elimination of trade taxes over time;

—reform of existing domestic indirect taxes to transform them into comprehensive consumption taxes on goods and services: this should cover both national and subnational taxes;

—a moderately progressive personal income tax;

—a corporate income tax at a rate equivalent to the highest marginal rate of the personal income tax.

---

21. Harberger (2003).

22. Harberger (2003); Bird and Zolt (2005).

23. For the United States, see Pechman (1985); for Chile, see Engel, Galetovic, and Raddatz (1999).

24. Harberger (2003); Bird and Zolt (2005).

Probably the most important aspect of the advice for developing countries in designing their tax systems is to keep the administrative dimension at the center rather than the periphery of reform efforts. Poor administrative capacity creates a wedge between the structure of the tax on paper and what actually works in practice. Apart from eroding revenue productivity, poor administration results in the perpetuation and even the spread of the informal economy, significant deadweight losses, and the violation of horizontal equity.

Tax policy, or for that matter any policy, stands on the tripod of architecture, engineering, and management.[25] Architecture provides the design of the tax system to be achieved, which is guided by the objectives of tax policy. Engineering provides the mechanics to achieve it, and these are provided by the nature of institutions and systems involved in tax collection. Management provides the implementation strategy and action, which, among others things, depends on the political support and vision and the nature of administrative agencies and the information system. The three legs of the tripod are interdependent. A tax policy is only as good as it is administered; so it is important to design the tax system keeping the administrative capacity in mind. Similarly, the nature of tax institutions and systems will have to be adapted to conform to the design of the tax system and the implementation capacity. Further, administrative capacity should be continuously augmented to keep pace with changing requirements of tax policy. In other words, reform of the tax system involves both its structure and operations, is a continuous process, and has to be calibrated constantly. A complementary action in this regard is the building of proper information system.

Evolution of Indian Tax System

The basic framework for the tax system in independent India was provided in the constitutional assignment of tax powers. The important feature of the tax assignment is the adoption of the principle of separation in tax powers between the central and state governments. The central government has the power to levy the major broad-based and mobile tax bases, which include taxes on nonagricultural incomes and wealth, corporate income taxes, customs duties, and excise duties on manufactured products. Over the years, the last item has evolved into a manufacturers' VAT on goods. The major

25. Bird and Zolt (2005).

tax powers assigned to the states include taxes on agricultural incomes and wealth, sales taxes, excises on alcoholic products, taxes on motor vehicles and on transport of passengers and goods, stamp duties and registration fees on transfers of property, and taxes and duties on electricity. States also have powers to levy taxes on entertainment and on income earned by engaging in a profession, trade or employment; some states have retained these powers for themselves, while others have assigned them to local bodies. [26] Although the state list also includes property taxes and taxes on the entry of goods into a local area for consumption, use, or sale, these have been assigned to local bodies. Until 2003 India's constitution did not explicitly recognize and assign to any level of government the power to tax services, However, since all residuary tax powers were assigned to the central government, in 1994, this authority became the basis for levying a tax on selected services. In 2003 an amendment to the constitution specifically assigned the power to tax services to the central government. [27]

Tax policy in India has evolved as an important component of fiscal policy that played a central role in the planned development strategy. In particular, tax policy was the principal instrument for transferring private savings to public consumption and investment. [28] Tax policy was also used to encourage savings and investment, reduce inequalities of income and wealth, foster balanced regional development, encourage small-scale industries on the assumption that they are employment intensive, and influence the volume and direction of economic activities in the country.

The evolution of tax policy within the framework of an industrialization strategy based on the public sector, heavy industry, and import substitution has had several implications. First, tax policy was directed to raise resources for the large and increasing requirements of public consumption and investment irrespective of the efficiency implications it entailed. Second, the objective of achieving a socialistic pattern of society, combined with the large oligopolistic rents generated by the system of licences, quotas, and restrictions, necessitated steeply progressive tax structure in both direct and indirect taxes. Third, the pursuit of a multiplicity of objectives enormously complicated the tax system with adverse consequences on efficiency and horizontal

26. While this tax applies to individuals based on the income earned, it is considered distinct from income tax, since the total tax leviable is limited by a cap spelled out by India's constitution.

27. The 88th Amendment to the Constitution of India assigns the power to levy a service tax to the central government, with the proceeds being collected and appropriated by the central and state governments, in accordance with principles formulated by the Parliament.

28. Bagchi and Stern (1994).

equity. It also opened up large avenues for evasion and avoidance of taxes. The disregard for efficiency considerations was a part of the import-substituting industrialization strategy. Fourth, not only did all of this require differentiation in tax rates based on arbitrary criteria, but plan priorities also legitimized selectivity and discretion in tax policy and administration. Once selectivity and discretion were accepted as legitimate, it mattered little whether these were exercised as intended. This provided enough scope for the special interest groups to influence tax policy and administration. Fifth, the influence of special interest groups, changing priorities, and the lack of an information system and scientific analysis led to ad hoc and often inconsistent calibration of policies. Finally, the poor information system was the cause of selective application of the tax system as well as its effect.

This section summarizes the evolution of the major central taxes and provides an overview of the state taxes. For the central government, the major direct taxes are personal income and corporate taxes; the major indirect taxes are excise duties, customs duties, and service tax At the state level, the major initiative in recent times has been the introduction of the VAT, and the discussion limits itself to this measure.

Reform of Central Taxes

The systematic evolution of the tax system in independent India started with the implementation of the report of the Taxation Enquiry Commission.[29] In fact, this was the first comprehensive attempt to review the existing tax system and design a system that would cover central, state, and local taxes. It was intended to fulfill a variety of objectives such as raising the level of savings and investment, transferring resources from the private sector to public sector, and achieving a desired state of redistribution. The commission report was available in 1953–54, but because of the ideological orientation of the Second Five-Year Plan (1956–60), Nicholas Kaldor was invited to produce another report on Indian tax reform. This report, published in 1956, was used (rather incompletely) to raise resources for the Second Five-Year Plan. Kaldor recommended the implementation of an expenditure tax to curb consumption and raise the level of saving, which was abysmally low at about 10 percent of gross domestic product (GDP).[30] However, this tax had to be withdrawn in 1957–58 because it did not generate the expected revenues.

29. Government of India (1953).
30. Government of India (1956).

With the adoption of a planned-development strategy in a mixed economy framework, raising more resources and achieving the desired state of redistribution became an obsession, which led policymakers to design the income tax system with confiscatory marginal rates. The consequent disincentives, as well as the high rate of return on tax evasion, low probability of detection, and an ineffective legal system that failed to impose penalties within a reasonable time period, led the Direct Taxes Enquiry Committee in 1971 to recommend a significant reduction in marginal tax rates.[31]

On the indirect taxes side, a major simplification exercise was attempted by the Indirect Taxes Enquiry Committee.[32] Implementation of the important recommendations of this committee, however, were not initiated until 1986.

Systematic and comprehensive attempts to reform the tax system at the central level started only after market-based economic reforms were initiated in 1991, when the Tax Reforms Committee (TRC) laid out a framework and a road map for reforming both direct and indirect taxes.[33] Subsequent reports providing the analytical basis for reform in the new millennium were issued in 2002 and 2004.[34] In many ways the reforms since 1991, with their emphasis on simplicity and efficiency, are a marked departure from the past. In fact, the 2002 task force reports built on the recommendations of the TRC, which are summarized below.

The tax reforms initiated since 1991 have been a part of the structural reform process that followed the economic crisis of 1991. In keeping with the best-practices approach, the TRC combined economic principles with conventional wisdom in recommending comprehensive tax system reforms. The report is in three parts. In the first interim report, the committee set out the guiding principles of tax reform and applied them to important taxes, namely, taxes on income and wealth, tariffs, and taxes on domestic consumption. The first part of the final report was concerned mainly with the much neglected aspect of reforms in administration and enforcement of both direct and indirect taxes. The second part of the report dealt with restructuring the tariff structure. In keeping with the structural adjustment of the economy, the basic principles outlined in the recommendations are to broaden the tax base, lower marginal tax rates, reduce rate differentiation, simplify the tax structure, and undertake measures to make the administration and enforcement of the tax system more effective. The reforms were to be calibrated to bring about revenue neutrality in the short term and to

31. Government of India (1971).
32. Government of India (1977).
33. Government of India (1991).
34. Government of India (2002a, 2002b, 2004b).

enhance revenue productivity of the tax system in the medium and long term. The overall thrust of the TRC was to decrease the share of trade taxes in total tax revenue; increase the share of domestic consumption taxes by transforming the domestic excises into a VAT, and increase the relative contribution of direct taxes.

The important proposals put forward by the TRC included reducing the rates of all major taxes—customs, individual and corporate income taxes, and excises—to reasonable levels, maintaining progressivity but without inducing evasion. The TRC recommended a number of measures to broaden the tax base by minimizing exemptions and concessions, drastically simplifying laws and procedures, building a proper information system, and computerizing tax returns, and thoroughly modernizing administrative and enforcement machinery.

In the case of customs, the TRC recommended tariff rates of 5, 10, 15, 20, 25, 30, and 50 percent to be achieved by 1997–98. Implementing this recommendation meant a considerable rationalization from the prevailing structure, which had more than 100 rates ranging up to 400 percent. The tariff rate was to vary directly with the stage of processing of commodities, and among final consumer goods, with income elasticity of demand (higher rates on luxuries). In hindsight, it is easy to criticize the excessive rate differentiation (seven rates) as well as the degree of protection depending on the stage of processing. Joshi and Little for example, call this "a totally unprincipled principle, for it has no foundation in economic principles."[35] In addition to continued complexity, the proposed tariff structure created very high differences in effective rates and provided a higher degree of protection to inessential commodities.

The TRC recommendation also fell far short of developing a coordinated domestic trade tax system in the country. This, in a sense, is understandable, as the committee had no mandate to reform state taxes. However, the committee was aware of the serious problems of avoidance and evasion of sales taxes levied by the states predominantly at the manufacturing stage. Therefore, it did recommend the extension of the central government's VAT to the wholesale stage with the revenues from the extended levy beyond the postmanufacturing stage assigned to the states.

By all accounts, the tax system at the central level was considerably simplified and rationalized by 2005, although these reforms were neither uniform nor consistent and the system was far from perfect.[36] Some areas

35. Joshi and Little (1996, p. 74).
36. Acharya (2005).

still need require reforms, and these are discussed later. Although a broad account of the history of tax reform has been given here, it is important to understand the evolution of the tax structure for each of the central government's major taxes: personal income tax, corporation income tax, Union excise duties, and customs.

Reform of Direct Taxes

At the central level, the changes in the income tax structure until the mid-1970s were largely ad hoc, dictated by the exigencies of bringing about a socialistic pattern of society. In 1973–74, the personal income tax had eleven tax brackets with rates monotonically rising from 10 percent to 85 percent. When a surcharge of 15 percent was taken into account, the highest marginal rate for persons with income above Rs. 0.2 million was 97.5 percent.[37] In fact, the increase in income tax rates to confiscatory levels was completed immediately after the split in the Congress party in 1969 and appeared to be a part of the effort to give the party a pro-left image.[38]

The policy was similar in the case of corporate taxation. The classical system of taxation involved taxing the profits in the hands of the company and dividends in the hands of the shareholders. A distinction was made between widely held companies and different types of closely held companies, and the tax rate varied from the base rate of 45–65 percent in the case of some widely held companies. Although nominal rates were high, the effective rates were substantial lower due to generous depreciation and investment allowances. In fact some companies benefited from the preferences so much that they did not pay any corporate tax year after year.

The Direct Taxes Enquiry Committee succinctly described the impact of the confiscatory tax system in 1971. It attributed the large-scale tax evasion to confiscatory tax rates and recommended reducing marginal rates to 70 percent. This change was implemented in 1974–75, when the tax was brought down to 77 percent including a 10 percent surcharge. Simultaneously, however, the wealth tax rates were increased. In 1976–77, the marginal rate was further reduced to 66 percent, and the wealth tax rate was

---

37. For incomes from capital alone, with a wealth tax of 5 percent, the above tax structure meant that there was a ceiling on income at Rs. 250,000; this was the desired goal as explicitly recorded in the budget speech of 1971–72, by Y. B. Chavan.

38. Indira Gandhi, presenting the 1970–71 budget, stated, "Taxation is also a major instrument in all modern societies to achieve greater equality of incomes and wealth. It is, therefore, proposed to make our direct tax system serve this purpose by increasing income taxation at higher levels as well as by substantially enhancing the present rates of taxation on wealth and gifts."

reduced from 5 percent to 2.5 percent. In 1979–80, the income tax surcharge was increased, and the wealth tax rate returned to a maximum of 5 percent. A major simplification and rationalization initiative, however, came in 1985–86, when the number of tax brackets was reduced from eight to four, the highest marginal tax rate was brought down to 50 percent, and wealth tax rates came down to 2.5 percent.

The last wave of reforms in personal income taxation was initiated on the basis of the recommendations of the TRC. Under the reforms, there were only three tax brackets, of 20, 30, and 40 percent, starting in 1992–93. Financial assets were excluded from the wealth tax, and the maximum marginal rate was reduced to 1 percent. Further reductions came in 1997–98, when the three rates were brought down further to 10, 20, and 30 percent. In subsequent years, the need for revenue has led to a general surcharge and additional surcharge of 2 percent dedicated to primary education, the latter applicable on all taxes.

The basic corporate tax rate was reduced to 50 percent, and rates applicable to different categories of closely held companies were unified at 55 percent. Following the recommendations of the TRC, the distinction between closely held and widely held companies was done away with and the tax rates were unified at 40 percent in 1993–94. In 1997–98, the corporate rate was further reduced, to 35 percent, and the 10 percent tax on dividends was shifted from individuals to companies. Since then the measures adopted have lacked direction. The dividends tax rate was increased to 20 percent in 2000–01, then reduced again to 10 percent in 2001–02 and levied on shareholders rather than the company. The policy was reversed once again in 2003–04, with the dividend tax imposed on the company.

A major problem that has haunted the tax system and reduced the tax base is the generous tax preferences. The Advisory Group on Tax Policy and Tax Administration needed twenty-five pages in its report to list the personal income tax preferences, and the Task Force on Tax Policy and Tax Administration also made a detailed list of these concessions.[39] Among the tax preferences are incentives and concessions for savings, housing, retirement benefits, investment in and returns from certain types of financial assets, investments in retirement schemes, and income of charitable trusts. These tax preferences have not only distorted the after-tax rates of return on various types of investments in unintended ways but have also significantly eroded the tax base.

---

39. Government of India (2001a, pp. 125–50).

The major corporate tax preferences are investment and depreciation allowances. Tax incentives were also provided for businesses locating in underdeveloped areas. As a result, some companies planned their activities to take full advantage of the generous concessions and fully avoid the tax. This form of tax avoidance by "zero-tax" companies was minimized by the introduction of a minimum alternative tax (MAT) in 1996–97. Even as companies can take advantage of the tax preferences, they are required to pay a tax on 30 percent of their book profits. In subsequent years, a provision was incorporated allowing those companies paying a MAT to take a partial credit against income tax liabilities in following years. Since the MAT meant that a lot of the other preferences accorded in the tax statute like accelerated depreciation were not available to business units, the partial credit mechanism sought to dilute the impact of the MAT on business units that were liable for the MAT only sporadically.

While tax reforms were calibrated on the basis of a consistent theoretical framework until the mid 1990s, some of the subsequent changes were ad hoc. The prime example is the decision to introduce the MAT instead of phasing out tax preferences. Setting the tax rate on corporate profits higher than the highest marginal rate on personal income is another example. Similarly, to improve tax compliance and create an audit trail, a securities transactions tax was introduced in April 2004 and tax of 0.1 percent on all cash withdrawals above Rs. 25,000 from current accounts of commercial banks was introduced in April 2005. These measures, however, are retrograde. The former hinders the development of stock market and discriminates against investments in shares. The latter penalizes small and medium-size firms, which have to withdraw large amounts of cash just to pay the salaries of their employees.[40]

Personal income tax rates have remained stable since 1997–98, at 10, 20, and 30 percent, with some changes in the associated tax brackets. A surcharge of 5 percent of the income tax payable was imposed in 2002–03 in the wake of the Kargil war and was discontinued the following year. It was replaced, however, with a separate 10 percent surcharge imposed on all taxpayers with taxable incomes above Rs. 850,000; the level was raised to Rs. 1 million in the 2005–06 budget. Further, all taxes are topped up by a 2 percent education cess—a surcharge dedicated to an education fund from 2004–05 onward. Although the income exemption limit has remained at Rs. 50,000 since 1998–99, the generous standard deduction and the

40. Arbalaez, Burman, and Zuluaga (2002) for discussion of effects of such a tax in Columbia.

exemptions on dividends and interest on government securities up to specified limits have effectively increased the threshold substantially. The 2004–05 budget did not raise the exemption limit but provided that those with incomes under Rs. 100,000 need not pay the tax. The budget still retained the existing tax brackets, however, which gave rise to a peculiar problem—those with taxable incomes above Rs. 100,000 were left with lower after-tax incomes than those with incomes marginally lower than Rs. 100,000, requiring an ad hoc correction. The budget for 2005–06 raised the exemption limit itself to Rs. 100,000, abolished the standard deduction, and made marginal changes in the tax brackets. The exemption limit was increased to Rs. 135,000 for women and to Rs. 185,000 for senior citizens. Savings in a variety of instruments including pension funds up to Rs. 100,000 were made deductible from taxable income.

The Income Tax Act has a provision to assess the value of identifiable perquisites provided by companies to their employees and to include the same in the taxable income of the individual. The budget for 2005–06 goes a step further and classifies a range of other expenses by the company, which provide indirect perquisites to the entire group of employees but are not directly assignable to any single employee. A specified proportion of each of these benefits is to be taxed at a rate of 30 percent through a fringe benefits tax, to be paid by the employer. Benefits covered include entertainment, conferences, employee welfare, sales promotion including publicity, conveyance, tour and travel (including foreign travel expenses), and use of the telephone.

The structure of corporate income taxes has also remained stable since 1997–98, when the rate was reduced to 35 percent. As described earlier, however, there have been frequent changes and inconsistency in taxing dividends. In 2005–06, the corporate income tax was reduced to 30 percent on domestic companies. A surcharge of 10 percent (without any conditions regarding installed capacity increases) is also chargeable. The depreciation rate has been reduced to 15 percent in the case of general plant and machinery, but initial depreciation is set at 20 percent, thereby reducing the overall benefit of lowering corporate income tax rates.

The most important reform in recent years is in tax administration. Expansion of the scope of tax deduction at source is one of the significant measures taken to reach the "hard to tax" groups. Further, every individual living in a large city and covered under any one of the six conditions (ownership of house, ownership of a car, membership in a club, ownership of credit cards, foreign travel, and a subscriber of a telephone connection) is necessarily required to file a tax return. The government is also issuing permanent account numbers and strengthening the tax information system. Strengthening the information system, along with processing and matching the information from various sources on a selective basis is an important initiative that is likely to improve tax compliance.

Reform of Indirect taxes

UNION EXCISE DUTIES. After independence, excise duties were levied on selected goods to raise revenue. Over the years, as the revenue requirement increased, the list of commodities subject to tax was expanded. In the initial years, for reasons of administrative convenience, the taxed commodities tended to be raw materials and intermediate goods rather than final consumer goods.[41] As pressure to raise revenue increased, final consumer goods were included. In 1975–76 the tax was extended to all manufactured goods.

By this time the structure of excise duties was complex and highly distortionary. Some commodities were subject to specific duties and others to ad valorem taxes; on the latter alone there were twenty-four different rates ranging from 2 to 100 percent (tobacco and petroleum products were taxed at even higher rates). The process of converting specific duties to ad valorem rates was more or less completed by 1993–94.[42] The number of rates did not decrease, however, which led to several classification disputes. In effect, the excise duty became a manufacturers' sales tax administered on the basis of goods cleared from the warehouse. "Cascading" from the tax resulted not merely from its preretail nature but also because it was levied not only on final consumer goods but also on inputs and capital goods. The tax system was complex and opaque, and a detailed analysis showed significant variation in the effective rates.[43]

Although the Indirect Tax Enquiry Report issued in 1977 provided a detailed analysis of the allocative and distributional consequences of union excise duties, its recommendations were not implemented for almost a decade. The rationalization recommendations included converting specific duties into ad valorem taxes, unifying rates, and introducing an input tax credit to convert the cascading manufacturers' sales tax into a manufacturing-stage value-added tax (MANVAT). The interesting part of the reform was that there was virtually no preparation and the introduction of modified value-added tax (MODVAT) was a process of "learning by doing." This

41. Government of India (1977).
42. Thereafter only a few commodities remained on specific duties; tea, cement, and cigarettes are notable among these.
43 . Ahmad and Stern (1983).

was a strange combination of taxation based on physical verification of goods with provision of an input tax credit. The coverage of the credit mechanism also evolved over time. It began with selected items, with credit based on a one-to-one correspondence between inputs and outputs. It was only by 1996–97, that it covered a majority of commodities in the excise tariff and incorporated comprehensive credit. Nowhere else in the world can one find VAT introduction so complicated in its structure, so difficult in its operations, and so incomplete in its coverage. In fact, the revenue from the tax as a ratio of GDP declined after the introduction of MODVAT.

Further reform of the excise duties came with the implementation of the recommendations of the TRC. The measures included gradual unification of rates and greater reliance on account-based administration. In 1999–2000, eleven tax rates were merged into three, with a handful of "luxury" items subject to an additional nonrebatable tax (6 and 16 percent). The three rates were merged into a single rate in 2000–01 to be called a central VAT (CenVAT), along with three special additional excises of 8, 16, and 24 percent for a few commodities. Further, the tax base was widened; some exemptions were replaced by a tax at 8 percent. Some simplification of the tax on the small-scale sector was also attempted. Small businesses could either take an exemption or pay tax at a concessional rate of 60 percent of tax due, with access to the tax credit mechanism. This option, however, was withdrawn from the budget of 2005–06.

CUSTOMS DUTIES. Contrary to the general patterns seen in low-income countries, where an overwhelming proportion of revenues is raised from international trade taxes, revenue from this source was not very large in the initial years of independent India, largely because imports were restricted.[44] In addition, high and differentiated tariffs, with rates varying with the stage of production (lower rates on inputs and higher rates on finished goods) and income elasticity of demand (lower rates on necessities and higher rates on luxury items) not only resulted in high and widely varying effective rates of protection, but provided large premiums for inefficiency and caused unintended distortions in the allocation of resources.

By the mid-1980s, the tariff rates were very high and the structure quite complex. The government's Long-Term Fiscal Policy (LTFP) presented in the Parliament in 1985–86 emphasized the need to reduce tariffs, apply fewer and more uniform rates, and reduce and eventually eliminate quantitative restrictions on imports. The reforms undertaken, however, were not

44. Chelliah (1986).

comprehensive. Rationalization in the rates was attempted for specific industries such as capital goods, drug intermediates, and electronic goods. In
fact, contrary to the LTFP recommendations, the tariffs were raised for
revenue reasons, and the weighted average rate increased from 38 percent
in 1980–81 to 87 percent in 1989–90.[45] Thus, by 1990–91, the tariff structure
ranged from 0 to 400 percent. More than 10 percent of imports were subject
to tariffs of 120 percent or more. Wide-ranging exemptions, reflecting the
influence of various special interest groups on tax policy, often granted
outside the budgetary process, further complicated the system and made it
ad hoc.

The reform of import duties in earnest began in 1991–92 when all duties
on nonagricultural goods above 150 percent were reduced to this level.
This "peak" rate was lowered over the next four years to 50 percent,
and then to 40 percent in 1997–98, 30 percent in 2002–03, 25 percent in
2003–04, and finally to 15 percent in 2005–06. Along with relaxation of
quantitative restrictions on imports and exchange rate depreciation, the
change in the tariffs constituted a major change in the foreign trade regime
in the country.

The number of major duty rates was reduced from twenty-two in
1990–91 to four in 2003–04. Of course, some items are outside these four
rates, but 90 percent of the customs is collected from items under the four
rates. At the same time, a special additional duty was imposed on goods
imported into the country on the rationale that if the commodity was
domestically produced and sold interstate, it would have attracted the tax
rate of 4 percent. This duty was abolished in January 2004, only to be rein-
troduced in 2005–06. Thus, the direction of reforms was not always consistent, but overall the thrust has been to reduce the rates and reduce their
dispersion. However, tariffs rates still vary with the stage of processing,
and this practice has caused very high effective rates of protection on assem-
bly of consumer durables and luxury consumption items.

SERVICE TAX. An interesting aspect of the tax system in India is that except for a few specified services assigned to the states such as the entertainment tax, passengers and goods tax, and the electricity duty, the services
were not specifically assigned to either the center or the states. This omission
violated the principle of neutrality in consumption as it discriminated against
the goods component of consumption. Because services are relatively more
income elastic, the tax system is rendered less progressive when these are not
taxed. An even more important argument for taxing services is to enable a

45. Government of India (1991).

coordinated calibration of a consumption tax system on goods and services because services enter into goods production and vice versa.

Although there was no specific authority to tax services, the central government levied taxes on three services in 1994–95: insurance other than life insurance, stock brokerages, and telecommunications. The list was expanded in succeeding years and now includes more than eighty services. The initial 5 percent tax rate was increased to 8 percent in 2003–04 and to 10 percent in 2004–05. The Expert Group on Taxation of Services recommended extending the tax to all services, providing an input tax credit for both goods and services, and eventually integrating the services tax with the CenVAT.[46] With these reforms, the tax system can effectively be called a manufacturing-stage VAT. The exceptions were to be two small lists— one, a list of exempt services, and the other, a negative list of services, where the tax credit mechanism would not cover taxes paid on these services. The recommendation on the levy of general taxation of services has not been implemented, and the tax continues to be levied on selective services. However, the recommendation pertaining to the extension of input tax credit for goods entering into services and vice versa has been implemented.

State-Level Tax Reforms

Tax reforms at the state level were not coordinated with those at the center. While individual state governments tried to appoint committees from time to time and reform their tax structures, no systematic attempt was made to streamline the reform process even after 1991 when market-oriented reforms were introduced. Most of the reform attempts were ad hoc and were guided by revenue needs rather than attempts to modernize the tax system. In some cases, even when systematic studies were done, the recommendations were rarely implemented.[47] Increasing budget pressures and, in some cases, conditions imposed by multilateral lending agencies or the need to meet targets set by the medium-term fiscal reforms facility instituted by the eleventh Finance Commission helped to accelerate the pace of tax reforms in the states in the latter half of the 1990s. The major landmark in coordinated tax reform at the state level was the simplification and rationalization of the

---

46. Government of India (2001b).

47. The National Institute of Public Finance and Policy has conducted several studies on the tax systems in various states since 1980, including Assam, Bihar, Kerala, Madhya Pradesh, Punjab, and Tamil Nadu, Uttar Pradesh had a tradition of appointing a tax reform committee every five years. Sometimes, the studies were repeated after some years. These recommendations continue to be pertinent, suggesting that very few have been translated into policy.

sales tax system, beginning in 1999 and the introduction of a VAT in twenty-one states on April 1, 2005, to replace the existing cascading sales tax.

Although good progress has been made in converting the central government's excise duties into a manufacturing-stage VAT, the reform in the states' sales tax systems has lagged behind. These reforms are critical from the viewpoint of efficiency, for they contribute over 60 percent of states' tax revenues. Moreover, to have a coordinated consumption tax system in the country, reforms in the state sales tax systems should be considered along with reforms of the central excise duty regime.

A systematic discussion on evolving a coordinated consumption tax system in the country was initiated in the "Report on Reform of Domestic Trade Taxes in India," prepared by the National Institute of Public Finance and Policy (NIPFP) in 1994. It examined alternative models for a coordinated consumption tax system for India and studied the feasibility of centralizing sales taxes and unifying the levy with excise duties; giving the states the power to levy all domestic indirect taxes with a corresponding reduction in tax devolution; and evolving an independent dual VAT at the central and state levels with no credit for the payment of the central taxes by the states and vice versa. The report favored the last solution as the most practicable in the Indian context because it maintains a balance between subnational fiscal autonomy and the central government's fiscal capacity to undertake any desired interstate redistribution. Burgess and Stern had reached a similar conclusion in 1993, while an analysis by Joshi and Little in 1996 favored either centralization or assigning all indirect taxes either to the center or to the states.

Considerations of fiscal autonomy and demands on the central government to effect sizable interregional resource transfers as well as the political acceptability tilted the decision in favor of the dual VAT scheme as a medium-term goal.[48] While a centralized tax on goods and services is desirable for creating a harmonized consumption tax system, it can be considered only as a long-term goal. In the medium term, as part of the initiative to introduce a dual VAT, it has been decided to convert the cascading state-level sales taxes into a destination-based VAT.

There are a number of arguments for replacing the prevailing state sales tax with a destination-based VAT, that is, a VAT system where the tax accrues to the state where the good is finally consumed. In most states, sales taxes are levied only at the first point of sale, that is, either sale by a manufacturer

48. NIPFP (1994); Rao (1998).

of a good or by an importer of the good in the state, and this makes the base narrow. The multiplicity of rates makes the tax system complex. The taxation of inputs and capital goods contributes to cascading, vertical integration of firms, and opaqueness. In an imperfect market characterized by markup pricing, the taxes on inputs and capital goods result not only in a tax on tax but also a markup on the tax, with consumers paying much more than the revenues collected by the government. Interstate competition in providing liberal tax incentives, besides distorting resource allocation, involves significant cost to the exchequer in tax expenditures. The tax on interstate sales combined with input and capital goods taxation has caused significant interstate tax exportation from richer to poorer states. In addition, in many states, the urban local bodies impose a tax, known as *octroi*, on the entry of goods into a local area for consumption, use, or sale. Thus the country was divided into several tariff zones, limiting the scope and the gains from a common domestic market. Above all, with independent and overlapping commodity tax systems at the central and state levels, developing coordinated and harmonized domestic trade taxes has become difficult.

As a part of the dual VAT design, therefore, the NIPFP study group recommended that a separate destination-based, consumption-type, retail-stage VAT replace the existing state sales taxes. To persuade the states to rationalize their tax systems along the lines recommended by the study group, the government of India appointed a State Finance Ministers' Committee to make recommendations to phase in the VAT within a given time frame. The committee, which was subsequently transformed into the Empowered Committee of State Finance Ministers, recommended that the states adopt floor rates to minimize the "race to the bottom." The committee's recommendation that the VAT be implemented in 2003 was postponed repeatedly, until April 2005.

Although characterized as adoption of VAT, the reform in April 2005 only extends the sales tax up to the retail stage with credit allowed for taxes paid on intrastate purchases used for all intrastate and interstate sales. The interstate sales tax, that is, the central sales tax, will continue in the same form, although a pending proposal would phase it out over a two-year period. In this sense, the reform is only a transitional measure to achieve the ultimate objective of having a destination-based, retail-stage VAT.

The salient features of the April 2005 reform are summarized here:

—The tax is levied at two rates (except for bullion, specie, and precious metals, which are taxed at 1 percent). Basic necessities (about 75 items) are exempted. Most items of common consumption, inputs, and capital goods (about 275 items) are taxed at 4 percent, and all other items are taxed at 12.5 percent. Gasoline and diesel fuel (which contribute about 40 percent of the sales tax) are kept outside the VAT regime, and a floor rate of 20 percent is to be levied on them.

—The tax credit facility covers inputs and purchases as well as capital goods for both manufacturers and dealers. Credit for taxes paid on capital goods can be used over three years of sales.

—The tax credit mechanism operates fully only for intrastate sales. In interstate transactions, the exporting state is supposed to give an input tax credit for purchases made locally, against the collection of the central sales tax. The central sales tax credit in the importing state, or other mechanisms of zero-rating of interstate sales, will be introduced in two years, when the central sales tax in its present form will be phased out. In the meantime, an information system on interstate trade will be built up.

—The central government has agreed to compensate the states for any loss of revenue at rates of 100 percent in the first year, 75 percent in the second year, and 50 percent in the third year. The loss will be calculated by estimating the difference between the projected sales tax revenue using 2004–05 as the base and the actual revenue collected. The projected revenues will be estimated by applying the average of the best three years' growth rates during the last five years.

—Tax incentives given to new industries by different states could be continued so long as it does not break the VAT chain. Many states propose to convert tax holidays into deferment of the tax.

—All dealers with annual turnover above Rs. 500,000 are required to register for the VAT. However, the states may levy a simple turnover tax not exceeding 2 percent on those dealers with turnover up to Rs. 5 million. Such dealers, paying the turnover tax, do not have to keep detailed accounts of their transactions. But these small dealers will not be a part of the VAT chain, and no credit will be available for the taxes paid on purchases from these dealers. They may therefore voluntarily register as regular VAT dealers.

Altogether, as of April 2005 eighteen states and five Union Territories have committed themselves to implementing the VAT. Haryana began to implement the VAT in April 2004, but with three main rates (4 percent, 10 percent, and 12 percent). Eight states, including Gujarat, Madhya Pradesh, Tamil Nadu, and Uttar Pradesh, have stayed out of the system. These are some of the larger states with significant industrial bases. Given the perceived incentives of VAT regime in the form of input tax credit, there are pressures on these states to join in as well.

Issues of Design and Implementation

The introduction of the VAT is a major reform exercise, and it is not surprising that the measure would lead to some confusion and uncertainty. Two sets of issues need to be highlighted. One is the ad hoc manner in which the tax has been introduced, which can be seen in the lack of preparedness on the part of many of the states on the one hand and in the lack of firm decisions on the design and structure of the tax, even a few months after it was introduced, on the other. Education and awareness programs for dealers and the public have been largely inadequate in a number of states. Some states started off the new regime without the rules and forms in place. Even tax officials are not clear about many issues. In other words, this switchover can in no terms be called a planned switchover.

The second issue involves three shortcomings in the design of the tax itself. First, the difference of 8.5 percentage points between the tax rates on inputs and outputs (4 percent and 12.5 percent) tends to reduce tax compliance. In fact, it is inappropriate to specify a lower rate on inputs in a VAT system because full credit is available for taxes paid on inputs used in the production against the tax payable on the final product. No other country in the world operating a VAT system permits concessional treatment of inputs. Many commodities are used as inputs as well as final consumer goods, and the lower rate implies a loss of revenue when goods classified as "inputs" are sold for final use. Further, a manufacturer might prefer to pay the input tax at 4 percent, suppress his sale, and evade the larger tax on the final product. The large tax differential also encourages intense lobbying to shift more items from the higher rate to the lower rate category. From the viewpoint of better tax compliance, it would have been better to choose rates like 4 percent and 10 percent.

Second, it would have been better to stipulate the two tax rates as floor rates rather than uniform rates. The only condition should have been that no state should levy the tax at more than two rates, and the items under the two categories could have been specified. This approach would have provided a degree of autonomy to the states and potentially reduced the need for compensation.

The third important issue is the decision to apply the VAT on the maximum retail price (MRP) at the first point on pharmaceuticals and drugs in

West Bengal and Maharashtra. This was possibly done to accommodate the existing trade practices organized through commissions; once MRP is taken as the base, there cannot be more value added at later stages. This goes against the principle of VAT—of collecting the tax at different stages of value added with credit given for the tax paid at the previous stage. Further, this special treatment for pharmaceuticals puts two different mechanisms in place for taxation within the same state and for certain dealers, a complication both for administration and compliance.

Trends in Indian Tax Revenues

This section analyzes the trends in tax revenue in India, focusing on the changes in the level and composition of tax revenue since 1991, when systematic reforms were set in motion. The analysis shows that despite systematic reforms, the revenue productivity of the tax system has not shown any appreciable increase—a reduction in customs duties has not been offset by any internal indirect taxes.

The aggregate trends in tax revenue in India show four distinct phases (table 1; figures 1 and 2). In the first phase, the ratio of tax revenue to GDP steadily increased, from 6.3 percent in 1950–51 to 16.1 percent in 1987–88. In the initial years of planning, an increase in this ratio was needed to finance large public sector plans, and an increase was relatively easy because it started from a low base. In addition, rising imports and the extension of manufacturing excises to raw materials and intermediate goods, and later to all manufactured goods, increased the buoyancy. That buoyancy was maintained in the later years in this phase as the economy attained a higher growth path and quantitative restrictions on imports were replaced by protective tariffs following initial attempts at liberalization in the late 1980s.

The second phase started with a recession caused by the severe drought of 1987 and was marked by stagnation in revenues. This was followed by a decline in the tax ratio following the economic crisis of 1991 and the subsequent reforms in the tax system, including a reduction in tariffs. Thus, in the third phase, the tax ratio declined from 15.8 percent in 1991–92 to its lowest level of 13.4 percent in 1997–98 and fluctuated around 14 percent until 2001–02. Although the tax ratio has trended upward since then, it has yet to reach the levels that prevailed before systematic tax reforms were initiated in 1991.

FIGURE 1. Trends in Direct and Indirect Taxes

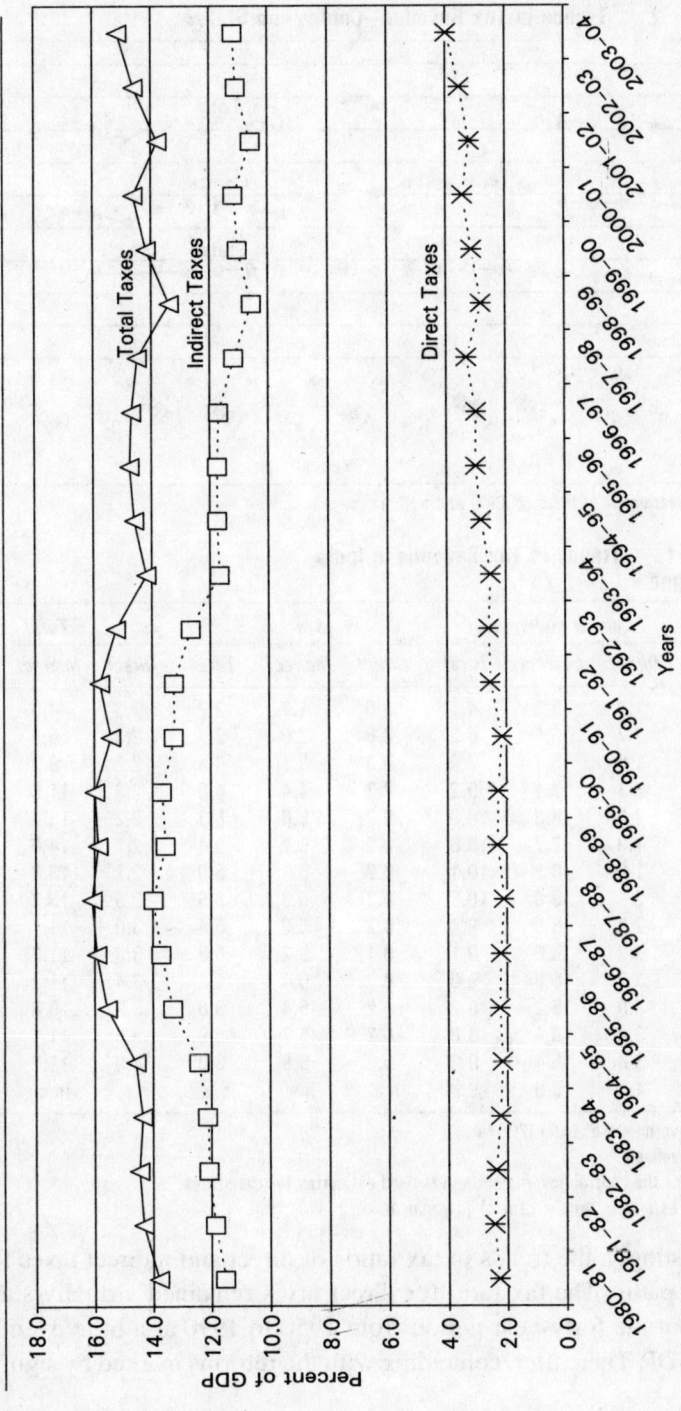

Source: Government of India (2004a) and authors' calculations.

FIGURE 2. Trends in Tax Revenue—Centre and States

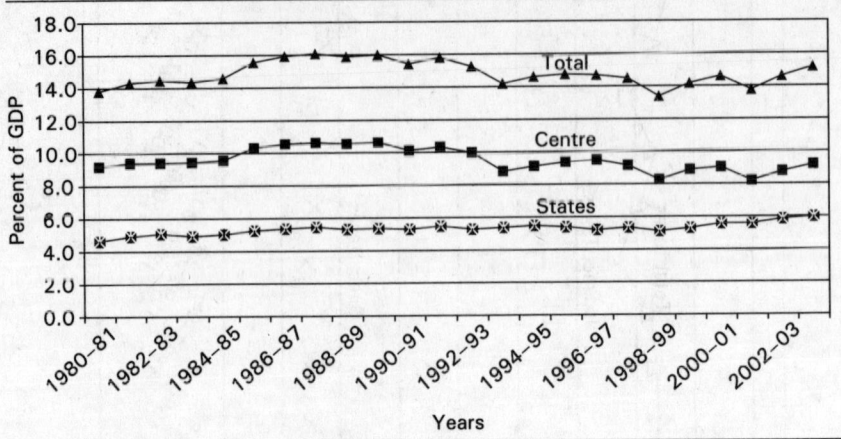

Source: Government of India (2004a) and authors' calculations.

TABLE 1. Trends in Tax Revenue in India
Percent of GDP

Year	Central government			States			Total		
	Direct	Indirect	Total	Direct	Indirect	Total	Direct	Indirect	Total
1950–51	1.8	2.3	4.1	0.6	1.7	2.2	2.3	4.0	6.3
1960–61	1.7	3.5	5.2	0.6	2.0	2.7	2.3	5.5	7.9
1970–71	1.9	5.1	7.0	0.3	3.1	3.4	2.2	8.2	10.4
1980–81	2.1	7.1	9.2	0.2	4.4	4.6	2.3	11.5	13.8
1985–86	2.0	8.3	10.3	0.2	5.0	5.3	2.2	13.3	15.6
1987–88	1.9	8.7	10.6	0.2	5.2	5.4	2.1	14.0	16.1
1990–91	1.9	8.2	10.1	0.2	5.1	5.3	2.2	13.3	15.4
1991–92	2.4	8.0	10.3	0.2	5.3	5.5	2.6	13.3	15.8
1995–96	2.8	6.5	9.4	0.2	5.2	5.4	3.0	11.7	14.8
1997–98	3.2	6.0	9.1	0.1	5.2	5.3	3.3	11.2	14.5
2000–01	3.3	5.8	9.0	0.2	5.4	5.6	3.4	11.2	14.6
2001–02	3.0	5.2	8.2	0.2	5.4	5.6	3.2	10.6	13.8
2002–03	3.4	5.4	8.8	0.2	5.7	5.9	3.5	11.1	14.6
2003–04[a]	3.8	5.4	9.2	0.2	5.8	6.0	4.0	11.2	15.2
2004–05[b]	4.3	5.6	9.9	n.a.	n.a.	n.a.	n.a.	n.a.	n.a.

Source: Government of India (2004a).
n.a. Not available.
a. Actual for the central government and revised estimates for the states.
b. Revised estimates for the central government.

Interestingly, the trends in tax ratios of direct and indirect taxes follow different paths. The tax ratio for direct taxes remained virtually stagnant throughout the forty-year period from 1950 to 1990 at a little over 2 percent of GDP. Thereafter, coinciding with the reforms marked by significant reduction in the tax rates and simplification of the tax structure, direct taxes increased sharply to over 4 percent of GDP in 2003–04 and were expected to be about 4.5 percent in 2004–05. In contrast, much of the increase in the tax ratio during the first forty years of planned development in India came from indirect taxes, which more than tripled, from 4 percent of GDP in 1950–51 to 13.5 percent in 1991–92. Since then, however, revenue from indirect taxes has fallen back to around 11 percent of GDP.

The decline in the total tax ratio observed since 1987–88 has occurred mainly at the central level, since center accounts for about 60 percent of the total. Notably, tax ratios of both central and state governments increased sharply between 1950–51 and 1985–86. Thereafter, the tax ratio at the state level was virtually stagnant at about 5.5 percent until 2001–02, when it increased modestly. In contrast, the central tax ratio increased to its peak in 1987–88, and remained at that level until the fiscal crisis of 1991–92, when it declined sharply until 2001–02; by 2004–05, it had nearly recovered its pre-1991 level. Within the central level, the share of direct taxes has shown a steady increase from less than 20 percent in 1990–91 to more than 43 percent in 2004–05.

Analysis of Central Taxes

Interestingly, the comprehensive tax reform at the central level was the direct consequence of economic crisis. As Bird stated after observing tax reforms in many countries, "fiscal crisis has been proven to be the mother of tax reform."[49] Unlike most ad hoc reforms undertaken in response to economic crises, the tax reforms in India were made systematically after a detailed analysis; since the reform package was introduced in 1991, the direction of reforms has continued. Thus the decline in central tax revenues as a share of GDP—from 10.1 percent in 1990–91 to 8.2 percent in 2001–02, before recovering to about 10 percent in 2004–05—came as a surprise and prompted many to ask whether the tax reform itself was responsible. The contrary view is that the ratio declined despite the reforms.

The disaggregated analysis of the trends in central tax revenue presented in table 2 and figure 3 shows that the sharpest decline in the tax–GDP ratio was in indirect taxes—both customs duties and central excise duties. The former declined by about half, from 3.6 percent in 1991–92 to 1.8 percent in 2004–05. Revenues from excise duties fell by 1 percentage point, from 4.3 percent to 3.3 percent during the period. The tax ratio for both taxes has been stable since 2001–02. Indicators suggest that while tax ratio for customs

49. Bird (1993).

duties may continue to decline as tariff levels are further reduced, the tax ratio for internal indirect taxes is likely to increase if reforms to expand the coverage of the services tax and integrate it with CenVAT are undertaken and significant improvement is achieved in tax administration.

TABLE 2. Level and Composition of Central Tax Revenue

	Personal income tax	Corporate income tax	Direct tax	Customs	Excise	Indirect tax	Total
As a percent of GDP							
1985–86	1.0	1.1	2.1	3.6	4.9	8.8	10.9
1990–91	0.9	0.9	2.0	3.6	4.3	8.2	10.1
1995–96	1.3	1.4	2.8	3.0	3.4	6.5	9.4
2000–01	1.5	1.7	3.3	2.3	3.3	5.8	9.0
2001–02	1.4	1.6	3.0	1.8	3.2	5.2	8.2
2002–03	1.5	1.9	3.4	1.8	3.3	5.4	8.8
2003–04	1.5	2.3	3.8	1.8	3.3	5.4	9.2
2004–05	1.6	2.7	4.3	1.8	3.3	5.6	9.9
2005–06	1.9	3.1	5.0	1.5	3.5	5.5	10.5
As a percent of total tax revenue							
1985–86	9.2	10.1	19.3	33.0	45.0	80.7	
1990–91	9.3	9.3	19.2	35.9	42.6	80.8	
1995–96	14.0	14.8	30.2	32.1	36.1	69.8	
2000–01	16.8	18.9	36.2	25.2	36.3	63.8	
2001–02	17.1	19.6	37.0	21.5	38.8	63.0	
2002–03	17.0	21.3	38.4	20.7	38.1	64.5	
2003–04	16.3	25.0	41.3	19.1	35.7	61.3	
2004–05[a]	16.6	27.1	43.9	18.4	32.9	56.1	
2005–06[b]	17.9	29.9	47.9	14.4	32.8	52.1	

Source: *Receipts Budget, Union Budget* (various years).
a. Revised estimates.
b. Budget estimates.

In contrast to the indirect taxes, revenue from centrally imposed direct taxes has increased significantly. Both personal and corporate income taxes have more than doubled as a ratio of GDP (see table 2). The major reason given for the increase is improved tax compliance arising from reduction in marginal tax rates.[50]

That increase also increased the importance of direct taxes in the total revenue picture. In 1991–92, direct taxes constituted less than one-fifth of the total tax revenue of the central government. In 2004–05, direct taxes accounted for 44 percent of the total and were estimated at 48 percent

50. Of course, there is some independent evidence on the improvement in tax compliance since 1991; see Das-Gupta and Mookherjee (1997) and Das-Gupta (2002).

FIGURE 3.   **Ratio of Central Taxes to GDP (as percent of GDP)**

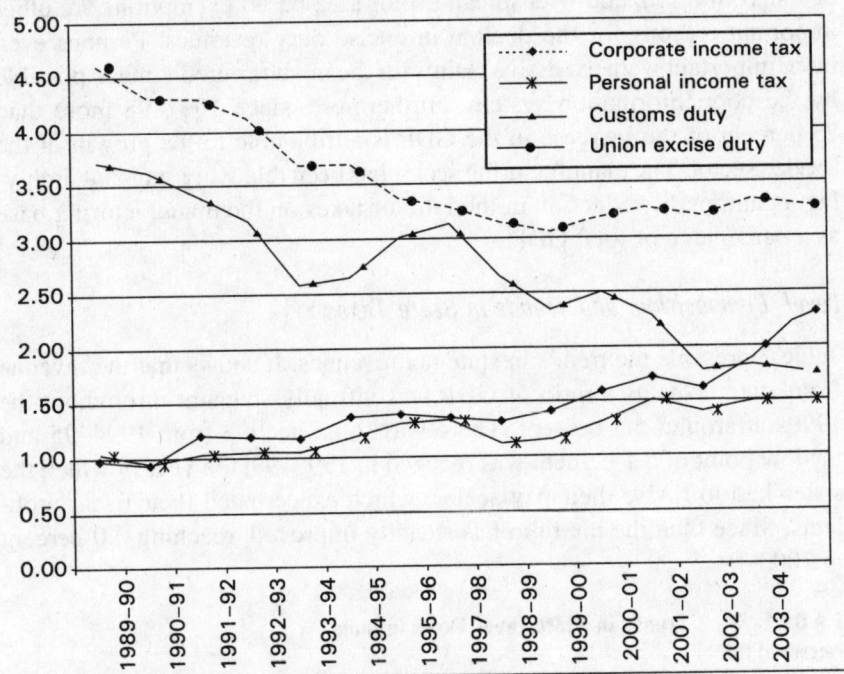

Source: Government of India (2004a) and authors' calculations.

for 2005–06. There has been a commensurate decline in the share of indirect taxes in total revenue, from 80 percent in 1991–92 to 56 percent in 2004–05 (see table 2).

The decline in the share of customs revenue might have been even greater but for the hesitancy on the part of the Finance Ministry in the face of demands from the domestic industry for protection against imports. The declining trend in customs revenue is likely to continue. Although imports have grown significantly since liberalization, it has not been enough to balance the lost customs revenues.[51] One reason for this could be the large-scale exemptions. Although the coverage of exemptions has not been expanded in a major way, the expansion in the base that should have accompanied a reduction in the rates of tax was not accomplished.

One explanation for the declining trend in excise duties throughout the 1980s is that the rate structure assumed was not revenue neutral when the input tax credit was allowed. Continued exemption of the small business

51. Panagariya (2005).

sector, expansion of its definition to include businesses with annual turnover of Rs. 10 million, and widespread use of area-based exemptions are other important reasons for the decline in excise duty revenues. Perhaps even more important were excessive claims for the input tax credit, made possible by the poor information system. Furthermore, since 1997–98 more than 75 percent of the increase in the GDP is attributable to the growth of the service sector. The manufacturing sector has been relatively stagnant, implying an automatic reduction in the ratio of taxes on the manufacturing base as a percentage of total GDP.

Level, Composition, and Trends in State Taxes

Table 3 presents the trends in state tax revenues. It shows that the revenue from state taxes as a ratio of GDP was virtually stagnant throughout the 1990s at around 5.5 percent. There was some decline from 1994–95 and the low point of 5.1 percent was reached in 1998–99, the year in which the states had to revise their pay scales, which exacerbated their fiscal problems. Since then the tax ratio has steadily improved, reaching 6.0 percent in 2003–04.[52]

TABLE 3. Trends in State Level Taxes in India
Percent of GDP

Year	Direct taxes	Sales tax	State excise duty	Stamps and registration	Taxes on transport	Other indirect taxes	Total indirect taxes	Total taxes
1985–86	0.2	3.1	0.7	0.4	0.5	0.3	5.0	5.2
1990–91	0.2	3.2	0.9	0.4	0.5	0.3	5.1	5.5
1991–92	0.2	3.4	0.9	0.4	0.5	0.4	5.4	5.7
1992–93	0.2	3.2	0.9	0.4	0.5	0.3	5.1	5.5
1993–94	0.2	3.3	0.9	0.4	0.5	0.3	5.2	5.5
1994–95	0.2	3.3	0.8	0.5	0.5	0.3	5.3	5.5
1995–96	0.2	3.0	0.7	0.5	0.4	0.5	5.2	5.4
1996–97	0.2	3.2	0.7	0.5	0.4	0.3	5.1	5.2
1997–98	0.1	3.2	0.8	0.5	0.4	0.3	5.2	5.4
1998–99	0.1	3.1	0.8	0.4	0.4	0.3	5.0	5.1
1999–00	0.1	3.2	0.8	0.4	0.4	0.3	5.2	5.3
2000–01	0.2	3.5	0.8	0.4	0.4	0.4	5.4	5.7
2001–02	0.2	3.4	0.8	0.5	0.5	0.4	5.4	5.7
2002–03	0.2	3.5	0.8	0.6	0.5	0.3	5.7	5.9
2003–04	0.2	3.6	0.8	0.5	0.6	0.3	5.8	6.0

Source: Government of India (2004a).

52. The tax ratios do vary significantly across states, however, with the southern states of Kerala, Karnataka, and Tamil Nadu on average recording higher levels than the other states.

The sales tax is the predominant state tax, constituting about 60 percent of total state tax revenues. Not surprisingly then, the overall trend in states' tax ratio follows closely the trends in sales tax revenue. After reaching a low of 3.1 percent in 1998-99, the sales tax ratio increased marginally to 3.5 percent in 2000–01 and has remained at that level. Any attempt to improve the revenue productivity of states' tax system, therefore, is inextricably intertwined with the reform of the sales tax system; in this respect, the recent move toward a destination-based VAT is extremely important.

The state excise duty is a sumptuary tax on alcoholic products. In addition to the state excise duty, some states levy a sales tax on alcoholic products, which accounts for a good proportion of the state tax revenue. In regard to this excise duty, there has always been a problem of balancing regulatory and revenue considerations. The major components of the tax come from arrack and country liquor on the one hand, and "India Made Foreign Liquor" (IMFL), including beer, on the other. The duty is collected through a licence fee for licenses to sellers or through the auction of selling vends, and through taxes on the consumption of liquor. The problem with country liquor has been the brewing and consumption of illicit liquor, which not only has caused loss of revenue but has been an important health hazard. The problem with IMFL has been tax evasion. The Karnataka Tax Reforms Committee estimated that the amount of evaded tax may be as high as three times the actual revenue collected.[53] The way to deal with this problem has more to do with strengthening the tax administration and information system and less to do with the structure of the tax.

The principal source of stamp duties and registration fees is from the sale of immovable property, such as land and buildings. The levy of stamp duties in addition to registration fees, adds to the marginal tax rates, which are already very high. Not surprisingly, the most important problem with this tax is undervaluation of the property sold. Undervaluation of immovable property is aided by the lack of an organized market. Development of organized market for urban immovable property transactions is hindered by the high rate of stamp duties and registration fees and other policies such as the rent control act and the urban land ceiling act.[54] Until recently, the tax rates were as high as 12–15 percent on the value of transactions.[55]

53. Government of Karnataka (2001).
54. The Urban Land Ceiling Act was introduced to prevent hoarding of land in private hands. It is currently being repealed in most states.
55. NIPFP (1996).

Many of the states that reduced the rates have found the typical working of the "Laffer curve" phenomenon. In Karnataka, for example, the tax rate was reduced from 16 percent in 2001–02 to 8 percent in 2002–03, and revenue from stamp duties grew 30 percent.

The other important component of state taxes are the taxes on transport, consisting of a motor vehicles tax and a tax on transport of passengers and goods. For administrative convenience, many states have merged the latter with an additional motor vehicles tax. Also the motor vehicles tax on private noncommercial vehicles has been converted into a lifetime tax by adding up ten years' tax or by adopting a similar formula. The reform in this area should separate the motor vehicles tax from the passengers' and goods tax, and the latter should eventually become a part of the state VAT rather than a separate tax. Similarly, the entertainment tax, electricity duty, and luxury tax on hotels and restaurants should also be merged with the VAT.

At the local level there are two taxes of some significance. These are the taxes on property and in some states, *octroi*, the checkpost-based tax levied by urban local bodies. The major problem with urban property taxes, as in the case of registration fees, is undervaluation. Alternative models of reform, such as using the capital value or rental value for valuing the property, have been suggested. The ultimate reform depends on the development of an organized property market. In most cases the recommendations suggested have been to use the value as determined in some independent manner. For instance, one city has divided the entire city into different categories of localities, and fixed a rate per square foot of built-up area. This process dispensed with the need to undertake acceptable property valuation. For its part, *octroi* not only impedes internal trade and violates the principle of common market, but also is a source of corruption and rent seeking.

Analysis of the Trends and Economic Impact of the Tax System

In this section, the observed trends in different central and state taxes are explained in greater detail and the possible efficiency and equity implications of different taxes are analyzed. Specifically, the analysis seeks to answer a number of questions. Has tax compliance improved over the years in response to reductions in marginal tax rates? What other factors influence revenue productivity of the tax system? What are the efficiency and equity implications of the tax system?

Personal Income Tax

The increase in revenue productivity of the personal income tax is attributed to the improvement in tax compliance arising from the sharp reduction in marginal tax rates in 1991–92 and 1996–97. This is also the period when the growth of GDP itself had decelerated. The apparent stimulus of declining marginal tax rates is reflected in the negative correlation between effective tax rates and the ratio of income tax collections to GDP, akin to a Laffer curve.[56] While it is clearly difficult to attribute the increase in revenue productivity solely or even mainly to reduction in marginal tax rates, Das-Gupta and Mookherjee draw a tentative but important conclusion capturing improvement in overall performance of the tax system.[57] Similarly, Das-Gupta analyzes sixteen different structural, administrative, and institutional indicators, and concludes that the performance of the tax system has shown improvement: tax compliance indeed improved with the reduction in marginal tax rates.[58]

In a more recent analysis, Bhalla estimates the aggregate revenue elasticity at –1.43 percent and concludes that the 1996–97 tax cut was a huge success in increasing revenues.[59] Bhalla provides an estimate of compliance by comparing the data published by the income tax department, the coverage of which itself is narrow, with those from other sources, particularly the National Council of Applied Economic Research to establish that the number of people recording incomes within any given bracket for income tax purposes, is significantly lower than the numbers recorded by other surveys. This approach has problems, however, especially for proprietary firms and individual businesses where it can be hard to distinguish between expenditures of the firm and expenditures of the individual for personal needs.[60] Nevertheless, the paper helps to focus on the need for some informed debate and analysis in this area.

---

56. Effective tax rates are derived by applying the tax structure to reference income levels. Given the limited sample size, such an exercise would not be empirically sound and hence is not reported.

57. Das-Gupta and Mookherjee (1997).

58. Das-Gupta (2002).

59. Bhalla (2005).

60. The income tax act provides for some deductions in the case of business and traders. The deductions include expenditure on travel and entertainment. Expenses on telecommunications too are a case in point. While any income tax return would show some or all of these expenses as business expenses, in most other consumer surveys, these would figure as personal expenses. Given that the proportion of these expenses in total income is likely to

The important point is that improvement in revenue productivity of the personal income tax since 1996–97 cannot be attributed solely or even mainly to reduction in the marginal rate of tax. The information presented in table 4 shows that the main reason for the increase in revenues is the administrative arrangement extending the scope of tax deductions at source— an arrangement whereby the employer withholds the tax due on the income paid to the employees and directly remits the same to the government exchequer. The proportion of tax deducted at source (TDS) to total revenue collections actually declined from 42 percent in 1990–91 to 22 percent in 1994–95. It increased to 50 percent following the expansion in the scope of TDS in 1996–97 and to 67 percent in 2001–02 before declining marginally to 64 percent in 2003–04. As a proportion of GDP, the ratio of collections from TDS increased by 0.67 percentage points over the period considered. When compared with the increase of 0.56 percentage points in the ratio of personal income tax collections to GDP, the improved compliance appears to result largely if not solely from improved coverage or greater effectiveness of TDS as a tool for collecting taxes.

TABLE 4. **Contribution of TDS to Personal Income Tax Revenue**

Year	Tax deduction at source (percent)	Advance tax (percent)	Gross collections (Rs. crore)	Refunds (Rs. crore)	TDS as a percentage of GDP
1990–91	41.75	36.00	6,188.37	827.74	0.45
1991–92	48.22	33.29	7,523.97	794.79	0.55
1992–93	42.91	33.45	9,060.79	1,165.44	0.52
1993–94	19.65	51.77	14,106.25	4,045.96	0.32
1994–95	22.18	56.87	17,178.72	3,357.76	0.37
1995–96	22.21	50.01	22,949.61	6,462.48	0.42
1996–97	50.87	27.30	20,042.48	1,808.49	0.75
1997–98	50.87	24.10	19,270.19	2,169.60	0.64
1998–99	52.44	23.59	22,411.98	2,171.83	0.67
1999–00	53.69	24.58	28,684.29	3,029.79	0.80
2000–01	63.22	20.89	35,162.61	3,398.63	1.06
2001–02	67.10	19.23	35,358.00	3,354.00	1.04
2002–03	65.55	20.26	42,119.00	5,253.00	1.12
2003–04	64.03	20.04	48,454.00	7,067.00	1.12

Source: Government of India, *Report of the Comptroller and Auditor General (Direct Taxes)* (various years).

be higher in the "middle," and given the higher possibility of this group of agents being in the "middle," it appears that this definitional issue itself could induce the pattern observed in the paper. Other categories of taxpayers are also affected, including association of persons, which are formed voluntarily to earn incomes.

Interestingly, although it is tempting to attribute this observed trend to extension of TDS to interest, dividends, payments to contractors, and insurance commissions, the increase has come about mainly in TDS in salaries (table 5). The TDS in salaries in 1992–93 constituted only 25 percent of total TDS, increased to 50 percent in 1999–2000 and thereafter declined to 41 percent, as TDS from payments to nonresidents and others and payments to contractors increased substantially. Even after the refunds are adjusted, the share of TDS in total receipts continues to remain high and increasing. This implies that the contribution of TDS to incremental revenue is increasing as well.

TABLE 5.   Contribution to TDS
Percent

Contributor	1992–93	1997–98	1999–2000	2000–01	2001–02	2002–03	2003–04
Salaries	25.15	42.05	50.43	48.99	47.82	44.56	41.23
Interest	40.15	25.25	25.85	19.91	21.39	18.37	16.63
Dividend	5.90	3.41	1.99	1.20	0.81	3.00	2.21
Winnings in lotteries and races	1.02	0.66	0.78	0.29	0.23	0.37	0.41
Payments to contractors	11.85	17.90	19.83	14.92	13.06	13.83	17.56
Insurance commissions	1.21	0.97	0.93	0.72	1.05	1.05	1.01
Payments to nonresidents and others	14.71	9.77	0.18	13.98	15.64	18.83	20.94
Total TDS collections (Rs crore)	6,210	13,788	18,546	28,213	30,672	36,568	42,955

Source: Government of India, *Report of the Comptroller and Auditor General (Direct Taxes)* (various years).

The increase in the tax revenue thus has more to do with the rapid growth of the organized sector, expansion in the interaction of the financial sector with the rest of the economy, and administrative measures extending the TDS than with improved compliance arising from the reduction in marginal rates of tax. The extension of permanent account numbers to cover a larger number of potential taxpayers and the expansion of the tax information system (TIN) are expected to advance this cause further, by generating an extensive and reliable database. This finding, however, does not make a case for increasing the marginal tax rates, since such increases would be associated with significant efficiency costs for the economy, which would likely be corrected or mitigated through exemptions and concessions of various kinds.

The number of personal income tax assessees has increased significantly over the last decade. From 1999–2000 to 2003–04 alone, the number increased from 19.6 million to 28.8 million—a growth rate of more than 10 percent a year (table 6). Interestingly, the highest growth was seen in the income range of Rs. 200,000–500,000 (38.4 percent) followed by those above Rs. 1 million (16 percent). The important thing to note is that the number of taxpayers is still small considering the growing middle class. Although the number of taxpayers with income above Rs. 1 million is growing, it still constitutes a small number as well as a small proportion of the total. There were only about 100,000 taxpayers in this group, constituting about 0.3 percent of the total number of taxpayers.

TABLE 6. Income Tax Assessees by Income Range

Taxable income range (Rs. million)	Number of taxpayers (million)		Growth rate (percent)	Ratio of taxpayers in the range to total number of taxpayers	
	1999–2000	2003–04		1999–2000	2003–04
Less than 0.2	18.75	26.55	9.1	95.80	92.08
0.2–0.5	0.49	1.80	38.4	2.50	6.24
0.5–1	0.26	0.37	9.2	1.32	1.28
Above 1	0.06	0.01	16.0	0.30	0.36
Search and seizure assessments	0.015	0.012	(–)5.43	0.08	0.04
Total	19.59	28.83	10.2	100	100

Source: Government of India, *Report of the Comptroller and Auditor General (Direct Taxes)* (2005).

It is important to understand the impact of reductions in the marginal tax rate and in the number of rate categories since 1991–92 on the overall progressivity and equity of the tax system. Given that the reform involved sharp reduction in the marginal tax rates, the effective rate declines as the level of income increases. It would be tempting to conclude that progressivity has therefore declined and overall equity in the tax system has worsened over the years. Such a conclusion would be inappropriate, for it pertains only to progressivity among the taxpayers; with a sharp increase in the total number of people paying tax, the overall progressivity would have improved. In 2003–04, as many as 29 million people paid income tax, compared with about 3.9 million in 1989–90, and the tax paid doubled from less than 1 percent of GDP to almost 2 percent of GDP. The increase in the number of taxpayers indicates improvement in horizontal equity since more people with similar incomes now possibly pay the tax, and the fact that a larger proportion of incomes are noow subject to tax represents improvement in vertical equity as well.

Corporate Income Tax

Of the four major taxes considered, the revenue from the corporate income tax grew at the fastest rate during the 1990s, tripling as a percentage of GDP, from 0.9 percent in 1990–91 to 2.7 percent in 2003–04, despite significant reduction in the rates. The main reforms eliminated the distinction between closely held and widely held companies, reduced the marginal tax rate to align it with the top marginal tax rate of personal income tax, and rationalized tax preferences, namely, investment and depreciation allowances, to a considerable extent. In addition, the introduction of the minimum alternative tax has also contributed to revenues.

It would be instructive to analyze the contribution of different sectors to the corporate tax. According to the Prowess database, the manufacturing sector accounted for two-thirds of the corporate tax collections in 1994–95, but that amount declined to just 40 percent by 2004–05 (table 7). Within the manufacturing sector, the petroleum sector contributed the most (12.5 percent), followed by chemicals (6.5 percent) and the basic metals industry (6.1 percent). In contrast, textiles contributed only about 0.5 percent.

In contrast, public sector enterprises account for a growing share of collections, increasing from 19 percent in 1994–95 to about 38 percent in 2002–03. That means that over 40 percent of the increase in corporate tax revenues was collected from public enterprises (table 8). This increase is attributable in part to the fact that, unlike the private sector, public enterprises do not undertake elaborate tax planning to minimize their taxes.

Union Excise Duties

The declining ratio of Union excise duties to GDP since reforms were introduced is truly a matter of concern as the loss of revenue has been a constraint in further reducing import duties. Although the ratio has been stagnant at 3.3 percent for several years, that is significantly lower than the ratio in 1991–92 (4.1 percent).

Not only has the revenue productivity of Union excise duties declined, but the revenue shows an increased concentration in commodities that would be used in further production. Independent operation of excise and sales tax systems and confining the tax to goods and to the manufacturing stage

TABLE 7. Sectoral Contribution to Corporate Income Tax Collections

Percent

Sector	1994–95	1995–96	1996–97	1997–98	1998–99	1999–2000	2000–01	2001–02	2002–03	2003–04
Mining	2.41	5.20	10.55	11.47	12.88	18.66	22.45	18.27	21.97	13.92
Manufacturing	67.33	60.93	44.74	35.27	38.90	34.29	27.96	28.69	32.99	39.95
Food products	6.75	3.69	2.96	3.88	4.55	4.77	4.76	3.67	3.43	3.46
Textiles	1.92	0.83	0.81	0.72	0.56	0.55	0.64	0.37	0.47	0.52
Leather	0.04	0.04	0.04	0.04	0.05	0.11	0.07	0.02	0.02	0.03
Paper and wood	1.61	2.29	0.78	0.53	0.44	0.75	0.89	0.94	0.58	0.74
Petroleum products	11.75	12.21	7.55	5.50	9.42	6.28	4.97	7.46	11.13	12.48
Chemicals	17.21	13.98	8.67	7.58	6.89	5.74	5.41	5.43	6.00	6.46
Rubber and plastics	0.87	0.63	0.70	0.64	0.93	0.80	0.51	0.47	0.61	0.50
Nonmetallic minerals	1.20	1.82	0.82	0.53	0.46	0.38	0.57	0.40	0.30	0.48
Basic metals and products	3.84	4.70	4.32	3.08	3.60	4.45	4.22	2.95	2.86	6.09
Machinery	13.34	9.90	8.68	6.40	6.35	5.75	3.51	3.92	3.63	3.88
Transport equipment	8.80	10.84	9.41	6.37	5.65	4.61	2.41	3.06	3.96	5.31
Electricity, gas, and steam	0.34	1.70	1.70	8.80	11.49	7.51	9.09	6.49	5.57	1.91
Construction	2.44	1.73	1.38	1.17	1.38	1.27	1.17	0.97	0.89	1.31
Wholesale and retail trade	3.29	2.27	3.31	3.41	2.23	1.89	3.00	2.94	3.03	2.99
Hotels and restaurants	1.15	1.37	0.97	0.62	0.53	0.35	0.38	0.23	0.21	0.21
Transport services	0.36	2.27	2.12	2.07	1.39	1.42	1.91	1.50	1.49	1.27
Post and telecom	10.07	7.91	6.13	5.95	7.58	4.29	5.72	6.35	2.61	6.50
Financial intermediation	11.89	15.95	28.34	30.39	22.37	28.54	25.83	32.01	28.67	29.74
Real estate	0.01	0.03	0.03	0.02	0.01	0.02	0.01	0.02	0.02	0.03
Computer, R&D, and other business services	0.67	0.60	0.64	0.72	1.06	1.46	2.19	2.21	2.13	1.79
Social services	0.04	0.05	0.09	0.13	0.19	0.39	0.31	0.32	0.40	0.40
Proportion of total corporate income tax collections	50.06	62.16	77.39	80.82	64.54	62.21	61.95	72.62	80.38	65.09

Source: PROWESS database.

TABLE 8. **Contribution of Public Sector Enterprises to Corporation Tax**

Year	Corporate tax paid by public enterprises (Rs. crore)	Total corporate tax paid (Rs. crore)	Ratio of public sector tax to total (percent)
1990–91	1,229	5,335	23.0
1991–92	1,674	7,853	21.3
1992–93	1,804	8,899	20.3
1993–94	2,110	10,060	21.0
1994–95	2,581	13,822	18.7
1995–96	4,187	16,487	25.4
1996–97	5,193	18,567	28.0
1997–98	5,634	20,016	28.1
1998–99	6,499	24,529	26.5
1999–00	7,706	30,692	25.1
2000–01	9,314	35,696	26.1
2001–02	12,254	36,609	33.5
2002–03	17,430	46,172	37.8

Source: Government of India, *Public Enterprises Survey* (various years).

alone does not remove cascading, and final products in the manufacturing stage are not necessarily final consumer goods—goods transport vehicles being a prime example.

Table 9, which shows Union excise duty collections by commodity, highlights some interesting features with implications for both efficiency and equity of the tax system. One of the most important features is the commodity concentration. Three-fourths of all Union excise duties are paid by just five groups of commodities—petroleum products, chemicals, basic metals, transport vehicles, and electrical and electronic goods. One would normally expect this concentration to decrease as manufacturing diversified. This increased concentration imposes a disproportionate tax burden on different sectors of the economy. Moreover, this type of commodity concentration does not allow objective calibration of policies regarding excise duties as the Finance Ministry would not like to lose revenue from this lucrative source.

Another important feature of the pattern of excise revenue collections is that the overwhelming proportion is paid by commodity groups that are in the nature of intermediate products used in the production of goods or services that are not subject to excise. Besides petroleum products, a significant proportion of which is used in other manufacturing, the duties on all goods used as inputs to service providers, especially of services used in manufacturing activities, contribute to cascading and add to production costs. Transport vehicles and related industries are one such industry. These are a source of

TABLE 9. **Revenue from Union Excise Duties by Commodity Groups**

Percent

Commodity group	1990–91	1995–96	1998–99	1999–2000	2000–01	2001–02	2002–03	2003–04
Food products	4.0	3.5	4.8	4.4	4.5	3.7	3.6	3.2
Tobacco products	8.3	8.1	7.9	6.7	6.7	6.6	5.9	5.6
Minerals and ores	8.4	8.7	7.2	6.7	6.2	6.0	5.8	6.2
Petroleum products	13.9	12.4	22.5	29.6	32.9	38.3	40.4	41.0
Chemicals	11.1	14.4	11.1	9.8	10.2	9.9	9.3	8.9
Plastics and articles thereof	2.5	4.0	4.2	3.7	2.3	2.4	2.4	2.5
Rubber products	4.9	4.6	2.9	2.6	2.2	2.0	1.8	1.3
Leather and wood products	0.6	0.4	0.2	0.2	0.2	0.2	0.1	0.1
Textiles and garments	10.8	8.5	6.2	5.2	4.8	4.7	4.6	3.7
Basic metals	9.6	14.5	11.4	11.1	10.4	9.2	9.8	11.2
Electrical and electronic goods/tools	16.1	11.9	10.5	9.5	8.8	8.2	7.8	7.8
Transport vehicles	8.4	7.3	8.5	8.8	8.9	7.2	7.0	6.6
Miscellaneous	1.3	1.5	2.5	1.8	1.8	1.9	1.6	1.7

Source: Central excise data.

significant inefficiency in the system. This inefficiency also makes it difficult to speculate on the effect of the tax on different manufacturing enterprises and its effects on employment and incomes and thus to make judgments on the distribution of the tax burden.

A striking feature of excise duty collections is that, as in the case of corporate incomes taxes, a predominant proportion is paid by public sector enterprises (table 10). Another striking feature is the wide fluctuation in collections from public sector enterprises from year to year, ranging from a high of 53 percent in 1999–2000 to a low of 30 percent just two years later. The fluctuations are attributable to fluctuations in administered prices on items such as steel, coal, minerals and ores, and petroleum products. Prices for petroleum products also vary with international prices. In other words, the revenue from excise duties, which constitutes an important source of revenue for the central government, is vulnerable to pricing and output decisions of public enterprises. Given the government's significant dependence on this sector, the ability of public enterprises to forge an independent pricing policy too could be compromised.

TABLE 10. **Contribution of Public Enterprises to the Central Government's Excise Revenues**

Year	Public enterprises (Rs. crore)	Total collections (Rs. 10 crore)	Public enterprises as percentage of total
1990–91	9,656	24,514	39.4
1991–92	9,815	28,110	34.9
1992–93	12,180	30,832	39.5
1993–94	12,527	31,697	39.5
1994–95	16,414	37,347	44.0
1995–96	17,044	40,187	42.4
1996–97	22,193	45,008	49.3
1997–98	21,720	47,962	45.3
1998–99	23,132	53,246	43.4
1999–00	32,942	61,902	53.2
2000–01	20,824	68,526	30.3
2001–02	31,203	72,555	43.0
2002–03	34,610	82,310	42.1

Sources: Government of India, *Public Enterprises Survey* (various issues), and *Union Budget* (various years).

Customs Duties

The most important and in many ways most far-reaching reforms involved customs tariffs. Since 1991 imports subject to quantitative restrictions constituted 90 percent of total imports, and these restrictions have been virtually done away with. The import-weighted tariff rates have been reduced from 72 percent in 1990 to 15 percent currently. The peak import rate has been lowered from more than 150 percent in 1991 to less than 20 percent.[61]

A major problem from the viewpoint of efficiency is the continuation of differentiated rates of duty varying with the stage of production. The rates on raw materials and intermediate goods continue to be lower than those on consumer and capital goods. The import tariff reduction has continued to be guided by this "unprincipled principle": even the Kelkar Task Force on indirect taxes suggested that the rate differentiation should continue to be made on the basis of the stage of production.[62] Because it focuses on greater protection for "final use industries" compared with inputs and inter-mediate goods, this approach continues reliance on the self-sufficiency model of development as opposed to a comparative advantage model.

Table 11 presents the collection of customs by commodity from 1990–91 to 2003–04. Despite significant external liberalization, almost 60 percent of the duty is collected from just three commodity groups—machinery, petroleum products, and chemicals. Furthermore, the overwhelming pro-portion (over 75 percent) of the duties are collected from either machinery or basic inputs and intermediate goods. Thus, contrary to the fear, liberal-ization has not led to massive inflow of consumer goods. These data also imply that further reduction in the duties and greater uniformity in the structure of duties would have beneficial effects on the economy. A detailed econometric study shows that uniform reduction in tariffs has had favorable effects on production, exports, employment, and capital and that these gains are different across different sectors.[63]

The proportion of duties collected from machinery has increased signifi-cantly, from 19.5 percent in 1990–91 to 26.6 percent in 2003–04. This increase has occurred despite exemptions provided for import of machinery for several infrastructure projects. The conclusion is that external liberal-ization is leading to adoption of more modern machinery and technology in the production process, which would have a favorable effect on the pro-ductivity growth. Customs collections have also increased for food products. In contrast, revenue from iron and steel and other basic metals has shown a substantial decline over the years; these items have become more competitive in recent years, and therefore may be more attractive to buy in the domestic market rather than from foreign markets.

61. Virmani and others (2004).
62. The quotation is from Joshi and Little (1996).
63. Virmani and others (2004).

TABLE 11.   **Composition of Revenue from Customs Duties, by Commodity Group**
Percent

	1990–91	1995–96	1996–97	2000–01	2001–02	2002–03	2003–04
Food items	2.5	2.4	2.3	5.4	10.6	8.8	6.4
Tea and coffee	0.1	0.0	0.0	0.1	0.1	0.1	0.0
Beverages	0.1	0.1	0.1	0.1	0.2	0.2	0.1
Minerals and ores	1.4	0.7	0.5	1.3	1.6	1.8	1.7
Petroleum products	19.4	23.4	28.5	23.2	16.1	19.5	20.9
Chemicals	12.3	11.9	11.2	10.4	11.4	11.2	11.1
Of which:							
Pharmaceutical products	0.1	0.1	0.1	0.2	0.3	0.4	0.3
Plastics	6.4	4.9	4.7	3.0	3.1	3.1	3.1
Rubber	1.4	1.3	1.5	1.4	1.4	1.3	1.3
Paper	1.0	0.7	0.7	0.7	0.7	0.7	0.9
Textiles	2.2	1.3	0.9	1.0	0.9	1.0	1.4
Cement products	0.2	0.2	0.1	0.2	0.2	0.2	0.3
Ceramics	0.6	0.5	0.5	0.7	0.8	0.8	1.0
Iron and steel	10.2	6.6	5.2	3.8	3.8	3.7	4.6
Other basic metals	4.3	5.0	4.4	2.1	2.3	2.2	2.5
Machinery	19.5	20.8	18.8	23.6	24.8	26.4	26.6
Transport equipment	3.3	4.0	4.7	3.9	4.0	3.4	4.1
Others	15.2	16.2	15.9	19.3	18.1	15.9	13.9

Source: Customs department data.

Toward Further Reforms in the Tax System

In the last few years, various study groups and task forces have focused on the reforms in the tax system at the central level. The Advisory Group on Tax Policy and Administration for the Tenth Plan and the Kelkar Task Force (KTF) reports on direct and indirect taxes and more recently the KTF on the implementation of the Fiscal Responsibility and Budget Management Act have comprehensively examined the tax system and made important recommendations for reform.[64] All these are in conformity with the direction set by the TRC in 1991 and 1993, which called for broadening the tax base, reducing the rates, minimizing rate differentiation, and simplifying the tax systems. While there are differences on specific recommendations, these newer task force reports share broad agreement on the direction and thrust of reforms and on the need to reform tax administration and the tax information system.

64. Government of India (2001a, 2002a, 2002b, 2004b).

Tax reform is an ongoing process, and with the fiscal imbalance in India looming large, reforms to improve long-run revenue productivity will have to continue. The reforms will have to involve all aspects to the tax system, including the tax structure, administration, and institutions, and any reforms should move the system toward one that is general and rule based. In a democratic polity with so many special interest groups influencing policies, moving away from a culture of selectivity and discretion is difficult but can be achieved over a period of time.

Reform of Central Taxes

Personal income tax reforms should involve further simplification of the tax system by withdrawing tax exemptions and concessions on income from specified activities. It is also necessary to abolish the surcharge and to further simplify the tax by reducing the number of tax brackets. In fact, there is considerable virtue in having a single tax rate with an exemption limit, as many of the transitional economies have found. In any case, the ability of the income tax system to bring about significant redistribution is limited, and if it is taken that equity in fiscal policy should focus on increasing the incomes of the poor rather than reducing the incomes of the rich, the objective is better achieved by allocating and targeting adequate resources to human development rather than creating disincentives to work, save, and invest. Moving toward a single tax rate may not be politically feasible at this juncture, however, but it may be possible to reduce the number of tax rates to two, with a small reduction in the marginal tax rate (say, 25 percent).

On the corporation tax, base broadening involves getting rid of the tax concessions and preferences. In particular, the exemption for profits from exports, free trade zones, and technology parks, as well as exemptions for area-based development and for infrastructure should be phased out. Similarly, the current depreciation allowance, even after the proposed reduction in 2005–06 is quite generous, and there is a case for reducing it to more realistic levels while at the same time reducing the tax rate to align it with the marginal tax rate on personal income tax. It is most important, however, to avoid flip-flop in tax policy. The history of dividend taxation, in particular, has been full of contradictory policy stances from one year to another. The issue of whether companies or individual shareholders should pay the dividend tax must be settled. The most satisfactory solution is to have partial integration of the tax with personal income tax. However, if for administrative reasons, it is thought to be better to collect the tax from the company, then the tax rate applicable on dividends should be determined on the basis of the difference between the marginal tax rate of personal income tax and the effective rate of the corporate tax.[65]

The other important issue involving the corporate income tax is the differential between the rates applicable to domestic and foreign companies. Part of the rationale for a differential is involves the dividend tax, which is payable by domestic companies alone. The rationalization of these two aspects therefore needs to go together.

With regard to import duties, reform should move in the direction of further reduction and unification of the rates. As most nonagricultural tariffs fall between 0 and 15 percent, a uniform tariff of 10 percent would considerably simplify and rationalize the system.[66] Equally important is the need to get rid of a plethora of exemptions and concessional treatment for various categories including imports for special projects. A minimum tariff of 5 percent on all currently exempt goods could be introduced as a first step in rationalizing the duty to bring it in line with the above recommendation.

Wide-ranging exemptions are also a problem with excise duties. Therefore, one of the most important base-broadening measures should be to reduce the exemptions. In particular, the exemptions given to small-scale industry have not only eroded the tax base but have inhibited the growth of firms into an economically efficient size. Similarly, various exemptions given to project imports have significantly eroded the tax base. This has also infused the tax system with selectivity and discretion. The rate structure should be rationalized by converting the remaining items subject to specific duties to ad valorem and by unifying the rates toward a single CenVAT rate.

The next step is to fully integrate the taxation of services with the CenVAT. This would require extending the service tax to all services excluding a small list of exemptions and a small negative list, as recommended by the Expert Group on Service Taxation.[67] This step would help in assessing the potential from service taxation. At the next stage, the taxes on services could be unified with the CenVAT to evolve a manufacturing-stage VAT on goods and services. Since credit for the tax paid on both goods and specific services is already provided, universal tax coverage of services, together with a tax credit mechanism and its integration with CenVAT, would

65. The rationale for a separate taxation of dividends is that the effective rate of the corporate tax is lower due to tax preferences and therefore the difference should be taxed to put corporations on the same footing as unincorporated businesses, which pay the tax at personal income tax rates.

66. Panagariya (2005); Acharya (2005).

67. Government of India (2001b). This expert group was headed by M. Govinda Rao, one of the authors of the current paper.

rationalize the tax system considerably. Not only would this tax have a broader base and increase revenues in the short term, but overall revenue productivity would be improved.

It should be noted, however, that restricting the CenVAT to the manufacturing stage alone, as the system currently does, creates a need to have a number of agents in the system that do not collect and pay taxes but that are entitled to issue VAT invoices. Wholesalers are authorized to issue multiple VAT invoices on their sales against the single invoice of their purchases, in order to facilitate the credit mechanism for small and medium manufacturers, who may not always buy from other manufacturers. This constitutes a weak link in the chain of invoices since these agents are difficult to monitor and administer. Integrating services into the credit mechanism could further exacerbate this problem, since a larger number of agents would seek to purchase from agents other than manufacturers. This is a problem that needs to be addressed. The solution discussed by the TRC of expanding the coverage of CenVAT to wholesalers, with the revenue being assigned to the states, is one option. An administrative alternative could be devised by mandating the filing of informational documents and periodic auditing of these dealers.

Evolving a Coordinated Consumption Tax System

One of the most important reforms needed in the indirect tax system is a coordinated consumption tax system for the country. Such a system is necessary to ensure fair distribution of the tax burden among different sectors and between goods and services, to improve revenue productivity, to minimize relative price distortions, and above all, to ensure a common market in the country without placing impediments on the movement of factors and products.

Such a system would require coordinated reforms at the central, state, and local levels. At the center, as mentioned above, the first step is to evolve a manufacturing-stage VAT on goods and services. At the state level, introduction of the VAT, initiated in April 2005, has to be completed. The most important step here involves extending the input tax credit mechanism not only to intrastate trade but also to interstate trade by introducing an appropriate zero-rating mechanism. This effort requires building an accurate information system on interstate transactions, a step that has been initiated. All the states and Union territories will have to adopt this information system. In addition, appropriate mechanisms will have to be found for enabling the states to levy the tax on services and integrating it with the VAT on goods, so as to arrive at a comprehensive VAT. An important problem that needs to be solved is devising a system for taxation of services with an interstate coverage, which would depend closely on the mechanism chosen for zero-rating interstate trade.

An important aspect from the viewpoint of efficiency in resource allocation is the continued cascading of the tax on petroleum products, which are kept outside the CenVAT system and are not part of the VAT system in states; although these commodities are subject to the levy, subsequent users cannot take credit for this tax. Petroleum products contribute over 40 percent of the revenues raised by both of both the taxes. Considering the use of these items for intermediate consumption, the extent of cascading and relative price distortion will continue to be high.

Extending the service tax to all services and then unifying it with CenVAT in a revenue-neutral manner would help bring down the CenVAT rate by about 3 percentage points and would thus reduce the overall tax burden. The CenVAT rate could be lowered to about 12 percent, with a special excise of 6 percent levied on luxury items for reasons of equity and revenue.[68] A 12 percent tax rate at the manufacturing stage would be equivalent to 8 percent at the retail stage, assuming that value added beyond the stage of manufacturing amounts to a third of the retail value of the commodity. The KTF on indirect taxes assumed that the overall consumption tax burden should not exceed 20 percent; thus, a 12 percent manufacturing-stage CenVAT would leave the states room for levying a VAT of about 12 percent at the retail stage. Along with the state-level VAT, it is important to integrate many specific taxes such as the entertainment tax, electricity duties, passengers and goods taxes, and the luxury tax on hotels. Turnover taxes, surcharges, and additional taxes should be eliminated as there should be no need for them.

The major indirect tax reform at the local level relates to the abolition of *octroi*. There is no place for *octroi* in any modern tax system. The problem, however, is one of finding an alternative source of revenue. In many other countries, a property tax is a mainstay of local finances, and reform in this area should help in raising revenue productivity. Yet, a property tax alone may not suffice. A better option may be to allow urban local bodies to piggyback on the VAT collections within their jurisdictions. This approach should avoid tax cascades and minimize tax spillovers from the urban jurisdictions to nonresidents.

68. Acharya (2005).

Reform in Tax Administration

Until recently, the focus of tax reform in India was on "what to do," rather "how to do." The administrative dimension has been on the periphery rather than at the center of tax reform.[69] The TRC and other study groups emphasized the need for tax administration reform to some extent, but it is the KTF that has brought administrative reform front and center.

Not surprisingly, poor tax administration has led to low levels of compliance and high compliance costs. The virtual absence of data on both direct and indirect taxes even at the central level has made it difficult not only to enforce the tax laws but to gather the analytical data necessary to make appropriate changes in the tax structure. The complexity of the tax structure and the poor information system meant that the tax system often acquired the character of negotiated payments—a situation that encouraged corruption and rent seeking.[70]

The only estimate of compliance cost is by Das-Gupta, who has estimated that the cost of compliance is as high as 49 percent of personal income tax collections and between 6 and 15 percent of corporate tax collections.[71] Das-Gupta found that the bulk of these costs were the legal costs incurred to meet the requirements of the Income Tax Act. While these estimates should be taken with a note of caution as the author himself has reservations on the adequacy and quality of the sample analyzed, the important point is that the compliance cost in Indian income taxes is extremely high.

Another example of the poor state of the tax information system is that even as the coverage of TDS was extended, there was virtually no way to check whether those deducting the tax at source filed the returns and actually paid the tax. According to the report of the Comptroller and Auditor General, in 2003–04, only 499,000 returns were filed although there were 626,000 TDS assessees. In other words, more than 20 percent of the TDS assessees did not file returns. Even this is a vast improvement from the previous year when almost 80 percent of the TDS assessees did not file returns.

Recent initiatives on building the computerized information system for direct taxes grew out of the recommendations of the KTF. The Central Board of Direct Taxes outsourced the function of issuing permanent account numbers, which now number more than 36 million; this process has facilitated the compiling of information on all taxpayers. The Tax Information

69. Bird (1989).
70. Government of India (1993, 2002a, 2002b).
71. Das-Gupta (2004a, 2004b).

Network, established by the National Securities Depository Limited, has focused initially on ensuring that TDS assessees do in fact file returns, and matching and cross-checking the information from banking and financial institutions to ensure that the taxes paid according to the returns are in fact credited into government accounts in the banks. The Online Tax Accounting System, implemented in July 2004, has helped expedite the number of refunds processed, from 2.6 million in 2002–03 to 5.6 million in 2003–04. Large companies such as Infosys Ltd can now upload one disk for filing the TDSs of their employees instead of filing large number of separate TDS returns. In short, in the last four years, collections of direct taxes have shown annual growth of over 20 percent a year, and the contribution of the improved information system in this growth has not been insignificant.

Similar initiatives have been taken in regard to indirect taxes. The customs e-commerce gateway (ICEGATE) and the Customs Electronic Data Interchange System (ICES) have helped to improve the information system and speed up clearance processes. In 2003–04, ICES handled about 4 million declarations in automated customs locations, which constituted about 75 percent of India's international trade. The technical assistance from the Canadian International Development Agency has helped the excise department to establish and build capacity in modern audit systems and computerized risk assessments for detailed audits. This is a step toward building expertise in areas requiring significant technical knowledge. Both the direct and indirect tax departments could gain from building expertise through functional specialization in such identified areas requiring technical and focused knowledge.

A computerized information system would help to put together data from a variety of relevant sources and lead to better administration and enforcement of the tax laws, improve the tax compliance, and reduce compliance costs particularly as it would reduce the need for tax officials to deal directly with taxpayers. An important constraint on how quickly a computerized system can be put in place is the fact that many of the senior officers are not familiar with computers and display a natural hesitancy, and often unwillingness, to adapt to new technology. There have to be several orientation workshops to manage this change well.

Another critical element in tax administration is the networking of the information from various sources. As mentioned earlier, systems have to be evolved to put together information received from various sources to quantify the possible tax implications from them in a legally acceptable manner to improve tax enforcement. The first step is to collect the information; the second is for the relevant tax agencies at both the central and state levels to exchange information to ensure a measure of consistency among the returns filed. It is only through a properly organized and computerized information system and returns that it will be possible to enforce the tax and improve the tax compliance.

Concluding Remarks

The foregoing analysis shows that India has made significant progress in tax reforms, particularly in tax administration, which has helped raise the ratio of tax revenues to GDP close to the levels that prevailed before significant reductions were made in customs duties. These reforms are only the beginning; considerable distance must still be covered in reforming the tax system. In other words, tax reform, including administrative reforms, is a continuous exercise for improving revenue productivity, minimizing distortions, and improving equity.

Coordinated reforms should be undertaken at the central, state, and local levels. A major objective should be minimization of distortions and compliance costs. In fact, the subnational tax system should be revised so that the principles of a common market are not violated. Taxes on domestically traded goods and services should be coordinated in the spirit of cooperative federalism. Domestic and external trade taxes should also be coordinated to ensure the desired degree of protection to domestic industry and the desired burden of consumption taxes on the community are achieved.

Broadening the base of both central and state taxes and keeping the tax structures simple—within the administrative capacity of the governments— is an important international lesson that should be incorporated in further reforms. Phasing out exemptions for small-scale industry, minimizing exemptions and concessions to industries in the services sector, and minimizing discretion and selectivity in tax policy and administration are all important not only for the soundness of the tax system but to enhance its acceptability and credibility.

Although the customs duties have been significantly reduced, India's economy is still highly protected. Further reduction in tariffs, as well as further unification and rationalization, is necessary. Because these reductions will certainly entail loss of revenue, a corresponding improvement must be made in the revenue productivity of all taxes. The conversion of the prevailing sales taxes into a destination-based, consumption-type VAT by the states must be carried out with vigor and completed within the next few years. This will require a complete phaseout of the central sales tax. Finalizing the mechanism to relieve taxes on interstate transactions, and building a proper information system for the purpose, is crucial to improving both revenue productivity and the efficiency of the tax system.

The most important reform is in tax administration. It is important to remember that "tax administration is tax policy."[72] Making the transition to information-based tax administration, online filing of tax returns, and compiling and matching information are key to administrative reform. Tax administrators should also assist taxpayers in a timely fashion and help them to reduce their compliance costs.

72. Casanegra (1990).

Comments and Discussion

Shankar Acharya: I enjoyed very much the paper by Govinda Rao and Kavita Rao (henceforth Raos), partly because I have recently published a survey of Indian tax reform.[1] So, I was interested to see in what way the Raos' perspectives were different from mine. I was glad to find that there were some differences, which give me an opportunity to comment. However, I must emphasize that there is an enormous amount of commonality between what they say and what I have written. So, although I dwell on the differences in these brief comments, the much broader areas of agreement have to be taken as understood.

To begin with, I liked the section of the paper on evolving paradigms of tax reform. I share the Raos' puzzlement as to why the vast literature on optimal taxation has had relatively limited impact on actual tax policy, not just in India but the world over. However, I was a little disappointed with the apparent lack of application of this useful taxonomic section to the description of Indian tax reform in subsequent parts of the paper. More broadly, I was disappointed by the absence of an analysis of the *economic impact* of tax reforms in India, other than in terms of the usual trends in revenue from different kinds of taxes. Of course, such an assessment of economic impact is very difficult to do, especially given the paucity of extant research studies in India on this theme. But then the heading referring to analysis of the economic impact is misleadingly ambitious.

Turning to the evolution of the Indian tax system, I broadly agree with the Raos' treatment, except for one very important judgment. They claim, "Systematic and comprehensive attempts to reform the tax system at the central level started only after market-based economic reforms were initiated in 1991." That is simply wrong. As I have detailed elsewhere, modern tax reform was really launched in India during V. P. Singh's two year stewardship of the finance ministry (1985–87) in Rajiv Gandhi's Congress government.[2] In his budget for 1985–86, Singh undertook the most comprehensive reform of direct taxes to date: the top marginal income tax rate was cut from 62 to 50 percent; the number of income tax slabs were halved from eight to four;

1. Acharya (2005).
2. Acharya (1988, 2005).

estate duty was abolished; the top wealth tax rate was reduced from 5 to 2 percent; and the basic rate of company tax was lowered to 50 percent.

Second, in his budget for 1986–87, V. P. Singh introduced MODVAT in thirty-seven chapters of the Central Excise Tariff and made a clear commitment to extend VAT principles to the remainder of the manufacturing sector. This was a huge stride forward in the reform of India's indirect taxes. Third, these reforms of direct and indirect taxes were coordinated and stressed the importance of simplicity, stability, and predictability in tax policy. Fourth, and perhaps most interesting, these tax reforms were embedded explicitly in a medium-term fiscal policy paper, entitled *The Long-Term Fiscal Policy* (LTFP), which was presented to Parliament in 1985.[3] It was the first (and until 2004, the only) time that a coherent program of tax reform intentions was articulated in India within a macroeconomic fiscal framework. Against this background, the Raos are clearly incorrect in asserting that comprehensive tax reform in India started after 1991. Of course, the later reports of the Tax Reforms Committee (1991–93) did a far more systematic job of analyzing and presenting a tax reform program for the 1990s, but that program and its subsequent implementation was greatly facilitated by the earlier V. P. Singh reforms.

Where the Raos are right is in their characterization of some of the post-1990s tax policy as "ad hoc" and lacking a "consistent theoretical framework." In this context, they mention the minimum alternate tax, the securities transaction tax of 2004, the cash withdrawal tax of 2005, and the "frequent changes and the lack of direction" in the taxation of dividends. The benign influence of the V. P. Singh–LTFP reforms and the Tax Reforms Committee–Manmohan Singh reforms had clearly waned by the turn of the millennium. Rather curiously, the Raos are neutral in their description of the 2005 fringe benefit tax, which has come in for a great deal of criticism from both industry and fiscal experts.[4]

The final section of the Raos' paper on future tax reforms has several good ideas but also suffers from some weaknesses. First, the paper is oddly noncommittal on possibly the most important recent tax policy proposal, namely the integrated goods and services tax (GST) proposed by the Kelkar Task Force on implementation of fiscal responsibility legislation.[5] Its most far-reaching recommendation was to implement a nationwide GST, basically a value added tax with a unified base and explicit sharing by states and

3. Government of India (1985).
4. See, for example, Acharya (2006).
5. Government of India (2004b).

central government of what is essentially a single, integrated, destination-based, value added tax. This important proposal has received considerable support, despite some questions about its constitutional validity. It would have been helpful if the Raos had articulated a considered view of this very important proposal.

Second, their paper has quite rightly bemoaned the presence of a large number of tax preferences and exemptions in all the major taxes. It would have been useful if the authors had delineated some sort of a road map for phasing out some of the more serious schemes of exemptions. This is particularly important in a climate where the political appetite for such exemptions continues unabated, as evidenced by the widening domain of area-based exemptions, including the recently notified income tax exemptions for special economic zones. Third, on tax administration, it might have been desirable for the paper to outline the priority steps that need to taken in this critically important area. This is especially so given the provenance of the authors from the National Institute of Public Finance and Policy, perhaps the foremost nongovernmental institution with detailed knowledge of administrative practices and lacunae in regard to the major taxes.

Fourth, I come to the reform of capital taxation, particularly the issue of taxing equity capital gains. The fact is that taxation of equity capital gains (or rather its exemption!) today is very concessional compared with taxation of other kinds of capital gains and other kinds of capital income. More broadly, there is surely a serious problem of fairness when long-term equity capital gains are exempt and there is no taxation of dividends in the hands of the recipient, while all forms of labor income fall into the tax net at a fairly modest level. The Raos do not accord adequate attention to this issue.

Finally, let me mention a big problem with India's long-run record of tax reform. While the ridiculously high customs duties of 1990 (and earlier) have been rightly reduced in a phased way, the replacement of declining customs revenue by a moderately high-yielding domestic trade tax, namely Excise/MODVAT, has been a serious failure. This issue, its causes, and its resolution required greater attention by Raos.

Perhaps they will take on the challenge posed by the lacunae pointed out above in a follow-up paper. I certainly hope so.

T. N. Srinivasan: I too enjoyed reading this "double Rao" or "Rao squared" paper. It presents a comprehensive description, historical antecedents and the evolution of Indian tax policy, quantitative implications thereof, and also what is best described as a glacial pace of tax reform, although after 1985 or 1987 it shifted from being glacial to gradual.

Much of the paper is about the central government's policy, although it does cover state-level developments in the aggregate, rather than state by state. The authors rightly point out that state-level reforms, such as they were, did not coincide with those at the center. There was no systematic attempt to streamline the reform process even after 1991, and most reform attempts were ad hoc and guided more by revenue exigencies than by any general principles.

Let me begin by asking how one might try to evaluate tax policy and its reform in federal India. There is an enormous and growing diversity among and within large states. Also the domestic and global economic and political context for policymaking has changed dramatically. First, does it make sense to talk about tax policy in isolation from fiscal policy narrowly and from other government interventions in the economy more generally? After all, in India state control over the economy was intrusive and extensive, and the state articulated and tried to implement a development strategy in which private sector participation was heavily circumscribed. In such a context, tax policy is just *one* instrument among many that the state uses or could use in steering the development of the economy. For example, public sector production that makes profits is an alternative to leaving that production activity in the private sector and taxing the profits of the private sector. In general, there are many instruments of public policy that are alternatives to narrowly defined tax policy. This means that one cannot think in terms of reform just of one segment of public policy without at the same time considering the whole panoply of state intervention in the economy.

The political economy in India, or in the states of India, is not the same as that of Brazil or that of Brazilian states. To believe that positive findings or normative pronouncements on fiscal policy are valid for all countries and all the time is just daydreaming. I am saying this only to caution that drawing policy inferences from a crude cross-country (or cross-states) regression is unlikely to be informative or meaningful. Fortunately the authors themselves report only one such regression. I am not convinced even that is particularly informative.

The authors say that in the initial years the tax policy was guided by the need to increase the level of savings and investment in the economy. However, they provide absolutely no empirical evidence that it in fact did. As we all know, in India, the largest component of savings is household savings, and a large proportion of household savings is direct savings in the form of physical assets. In what ways do the tax policy instruments influence the *direct* savings? All that policy seems to have done is to shift the composition of *financial* savings. Whether you hold your savings in the form of an insurance policy or bank deposit or equity is certainly influenced by the structure of incentives on different forms in which savings are held. However, it is hard to demonstrate empirically that aggregate savings have been influenced by differentials in incentives. The authors are right, of course, in saying that the nationalization of banks and insurance was primarily intended for transferring private resources into public hands for good or bad use. In my view, quite a bit of it was bad use. The basic point is that there is no empirical analysis that has carefully analyzed the impact of tax policies at the central and state level on household savings and their composition or on private investment and its sectoral composition.

The authors say that redistributive considerations heavily influenced tax policy. Again, they do not provide any empirical evidence for this assertion. As they themselves point out, the effective redistribution achieved through tax policy was in fact negligible. This fact was widely known early on. And the worthies who constituted the various tax reform commissions have also pointed this out. Yet only very late in the history of the last sixty years, have marginal rates been brought down.

More generally, if one were to focus on redistributive aspects of tax policy, one has to take an integrated view of all direct taxes, such as the personal income tax, the corporate tax, and the wealth tax, including what used to be taxes on particular forms of wealth in the old days. Unless one takes an integrated view of taxes and expenditures, it is very difficult to say anything meaningful about the redistributive effect of the whole tax expenditure system. In fact, the paper makes absolutely no mention of tax integration or of the debates that have gone on elsewhere in the world on integration of corporate tax or on personal income tax, for example.

I doubt whether my dear friend Al Harberger ever said, as the authors claim he said, that the tax reformers should pay less attention to economic theory and more to best-practice experience. If he did, perhaps, he was referring to the virtually useless optimal tax theory of the first best. But even if one were to confine oneself to positive analysis, it has to be recognized that interventions that do not distort private decisions, like lump-sum taxes and subsidies, are not available in any economy. Tax, subsidy, expenditure, and public production policies are likely to be distortionary. But they influence private decisions to consume, invest, export, and import in various ways. Any positive analysis has to address the complex interaction of all the effects of policy.

What about normative analysis? One could take the simplistic first-best optimal tax theory perspective: the policymaker is a Stackleberg leader who is omniscient—that is, who has all the necessary information—and omnipotent, that is, who has no constraints on his choice of policy instruments. The private sector responds to his policy announcement as a follower. Of course, being omniscient, he knows how the private sector would respond and uses this information in choosing and announcing the optimal tax policy. This is a never-never land. It seems to me this is the theory that Al probably had in mind when he said to forget it. The theory or model we would want to use, if we want to analyze the tax policy in India, would allow for information asymmetries, both among levels of government and between governments and the private sector, and also for constraints on policy choices.

The authors' cryptic remark on welfare effects of external tariff reduction, as opposed to its elimination, is unclear. It is possible that they have in mind some nonlinear welfare response to a tariff change, or some kind of a second-best situation, in which, because other distortions remain, welfare does not change in the expected direction as tariff is reduced. In any case, they rightly point out that no economic logic lies behind the recommendation of the Tax Reforms Committee in favor of multiple tariff levels. I may add such economic illiteracy continues even today, with respect to privatization, for example.

Let me conclude with my approach to tax reform. I will start with what I think is the most essential; namely, the assignment of tax bases and expenditure responsibilities between the center and the states laid out in our constitution, enacted in 1950. The constitution also mandated the appointment of a finance commission every five years or so. We created in the same year an extraconstitutional body, the planning commission, which also makes transfers to states. However today's economy is not that of the 1950s. If the rituals of five-year plans, annual plans, and the "approval" of state plans by the planning commission (let alone the bureaucracy of state planning commissions and planning boards) are no longer relevant, any reform of the planning process will also involve, among other things, reform of the process of transfers from the central planning commission.

Second, we have yet another means of transfers to states, namely, through assistance for the centrally sponsored schemes. These are meant to address interstate externalities and spillovers. Unfortunately externality is often the last resort for the scoundrels among economists—if they can find no other way of justifying a transfer scheme, they invent externalities! Anyway, whether the transfers through these schemes are mere distortions or address genuine externalities, they have to be thought through.

Third, we do not have the analogue of the interstate commerce clause of the U.S. Constitution in our constitution. As Ajay Shah rightly pointed out, India is not a common market. To conclude, one has to think through what the fundamental economic structure of the economy currently is and the roles which the governments at various levels are playing in it, if we want to make progress in tax reform.

General Discussion

Ajay Shah said it was useful to analyze where the tax system was going wrong. Several measures currently in place had adverse efficiency effects, Shah said, including the 2 percent cess, or surcharge, on all taxes that is earmarked for education. Similarly, the subsidy to promote the universal service objective in telecommunications was funded by taxes on telephone usage and interconnections between fixed and cell phones. These specialized taxes were in place, Shah said, even though we know that it is more efficient to fund education and universal service obligations out of general tax revenue. Shah added that because of its bad design and implementation, the value added tax also failed to yield the desired efficiency results. The transactions tax, which started with a security transactions tax, is yet another example of inefficient taxation. The recent plans by the Maharashtra government to introduce very high stamp duties on Mumbai-based financial transactions were likely to be even more damaging, he said.

Shah then pointed out that the revenue implications of eliminating the remaining tariffs were not as dire as they might seem. The standard Indian data for customs revenue included not just the custom duty but also the countervailing duty. Therefore, the fiscal cost and the fiscal challenge of further customs reform were smaller than they appeared: even if the tariff moved to zero, the countervailing duty would still be collected. If the exemptions on the countervailing duty were eliminated carefully, Shah said, it would not be difficult for India to go to zero customs duty on everything very quickly.

Shah also commented on the implications of the developments in information technology. The tax information network set up in India was nothing short of revolutionary compared with what seemed feasible even five years earlier. Firms from all across the country file electronically, feeding directly into a single database and matching up with the tax deduction at source.

Shah concluded with the comment that research economists should be tilting at the windmills of fundamental tax reform. For example, they should question the idea that states are independent taxing authorities. A unified value-added tax required vesting this power entirely in the central government, he said.

Calling the paper very interesting, Partho Shome said it showed, for example, that progressivity in the tax structure in personal income tax had decreased only among a class of taxpayers but not overall. The paper also showed how the collection of the corporate income taxes, excise taxes, and custom duties was concentrated in a few sectors such as petroleum, chemicals, and metal industries and at the very low end from textiles. The paper also put great emphasis on the need to reform tax administration.

Shome went on to note that India's tax policy was moving "briskly" from (distortionary) indirect taxes to direct taxes. For the first time, this year the government budgeted more than 5 percent of GDP from direct taxes. Also, for the first time, revenue from direct taxes would be higher than the revenue from production taxes and import taxes. Shome also reminded the audience that countervailing duties do not cover state sales tax.

Shome then observed that even though one would like to make rules-based policies at the economywide level, such as a single custom duty rate, the actual policy choice was tempered by a variety of forces working at the sectoral level. For example, Indian tax policy was influenced by what competitor countries are doing in the specific sectors. India's excise and custom duties in the textiles sector, for example, were influenced by what China, Pakistan, Bangladesh, and Vietnam did in that sector.

Shome said that at the same time, the system was extremely sensitive to the needs of domestic industries. The expression policymakers used here was "Is there a domestic angle?" One had to be very careful about employment effects and capital effects. The practice of consulting with representatives of both big corporations and small enterprises was bound to influence the eventual choice of policy.

Shome stated that the export objectives were yet another determinant of that policy. Such policies led to the establishment of export-oriented units and special economic zones, which immediately protected all enterprises with a cut in various taxes and provision of infrastructure. The country's export strategy also led to policies that ensure that exports have "free-trade" status. That in turn led to numerous schemes to free the exports from custom duties on the imported input. Thus there were advance licenses that allowed inputs to be imported free of duty. There were duty drawbacks whereby the company paid the duty but later received drawbacks against it. Then there was the passbook scheme organized by the Ministry of Commerce, where companies had accounts from which they could automatically deduct the customs duties they paid. In addition, there was a target zero tax scheme, linked to how much exports increase each year. Under yet another scheme, a company that exported a certain amount could import capital goods without paying duty. These were not all, Shome said. They were so numerous and so complex, he added, that he could not hold them in his memory.

Shome pointed to regional balance and development and social infrastructure as yet additional factors that influence policy. Special needs of regions such as Jammu and Kashmir, Special Category States that have been newly formed, and the northeastern states must be taken into account. Charities and trusts have to be considered, as stipulated in the Income Tax Act. As a result, Shome said, the efficiency of implementation was quite low, to put it mildly.

Regarding the fringe benefit tax, Shome noted that before it was enacted, there was a perquisites tax in the personal income tax, similar to the one that existed in most developed countries in Europe and in the United States and Canada. The government felt that the self-assessment and self-declaration of perquisites did not work. The alternative was to fix the problem through the corporate route. The government could identify a positive list of fringe benefits and tax them at the corporate level, although the incidence should be on the individuals who received the benefits. In fact, what is being shown from industry information is that quite a few of the fringe benefits are being rewritten in the salary structure, because the corporations cannot take these deductions any more, Shome said.

Turning to tax administration, Shome said while many initiatives were under way in this area, he would limit himself to the VAT. One thing that is often mentioned is the removal of the central sales tax, which was imposed on interstate trade. But it can be removed only with the full development of the information exchange system, which was being done. Shome concluded with a remark about the unified goods and services tax. One should remember, he said, that under the GST, services and goods would have to become creditable against each other at both central and state levels. That would require a major constitutional amendment, almost like a constitutional convention. So, as a first goal, it may be better to discuss a kind of national VAT with two parallel VATs at the central and state level. Even that would require constitutional amendment.

Reacting to one of Shome's points, Surjit Bhalla argued that economists should resist the political economy pressures that push toward bad policies. If the only way to make textiles competitive with China is to have a special tax rate, Bhalla said, then economists should oppose the special tax. T. N. Srinivasan responded that when recommending policies, economists could not entirely ignore the presence of political-economy pressures. There was someplace in between presuming to describe the political economy, on which you have no competence, and at the other end, ignoring it completely, when it is staring you in the eye, Srinivasan said.

Rajnish Mehra raised a question on the relationship of the tax system to the Indian stock market valuation. Suppose, he said, one wants to assess whether the Indian market is overvalued. One of the parameters needed is the tax rate on dividend distribution. This rate was 56 percent in 1990 and went down to 10 percent in 1997–98. A permanent cut in dividend tax rates would hugely increase asset valuation. Perhaps, if the market views this tax drop to 10 percent as a permanent tax cut, that might explain some of the valuations that we are seeing. In response, Shankar Acharya stated that perhaps one of the reasons why there was so much variation in the dividend payment was that the taxation on dividends had changed about six times in the last twenty years in India. But he acknowledged that there were a lot of other factors as well.

Bhalla asked Shome what the rationale for the fringe benefit tax was, how effective it had been, and how much revenue had the government been able to raise from it in absolute terms and as a percentage of the total revenue?

Arvind Panagariya asked Shome whether he was asserting that under the current government the country would move substantially to direct taxes as the source of revenue and deemphasize indirect taxes? And if so, would Shome also say that if he were designing the tax system from scratch, he would actually not even bother to have indirect taxes?

Kavita Rao took issue with the suggestion by Shah that India should now think about taking the power to tax final consumption away from the states and vesting it entirely in the center to achieve a unified goods and services tax. There was surely some gain in harmonizing the tax structure, laws, procedures and rules, and even tax administration, Rao said, but do we want a single nationwide tax system that guides the allocation of resources across all states? Rao added that this was not a politically feasible solution. If we wish to let the states choose their own levels of services according to local preferences, it is not feasible to have a national, homogenous, and uniform centralized tax system, Rao said.

Govinda Rao joined Kavita Rao in responding to the discussants' comments. He began by stating that Acharya had raised a very important question about when the tax reform began. In his view, the fundamental tax reform started in 1991. He did not deny that there had been significant simplification of direct taxes before to 1991. The government had actually introduced the MODVAT before then he said, and this had been accompanied by analysis and discussions within the Finance Ministry. But that was not enough. In 1991, there were something like fifteen income tax rates and twenty excise tax rates. A large number of commodities were still subject to specific rates. There was a plethora of rates in customs duty. Therefore, fundamentally speaking, there had not been any tax reform prior to 1991. In contrast, the reform during the 1990s proceeded according to a clearly laid out roadmap and with appropriate preparations made at various levels.

Shome had the final word. He made three points. First, regarding Bhalla's question on the fringe benefits tax, the rationale had been explained in the Finance Act itself. As Shome had indicated earlier, the perquisites tax had not been working well. It yielded no revenue from loss-declaring firms. So, to improve equity within the corporate sector, the government introduced the fringe benefit tax. As far as the revenue was concerned, the tax was still in an experimental stage and he would not venture to hazard a guess as to how much revenue might be collected.

Second, Shome stated that at the moment the government was indeed moving toward greater reliance on direct taxes. But if it could do something like the goods and services tax and implement a broad-based consumption tax at the national level, which would necessitate a constitutional amendment, Shome said the government would probably return to the broad-based consumption tax. If the central and state taxes were consolidated and one looks at what the center is collecting from excise up to manufacturing and what the states are collecting from the sales tax, then the indirect tax revenues are quite high—higher than the direct tax component.

Finally, Shome commented on the controversy between Acharya and Govinda Rao on the timing of the tax reform. He said the controversy had reminded him of a parallel controversy on when and which country first implemented the VAT. The French started it in the early 1960s on certain items. Then, a couple of years later, Brazil introduced a very comprehensive VAT at the level of the states, addressing even the issue of how to tax the interstate trade. Shome noted that in his view, although France was the first to adopt the VAT technically speaking, Brazil was the one to first adopt it meaningfully.

References

Acharya, Shankar. 1988. "India's Fiscal Policy." In *The Indian Economy: Recent Developments and Future Prospect*, edited by Robert E. Lucas and Gustav F. Papanek. New Delhi: Oxford University Press.

———. 2005. "Thirty Years of Tax Reform in India." *Economic and Political Weekly* 40 (May 14): 2061–69. Reprinted in Shankar Acharya, 2006, *Essays on Macroeconomic Policy and Growth in India*. New Delhi: Oxford University Press.

———. 2006. "The Year of Bad Taxes." *Business Standard*, January 24.

Ahmad, Ehtisham, and Nicholas Stern. 1983. "Effective Taxes and Tax Reform in India." Discussion Paper 25. Development Economics Research Centre, University of Warwick.

———. 1991. *Theory and Practice of Tax Reform in Developing Countries*. Cambridge: Cambridge University Press.

Arbalaez, M. A., L. E. Burman, and S. C. Zuluaga. 2002. "The Bank Debit Tax in Columbia." Documentos de trabajo, FEDESAROLLO 000828 (ftp://ftp.fedesarrollo.org.co/pub/documentos/wp_mmgonzalez_web/Tercer_ informe_Zuluaga-Arbalaez-Burman.pdf).

Auerbach, Alan J., and Joel Slemrod. 1997. "The Economic Effects of the Tax Reform Act of 1986." *Journal of Economic Literature* 35 (June): 559–632.

Bagchi, Amaresh, and Nicholas Stern. 1994. *Tax Policy and Planning in Developing Countries*. New Delhi: Oxford University Press.

Bagchi, Amaresh, and Pulin Nayak. 1994. "A Survey of Public Finance and the Planning Process: The Indian Experience." In *Tax Policy and Planning in Developing Countries*, edited by Amaresh Bagchi and Nicholas Stern. New Delhi: Oxford University Press.

Bhagwati, Jagdish N., and Bent Hansen. 1973. "A Theoretical Analysis of Smuggling." *Quarterly Journal of Economics* 87 (2): 172–87.

Bhalla, Surjit. 2005. "Tax Rates, Tax Compliance and Tax Revenues: India, 1988–2004" (www.oxusresearch.com/downloads/ce070704.pdf).

Bird, Richard. 1989. "The Administrative Dimension of Tax Reform in Developing Countries." In *The Theory and Practice of Tax Reform in Developing Countries*, edited by Malcolm Gillis, pp. 315–45. Durham: Duke University Press.

———. 1993. "Federal Provincial Taxation in Turbulent Times." *Canadian Public Administration* 36, pp. 479–96.

———. 2005. "Value-Added Taxes in Developing and Transitional Countries: Lessons and Questions," International Studies Program Working Paper Series 0505, Andrew Young School of Policy Studies, Georgia State University.

Bird, Richard, and Oliver Oldman. 1990. *Taxation in Developing Countries*. Baltimore: John Hopkins University Press.

Bird, Richard M., and Eric M. Zolt. 2005. "Redistribution via Taxation: The Limited Role of the Personal Income Tax in Developing Countries," International Studies

Program Working Paper Series 0507, Andrew Young School of Policy Studies, Georgia State University.

Boskin, Michael J., and Charles E. McLure Jr., eds. 1990. *World Tax Reform: Case Studies of Developed and Developing Countries.* San Francisco: ICS Press.

Burgess, Robin, and Nicholas Stern. 1993. "Taxation and Development." *Journal of Economic Literature* 31 (2): 762–830.

Casanegra de Jantscher, Milka. 1990. "Administering VAT." In *Value Added Taxation in Developing Countries. A World Bank Symposium*, edited by Malcolm Gillis, Carl S. Shoup, and Gerardo P. Sicat. Washington: World Bank.

Centre for Monitoring Indian Economy. 2005. Prowess Release 2.5, dated October 2005.

Chelliah, Raja J. 1986. "Change in the Tax Structure: A Case Study of India." Paper presented at the 42nd Congress of the International Institute of Public Finance, Athens, Greece.

Das-Gupta, Arindam. 2002. "Central Tax and Administration Reform in the 1990s: An Assessment." In *Development, Poverty and Fiscal Policy: Decentralisation of Institutions*, edited by M. Govinda Rao. New Delhi: Oxford University Press.

———. 2004a. "The Compliance Cost of the Personal Income Tax in India, 2000–2001: Preliminary Estimates." NIPFP Working Paper 9. National Institute of Public Finance and Policy, New Delhi. March.

———. 2004b. "The Income Tax Compliance Cost of Corporations in India, 2000–2001." NIPFP Working Paper 8. National Institute of Public Finance and Policy, New Delhi. March.

———. 2004c. "The VAT versus the Turnover Tax with Non-Competitive Firms." NIPFP Working Paper 21. National Institute of Public Finance and Policy, New Delhi. July.

Das-Gupta, Arindam, and Dilip Mookherjee. 1997. "Design and Enforcement of Personal Income Tax in India." In *Public Finance, Policy Issues for India, Themes in Economics*, edited by Sudipto Mundle. New Delhi: Oxford University Press.

Ebrill, Liam, and others. 2001. *The Modern VAT.* Washington: International Monetary Fund.

Emran, M. Shahe, and Joseph Stiglitz. 2004. "Price Neutral Tax Reform with an Informal Economy." Public Economics 0407010, Economics Working Paper Archive at WUSTL (http://econwpa.wustl.edu:8089/eps/pe/papers/0407/0407010.pdf).

———. 2005. "On Selective Indirect Tax Reform in Developing Countries." *Journal of Public Economics* 89 (April): 599–623.

Engel, Eduardo-M-R-A, Alexander Galetovic, and Claudio-E. Raddatz. 1999. "Taxes and Income Distribution in Chile: Some Unpleasant Redistributive Arithmetic." *Journal of Development Economics* 59 (June): 155–92.

Gerxhani, Klarita. 2004. "The Informal Sector in Developed and Less Developed Countries: A Literature Survey." *Public Choice* 120 (September): 267–300.

Gillis, Malcolm, ed. 1989. *Tax Reform in Developing Countries.* Durham: Duke University Press.

Gordon, Roger, and Wei Li. 2005. "Tax Structure in Developing Countries: Many Puzzles and a Possible Explanation." NBER Working Paper 11267. National Bureau of Economic Research, Cambirdge, Mass.

Government of India. 1953. *Report of the Taxation Enquiry Commission.* New Delhi: Ministry of Finance.

———. 1956. *Indian Tax Reform.* New Delhi: Ministry of Finance.

———. 1971. *Direct Taxes Enquiry Committee: Final Report.* New Delhi: Ministry of Finance.

———. 1977. *Report of the Indirect Taxation Enquiry Committee.* New Delhi: Ministry of Finance.

———. 1985. *Long Term Fiscal Policy.* New Delhi: Ministry of Finance.

———. 1991. *Tax Reforms Committee, Interim Report.* New Delhi: Ministry of Finance.

———. 1993. *Report of the Tax Reforms Committee.* New Delhi: Ministry of Finance.

———. 2001a. *Report of the Advisory Group on Tax Policy and Tax Administration for the Tenth Plan.* New Delhi: Planning Commission (planningcommission. nic.in/aboutus/committee/wrkgrp/tptarpt.pdf).

———. 2001b. *Report of the Expert Group on Taxation of Services.* New Delhi: Ministry of Finance.

———. 2002a. *Report of the Taskforce on Direct Taxes.* New Delhi: Ministry of Finance (finmin.nic.in/kelkar/final_dt.htm).

———. 2002b. *Report of the Taskforce on Indirect Taxes.* New Delhi: Ministry of Finance (http://finmin.nic.in/kelkar/final_idt.htm).

———. 2004a. *Indian Public Finance Statistics.* New Delhi: Ministry of Finance.

———. 2004b. *Report of the Task Force on Implementation of the Fiscal Responsibility and Budget Management Act, 2003.* New Delhi: Ministry of Finance (finmin.nic.in/downloads/reports/frbm/start.htm).

———. Various years. *Report of the Comptroller and Auditor General (Direct Taxes).* New Delhi.

———. Various years. *Union Budget.* New Delhi: Ministry of Finance.

———. Various years. *Public Enterprises Survey.* New Delhi: Ministry of Industry, Department of Public Enterprises.

Government of Karnataka. 2001. *First Report of the Tax Reforms Commission.* Bangalore: Finance Department.

Harberger, Arnold C. 1990. "Principles of Taxation Applied to Developing Countries: What Have We Learned?" In *World Tax Reform: Case Studies of Developed and Developing Countries,* edited by Michael J. Boskin and Charles E. McLure, Jr., pp. 25–46. San Francisco: ICS Press.

———. 2003. "Reflections on Distributional Considerations and the Public Finances." Paper prepared for a course on Practical Issues of Tax Policy in Developing Countries, World Bank, April.

Hatta, Tatsuo. 1986. "Welfare Effects of Changing Commodity Tax Rates towards Uniformity." *Journal of Public Economics* 29: 99–112.

Hines, James R., Jr. 2004. "Might Fundamental Tax Reform Increase Criminal Activity?" *Economica* 71: 483–92.

Joshi, Vijay, and Ian M. D. Little. 1996. *India's Economic Reforms, 1991–2001.* New Delhi: Oxford University Press.

Keen, Michael, and Jenny E. Ligthart. 2002. "Coordinating Tariff Reduction and Domestic Tax Reform." *Journal of International Economics* 56 (March): 489–507.

Martin, Lawrence, and Arvind Panagariya. 1984. "Smuggling, Trade and Price Disparity: A Crime Theoretic Approach." *Journal of International Economics* (November): 201–17.

National Institute of Public Finance and Policy (NIPFP). 1994. *Reform of Domestic Trade Taxes in India: Issues and Options.* New Delhi: NIPFP.

———. 1996. *Report of the Committee of State Finance Ministers on Stamp Duty Reform.* New Delhi: NIPFP.

Panagariya, Arvind. 2005. "India's Trade Reforms." *India Policy Forum 2004*, pp. 1–57. Brookings and New Delhi: National Council of Applied Economic Research.

Panagariya, Arvind, and Dani Rodrik. 1991. "Political Economy Arguments for Uniform Tariffs." *International Economic Review* 34 (3): 685–703.

Pechman, Joseph A. 1985. *Who Paid the Taxes—1966–85?.* Washington, D.C.: Brookings.

Rajaraman, Indira. 2004. "Fiscal Developments and Outlook in India." NIPFP Working Paper No. 15. National Institute of Public Finance and Policy, New Delhi.

Rao, Govinda M. 1992. "Reform of Indirect Taxes in Developing Countries: Selected Issues." *Asian Development Review* 10 (2): 144–58.

———. 1998. "Reforms in Tax Devolution and Evolving a Co-ordinated Tax System." *Economic and Political Weekly* 33 (July 18–24/25–31): 1971–76.

Stern, Nicholas. 1987. "The Theory of Optimal Commodity and Income Taxation: An Introduction." In *The Theory of Taxation for Developing Countries*, edited by David Newbery and Nicholas Stern, pp. 22–59. Washington: World Bank.

Virmani, Arvind, and others. 2004. "Impact of Tariff Reforms on Indian Industry: Assessment Based on a Multisector Econometric Model." ICRIER Working Paper 135 (econpapers.repec.org/paper/indicrier/135.htm).

SHEETAL K. CHAND
University of Oslo

KANHAIYA SINGH
National Council of Applied Economic Research

How Applicable Is the Inflation-Targeting Framework for India?

A key component in stabilizing an economy is keeping the rate of inflation within acceptable bounds and doing so in a manner that does not detract from other goals. This is a difficult exercise, and there have been many failures both in the advanced economies and especially in emerging economies. The record of inflation control in India, while not unsatisfactory, could have been better. Inflation in the first half of 2005–06 is around 5 percent, which is relatively high in the current global environment of mild inflation and, contingent on the handling of the ongoing oil price increases, could easily ratchet upward. The issue of inflation control in India is therefore important. In recent years, several countries have adopted the inflation-targeting framework (ITF) approach, which is now being strongly recommended to others as a best-practice approach for keeping inflation under control. Although it is still too early to tell whether or not the approach has been decisive in reducing inflation rates—its introduction coincided with a period of exceptional weakness in commodity prices following the break up of the Soviet Union—a strong theoretical case has been made for it.[1] Detailed operational guidelines and procedures have also been developed for its application.[2]

Essentially the ITF approach consists of setting an inflation target, aligning monetary policy to ensure its attainment, and doing so in a manner that is both transparent and accountable. The target is set publicly and considerable information is made available to the public regarding the modalities

The authors are indebted for helpful comments from participants and especially Barry Bosworth, Ken Kletzer, Rajnish Mehra, and Partha Sen who are not, however, responsible for any remaining errors and omissions.
1. See especially Svensson (1997).
2. See, for example, various reports of the Bank of England. Bernanke and others (2001) provide some useful historical details.

for achieving it in an attempt to establish credibility and to manage inflation expectations. A major advantage claimed for the ITF is that it enables focusing on the inflation target in a nonmechanical, flexible way that can take account of various contingencies and possible trade-offs with other objectives such as the level of economic activity.

For a country to be able to apply the ITF successfully, it must have strong fiscal and financial institutions and a balanced exposure to foreign exchange risks. Questions have therefore been raised about whether many emerging economies qualify for the ITF. Some of them, including India, have large fiscal deficits, and others such as China have weak banks and financial institutions. Moreover, most of them appear to exhibit a "fear of floating" and intervene to stabilize the exchange rate, thereby compromising the practice of inflation targeting. However, some have argued that, provided the authorities in these economies are sufficiently motivated to want the benefits of inflation targeting, they should not delay but use the introduction of the ITF as an incentive device to promote needed reforms in economic structure.[3] It is presumably in this spirit that the International Monetary Fund (IMF) and other agencies have been encouraging emerging economies to adopt the ITF.[4]

In making these recommendations, it is taken for granted that the ITF is an appropriate institution for emerging economies such as India. But this assumption may be questionable. The issue is not that of denying the importance of a low inflation rate; indeed, for India it has been amply demonstrated that the lower the inflation rate the more favorable the growth outcome.[5] The issue, which this paper focuses on, is whether lower inflation is best brought about through the adoption of ITF. At the heart of the ITF is a specific view of the inflation-generating process determined largely by demand, a conviction that the most efficient way of dealing with it is through an interest rate rule, and the belief that the public's inflation expectations can be managed. From this follows the prescription that the central bank, as the custodian of interest rate policy, should play a dedicated and dominant role in promoting the inflation objective.

But what if the inflation-generating process differs from that commonly assumed to hold for the advanced economies? For example, supply shocks and price management could feature more prominently than demand effects, while the latter could be influenced by a different array of instruments.

---

3. See Mishkin (2004), among others.
4. See, for example, IMF (2005).
5. Singh and Kalirajan (2003) provide a demonstration.

Expectations could also be more difficult to manage, especially if the economy is large, diverse, and segmented as is India's. But aside from these considerations, emerging economies may have good reasons for not wanting to free up fully the process of interest and exchange rate determination by the market. They may fear being exposed to persistent deviations in the exchange and interest rates from equilibrium levels and also to greater volatility in them, since they lack the hedging capabilities and facilities present in the advanced economies. All this implies that these emerging economies may find it more prudent and welfare enhancing f to pursue a strategy other than the standard ITF for controlling inflation, at least until they reproduce conditions favorable for an ITF.[6] They will then have to seek nominal anchors elsewhere.

In analyzing these issues, this paper first presents the rationale for the ITF and examines a standard theoretical formulation based on Svensson's work. The central proposition of this formulation is tested on Indian data and found inadmissible. Rather than accept the implication of that specification that demand does not affect the inflation rate, an alternative structure for determining inflation is then developed. This shows how demand may play a role in influencing the inflation rate as part of a broader scheme, and the choices of instruments for dealing with inflation. Testing on Indian data is more favorable to the alternative specifications developed. In light of the findings, the paper then examines how best to ensure an adequate inflation performance and the implied institutional allocation of responsibilities. A sharp distinction is drawn between "flow" responsibilities concerning operations in the goods market for which a combination of fiscal, credit, and supply-price management policies may be appropriate and "stock" responsibilities involving balance-sheet operations to influence asset valuations in desirable directions. As will be seen, this distinction determines a specific allocation of responsibilities in the Indian context between the government and the central bank.

A Rationale and Test of ITF Using Indian Data

Controlling inflation has traditionally been viewed as a matter of anchoring the money supply. The issue arises specifically with fiduciary money, since

6. However, concerns over interest rate and exchange rate misalignments and volatilities, including especially their divergent asset market and goods market effects, could limit interest in the ITF.

its amount can be increased at virtually no cost. This section briefly reviews the evolution of views as to what constitutes a good anchor, culminating in the inflation forecast targeting rule.

Why an ITF?

In a textbook closed economy, controlling the money stock is a sufficient anchor, while in an open economy, the traditional approach to anchoring the money supply is to peg the exchange rate. Observing the peg enforces the needed discipline on the central bank as it cannot expand the money supply excessively without suffering a loss of international reserves, which will threaten the peg. However, the increasing trend to capital market liberalization renders the exchange rate peg more vulnerable to large swings in capital flows. Following a number of spectacular failures in both developed and emerging economies to maintain the peg in the face of speculative pressures, pegged exchange rates were largely abandoned in favor of floating exchange rates.

Since a floating exchange rate regime confers considerable independence on monetary policy, the issue of its anchor had to be resolved anew; generally an anchor was achieved through adoption of money supply targets. Financial innovations, however, have made money demand growth unstable and unpredictable, and thus the experience with monetary targeting has not been satisfactory. Pursuit of a given rate of growth in a selected monetary aggregate could result in unacceptable inflation rates.

As monetary targeting is abandoned, emphasis is increasingly being placed directly on the inflation rate. If the principal consequence of undisciplined monetary policy is the generation of unacceptable inflation rates, an alternative to attempting to control an elusive monetary aggregate would be to target the inflation rate, and to seek instruments that would realize it. In pursuit of the inflation target, the central bank must be free to use its interest rate instrument, since this is the only alternative to money supply targeting available to it. But this in turn implies that the central bank cannot be diverted by any simultaneous need to influence the exchange rate. Ruling out the exchange rate, interest rates, and monetary aggregate as potential anchors implies that the anchoring role is instead performed by the inflation target.

Beginning with New Zealand, an increasing number of countries have adopted inflation targeting. There is little doubt that the ITF countries have improved their inflation record after adopting this framework (table 1). The actual mechanism that reduced inflation is an open question, however.

TABLE 1. Coefficient of Variation of Exchange Rate in United States, Japan, India, and Selected Inflation-Targeting Countries

	ITF date	Exchange rate variation			CPI inflation (mean)		
		During 3 years before ITF	During first 3 years after ITF	During full period after ITF	During 3 years before ITF	During first 3 years after ITF	During full period after ITF
Brazil	Q2-1999	20.86	17.08	24.28	6.83	6.78	8.34
Chile	Q1-1991	11.17	7.81	23.57	19.45	17.69	7.25
South Africa	Q1-2000	13.15	20.25	22.70	6.60	7.04	5.51
Israel	Q1-1992	9.07	8.35	19.23	18.64	11.90	2.03
Peru	Q1-1994	40.44	6.95	16.67	721.51	15.21	6.49
Czech Republic	Q1-1999	10.00	4.79	16.29	8.84	3.60	2.58
Iceland	Q1-2001	8.77	14.18	16.18	3.41	4.36	4.12
New Zealand	Q1-1990	5.70	0.07	15.89	9.17	2.57	2.28
Hungary	Q1-2001	12.47	13.33	15.41	11.27	6.41	11.32
Australia	Q4-1994	6.06	6.59	15.21	1.61	2.32	2.68
Sweden	Q1-1995	15.20	7.35	14.76	3.46	0.98	1.16
Switzerland	Q1-2000	5.40	8.60	13.78	0.54	1.06	0.92
Norway	Q1-2001	7.52	12.59	13.67	2.64	1.98	1.82
Colombia	Q3-1999	21.90	10.57	13.39	17.42	8.14	7.49
Mexico	Q1-1999	10.86	2.66	8.15	23.56	10.38	7.80
Poland	Q4-1998	12.67	5.99	7.73	16.11	7.77	5.02
Canada	Q1-1992	5.78	5.63	7.72	3.14	1.21	1.83
Korea	Q1-1998	30.26	8.28	7.57	4.95	3.09	3.51
United Kingdom	Q1 1993	8.25	2.78	6.74	6.02	2.51	2.52
Thailand	Q2-2000	4.70	3.72	4.73	3.62	1.39	1.72
United States[a]	Q1-1995	2.49	5.04	6.14	2.87	2.50	2.46
India[a]	Q1-1995	9.37	7.71	12.56	9.80	8.87	6.41
Japan[a]	Q1-1995	10.48	13.26	10.50	1.36	0.70	-0.05

Source: Basic data come from IMF (2005).

Note: All variations are reported in US$, except for variations for the United States, which are reported in special drawing rights. Data exclude the crisis period for Brazil, and 1997–2000 for Thailand. Chile had a crawling peg before 1991. Mexico has an oil fund.

a. Countries do not have an inflation-targeting framework.

Was it the intention to target inflation, was it the inflation-targeting framework, or were some other exogenous factors responsible?

The rigorous implementation of the ITF would imply increased volatility in variables such as the exchange rate. A close look at the quarterly variation in exchange rates during the three years before and the three years after implementation of the ITF indicates a mixed outcome (see table 1 and figure 1, where variation in the U.S. dollar is reported with respect to special drawing rights, while variation in the currencies of other countries is reported with respect to the U.S. dollar). For most of the ITF countries (with the exception of Hungary, Iceland, Norway, South Africa, and Switzerland), the volatility in nominal exchange rate, measured as a coefficient of variation with respect to the U.S. dollar, was reduced during the first three years of implementation.

When a longer period after implementation of the ITF is considered, however, the coefficient of variation increases considerably beyond the initial three-year period in almost all cases. One explanation is that the countries have, contrary to the ITF requirements, engaged in a "dirty" peg of their domestic currency to the dollar as a way to reduce inflation, since the United States is a low-inflation, low-interest-rate country. Most of the ITF countries appear to have adopted this strategy in the initial period following the adoption of the ITF. Having achieved reasonable stability, monetary policy is then better aligned with ITF requirements; that situation is reflected in a more volatile exchange rate during the later periods. Such volatility could also be partially attributable to an increase in the volatility of the U.S. dollar. While it is difficult to fully disentangle the contributions of these alternative explanations, the data give some support to the implication that the ITF leads to volatile asset markets, indicating that at least some of the countries were more rigorous in their application of the ITF.

In general, for countries to be able to abandon traditional anchors in favor of inflation targeting, their economies must have the capacity to tolerate wide swings in nominal interest rates and in the nominal exchange rate. On the stock side, these swings will exert valuation effects. They may contribute to mismatches between different categories of assets and liabilities on balance sheets. This could generate various problems both in the financing and production spheres as became readily apparent during the Asian crisis of the late 1990s. Firms that borrow short in one currency and invest long in another may find their net worth wiped out. Declines in asset values affect both the ability of firms to borrow from banks and the desire of individuals to spend. Deterioration in investment and consumption activities will then act as a drag on output growth.

FIGURE 1. Coefficient of Variation of Exchange Rate in United States, Japan, India, and Selected Inflation-Targeting Countries

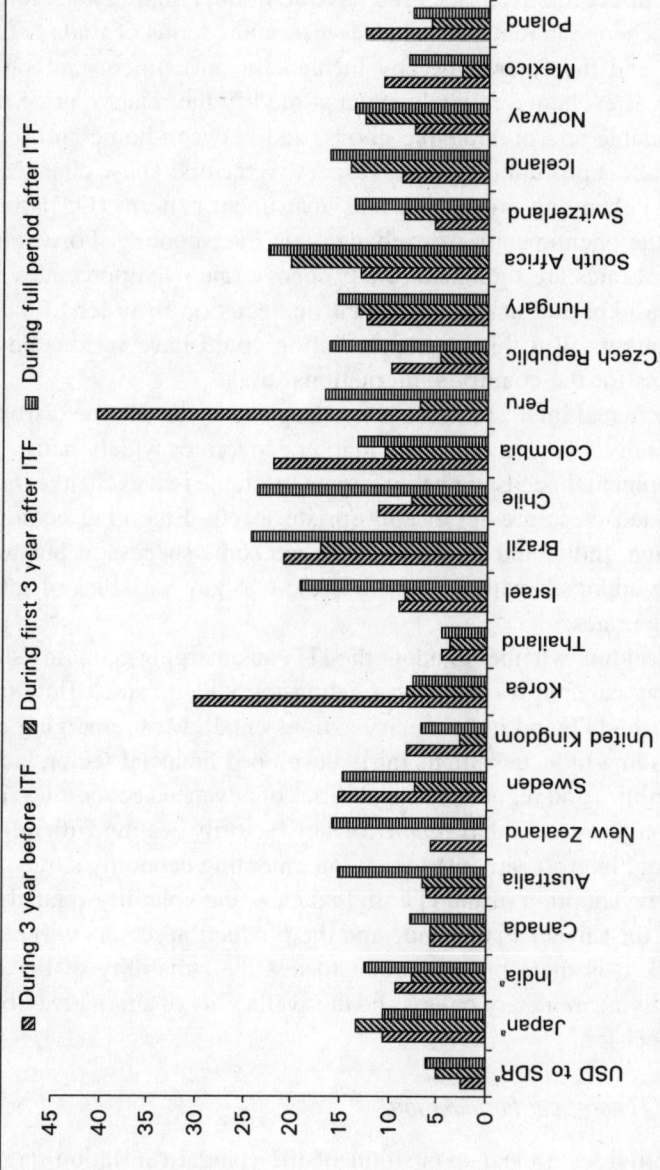

▨ During 3 year before ITF   ▨ During first 3 year after ITF   ▤ During full period after ITF

Source: Basic data come from IMF (2005).
Note: All variations are reported in US$, except for variations for the United States, which are reported in special drawing rights. Data exclude the crisis period for Brazil, and 1997–2000 for Thailand. Chile had a crawling peg before 1991. Mexico has an oil fund.
a. Countries do not have an inflation-targeting framework.

In a world of sticky prices, nominal swings in interest and exchange rates also imply corresponding fluctuations in their real counterparts. These fluctuations affect relative prices and have additional implications for flow behavior. A change in real interest rates affects the terms of trade between the present and the future, thereby influencing investment and savings behavior. Real exchange rate adjustments modify the relative price ratios between tradable and nontradable goods, and between home and foreign goods, that affect profitability in the respective sectors. These changes also contribute to changing production and investment patterns. Of particular concern is the phenomenon of exchange rate overshooting. For example, when interest rates are tightened, the exchange rate overappreciates so as to induce an expectation of subsequent depreciation in order to balance financial markets. But this overappreciation could have serious adverse consequences for the country's international trade.

Volatility in real interest rates and exchange rates can thus be disruptive. Not surprisingly, many in emerging market economies widely believe that their developmental needs are better served by stable real exchange interest rates, provided these are set at appropriate levels. Emerging economies such as China, India, and Malaysia have had some success in pursuing a less volatile approach with respect to these two key variables of interest and exchange rates.

Before deciding whether to adopt the ITF, an emerging economy should establish how capable it is of withstanding the volatile stock-flow implications that the ITF and its monetary actions entail. Most emerging economies, including India despite its fairly developed financial sector, lack the hedging facilities and regulatory capabilities of advanced economies. However, if the only instrument available for satisfactorily dealing with inflation is the nominal interest rate instrument, an emerging economy's only alternative may be adoption of the ITF. In that case, the volatility-related costs incurred on the financial stock side and the production sectors will have to be tolerated. It is therefore important to test the suitability of the ITF's mode of applying monetary policy, and the availability of alternatives, before making a decision.

A Standard Theoretical Formulation

Svensson provides a clear exposition of the standard inflation-targeting approach, which is used as the reference in the following discussion.[7] He

7. Svensson (1997).

assumes a closed economy, and although in other papers he relaxes that assumption, that is not essential for our purposes here.[8] Since our concern is with the assumed transmission mechanism that links the monetary policy instrument with the domestic rate of inflation, the analysis of the simpler closed-economy case could be regarded as embedded in a more comprehensive open-economy model. Simplifying even further, we assume, with Svensson, that the focus is on pure inflation targeting without any trade-offs with other objectives.

THE SVENSSON VERSION. The model structure is as follows:

(1)
$$\pi_{t+1} = \pi_t + \alpha_1 x_t + \varepsilon_{t+1}$$

(2)
$$x_{t+1} = \beta_1 x_t - \beta_2 (i_t - \pi_t) + \eta_{t+1}$$

where $\pi_t = p_t - p_{t-1}$ is the inflation rate in year t, p_t is the log of the price level, x_t is the output gap defined as the log of actual to potential output, i_t is the monetary policy instrument, and ε_t and η_t are i.i.d. shocks in year t that are not known in year $t-1$. All coefficients are nonnegative; $\beta_t < 1$.

The formulation of this model is based on stylized empirical factors as they pertain to the advanced industrial economies. Equation 1 determines inflation as a function of the preceding period's inflation rate, output gap, and a stochastic shock. Equation 2 indicates that the output gap is a positive function of the previous period's output gap and negatively affected by the ex post real interest rate.

The model yields a reduced form solution for the inflation rate on taking note of the assumed stylized lag structure and making the relevant substitutions. The important point is that there is a one-year lag between the output gap and the inflation rate, while the output gap responds to the previous year's real interest rate. In other words, the central bank, in setting the nominal interest rate, can only influence inflation two years down the road.

(3)
$$\pi_{t+2} = a_1 \pi_t + a_2 x_t - a_3 i_t + (\varepsilon_{t+1} + \alpha_1 \eta_{t+1} + \varepsilon_{t+2})$$
where
$$a_1 = 1 + \alpha_1 \beta_2, \, a_2 = \alpha_1 (1 + \beta_1), \, a_3 = \alpha_1 \beta_2.$$

8. Svensson (2003) reviews several variants of the basic model. See also Aghenor (2002) for an exposition. The main effect of opening the economy is to introduce another channel of influence through the exchange rate on the domestic rate of inflation. Since the exchange rate is floating, the effect would be in the same direction as the monetary action; for example, an appreciation accompanying a monetary tightening would accelerate the improvement in the inflation rate.

The solution shows that the inflation rate that will prevail at time $t + 2$ will be determined by the current profile of the specified key variables and the relevant shocks that occur over the next two periods. Since those shocks cannot be anticipated, the inflation rate expected at time $t + 2$ will be a function only of current variable values and the interest rate instrument setting. An optimal inflation-targeting rule is obtained by minimizing the present expected value of an intertemporal loss function

(4)
$$E_t \sum_{\tau=t}^{\infty} \delta^{\tau-t} L(\pi_\tau)$$

where $\delta \in (0, 1)$ is the discount factor.

The loss function for each period is specified as the squared deviation of the inflation rate from the target level π^*.

(5)
$$L(\pi_\tau) = \frac{1}{2}(\pi_\tau - \pi^*)^2$$

The decision problem is to select a time path of nominal interest rates that will minimize the expected sum of discounted squared future deviations of inflation from the target, subject to the constraint imposed by equation 3. This is a potentially complicated exercise in dynamic programming, but Svensson shows how the problem can be simplified by using the lag structure. Since the central bank can only influence the inflation rate two periods ahead, the optimal interest rate in year t is found as the solution to a period-by-period problem.

(6)
$$\text{Min}_{i_t} E_t \delta^2 L(\pi_{t+2})$$

The first-order condition for minimizing equation 6 with respect to i_t is

(7)
$$\frac{\partial E_t \delta^2 L(\pi_{t+2})}{\partial i_t} = -\delta^2 a_3 (E_t \pi_{t+2} - \pi^*) = 0$$

The condition is met if the expected rate of inflation two years hence equals the target rate. This is equivalent to equating the current two-year inflation forecast (given by equation 3) to the target rate. On setting this forecast equal to the target rate, the following optimal policy rule for the nominal interest rate is derived

(8)
$$i_t = \pi_t + b_1(\pi_t - \pi^*) + b_2 x_t$$
where

$$b_1 = \frac{1}{\alpha_1 \beta_2}, b_2 = \frac{1 + \beta_1}{\beta_2}$$

It is an inflation *forecast* targeting rule, which corresponds to the strict inflation-targeting version of the well-known Taylor rule.[9] However, unlike the Taylor rule, where the coefficients would either be arbitrary or somehow estimated from past data, Svensson's derivation is based on the postulated underlying structure of the economy. His rule sets the interest rate by reference to the deviation of the current inflation rate from the target rate. As he points out, this is not because current inflation is targeted, which it cannot be since it is predetermined, but because current inflation is one of the inputs in predicting future inflation (see equation 3). The ITF targets the inflation rate through the adoption of a relatively flexible approach centered on the interest rate as the preferred instrument of choice. It attempts to cope with inherent uncertainties arising from the complexity of the economy that precludes rigid targeting, through the adoption of a so-called flexible "rule." While the rule is optimal in the sense of being derived from minimizing a loss function, it is a far cry from the optimal "control" approach to targeting that was pursued and abandoned in the 1970s.

Equation 8 implies that in a steady state in which the inflation target is attained and the output gap is zero, the nominal interest rate should equal the target rate of inflation. This implies a zero real rate of interest, but it is straightforward to ensure some positive target real interest rate level by including it in equation 2, which then yields the desired term in equation 8. Notice also that the specification of the structural equation 2 provides only for a real interest term as the principal influence on the output gap. In particular, no role is specified for fiscal policy, indicating either that it is impotent or that it has no part to play in inflation control, which is implicitly assigned to monetary policy.

A Test of the Svensson Model

The foregoing discussion raises three important issues, which need to be resolved to select a consistent macroeconomic policy procedure. These issues include the persistence of inflation and its lag structure, the effect of

9. Taylor (1993).

the output gap and its lag structure, and how they relate to the underlying actual process of inflation in the case of India. The discussion here is based on annual data because quarterly data are not available for a sufficiently long period. First we examine the time series behavior of inflation and then test the structure suggested by Svensson. In undertaking the estimation, particular attention is paid to the inflation equation 3. The variables used in the empirical analysis are described in table A-1 and their descriptive statistics are presented in table A-2. An augmented Dicky-Fuller test is used to check the stationary properties of the variables, and the final outcomes are reported in table A-2. The normal convention in this paper is to prefix a variable with 'L' to indicate that the variable is taken in log and by D to indicate that the variable is taken in first difference. Thus, a prefix DL means first difference of the logged value of the variable. As a general practice in this paper, the estimations (particularly for modeling inflation) are carried out taking data from 1970–71 to 2002–03, while data from 2003–04 to 2004–05 are used to check the predictive power of the models.

Inflation ($DLWP$) is defined as the first difference of log wholesale price index (WPI). The selection of this particular price index is guided by several factors. The most important reason is that macroeconomic policy decisions in India are based on movements in the WPI; moreover, this index has the largest basket of commodities and is therefore most representative of economic activities. In addition to the WPI, four other price indexes are published in India. Three are consumer price indexes (CPIs) targeted to three different groups of consumers. The fourth is the gross domestic product (GDP) deflator.

The difference between the CPI and WPI also stems from the different composition of the basket of commodities and the weight given to them. For instance, the WPI includes manufactured goods with a weight (1993–94 base) of 63.75 percent in the basket, while primary articles account for 22 percent. In contrast, the CPI has a weight of about 57 percent for food articles alone. Thus, the WPI has a lesser weight for volatile elements and can be considered a closer proxy of core inflation. Finally, the WPI captures larger components of imports, which reflects on domestic inflation.

The GDP deflator is an implicit price index, which can be derived from the national accounts for GDP, consumption, or investment. Covering all three sectors of services, industry, and agriculture, it largely represents producer prices. However, the GDP deflator can be known only with a lag of two to three years after accounts are final. Nor is the GDP deflator well understood by the economic agents compared with the directly published prices indexes. Furthermore, in the context of monetary policy analysis, information on price movements is needed at quick intervals to allow policy-makers to forecast inflation trends and to take corrective measures. Probably for these reasons, the GDP deflator is not a popular measure of the price index for analyzing the Indian economy.

The WPI includes service charges from wholesalers and retail profits; it covers 447 commodities spread over primary articles, fuel products, and manufactured items. It does not include the services sector per se; nor does it account for price effects of efficiency gains. However, it can be argued that WPI implicitly captures the effect of service sector prices, including asset prices, because of its wide coverage of commodities albeit with different lags. For example, an increase in real estate prices would increase rentals and consequently increase the prices of traded goods. Similarly, a booming stock market would lead to increases in deposit rates and consequently lending rates, which may affect the commodity prices.[10] For the monetary authorities to be fully aware of the broadest possible inflation coverage, any model of inflation must be able to explain price variations as a whole. Therefore, the WPI has been adopted as the preferred price index in this study. Henceforth, any reference to price index or inflation in this paper means the WPI unless otherwise specifically stated.

An evaluation of the inflation series shows that it is a stationary process, and its autocorrelation function in table 2 and figure 2 indicate that the series has poor persistence. Neither of the two widely used criteria, Box-Pierce and the Ljung-Box statistic, support persistence. The first and fourth lags are significant at 10 percent only, but the fourth lag is negative. The standardized spectral density at zero frequency, presented in table 3 along with standard errors, also indicates no significant evidence of persistence.

Taking four lags, we present an ARMA (4, 1) forecasting model for the series in table 4, the lag structure being selected by Akaike information criteria and the Schwartz Bayesian criteria starting with six lags. In this formulation too, the evidence for persistence is not strong; the sum of the lagged coefficients is negative. The moving-average term, however, is significant, positive, but less than one. Clearly, any shock to the inflation series dies down very soon.

To test equation 3, we require a time series on the stationary output gap and a measure of the interest rate, which is close to policy rates. To obtain a series on potential output we employ a widely accepted method of filtering

---

10. Nevertheless, this does not mean that India should not strive to create a better time series to capture effects of the services sector adequately. The government has already set up a committee to improve the WPI and develop a producer price index covering a wider spectrum of inputs.

TABLE 2. Autocorrelation Coefficients of *DLWP*

Order	Autocorrelation coefficients	Standard error	Box-pierce statistic	Ljung-box
1	0.296	0.172	2.973 [0.085]	3.243 [0.072]
2	−0.171	0.186	3.972 [0.137]	4.367 [0.113]
3	−0.149	0.190	4.728 [0.193]	5.245 [0.155]
4	−0.270	0.194	7.214 [0.125]	8.228 [0.084]
5	−0.117	0.205	7.680 [0.175]	8.807 [0.117]
6	0.173	0.207	8.696 [0.191]	10.113 [0.120]
7	0.182	0.211	9.823 [0.199]	11.615 [0.114]
8	−0.064	0.215	9.962 [0.268]	11.808 [0.160]
9	−0.101	0.216	10.307 [0.326]	12.304 [0.197]
10	−0.010	0.217	10.310 [0.414]	12.310 [0.265]
11	0.010	0.217	10.314 [0.502]	12.315 [0.340]

Note: Numbers in brackets are *p*-values.

FIGURE 2. Autocorrelation Function of *DLWP*, Sample from 1971 to 2004

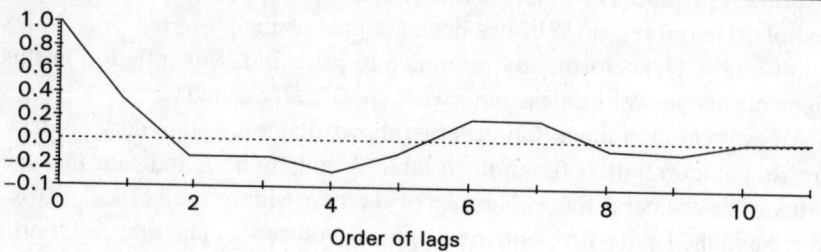

Order of lags

TABLE 3. Standardized Spectral Density Functions of *DLWP* at Zero Frequency with Estimated Asymptotic Standard Errors, Sample from 1971 to 2004

	Bartlett weights	Turkey weights	Parzen weights
Standardized spectral density functions of *DLWP*	0.765	0.699	0.79
Asymptotic standard errors	0.525	0.509	0.487

TABLE 4. Distributed Lag Model with ARMA (4, 1), 1971–2004

$DLWP = 0.121^* - 0.126\ DLWP\ (-1) - 0.250\ DLWP\ (-2)^{***} + 0.0261\ DLWP\ (-3) - 0.331\ DLWP\ (-4)^*$
(0.024) (0.135)   (0.126)   (0.124)   (0.124)

Moving average term: $U = E + 0.487\ E\ (-1)^*$
                (0.145)

$a = a2 + a3 + a4 + a5 = -0.680\ (0.284)^{**}$

$R^2 = 0.42$; $\bar{R}^2 = 0.28$; SER = 0.035; root mean sum-sq prediction errors = 0.0284.
*Significant at the 1 percent level; **Significant at the 5 percent level; ***Significant at the 10 percent level. Standard errors are in parentheses; *p*-values are in brackets.

the output series (real gross domestic product, RGDP, or Y) using the Hoderick-Prescott filter with penalizing parameter λ equal to 7 as suggested by Harvey and Jaeger.[11] Thus, the real output gap ($GAPHP$) is calculated as $GAPHP = LY - LYHP$, where $LYHP$ is the log of the filtered series of real GDP. The deposit interest rate variable $DR1$ is not stationary, but it is kept in the model as required by the theory. However, the residuals of the regression are tested for unit root to see the consistency of the regression. The results are presented in table 5 as models A-1 and A-2. Model A-1 has exactly the same lag structure as equation 3 whereas model A-2 has the full set of lags and encompasses the spirit behind equation 1. Given the theoretical construct of equation 3, we do not expect the regressors to be correlated with the error term. The same conclusion is supported by the diagnostic tests. Neither of the two regressions are significant, however (see F-test), although A-2 appears to be better specified. Our interest is more in the sign and significance of the lagged output gap term ($GAPHP$). Clearly, for the sample period, the output gap is not significant in explaining inflation.

However, it may be argued that during most of the sample period, the Indian economy remained supply-driven, with all kinds of controls clamped on by the government. To see the effects of the controls, we run a rolling regression with a window size of fifteen, using the same set of variables; the results are recorded in figures 3, 4, 5, and 6. The lagged output gap is not significant enough to explain current inflation, although the signs are correct.

FIGURE 3.   Result of Rolling Regression with Variables in Model A-1

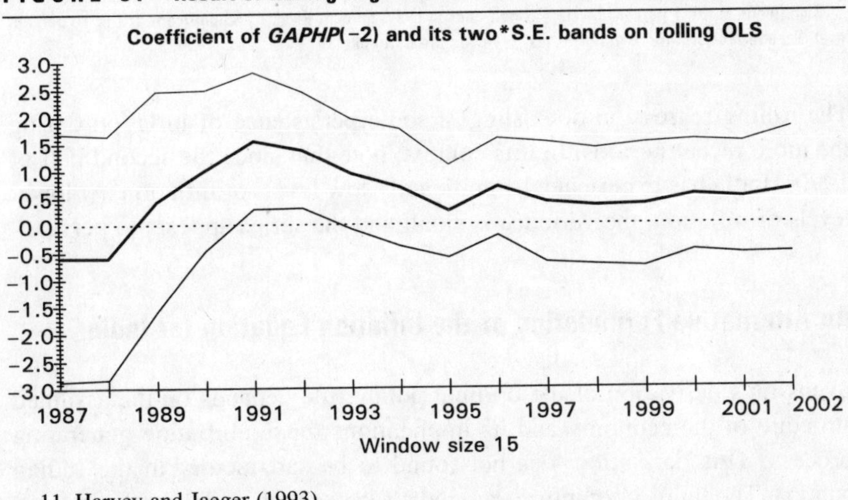

Coefficient of $GAPHP(-2)$ and its two*S.E. bands on rolling OLS

Window size 15

11. Harvey and Jaeger (1993).

TABLE 5. Regression Results with Svensson's Lag Structure: Selected Models

Regressor/Dependent variable	1972–73 to 2002–03 Model A-1 DLWP	1972–73 to 2002–03 Model A-2 DLWP
Intercept	0.171 (0.053)*	1.124 (0.072)***
DLWP (−1)		0.392 (0.262)
DLWP (−2)	−0.092 (0.242)	−0.151 (0.288)
GAPHP (−1)		0.351 (0.697)
GAPHP (−2)	0.570 (0.690)	0.630 (0.759)
DR1 (−1)		−0.348 (1.460)
DR1 (−2)	0.987 (0.529)	−0.401 (1.456)
Summary statistics		
R^2	0.184	0.270
$\bar{R}^2$	0.091	0.071
SER	0.050	0.051
F statistic, $F(k-1, n-k)$, n = 31, k = no. of regressors including intercept	1.96 [0.66]	1.37 [0.27]
Diagnostic tests		
LM (1) serial correlation	2.08 [0.15]	0.21 [0.65]
LM (2) serial correlation	2.08 [0.05]	1.24 [0.54]
ARCH (2) test CHSQ (3)	11.92 [0.00]	3.85 [0.14]
Functional form CHSQ (1)	4.46 [0.04]	1.68 [0.20]
Normality CHSQ (2)	1.22 [0.54]	3.58 [0.17]
Predictive failure CHSQ (2)	0.83 [0.66]	0.32 [0.85]
Residual unit root		
Test statistics (DF)	−3.49	−5.88

Note: Predictive failure tests are conducted by breaking the sample at 2002. Unit root test statistics are presented corresponding to the SBC model selection criteria in a unit root test with second order ADF.

*Significant at the 1 percent level. **Significant at the 5 percent level. ***Significant at the 10 percent level. Standard errors are in parentheses; p-values are in brackets.

The rolling regression does suggest some persistence of inflation during the more recent periods. In this context, note that since the second half of 1990s, India has experienced significantly low levels of inflation. At lower levels of inflation, the variance is small and the series appears to persist.

An Alternative Formulation of the Inflation Equation for India

Svensson's derivation of the optimal policy rule depends on the assumed structure of the economy and its implications for the inflation-generating process. This derivation was not found to be satisfactory in the Indian context. The failure to capture demand effects in that model need not mean

FIGURE 4.   **Result of Rolling Regression with Variables in Model A-2**

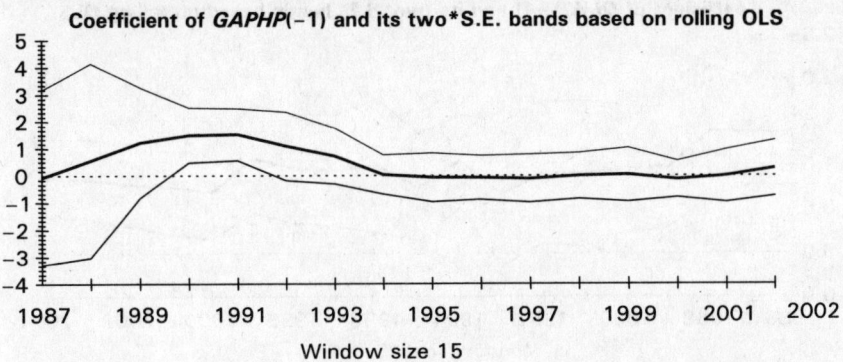

Coefficient of *GAPHP*(–1) and its two*S.E. bands based on rolling OLS

Window size 15

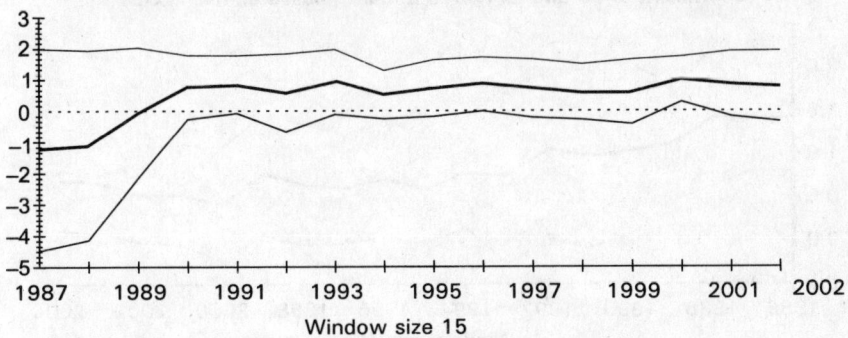

Coefficient of *GAPHP*(–2) and its two*S.E. bands based on rolling OLS

Window size 15

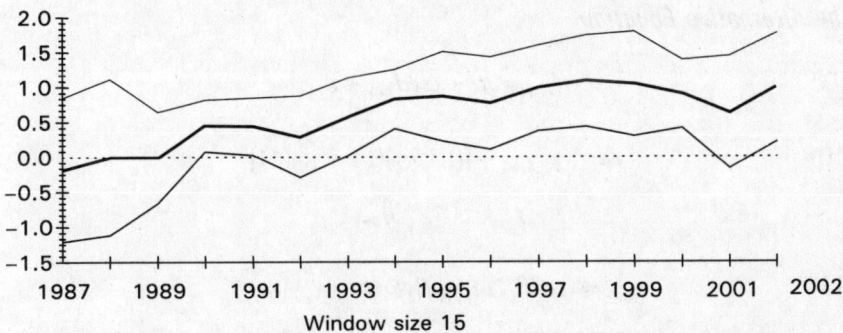

Coefficient of *DLWP*(–1) and its two*S.E. bands based on rolling OLS

Window size 15

that they are unimportant, however; the outcome could be the result of structural misspecification. The focus here is on replacing Svensson's postulated structure, with its Phillips curve, with an alternative that might better accord with conditions in India.

FIGURE 5. Result of Rolling Regression with Variables in Model B-1

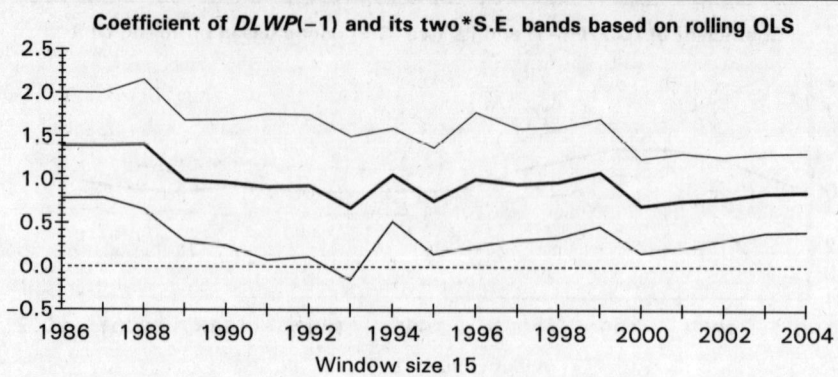

Coefficient of *DLWP*(–1) and its two*S.E. bands based on rolling OLS

Window size 15

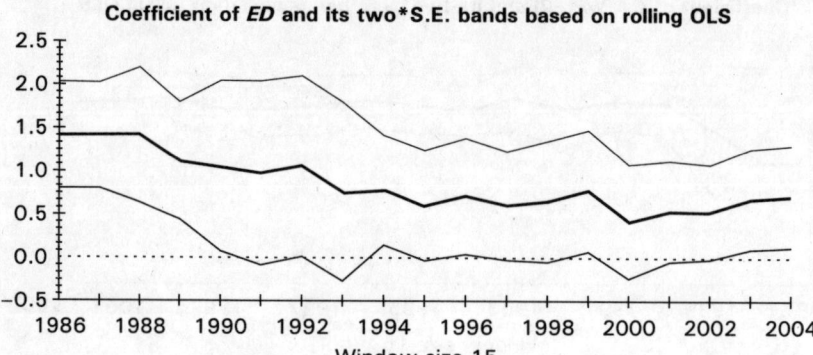

Coefficient of *ED* and its two*S.E. bands based on rolling OLS

Window size 15

The Alternative Equation

$$(9) \qquad \pi_{t+1} = \pi_t + \alpha ed_{t+1} + \varepsilon_{t+1}$$

$$(10) \qquad ed_{t+1} \equiv y_{t+1} - [(1+\pi_t)(1+\hat{q}_{t+1}) - 1]$$

$$y_{t+1} - (\pi_t + \hat{q}_{t+1})$$

$$(11) \qquad y_{t+1} = c + \beta_1 Dd_t - \beta_2 D(i_t - \pi_t) + \eta_{t+1}$$

In addition to the variables defined earlier, *ED* is the growth rate of nominally valued aggregate excess demand, *d* is the budget deficit ratio, *y* is the nominally valued GDP growth rate, and $\hat{q}$ is the growth rate of potential output. *D* is the difference operator. All coefficients are positive, $\alpha \leq 1$ and the stochastic terms have the same interpretation as before.

FIGURE 6. Rolling Diagrams of Regression for Model D-3: *DLWP* on *INPT*, *DLWP*[1], *ED*[0], *DLPEO*[0], *DLPMO*[0], *DLWOP*, *DLM1DIS*[0–1], *DRAINR*[0], *DLFERUWB* [0], and *DLWAGPI*[0]

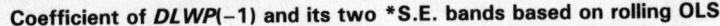

Coefficient of *DLWP*(–1) and its two *S.E. bands based on rolling OLS

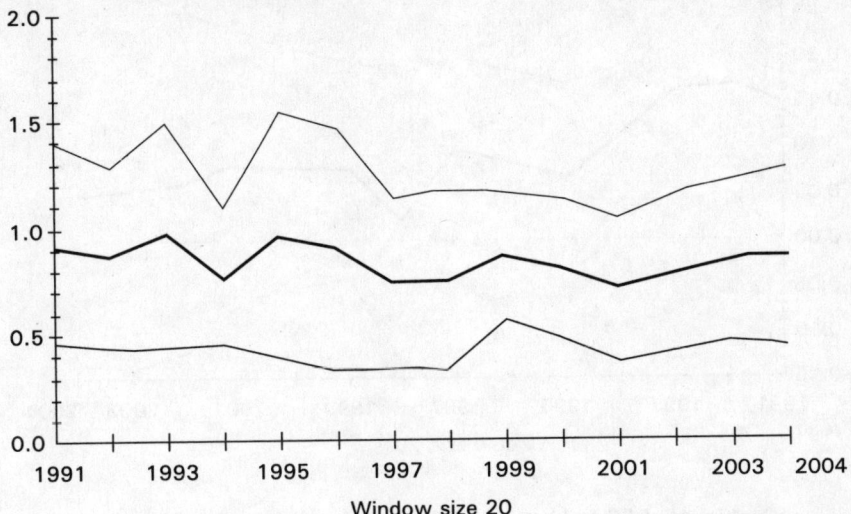

Window size 20

Coefficient of *DLM1DIS* and its two *S.E. bands based on rolling OLS

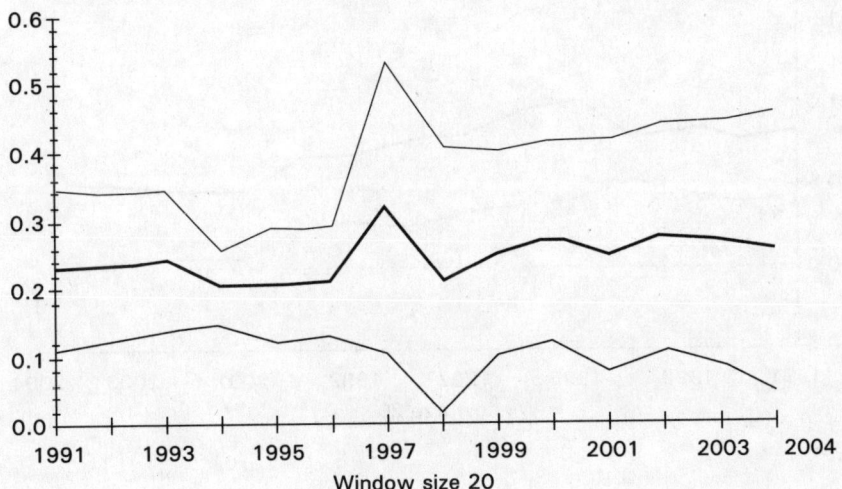

Window size 20

(Figure 6 continued)

(Figure 6 continued)

Coefficient of *DLM1DIS*(–1) and its two *S.E. bands based on rolling OLS

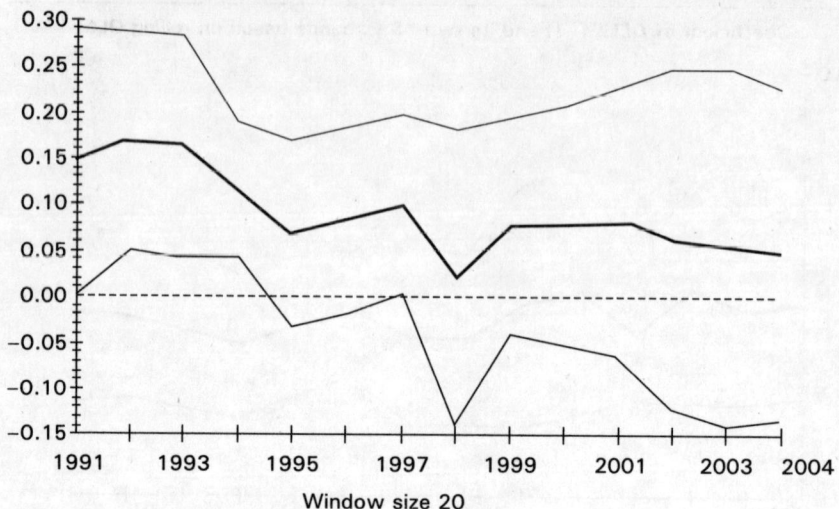

Window size 20

Coefficient of *ED* and its two *S.E. bands based on rolling OLS

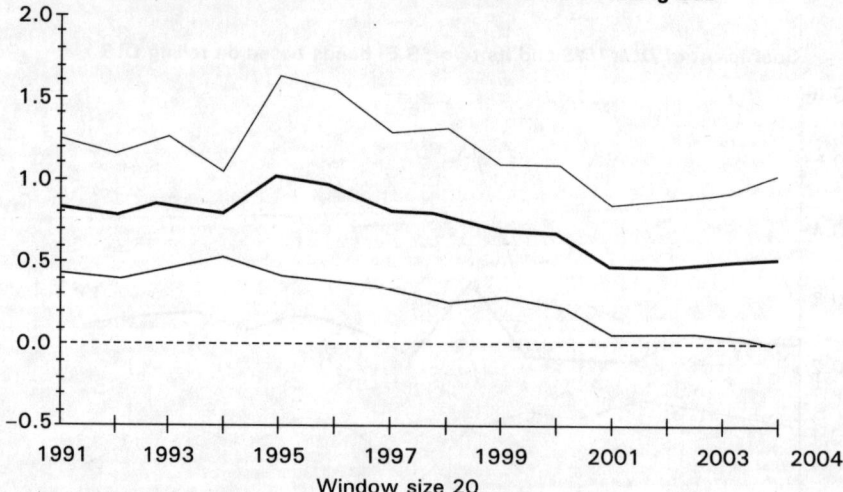

Window size 20

(Figure 6 continued)

(Figure 6 continued)

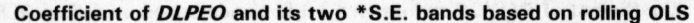

Coefficient of *DLPEO* and its two *S.E. bands based on rolling OLS

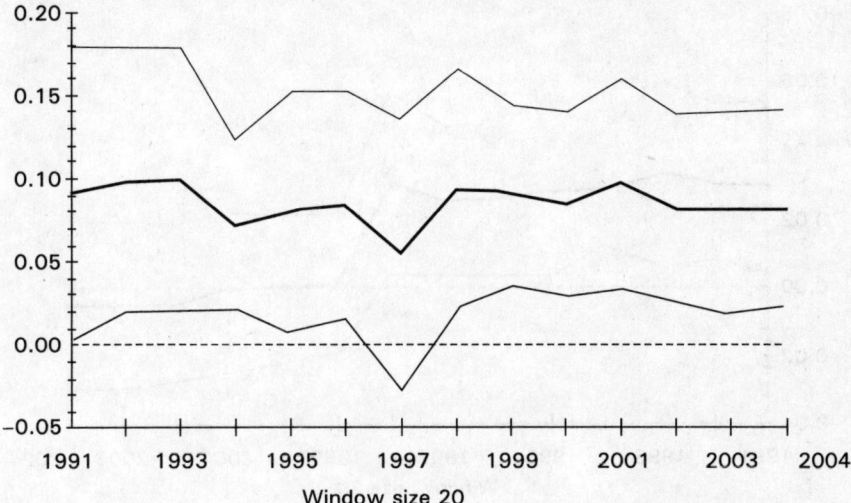

Window size 20

Coefficient of *DLPMO* and its two *S.E. bands based on rolling OLS

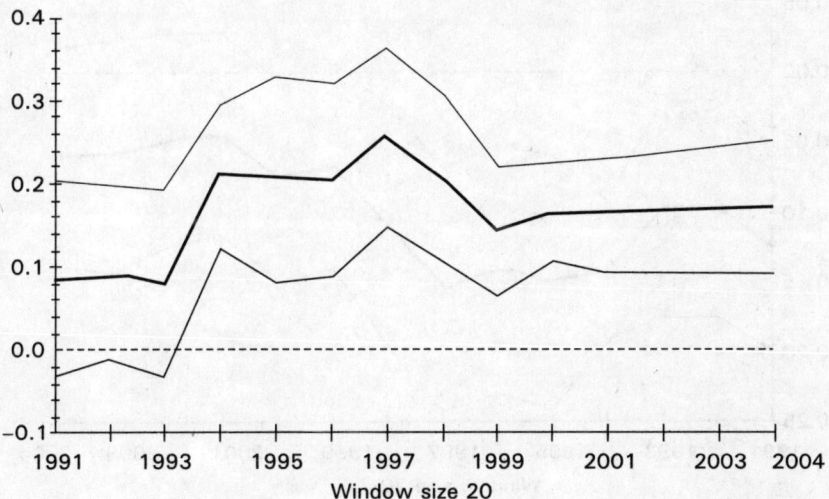

Window size 20

(Figure 6 continued)

(Figure 6 continued)

Coefficient of *DLWOP* and its two *S.E. bands based on rolling OLS

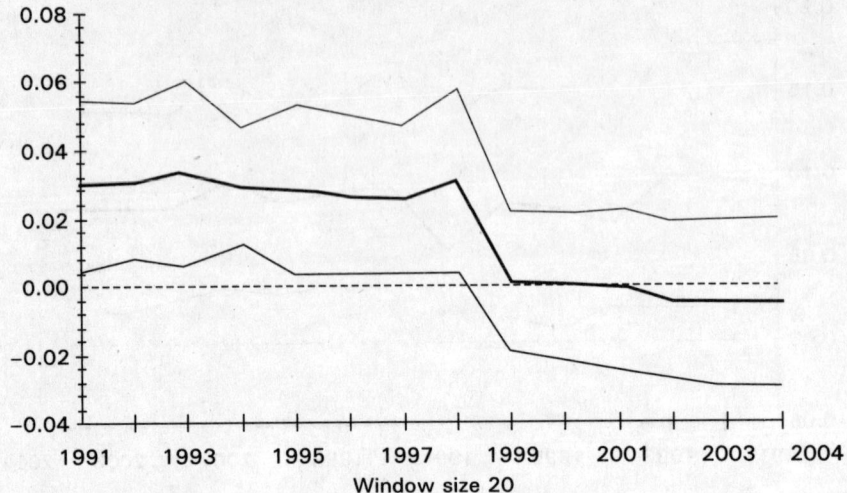

Window size 20

Coefficient of *DRAINR* and its two *S.E. bands based on rolling OLS

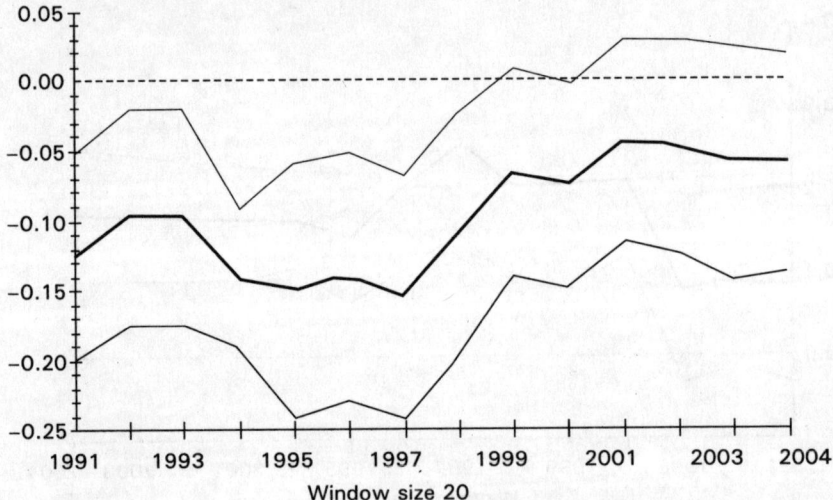

Window size 20

(Figure 6 continued)

(Figure 6 continued)

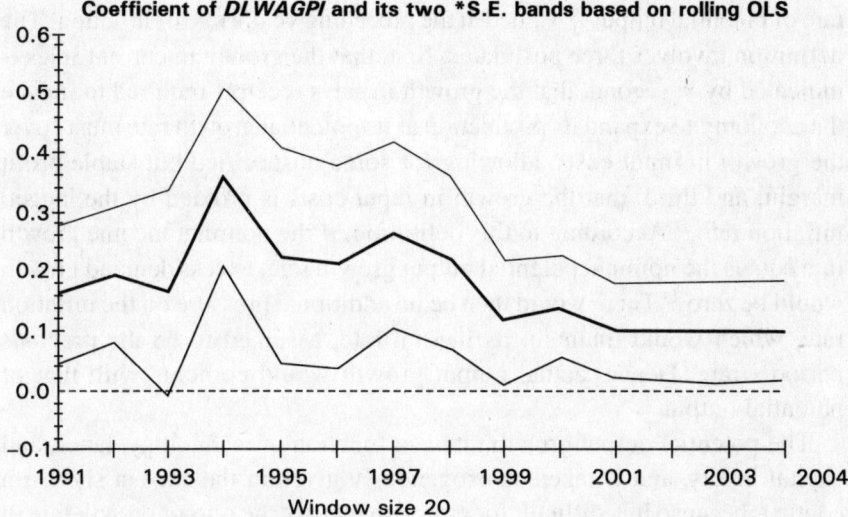

Coefficient of *DLWAGPI* and its two *S.E. bands based on rolling OLS

Window size 20

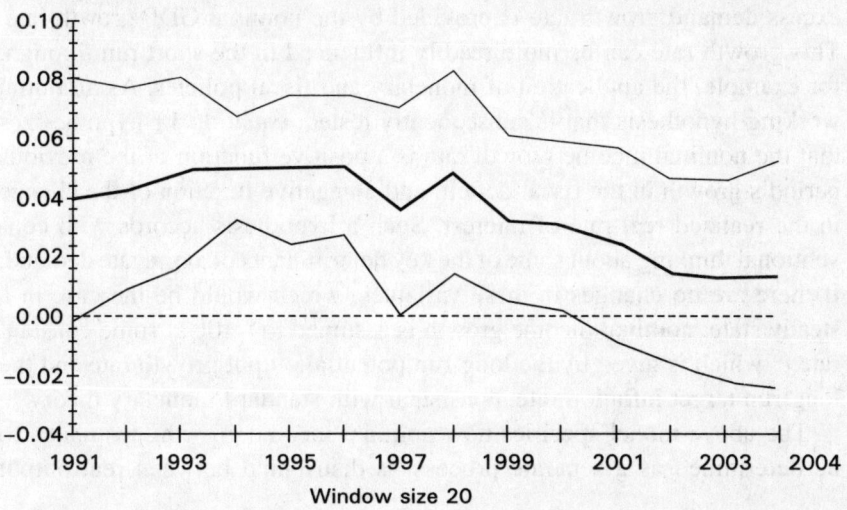

Coefficient of *DLFERUWB* and its two *S.E. bands based on rolling OLS

Window size 20

Equation 9 states that the inflation rate equals the previous period's inflation rate, a one-year lag being needed to allow for the type of inflation persistence found in India. If the growth in aggregate excess demand is other than zero, however, a proportion of that growth α will be reflected in the inflation rate. Aggregate excess demand growth is defined in equation 10 as the difference between the nominal GDP growth rate y and the growth rate of potential output $\hat{q}$ valued at the preceding year's rate of inflation. The definition involves three postulates: first, that the growth in current sales is indicated by y; second, that the growth in sales receipts required to induce the economy to expand its production at its potential growth rate must cover the growth in input costs, allowing for some unspecified but stable profit margin; and third, that the growth in input costs is proxied by the lagged inflation rate.[12] According to this definition, if the nominal income growth rate equals the nominal potential output growth rate, excess demand growth would be zero.[13] There would then be no additional pressure on the inflation rate, which would maintain its inertial rate, assumed to be the previous period's rate. Hence, actual output growth would coincide with that of potential output.

The potential output growth rate is a function of technology, labor, and capital inputs, and is taken as exogenously given in the current short-run context, because it is difficult for policy to modify the output growth rate in such a short time span. The other component of fluctuations in the nominal excess demand growth rate is provided by the nominal GDP growth rate. This growth rate can be more readily influenced in the short run through, for example, the application of monetary and fiscal policies. As an initial working hypothesis that is subsequently tested, equation 11 hypothesizes that the nominal income growth rate is a positive function of the previous period's growth in the fiscal deficit, and a negative function of the change in the realized real rate of interest. Such a hypothesis accords with conventional thinking about some of the key determinants of aggregate demand. If there are no changes in these variables, which would be the case in a steady state, nominal income growth is assumed to settle at some constant rate c, which is given by the long-run potential output growth rate and the long-run target inflation rate, consistent with standard monetary theory.

The above model specifies how nominal income growth, postulated to be determined as a separate process, is distributed between real output

12. The use of the previous period's rate of inflation in valuing potential output growth rates can be viewed alternatively as reflecting a specific process governing the expectations of suppliers.

13. Chand (1997) develops this structural specification. The exercise is that of decomposing nominal income, viewed as determined separately, into its output and price components; see also Gordon (1981). Imposing a Phillips-type linkage on the output and price components as in Svensson's derivation may not be consistent with the determination of nominal income from the demand side, resulting in a structural misspecification.

growth and the rate of inflation. Applying a proportion α to ED to indicate its impact on inflation assumes that the remaining proportion of excess demand will affect the output growth rate. Note that the specification in equation 11 provides for two potential policy instruments involving the fiscal deficit and the nominal interest rate. These are instruments traditionally invoked to influence aggregate demand, but in principle there could be additional or alternative policy instruments for managing aggregate demand. The selected specifications are tested in the next section.

Retaining the strict inflation-targeting goal of minimizing deviations between the forecast inflation rate and the target rate, what does the above model imply for the choice of instrument and the optimal setting? Undertaking a similar optimization procedure to Svensson's, first generate a solution for the inflation rate from equations 9, 10, and 11.

$$(12) \quad \pi_{t+1} = \pi_t - \alpha(\pi_t + \hat{q}_{t+1} - c) + \alpha\beta_2 D(\pi_t - i_t) + \alpha\beta_1 Dd_t + \alpha\eta_{t+1} + \varepsilon_{t+1}$$

Next, minimize the present discounted value of losses from deviations between the expected rate and the target inflation rate subject to equation 12.

$$(13) \qquad\qquad \text{Min}_{i_t, d_t} E_t \delta L(\pi_{t+1})$$

The first-order conditions with respect to the nominal interest rate instrument and the fiscal deficit are respectively

$$(14) \qquad \frac{\partial E_t \delta L(\pi_{t+1})}{\partial Di_t} = -\delta\alpha\beta_2 (E_t\pi_{t+1} - \pi^*) = 0,$$

and

$$(15) \qquad \frac{\partial E_t \delta L(\pi_{t+1})}{\partial Dd_t} = -\delta\alpha\beta_1 (E_t\pi_{t+1} - \pi^*) = 0$$

The conditions are met if the expected rate of inflation a year from now equals the target rate. Since this is equivalent to equating the inflation forecast given by equation 12 to the target rate, we can employ the target rate in equation 12 and solve for the optimum values for whichever of the two instruments is used for promoting the inflation target.

$$(16) \qquad Di_t = D\pi_t + \frac{1}{\alpha\beta_2}(\pi_t - \pi^*) + \frac{\beta_1}{\beta_2} Dd_t - \frac{1}{\beta_2}(\pi_{t-1} + \hat{q}_t - c)$$

(17) $$Dd_t = -\frac{(\pi_t - \pi^*)}{\alpha\beta_1} + \frac{\beta_2}{\beta_1}D(i_t - \pi_t) + \frac{1}{\beta_1}(\pi_{t-1} + \hat{q}_t - c)$$

Equation 16 is broadly similar to the standard model's equation 8 earlier: the more the current rate of inflation exceeds the target the higher the nominal interest rate should be set. However, the output gap does not appear in equation 16, where it has been replaced by a term involving the nominal value of potential output growth and also the fiscal deficit. Increasing the last stimulates excess demand, which raises the inflation rate, thereby requiring a higher nominal interest rate to offset it.

An interesting new element is the alternative model's optimal policy rule for the fiscal deficit. Should the forecast inflation rate be higher than the target, the fiscal deficit has to be reduced to lower excess demand and bring the forecast inflation rate back to target. However, if in the process the real interest rate is made higher, the reduction in the fiscal deficit will need to be restrained to counteract the interest rate's deflationary consequences.

Having two instruments directed at the same target gives an extra degree of freedom. Which instrument should be dispensed with? In accordance with well-established procedures in policy analysis (the Mundell rule), the instrument with a bigger impact on the target variable and milder side effects should be selected. From equation 12 the relative impacts on the target variable are determined by comparing the respective sizes of the β coefficients. But even if the fiscal deficit, ideally adjusted to remove feedback effects on it, is less potent than the nominal interest rate instrument, it may still be the preferred instrument for dealing with inflation insofar as its side effects are milder. Considerations that may be decisive in the instrument assignment would also be the scope for using interest rates to address other problems such as that of ensuring a stable exchange rate and preventing revaluation volatility in balance sheets.

Testing the Alternative Specification

We start here with estimation of equation 9 (the results are presented as model B-1 in table 6). Clearly, *ED* along with lagged inflation appears to explain a much larger part of inflation than was the case with the previous model, and the estimation results are also consistent. However, the coefficient estimates are much too large since they exceed unity, indicating the presence of some upward bias possibly involving linkages with omitted variables. Since the normality assumption is violated in model B-1, the significance of the variables was tested using Wald's maximum likelihood

TABLE 6.   Regression Results under Alternative Formulation: Selected Models

Regressor/ dependent variable	1972–73 to 2002–03 Model B-1 DLWP	1972–73 to 2002–03 Model B-2 DLWP	1972–73 to 2002–03 Model B-3 DLWP	1973–74 to 2002–03 Model B-4 ED
Intercept	−0.009 (0.016)	−0.009 (0.016)	0.190* (0.057)	− 0.034* (0.012)
DLWP (−1)	1.157 (0.198)*	−0.044 (0.138)	−0.067 (0.260)	
DDLWP (−1)			0.279 (0.194)	
DLYHP			−2.041** (0.960)	
ED	1.152 (0.204)*			
EDNP		1.151 (0.204)*		
DGAPHP				
DGAPHP (−1)				
DLCFGAP (−1)			−0.055 (0.079)	−0.057 (0.050)
DLCFGAP (−2)				0.108* (0.043)
DDR1 (−1)			0.443 (1.228)	− 2.383* (0.623)
DDR1 (−2)				1.693** (0.697)
DSBI (−2)				− 0.552 (0.339)
DLIPIG5				0.942* (0.181)
DLIPIG5 (−1)				0.366*** (0.174)
DGBG5 (−2)				1.480** (0.612)
DDLM1DIS (−1)				0.302* (0.064)
Summary statistics				
R^2	0.580	0.570	0.311	0.862
$\bar{R}^2$	0.550	0.539	0.167	0.800
SER	0.035	0.035	0.048	0.022
F statistic, F(k−1, n−k), n=31, k= no. of regressors including intercept	18.66 [0.00]	18.54 [0.00]	2.167 [0.09]	13.92 [0.00]
Diagnostic tests				
LM (1) serial correlation	0.11 [0.75]	0.04 [0.83]	0.08 [0.78]	0.83 [0.36]
LM (2) serial correlation	0.97 [0.61]	0.46 [0.79]	0.08 [0.6]	1.29 [0.52]
ARCH (2) test CHSQ (2)	0.06 [0.97]	0.32 [0.85]	0.49 [0.17]	0.16 [0.92]
Functional form CHSQ (1)	1.16 [0.28]	1.06 [0.30]	4.09 [0.04]	6.33 [0.01]
Normality CHSQ (2)	11.12 [0.00]	11.30 [0.00]	2.55 [0.28]	2.78 [0.25]
Predictive failure CHSQ (2)	0.07 [0.97]	0.05 [0.98]	0.01 [0.99]	0.68 [0.71]
Residual unit root				
Test statistics [DF/ADF (1)]	−4.94	−6.07	−5.20	−4.01

Note: Predictive failure tests are conducted by breaking the sample at 2002. Unit root test statistics are presented corresponding to the SBC model selection criteria in a unit root test with second order ADF.

*Significant at the 1 percent level. **Significant at the 5 percent level. ***Significant at the 10 percent level. Standard errors are in parentheses; p-values are in brackets.

criterion. The results indicated that both variables were highly significant. The rolling regression of lagged inflation is significant, and despite intermittent failure *ED* is also significant during most of the windows, particularly the recent period (figure 5).

An alternative and possibly more intuitive way of presenting equation 9 is to substitute equation 10 in equation 9 to yield a relationship between the current inflation and the difference between the nominal growth rate and the real potential growth rate. This difference is represented by the variable *EDNP*. This regression is presented as model B-2 in table 6. The estimated coefficient attaching to *EDNP* is virtually identical to that associated with *ED* in B-1. The importance of B-2 is that it relates the inflation process directly to the difference between the nominal income growth rate and the potential real growth rate but without imposing any valuation on the latter. The rate of inflation is now a proportion of the excess of nominal income growth over real potential growth. As a consequence the contribution of the lagged inflation term is reduced.

Rather than use *ED* we could use the parallel concept of the change in output gap (*DGAPHP*), which corresponds in growth rate terms to the output gap earlier employed. When this variable is used in model B-3, the sign is significantly negative. This is puzzling, given the conventional view that an increase in the output gap should be more inflationary.[14] Such a result indicates that this view needs to be reconsidered. The fact that a negative sign resulted from regressing the inflation rate on the change in the output gap suggests that nominal income is determined by a process separate from that of its constituents. Hence, since nominal income growth is the sum of the inflation rate and the rate of output growth, if the latter increases the former must decline as long as nominal income is unchanged, which would explain the estimated negative sign.

Next we estimate a reduced-form equation for inflation using equation 12 with the specified lag structure and present the results as model B-4. Neither the lagged growth in fiscal deficit nor the lagged change in interest rate affects current inflation. However, when the same variables are used to explain *ED*, they are found to be significant albeit with a different lag

---

14. In a more recent work, the Reserve Bank of India has estimated inflation using the output gap and claims to have obtained a positive relationship between the output gap and inflation (RBI 2004). However, this relationship is a very specific case where estimations are made without intercepts. The results are fragile to inclusion of an intercept term and, therefore, cannot be taken as robust.

structure (model B-5, table 5). The signs are also as expected. The determinants of *ED* must be established to identify and quantify the effects of demand-side variables on nominal income, and some testing is undertaken to establish the influence of additional variables and different lag structures.

Variables that affect *ED* through the external sector include growth rates in industrialized countries (*DLIPIG5*) and changes in GDP-weighted government bond yields (*DGBG5*). Five countries, France, Germany, Japan, the United Kingdom, and the United States (G5), are taken to represent industrialized countries. With increasing yield on international bonds, the domestic currency depreciates, thereby increasing exports. Similarly, with an increase in international output, demand on Indian exports increases. Both these factors lead to an increase in *ED*.

Looking at domestic financial intermediation, the domestic deposit rate (*DR1*) and lending rates (*SBI*) have opposite signs with two lags. A higher deposit rate indicates liquidity constraint and presumably restrains expenditures with one lag, while a higher lending rate reduces them with apparently two lags. Concerning monetary and fiscal influences, excess acceleration in narrow money growth (*DDLM1DIS*) and growth in fiscal deficit (*DLCFGAP*) are found to significantly affect *ED* , but with one and two lags respectively. Money growth might itself be affected by the fiscal growth with a lag, although the two growth rates are not contemporaneously highly correlated. In addition the lag structure of the two variables reduces the possibility of endogeneity. The finding that the first lag of the fiscal variable is not significant need not indicate that fiscal effects are unimportant, but rather that they have not been adequately represented. Aside from the issue of adjusting the fiscal deficit variable to exclude endogeneity effects so as to capture its discretionary aspect, the inclusion of the monetary acceleration term could primarily reflect fiscal influences, given the dominant role of the budget in the process of generating the money supply.

Expanding the Alternative Specification

Considering that the inflation models discussed so far have rather limited explanatory power and the standard errors of regression are high, it is important to explore other sources of inflation in India. The particular limitation comes from the inadequacy of demand-side variables such as *ED* in explaining inflation. An alternative approach to modeling the demand side would be to adopt the monetarist way of modeling inflation. In this approach, which continues to dominate the Indian literature, the price equation is obtained by inverting the demand for money equation.[15] However, a pure demand-type monetarist model can at best provide only a poor and incomplete specification of the inflation process in India, because inflation movements may not result simply from excess money over nominal income alone as predicted by such models. It is revealing that in the annual commentary on price and distribution in various issues of the *Economic Survey*, particularly during the 1990s, the discussion emphasizes supply-side effects.[16] Also several studies have demonstrated supply-side dominance in the inflationary process in India.[17]

Nonetheless, even though the supply of money is dominated by the fiscal deficit and its monetary financing requirements, no model of inflation in India can ignore money. This is in keeping with general observations elsewhere.[18] Further, given a desire to collect inflation taxes, the possibility of some discretion in conducting monetary policy cannot be ignored. It is also important to identify a potential monetary aggregate that can be treated as exogenous to the inflationary process. In the current study, narrow money (M1) is identified as the preferred aggregate based on causality tests.

Fewer attempts have been made in recent years in India to address supply-side aspects of price formation behavior involving such variables as nominal wages and prices of important inputs and intermediates at the aggregate level. Balakrishnan modeled manufactured prices through an error correction model, using annual data for 1952–80, and found that labor and raw material costs were both significant determinants of inflation in the industrial sector.[19] Joshi and Little modeled food and nonfood inflation separately using money, consolidated fiscal deficit, food production, nonfood production, and import prices as explanatory variables.[20] Callen and Chang modeled WPI-based annual inflation for the period 1957–58 to 1997–98, with output gaps in

15. Pradhan and Subramanian (1998), Arif (1996), and Rangarajan (1998) are three studies where a predominantly monetarist approach has been used. Most recent among these, Pradhan and Subramanian (1998) model the CPI for urban nonmanual workers (CPI-UNME) and the CPI for agricultural labor (CPI-AL), which is dominated by food items. The series on CPI-AL has already been rendered outdated (GOI 1994, 1996), however, and the CPI-UNME has limited application in conducting monetary policy because of its very small basket size, which is focused on a particular segment of the labor force.

16. The *Economic Survey* is the official document of the Ministry of Finance issued before the presentation of the annual budget of the Government of India.

17. See, for example, Bhattacharya and Lodh (1990) and Singh (2002).

18. See, for example, McCallum (1994).

19. Balakrishnan (1991, 1992, 1994). Balakrishnan uses a dataset of old vintage that probably cannot be updated due to discontinuation in data compilation. Therefore, the usefulness of such a study is necessarily limited.

20. Joshi and Little (1994).

industrial and agricultural components of GDP, treating them separately as well as combined.[21] They found that the lagged industrial gap was insignificantly positive, while the lagged agricultural output gap was significantly negative and the lagged combined output gap insignificantly negative. This led them to conclude that inflation in India is structural. They did not analyze the contemporaneous gaps, however.

Drawing on the above considerations, we adopt the following strategy: First, an input-based basic model is created. This is augmented by adding demand-side variables in three alternative forms: monetarism, a Phillips curve output gap analysis, and the alternative *ED* approach.

A general form of the price equation based on costs can be written as follows.

$$(18) \qquad P = \mu \prod_{i=1}^{n} X_i^{\alpha_i}, \ \sum_{i=1}^{n} \alpha_i = 1$$

Here, X_i is the cost of the ith factor, α is the share of the ith factor in total cost and μ is a constant capturing the markup. Taking logs and then differentiating yields an input-based inflation equation. In an economywide model, the selection of such variables is limited. Most such inputs may form part of the WPI basket. However, we select those sensitive components that are important in the production process of several other goods and thus proxy a wider range of inputs. We consider petroleum mineral oil as a key energy source, and we proxy energy prices using the international price of oil (*WOP*), as well as the domestic price of mineral oil (*WPIMO*). *DLWOP* and *DLWPMO* represent inflation rates in world oil prices and domestic oil prices. Both variables must be considered because the government of India controls domestic oil prices using several instruments, and the inflation rates for domestic oil prices and world oil prices are not synchronized. However, the world oil price can affect inflation in India through other channels such as the international prices of goods and services, the transport cost of Indian exports, and expectations about future prices.

To capture agriculture-specific effects, we choose the price of fertilizer (*WPIFZ*) as another key input. Edible oil (*WPIEO*) is considered as a critical input to manufactured food. The weights of mineral oil, edible oil, and fertilizer in the overall WPI are about 6.7 percent, 2.5 percent, and 3.9 percent, respectively. The weight of manufactured goods is 63.8 percent; that

---

21. Callen and Chang (1999) also model quarterly inflation using an index of industrial production-based output gap and report signs of the output gap term that are not consistent with standard expectations.

of fuel, power, and lubricants is 14.2 percent; food products, 15.4 percent; and nonfood primary products including minerals, 6.6 percent.

Edible oil inflation, which is part of the manufacturing sector, is not highly correlated with inflation in that sector, partly because a substantial part of it is imported. In line with expectations, mineral oil and edible oil price inflation are not themselves correlated (table A-2). Therefore, both can be allowed in the inflation model as supply-side variables, where they proxy a sensitive component of import prices in India.[22] In addition, we also use world consumer price inflation ($DLCPIW$), as reported by the International Monetary Fund in its *International Financial Statistics*, to capture the general inflation trend worldwide. The sign of $DLCPIW$ is positive and significant, indicating the wider interaction of the Indian economy with the rest of the world.

Regarding wage price inflation, wages of public sector employees ($WAGPI$) are used as the benchmark salary for workers in other sectors, since India has no series to represent general wage price inflation. However, public sector wages are likely to influence the wages elsewhere in the economy and so considered a suitable proxy for wage inflation at the aggregate level.

Finally, to see if it provides a suitable hybrid, money is introduced into model C-2 as excess money growth over its long-term trend growth rate ($DLM1DIS$). Treating money in this way yields the same coefficients with or without the long-term trend growth The advantage of this definition, however, is that it corresponds better to the meaning of discretionary money growth. In addition, the selection of narrow money is motivated by the finding that this aggregate precedes inflation in the sense of Granger causality, while other aggregates have bidirectional causality. Although the introduction of money in model C-2 improves the model significantly, the coefficients of monetary growth are small at 0.35 including both lags, a finding that indicates that the scope for purely monetary control on inflation is limited, at least in the short run (table 7).

Table 8 incorporates the two additional and alternative specifications of the demand side in the basic supply-side platform. Model D-1 clearly indicates the supply dominance on the economy's inflation rate. Most of the supply-side variables remain significant. While contemporaneous as well as lagged $DGAPHP$ remains negative, however, the size of the coefficients is reduced significantly. All the variables contained in model C-1 retain their signs as well as size. The model D-1 is statistically well estimated with high R^2 and good forecasting ability, but the size of the demand-side effects is difficult to know because the sign of $DGAPHP$ is negative.

22. Singh (2002).

TABLE 7. Regression Results of Input-Based Inflation Models: Selected Models

Regressor/Dependent variable	1972–73 to 2002–03 Model C-1 DLWP		1972–73 to 2002–03 Model C-2 DLWP	
Intercept	0.107	(0.013)	0.027***	(0.014)
DLWAGEPI	0.018	(0.063)	0.020	(0.061)
DLWFZ	0.113**	(0.049)	0.108**	(0.046)
DLPEO	0.175*	(0.034)	0.159*	(0.035)
DLPMO	0.115***	(0.061)	0.129**	(0.057)
DLWOP	0.040**	(0.016)	0.038**	(0.014)
DLCPIW	0.230*	(0.081)	0.123	(0.086)
DLM1DIS			0.150**	(0.073)
DLM1DIS (–1)			0.155***	(0.076)
Summary statistics				
R^2	0.858		0.889	
$\bar{R}^2$	0.822		0.850	
SER	0.022		0.020	
F statistic, $F(k-1, n-k)$, $n = 31$, $k =$ no.	24.16	[0.00]	22.10	[0.00]
of regressors including intercept				
Diagnostic tests				
LM (1) serial correlation	0.03	[0.87]	0.05	[0.83]
LM (2) serial correlation	4.15	[0.13]	4.20	[0.12]
ARCH (2) test CHSQ (3)	0.92	[0.63]	1.30	[0.52]
Functional form CHSQ (1)	0.30	[0.58]	0.57	[0.45]
Normality CHSQ (2)	0.41	[0.82]	2.46	[0.29]
Predictive failure CHSQ (2)	0.35	[0.84]	0.69	[0.71]
Residual unit root				
Test statistics (DF)	–4.94		–4.99	

Note: Predictive failure tests are conducted by breaking the sample at 2002. Unit root test statistics are presented corresponding to the SBC model selection criteria in a unit root test with second order ADF.

*Significant at the 1 percent level. **Significant at the 5 percent level. ***Significant at the 10 percent level. Standard errors are in parentheses; *p*-values are in brackets.

Model D-2 is obtained by superimposing input price inflation rates on demand-side effects captured in *ED*. The coefficient of *ED* is positive and highly significant, but its size is reduced from the one obtained in model B-1, which was excessive. The R^2 is more than 0.90, but the model is not acceptable statistically because of the problem of serial correlation in errors. Model D-2 can be augmented in a number of ways, as indicated in table 8, by including more variables such as deviations in rainfall (*DRAIN*) and growth in foreign exchange reserves (*DLFERU*). Inclusion of these variables improves the explanatory and predictive power of the models. It may be noticed that *DRAIN* and *DLFERU* are also supply-side variables, which are observed to be significant with appropriate signs only in the presence of demand-side variables and the lagged inflation. These variables did not

TABLE 8. Regression Results of Hybrid Inflation Models with Demand- and Supply-Side Variables: Selected Models

Regressor/ Dependent variable	1972–73 to 2002–03 Model D-1 DLWP		1972–73 to 2002–03 Model D-2 DLWP		1972–73 to 2002–03 Model D-3 DLWP		1972–73 to 2002–03 Model D-4 DLWP	
Intercept	0.008	(0.012)	−0.025	(0.011)	−0.043*	(0.013)	−0.042*	(0.009)
DLWP (−1)	0.294***	(0.161)	0.840*	(0.131)	0.693*	(0.196)	1.032*	(0.113)
ED	0.517*	(0.162)	0.797*	(0.142)	0.722*	(0.195)	0.932*	(0.118)
DGAPHP								
DGAPHP (−1)								
DLWAGEPI	0.012	(0.054)	0.093**	(0.042)	0.101***	(0.054)	0.102**	(0.037)
DLWFZ	0.158*	(0.038)						
DLPEO	0.095**	(0.038)	0.082*	(0.031)	0.100**	(0.040)	0.066*	(0.027)
DLPMO	0.078	(0.053)	0.152**	(0.031)	0.180*	(0.039)	0.161*	(0.025)
DLWOP	0.035**	(0.013)	0.013	(0.010)	0.028*	(0.014)		
DLCPIW	0.148***	(0.080)			0.173**	(0.082)		
DLM1DIS			0.207*	(0.046)				
DLM1DIS (−1)			0.121**	(0.053)				
DRAINR			−0.115*	(0.032)	−0.087***	(0.044)	−0.111*	(0.030)
DLFERU			0.034*	(0.013)	0.036**	(0.016)	0.033*	(0.011)
DDLM1DIS							0.161*	(0.031)
DDLM1DIS (−1)							0.191*	(0.033)
Summary statistics								
R^2	0.906		0.949		0.912		0.963	
$\bar{R}^2$	0.870		0.923		0.879		0.947	
SER	0.019		0.014		0.018		0.012	
F statistic, $F(k-1, n-k)$, $n=31$, $k=$ no. of regressors including intercept	26.42	[0.00]	37.29	[0.00]	27.26	[0.00]	58.50	[0.00]
Diagnostic tests								
LM (1) serial correlation	2.87	[0.09]	0.74	[0.38]	0.91	[0.98]	0.01	[0.93]
LM (2) serial correlation	8.20	[0.02]	1.89	[0.38]	5.90	[0.05]	0.88	[0.65]
ARCH (2) test CHSQ (2)	1.13	[0.57]	0.67	[0.72]	2.19	[0.35]	0.46	[0.79]
Functional form CHSQ (1)	0.62	[0.43]	0.00	[0.95]	0.26	[0.61]	2.95	[0.09]
Normality CHSQ (2)	3.13	[0.21]	1.01	[0.60]	3.13	[0.21]	0.99	[0.61]
Predictive failure CHSQ (2)	0.20	[0.91]	2.89	[0.24]	0.21	[0.90]	1.57	[0.46]
Residual unit root								
Test statistics [DF/ADF(1)]	−6.62		−5.62		−5.31		−5.25	

Note: Predictive failure tests are conducted by breaking the sample at 2002. Unit root test statistics are presented corresponding to the SBC model selection criteria in a unit root test with second order ADF.

*Significant at the 1 percent level. **Significant at the 5 percent level.***Significant at the 10 percent level. Standard errors are in parentheses; p-values are in brackets.

improve the results for the models shown in table 5. Therefore, they could be considered to be conditionally significant. Also, in models D-3 and D-4, we removed *DLWFZ* (fertilizer price inflation) in favor of oil price inflation to improve the model specification. The fertilizer price could be partly determined by the oil price, which is one of the key inputs and also by weather conditions (during favorable weather, farmers are tempted to use more inputs, which raises the fertilizer price).

Adding these additional variables improves the statistical properties. Therefore, on statistical grounds we select model D-3 for further analysis and run a rolling regression for all the variables on the right-hand side taking a window size of 20, which is reasonable given the number of variables in the model. The results of the rolling regression are presented in figure 6. Clearly, contemporaneous money growth, edible oil price inflation, mineral oil price inflation, *ED*, lagged inflation, and wage price inflation remain significant.

A Strategy for Controlling Inflation in India

The empirical results discussed in this paper indicate that the determination of the inflation rate in India does not correspond to the stylized profile of the demand-dependant Phillips curve trade-off prevalent in the advanced economies, and the associated use of the nominal interest rate as the chief instrument with which to influence the inflation rate. Nor did the (shorter-run) monetarist model perform well. An alternative model was developed to better portray demand-side effects on inflation, while allowing for supply-side phenomena. This model performed much better under conditions prevailing in India. The estimation results indicate that the transmission lag between the expenditure stimulus, represented by the excess demand variable *ED*, and the inflation rate is quite short. This finding suggests a more active use of demand-management policy in inflation control, for example, through the use of fiscal policy, since it is more feasible to adopt and maintain a fiscal stance that is geared to projected developments a year ahead than for, say, two or more years.

An issue that needs to be clarified is that of the determinants of *ED*. For estimation purposes we assumed that fiscal effects could be captured by the unadjusted fiscal deficit. The results obtained did not bear this out. More research will be needed to identify precisely how fiscal instruments affect aggregate demand. In particular, a fiscal measure is required that separates out feedback effects of the economy on the budget. Under Indian institutional conditions, it seems likely that fiscal effects are being captured by the growth in M1—for which budget deficit financing requirements are prominent—in a context of interest rate restraint.

In any case, given the size of the fiscal deficit and its undoubted stimulus and crowding out effects, one component of the suggested approach to inflation targeting in the Indian context would be to rely more on fiscal restraint. If the forecast rate of inflation is likely to exceed the target rate, both the fiscal deficit and its monetary financing would need to be reduced. Of course, simply reducing the monetary financing would not be adequate, either because with unchanged interest rates the increased supply of government paper would be monetized, or because interest rates would increase and some private sector crowding out would occur through that channel.

It is also apparent that safeguards would need to be built in to ensure that political expediency does not lead to a watering down of the commitment to restrain inflation. India has adopted the Fiscal Responsibility and Budget Management Act, which is expected to ensure fiscal discipline. That law eases the concern that relying on fiscal instruments is more open to short-term political expediency. It may still be necessary to develop further the mechanisms for ensuring sound fiscal policy. A simple way to achieve this is to require that the government and the central bank agree on the size of the fiscal deficit and the amount of permissible monetary financing. If the agreement cannot be upheld, then the central bank would be free to raise interest rates.

Another component of *ED* is private expenditures, which in an expenditure approach to inflation control may also need to be restrained. Using the interest rate for this purpose may not be advisable if it has undesirable side effects; for example, the exchange rate could appreciate in a persistent manner that damages export prospects and leads to excessive imports. Asset valuations could become so depressed that long-lasting adverse effects on capital accumulation are created. Regulating the flow supply of credit that finances investment expenditures by adjusting liquidity ratios may be more appropriate, especially since that approach is likely to have weaker, less direct adverse effects on stock asset valuations.

Abstracting from an active use of the interest rate for purposes of inflation control raises the issue of what role the Reserve Bank of India (RBI) would play, aside from regulating liquidity ratios? A useful application would involve portfolio side operations. A key objective for portfolio operations would be to maintain a desired real interest rate, with the nominal interest adjusted whenever the underlying inflation rate deviates from target. From time to time, shifts in liquidity preferences result in asset transactions that either press interest rates above or below the target long-term level. Accommodating liquidity preference shifts through appropriate open market operations helps keep interest rates stable. If, for example, interest rates were to be reduced to very low levels, there would be at least two effects: first, the reward from postponing consumption would be reduced, which would tend to stimulate current consumption, and second, the discount factor used in establishing the present values of assets would be lowered, which would increase asset values and could have undesirable distortions on the goods market.

In this connection, some recent institutional changes affecting the operations of the RBI are of interest. The inflow of remittances and foreign institutional investors has added to the foreign exchange reserves at an average annual rate of about 18 percent during the last ten years. Concerned over possible currency appreciation and potential adverse effects on exports, the RBI has been undertaking heavy sterilization, with the result that its holdings of domestic assets are almost depleted. A new instrument called a market stabilization scheme (MSS) has now been implemented, whereby the RBI prints money that is kept in a sterilized government account, and pays interest on the equivalent Treasury bills to buy foreign exchange assets from the domestic market. This maneuver enables the RBI to restrain appreciation, but at the cost of keeping interest rates above international levels, the current wedge being about 2 percentage points. This, of course, tends to attract capital inflows, given the market's perception that the RBI will keep exchange rates stable, which then requires some further sterilization and reserve accumulation. A potential for conflict thus exists between interest rate levels that are better geared to internal requirements and those needed as a consequence of international considerations. One way of resolving the conflict would be to apply regulatory and control devices of various sorts to prevent excessive capital inflows.

Conclusion

Key support for the inflation-targeting framework has emerged from two important experiences. First, financial sector reforms and globalization have led to the breakdown of the broad money demand equation in several countries, including India, which has rendered monetary targeting less reliable. The second key reason has been a broader agreement worldwide on maintaining a lower level of inflation as it is detrimental to sustainable growth for various reasons including uncertainties in investment and savings behavior.

The advantage of the ITF is the direct relationship between the inflation target and the objective of monetary policy. However, there is an important question about the efficacy of monetary instruments in targeting inflation, especially in the case of developing countries where a number of rigidities persist because of direct and indirect controls and constraints. The economy may not fully employ its resources and the concept of a nonaccelerating rate of unemployment may not apply. The supply-side dominance appears sufficiently prominent that monetary stance, which relies on influencing the demand side, may be a misjudged risky option. Monetary policy may end up tightening the supply too much, or it may be too proactive, adversely affecting current income flows. Furthermore, it carries potential asset and balance sheet valuation effects that could be disruptive, in addition to adverse real exchange rate developments.

Even advanced economies have been exposed from time to time to costly consequences from persistent deviations of interest and exchange rates from equilibrium levels, and from increased volatility. For example, the real appreciation of the euro by almost 60 percent against the dollar in recent years is an important factor in the erosion of competitiveness and the sluggish economic performance that much of Europe is experiencing today. Even though interest rates are low in Europe, with the European Central Bank essentially operating as an inflation targeter, rates have been even lower in the United States. In addition, for some time now, prospective inflation rates have appeared to be well below target, spawning a "fear of deflation" syndrome that has led to an unprecedented lowering of nominal interest rates in several advanced economies.[23] The low interest rates in turn have contributed to an excessive upward revaluation of assets in these economies, including especially real estate, where low rates appear to have fueled a less productive investment boom in that area, while excessively stimulating

---

23. The concern with deflation is understandable in an economy, such as Japan's, that has experienced a long period of stagnation. However, it is more difficult to explain these concerns in such economies as the United States, the United Kingdom, or even Australia, since they are, or have been, booming. The unexpectedly benign inflation performance appears to have contributed to this fear of deflation and led to historically low interest levels as inflation targeting would counsel. There is an asymmetry when monetary authorities avow that they are able to identify a deflationary prospect but not an inflationary asset price bubble. Nonetheless, the deflationary reading may have been inappropriate, which illustrates the importance of distinguishing between supply shocks to inflation—productivity growth, the "China factor," or appreciating exchange rates—and demand-side shocks. The fact that the aforementioned economies have simultaneously run very large current account deficits on their balance of payments suggests that demand pressures were potentially inflationary but were dissipated through higher imports, especially from China.

consumption. On occasion regulatory facilities have also been found wanting, as evidenced by the Long-Term Capital Management Hedge Fund crisis or recent concerns that hedge funds are too lightly regulated.

A more cautious approach to inflation targeting in India would rely on both monetary and fiscal instruments and be closely coordinated with other instruments such as government buffer stock and other supply-side operations. If the forecast rate of inflation were to exceed the target rate, both the fiscal deficit and its monetary financing and the general availability of credit flows would be reduced, but without necessarily raising real interest rates. Of course, safeguards would need to be installed to ensure that political expediency does not lead to a watering down of the commitment to restraining inflation.

APPENDIX

Table A-1.   List of Variables and Their Descriptions

CGAP	Combined gap between outlay and revenue (Rs. mn).
CPIG5	Consumer Price Index for trade-weighted geometric mean of G-5 countries. Base: 1993–94.
CPIW	Consumer Price Index for world. Converted Base: 1993–94.
DR1	One-three year commercial bank deposit rates (percent per year).
DRAINR	Variation of actual rain fall from normal (fraction).
DSBI	sbi-sbi(−1).
ED	dlyn − [(1 + dlwpl)*(1 + dlyhp) − 1].
FERURB	Foreign exchange reserves, including gold (current US$ mn).
FERUWB	Gross international reserves, including gold (current US$ mn).
GAPHP	ly − lyhp.
GBG5	International government bond (GB) rates. Average of the monthly (line 61 of IFS).
INPT	Intercept.
IPIG5	Industrial production index of G5 countries (trade-weighted geometric mean).
LYHP	hpf(ly, 7).
LYNHP	hpf(lyn, 7).
M1	Narrow money M1 (Rs. mn).
RGDP	GDP at market prices, in constant 1993–94 prices (Rs. mn).
SBI	Average lending rate of State Bank of India (percent per year).
T	Time trend.
USGB	U.S. government bond yield (percent per year). Source: IFS: M111.61.
WAGPI	Index of per capita remunerations of public sector employees (1993 = 100).
WOP	World oil (crude) price index. Converted Base: 1993–94 = 100. Source: IFS.
WPI	World price index of all commodities at 1993–94 prices. Source: ES.
WPIEO	WPI for edible oil (domestic).
WPIFD	WPI for primary food (domestic).
WPIFZ	WPI for fertilizer (domestic).
WPIMO	WPI for mineral oil (domestic).
Y	GDP at market prices, in constant 1993–94 prices (Rs. mn).
YN	GDP at market prices, in current LCU (Rs. mn).

TABLE A-2. Statistical Properties of Selected Variables, 1972–2004

Variable(s)	Maximum	Minimum	Mean	Std. deviation	Skewness	Kurtosis-3	Coef. of variation	Unit root test[a]
DLWP	0.2247	-0.0109	0.0762	0.0507	1.0484	1.1452	0.67	-4.41
ED	0.0716	-0.2000	-0.0028	0.0487	-1.8686	6.3217	17.46	-5.86
DLPEO	0.4021	-0.2422	0.0747	0.1341	-0.1985	0.1058	1.79	-7.66
DLPMO	0.5248	0.0000	0.1058	0.1134	1.9208	4.1505	1.07	-4.74
DLWOP	0.8520	-0.5508	0.0878	0.3070	0.7943	0.8114	3.50	-4.23
DLM1DIS	0.1034	-0.2474	-0.0071	0.0602	-1.7212	5.9565	8.48	-6.93
DRAINR	0.1617	-0.2472	-0.0353	0.1057	-0.2486	-0.6377	2.99	-7.42
DLWAGPI	0.2838	-0.0408	0.1178	0.0772	-0.0434	0.2544	0.66	-6.53
DLFERUWB	0.5912	-0.3928	0.1408	0.2328	-0.2968	-0.1007	1.65	-3.81
DGAPHP	0.0490	-0.0871	-0.0001	0.0246	-1.1346	3.2304	364.00	-8.05
DLCPIW	0.2443	0.0327	0.1186	0.0565	0.0618	-0.7032	0.48	-1.47
DLWPFZ	0.5770	-0.1395	0.0646	0.1356	2.0055	4.9481	2.10	-4.47

a. Critical value at 5 percent = –2.99. DLCPIW demonstrates a structural break at 1994–96 when inflation falls from previous high levels of around 20 percent to low levels of around 5 percent after 1996.

T A B L E A - 3. Correlation Matrix of the Selected Variables, 1972–2004

	DLWP	ED	DLPEO	DLPMO	DLWOP	DLM1DIS	DRAINR	DLWAGPI	DLFERUWB	DGAPHP	DLCPIW	DLWPFZ
DLWP	1.00											
ED	0.22	1.00										
DLPEO	0.57	0.54	1.00									
DLPMO	0.66	-0.18	0.07	1.00								
DLWOP	0.49	0.15	0.14	0.48	1.00							
DLM1DIS	0.06	0.09	0.00	-0.15	-0.12	1.00						
DRAINR	-0.15	0.01	-0.14	-0.14	-0.25	0.19	1.00					
DLWAGPI	0.12	-0.36	-0.37	0.32	0.09	-0.19	0.12	1.00				
DLFERUWB	0.05	0.26	0.09	0.02	0.18	0.07	-0.17	-0.18	1.00			
DGAPHP	-0.35	-0.29	-0.26	-0.17	-0.30	-0.20	0.66	0.14	-0.35	1.00		
DLCPIW	0.44	-0.04	0.18	0.09	0.00	0.24	0.24	0.16	-0.24	0.00	1.00	
DLWPFZ	0.65	-0.41	0.10	0.74	0.16	-0.05	-0.13	0.40	0.07	-0.05	0.28	1.00

Comments and Discussion

Rajnish Mehra*: The authors, whose analysis builds on their earlier work, have produced a thought-provoking paper.[1] They highlight many interesting issues regarding the policy implications of inflation targeting and draw upon the experience of countries that have adopted this framework. I do, however, take issue with the methodology of the study—that of testing an atheoretical model on historical data and then using it for policy analysis. My specific comments on the paper appear at the end of this discussion.

I begin by focusing on some of the issues raised in the paper and by making a distinction between targeting inflation and inflation targeting.

Targeting Inflation

The rational for targeting inflation is the lesson learned over the past three decades, about which there is broad consensus, that positive expected inflation, above some low rate, is welfare reducing.

There is less agreement on how this low inflation state should be achieved. In the late 1960s, the prevailing view, championed by Paul Samuelson and Robert Solow, advocated the use of control theory for formulating and implementing macroeconomic policy. A minority, notably Milton Friedman, argued against this, claiming that policy acted with long, variable, and unpredictable lags. With the advent of the Lucas Critique and the Time-Inconsistency literature, the later view has gradually prevailed.[2]

Today, most academics and policymakers accept the view that the economy is complex and that control theory is inappropriate for macroeconomic stabilization. It is also the view, articulated by Friedman and Phelps, that there is no long-run Phillips-curve trade-off.[3]

---

*I specially thank Henning Bohn, Barry Bosworth (the editor), John Donaldson, and Edward Prescott for their insightful comments. I am grateful to the participants of the India Policy Forum Conference for a stimulating discussion.
1. See, in particular, Chand (1997), McKibbin and Singh (2003), and Singh and Kalirajan (2003).
2. Kydland and Prescott (1977).
3. Friedman (1968); Phelps (1968).

Whether there is indeed a short-run Phillips-curve relationship and whether monetary policy can beneficially exploit this short-run trade-off between inflation and the output gap is a long-standing dispute that is still at the center of monetary policy discussions. Friedman and Lucas have argued that given the inherent complexity of the economy and our incomplete knowledge of it, monetary policy should be limited to achieving nominal stability. Their arguments are based on the view that although monetary policy has strong short-run real effects, there is no way to exploit them beneficially. They suggest that a response in the form of a k-percent rule for money growth is the best way to achieve nominal stability. Svensson and Woodford on the other hand, argue that there are (limited) short-run exploitable trade-offs.[4] In their analysis, they describe a framework involving optimal exploitation of the short-run trade-off.

Irrespective of one's position on the issues discussed above, the rational for targeting inflation is clear. *Lower inflation rates lead to better operating characteristics for the economy.* See, for example, figure 7, which plots the real growth of gross national product versus inflation for India for the postwar period.

FIGURE 7.   **Real GNP Growth Rate versus Inflation for India**

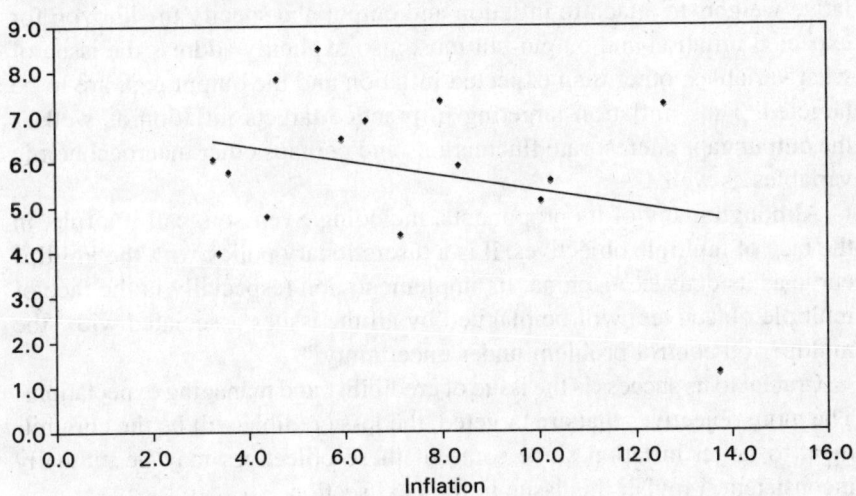

4. Svensson (1999); Svensson and Woodford (2004).

Inflation Targeting

What is inflation targeting? This is not an easy question to answer as there are many variations on the theme. As broadly accepted, it is a framework for monetary policy *whereby a short-term interest rate instrument responds to deviations of expected future inflation from the target rate and to deviations of output from its full-employment level.* It explicitly incorporates the type of Phillips-curve trade-off discussed earlier. An important feature of inflation targeting is the articulation of this policy—to clearly communicate to the public the plans and objectives of the monetary authorities. This is intended to serve as a quasi-commitment mechanism.

One variant—"the hard version"— is the original Svensson framework.[5] It argues that the central bank should concentrate only on inflation to the exclusion of any other objectives. There are a host of other variations— "the soft versions"—with inflation as only one of the targeted variables. The variants differ depending on what is included in the targeted set. Informal conversations with central banking officials in a number of countries lead me to believe that inflation targeting in practice is almost never implemented in its hard version.

Several questions must then be addressed before a soft version can be effectively implemented. The policymaker must not only articulate the relative weights to attach to inflation and output and specify the horizon for expected inflation and output but must also explicitly address the issue of what variables, other than expected inflation and the output gap, are to be targeted. Thus, inflation targeting in practice targets inflation as well as the output gap, interest rate fluctuations and perhaps other macroeconomic variables as well.

Although many of its proponents, including Svensson, call it a rule, in the face of multiple objectives, it is a discretionary policy with the Phillips curve as its deus ex machina. Its implementation (especially in the face of multiple objectives) will be plagued by all the issues associated with "the multiperiod control problem under uncertainty."[6]

Crucial to its success is the issue of credibility and managing expectations. The more objectives that are targeted, the less credible will be the commitment to target inflation since some of these objectives may be mutually inconsistent. I revisit this issue in the next section.

5. Svensson (1997). Henning Bohn suggested this "hard version" usage, which is the version "tested" by the authors in the paper.
6. By postulating a specific lag structure, Svensson and others convert the multiperiod problem to a sequence of static problems and circumvent some of these issues and their implications.

There is little doubt that a central bank can control inflation. This control, though not perfect due to macroeconomic shocks (such as oil supply shocks) involves costs, which may not be (politically) acceptable. Economic agents, of course take this into account when forming their expectations.

The United States does not explicitly target inflation; in contrast, Canada and the United Kingdom are explicit inflation targeters.[7] In all three countries inflation is low, but it is difficult to attribute this categorically to ITF programs. Ball and Sheridan examine a sample of twenty industrialized countries, seven of which are targeters and thirteen nontargeters.[8] They conclude that on a number of dimensions there is no evidence that inflation targeting improves economic performance. Others, notably Bernanke, King, Mishkin, Svensson and several central bankers (of course!) beg to differ. In the absence of credibility, inflation targeting is just another value-loaded term (with a positive valence).

The Indian Context

Implementing inflation targeting in India raises a number of issues, some technical, others more serious, which address credibility. These include:

—India lacks a comprehensive price index that adjusts for quality and technical innovation. This "measurement issue" could be a major impediment to implementing inflation targeting effectively. Current estimates are most likely upwardly biased.

—What is the evidence on the Phillips curve in India, given the structure of the labor force?

—To what extent will the policy of pegging the rupee to the dollar undermine the credibility of a central bank that promises to inflation target? Pegging the currency and inflation targeting are not in general, mutually consistent. If an inflationary shock mandates high rates in the one country, while low rates persist in the other, capital will flow to the high-rate country, putting pressure on the currency peg. To peg the rupee to the dollar, the Reserve Bank of India has engaged in a classic sterilization policy, buying foreign currency and bonds and offsetting these purchases by selling domestic bonds. Given that the domestic assets of the RBI are rapidly being

7. With Bernanke's appointment as the Chairman of the Federal Reserve, this will probably change as, unlike his predecessor, Bernanke has long supported the concept. It should be noted that by law the Federal Reserve is mandated to pursue maximum employment.

8. Ball and Sheridan (2003).

depleted, it is only a matter of time before the monetary base will be affected—with the concomitant effect on inflation.

—What is the role of current asset valuation levels? Inflation targeting in its hard version also precludes intervening in asset markets in case of a bubble. As Bernanke and Gertler emphasize: "Importantly, it also implies that policy should *not* respond to changes in asset prices, except in so far as they signal changes in expected inflation."[9] Asset valuations in India are at an all-time high. The Indian stock market had risen by more than 90 percent between June 2004 and June 2005 and continues to rise. Figure 8 illustrates this dramatic increase in valuation. The 15 percent decline in the stock index on May 17, 2004, surely had information content regarding fundamental valuations! Again this raises the issue of credibility.

—What about taxation. Given a large parallel economy and political considerations that preclude the taxation of certain sectors of the economy such as agriculture, an inflation tax may be a necessary evil. There is always a temptation for governments to let inflation exceed expectations and needless to say the populace is aware of this! Credibility issues once again are at the forefront of concern.

FIGURE 8. Market Value of Equity in the Indian Stock Market

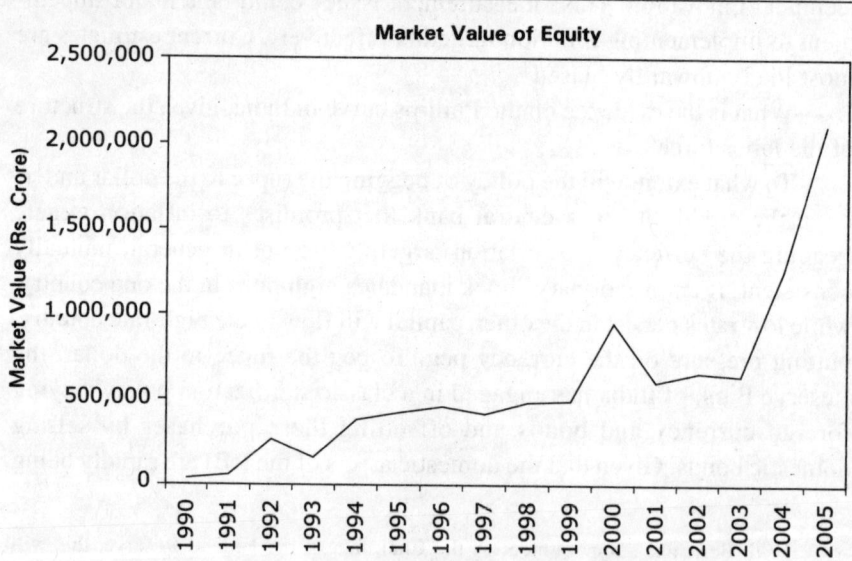

9. Bernanke and Gertler (1999, p. 18).

Inflation in India is currently running at about 5.6 percent with GDP growth at a healthy 8 percent. The current environment is ideal for embarking on an inflation targeting program. In the absence of a comprehensive price index, the core CPI should be targeted after allowing for a bias in measurement of, say, 1 percent. An advantage of this is that it avoids potentially destabilizing policy responses. The credibility issues raised above would have to be addressed in a transparent manner. The challenge would be to articulate a policy that is credible but not vacuous.

Comments and Quibbles

The paper addresses many, sometimes orthogonal, issues. This is both a strength and a weakness. On the positive side, it alerts the reader to a host of interesting questions; on the other hand, at times it appears to lack a unifying theme.

The paper starts out by "testing" a reduced form of the Svensson model. The authors conclude it does poorly when confronted with Indian data (see table 5). The authors then propose two alternative models: the first focuses on excess demand, where they essentially replace the output gap in the Svensson model with the fiscal deficit. The other is an input-based supply-side model that examines industrial commodities and their price effects on overall inflation. These extensions are completely ad hoc and atheoretical. The authors provide no justification, either empirical or theoretical, for their formulations. In fact the "excess demand" model is a radical change of the Svensson formulation—a change from "levels" to "growth rates." They find that these alternatives are an improvement in the sense that certain coefficients are "significant." I disagree with this as a research methodology especially for formulating policy.

Their key conclusion is that in the Indian context, the use of fiscal policy rather than monetary instruments is likely to be more effective in controlling inflation.

I remain skeptical. To quote Friedman, "Inflation is always and everywhere a monetary phenomena." The effectiveness of policies predicated on using fiscal instruments is an open question. The fiscal deficit is a far more difficult policy instrument to control—quickly and smoothly—than are monetary instruments. While the coordination of fiscal and monetary policy may sound good in theory, it can lead to undesirable outcomes since these policies act with differing lags and over different time intervals. The formulation in the paper implicitly assumes that these time intervals are identical.

The authors emphasize that Indian inflation in recent years appears to be motivated by supply rather than demand shocks. However, there is no evidence in the literature that ITF programs work better under supply-induced inflation than under demand-induced inflation, and I would argue that that this is not a relevant distinction at our current level of understanding. From a practical point of view, as mentioned earlier, the lack of a comprehensive price index in India that adjusts for quality and technical innovation is a major impediment to inflation targeting.

The authors also argue that a supply side model of inflation works best for India and that the lag between an expenditure stimulus and inflation is shorter for India. Unfortunately, they do not offer any cross-country comparison to substantiate this claim or indeed, their observation that the nominal interest rate appears to be a less powerful instrument in India than in other countries.

The paper notes that the ITF has had variable success across countries but does not provide data to support this, nor does it address whether the Indian subcontext resembles the countries for which the policy has been a success or where it has failed. There *are* differences between developed and emerging markets.[10]

In closing, I compliment the authors for initiating a serious debate on the relative merits of inflation targeting and its appropriateness as a policy prescription for India. Their paper will undoubtedly be an impetus for further research in this important area.

Kenneth Kletzer: The widespread popularity of inflation targeting as a framework for monetary policy quite naturally raises the question whether India should also adopt an inflation-targeting regime. The reputation of inflation targeting has been bolstered by the recent ability of the central banks of several industrialized countries to maintain low and stable inflation without neglecting real economic performance. Further, the adoption of the inflation rate as the nominal anchor by some emerging market central banks, particularly in Latin America, has met with some apparent success as well as providing useful learning experiences.

In this interesting and well-done paper, Chand and Singh ask whether inflation targeting would be appropriate for adoption by the RBI given the structure of the Indian economy. They emphasize that the analytical arguments for inflation targeting are based on specific models of the dynamics

---

10. See, for example, tables 1 and 2 in Fraga, Goldfajn, and Minella (2003), which highlight these differences.

of inflation and aggregate output fluctuations and that the nominal interest rate takes the central role as the instrument of monetary policy. The primary argument of Chand and Singh is that the basic assumptions of the macroeconomic models used to motivate a monetary policy regime targeting inflation with interest rate instruments fail to match the dynamics of inflation and output growth in India. Certainly, the empirical evidence presented in the paper demonstrates the poor relationship of the inflationary process underlying monetary policy analysis in advanced industrialized countries to the macroeconomic data for the Indian economy.

Much of the analysis and criticism of applying inflation targeting in emerging markets centers on countries with open capital accounts, raising concerns about the conflicting objectives of price level stabilization and nominal exchange rate stabilization, as well as the consequences of inflation stabilization for interest rate volatility. Chand and Singh raise these issues in their argument that India is not a good candidate for an inflation-targeting framework for monetary policy. At the same time, proponents of inflation targeting often emphasize the importance of building credibility around announced inflation goals in emerging market economies as several emerging market governments have adopted inflation-targeting regimes with varying degrees of discretion. Rather than reiterate the credibility question, Chand and Singh concentrate on the modeling issue—how does the inflationary and real growth process work in India.

In contrast with most emerging market economies that are candidates for inflation-targeting monetary regimes, India restricts international capital flows and has not liberalized financial capital outflows to any significant extent. An important and open question concerns the appropriate monetary policy framework for India in anticipation of further liberalization of the economy and integration with international financial markets. The motivating issue for the Chand and Singh paper is the analysis of appropriate choices of monetary policy rules for the Indian economy. In my view, an important challenge for macroeconomists considering India is the design of monetary policy for the transition from an economy that had repressed financial markets to one with an open capital account. That is, how should the monetary policy framework complement the on-going process of economic reform and liberalization in India. I turn to these broader issues after discussing the particulars of the Chand and Singh paper.

Chand and Singh focus their attention on the theoretical analysis of inflation targeting exemplified by the basic model used by Svensson.[11]

11. Svensson (1997).

A conventional reduced-form model leads to a simple nominal interest rate rule for a central bank that seeks to minimize deviations from a given inflation target. The policy rule derived by Svensson is a strict inflation-targeting version of the Taylor rule that specifies the nominal interest rate as an increasing function of the deviation of current inflation from the inflation target and of the output gap. Chand and Singh question whether such a model is an appropriate empirical representation of the structure of the Indian economy, providing econometric evidence that it is not. They propose an alternate model of the aggregate adjustment process for the Indian economy, derive a policy rule for an inflation-targeting central bank and ask whether a version of an inflation-targeting regime makes sense in this new model.

An important feature of the model given in equations 9–11 is the dependence of inflation on the difference between the nominal growth rates of GDP and potential GDP. This implies a proportional relationship between the expected change in inflation and the expected difference between the growth rate of real GDP and real potential GDP. This is a change in the interpretation of the output gap term in the basic model and implies that inflation remains constant if the growth rate equals the potential growth rate. The innovation in the proposed model appears in equation 11, which relates the growth rate of nominal GDP to the growth of the public sector budget deficit as a share of GDP and the change in the real rate of interest. Relating the real interest rate and real fiscal expansions to nominal output growth seems a bit unusual, although the relationship between fiscal policy growth, real interest rates, and the growth of real output can be disentangled with algebra along with an equation for the change in the inflation rate.

The major implication of the Chand and Singh model of inflation and optimal policy for a central bank that seeks to minimize a conventional loss function around an inflation target is that there are two policy instruments, the nominal interest rate, and the growth of the public sector budget deficit as a share of output. Their main observation about the dynamics of the macroeconomy for India is that fiscal policy is an important driving variable for real output growth and inflation. Their econometric analysis lends support to the inclusion of fiscal expansion in a traditional way in the short-run aggregate supply equation. In the derived optimal policy, the change in the nominal interest rate is increasing in the inflation rate as well as in the deviation of the current inflation rate from the targeted inflation rate given a constant deficit to GDP ratio. The interpretation of this model is that the nominal interest rate can be used to guide monetary policy built around an inflation target if the expansion of the fiscal deficit is exogenous. There are two instruments and either can be used. If fiscal policy is made autonomously (a reasonable assumption in my view), then the central bank can implement an inflation target using the nominal interest rate. The model is consistent with the claim that perpetual growth in the public sector budget deficit forces tighter monetary policies to contain inflation. The real interest rate rises with the growth of the deficit, although the model does not address policy sustainability. That is, not all the necessary conditions for an optimal policy are in the text; sustainability should restrict the fiscal policy variable so that its inclusion as a policy instrument is not redundant.

The econometrics reveals that the textbook model used as a benchmark does not perform well against Indian data. Introducing supply-side effects such as commodity price inflation and public sector wage growth is reasonable, as is the inclusion of changes in fiscal policy. The results do not really negate the applicability of an inflation-targeting regime until losses other than deviations from the inflation target are included in the derivation of optimal policy. The costs of real interest rate and output growth volatility are not included in the objective function of the central bank.

There are important reasons to think about using a nominal interest rate rule to meet the objectives of price and output growth stability in the case if India. Some of these are common to emerging market economies that have adopted inflation-targeting frameworks, notably Chile and Brazil. Those two experiences may be very useful for considering the applicability of inflation targeting for India. One caveat is that both countries liberalized capital account transactions some time ago. Lessons learned from other emerging market economies might be appropriate for India after the relaxation of controls on capital outflows. However, credibility should be crucial for the success of inflation-stabilizing discretionary monetary policy in any context. The route to achieving credibility is not easy to identify, although current thinking focuses on the importance of strong monetary institutions, a sound fiscal and financial environment, and transparency in central bank governance and policy.

One issue of importance is whether an inflation target that takes account of output growth makes sense before liberalization. A simple answer is that the more credible central bank policy is before international financial integration, the more able are monetary authorities to manage inflation and exchange rate volatility. The broad preconditions for adopting inflation targeting are reviewed by Chand and Singh.[12] These are the same conditions just listed as appropriate starting points for gaining credibility for price

12. Mishkin (2004) elaborates on each.

stability, and they are also reasonable preconditions for a successful liberalization of the capital account. Another issue of importance for an emerging market economy whose central bank is pursuing an inflation target is the need to give the inflation rate precedence over the nominal exchange rate. As Chand and Singh note, resistance to floating is a common feature of monetary policy in emerging markets, creating a conflict in the choice of a nominal anchor. The track record for the rupee and for exchange rate intervention in India suggests that monetary authorities care very much about exchange rate volatility. As a concern for inflation targeting, though, this should not be seen as a primary issue for now because the conflict between these objectives only comes into play with an open capital account.

In the Indian context, the first important barrier to adopting inflation targeting is the continuing growth of outstanding public debt and deficits as a share of GDP. But the debt and deficit of the public sector is a barrier to progress on any macroeconomic front. The potential monetization of deficits and debt interferes with any effort to establish credibility for maintaining low inflation with or without any manner of central bank independence. Financial repression plays a significant role for financing public sector deficits without rising inflation in India. Further financial market liberalization and reform will reduce the capacity of the government to deliver low inflation by issuing long-maturity public debt at modest interest rates, and full capital account liberalization should eliminate the government's ability to do so. A worry should be that any credibility gained by the RBI from its choice of monetary regime in the current fiscal situation with capital controls will be lost immediately at the very time that is needed most, with the liberalization of capital outflows.

The second precondition is a sound domestic financial sector with adequate prudential regulation and supervision. Again, this is also a condition for avoiding financial crises in an economy with free financial capital mobility and for improving the allocation of savings and investment and overall macroeconomic performance in the domestic economy. It may be useful to observe that the adverse conditions faced by the RBI for predicting the successful adoption of an inflation-targeting framework for monetary policy are the same deficiencies that arise in any discussion of macroeconomic policy for India. Indeed, the virtues of each transcend the particular choice of targets and instruments for monetary policy.

A tough question is how the central bank gains or maintains credibility in the environment of Indian fiscal policymaking. The literature on inflation targeting (and similar policies) raises the problem that a targeting regime may be doomed if monetary policy is subordinate to fiscal policy. Questions that need to be considered include how the RBI should conduct monetary policy when government debt is rising as a share of the economy at the same time that domestic financial reform is under way. Central bankers face the unpleasant task of an increasing prospect of inflating away outstanding domestic currency debt if efforts to improve domestic financial intermediation by reducing financial repression proceed. The critique of inflation targeting in emerging markets concerns countries that do not have effective capital controls, as does India. These countries are, therefore, susceptible to capital account reversals and unable to resist exchange rate fluctuations without sacrificing the inflation rate objective. These are not yet the issues for India; adopting a monetary policy regime to accompany fiscal reform, accommodate financial reform and meet the importance of stability of the inflation rate are major issues.

Partha Sen: This paper seeks to study the appropriateness (or otherwise) of adopting inflation targeting in India. Two sets of issues are addressed: Is inflation targeting the appropriate policy framework in developing countries? What is the process that determines inflation in India? The first issue is addressed rather perfunctorily. The paper's main focus is on the second one.

Here I address both issues but with more emphasis on the first. I shall argue that inflation targeting is not necessarily appropriate in developing economies—a position that Chand and Singh share (see table 1 and figure 1). Given this position, the inflation-generating process in India becomes (somewhat) less important.

Inflation targeting is the flavor of the month for monetary policymakers. Whether it will prove to be more durable, only time will tell. Theoretically, there is a weak case for it.[13] But as of 2005, about eight developed economies and thirteen emerging market economies are classified as having inflation-targeting regimes. Preliminary evidence suggests that it seems to work well in reducing inflation in both developed and developing countries.[14]

What does an inflation-targeting regime entail? Mishkin stipulates five conditions that such a regime must meet:

1) The public announcement of medium-term numerical targets for inflation; 2) an institutional commitment to price stability as the primary goal of monetary policy, *to which other goals are subordinated* (emphasis added); 3) an information inclusive strategy in which many variables, and not just monetary aggregates or the exchange rate, are used for deciding the setting of policy instruments;

13. See, for example, Buiter (2004).
14. Fraga, Goldfajn, and Minella (2003); Mishkin and Schmid-Hebbel (2005).

4) increased transparency of the monetary policy strategy through communication with the public and the markets about the plans, objectives, and decisions of the monetary authorities; and 5) increased accountability of the central bank for attaining its inflation objectives.[15]

Mishkin also notes the macroeconomic features of developing or emerging market economies that make them different from those with developed capital markets: "These are: 1) Weak fiscal institutions, 2) Weak financial institutions including government prudential regulation and supervision, 3) Low credibility of monetary institutions, 4) Currency substitution and liability dollarization; and 5) Vulnerability to sudden stops (of capital inflows)."[16]

Exogenous shocks are magnified in emerging economies because of their underdeveloped markets. Broner and Rigobon look at twenty-three developed and thirty-five emerging market economies and find that capital flows to the emerging market countries are 1.79 times more volatile than those to the developed countries, while the (left) skewness (that is, proneness to crises) is 1.5 times as high.[17] In addition to "fundamentals," emerging market economies experience more contagion and persistence.

It is important to note that most of the emerging market economies that have embraced inflation targeting have had a (recent) history of high (even hyper-) inflation. Among them, at least the Latin American countries are very open and suffer (more) from dollarization. Building credibility is very important for them because lack of credibility acts as a distortion and could cause reversal of very sensible policies.[18] But because of weak financial markets (and institutions, generally), the central bank cannot ignore fluctuations in interest rates, exchange rates, supply-side variables, and (of course) output. It is very difficult to claim that it is a regime of inflation targeting only—Mervyn King would rather not be an "inflation nutter," but at least he may have the choice that developing country policymakers often do not.

Thus is there a case for India adopting inflation targeting? Does one size fit all? In the Indian context one does not need to worry too much about low credibility of the central bank and dollarization (points three and four above). India's fiscal institutions have shown themselves to be very weak in the recent past and that could compromise the credibility of the Reserve

15. Mishkin (2004, p. 3).
16. Mishkin (2004, p. 5).
17. Broner and Rigobon (2004). Note that their data is annual (as is Chand and Singh's) and goes back to 1965. This perhaps understates the volatility in recent times as the emerging market economies have opened up their capital accounts.
18. Calvo has drawn attention to this in a macroeconomic context for over twenty years.

Bank of India in the future. This could be compounded by the further opening up of the capital account. In that scenario capital flow reversals (the
fifth point above) could become important, but right now it is not a source
of headache. But if credibility of the RBI is not an issue today and if, even
with an inflation-targeting regime, we would need to look at "other things"
(other than inflation, that is), where is the need for such a regime? This is
not to deny that the RBI should be given functional independence and its
policies should be less opaque.[19]

Let me turn to Chand and Singh's empirical work. It is motivated by
Svensson, who sets up a model for expository reasons and shows what an
inflation-targeting regime could achieve.[20] Chand and Singh accuse him of
looking at only demand variables and neglecting the supply side. While
that is literally true, it is not a criticism against inflation-targeting models
in general. Fraga, Goldfajn, and Minella discuss both supply shocks and
inflation of administratively priced goods—the message seems to be that
the original supply shocks should be accommodated (one time only).[21]

Chand and Singh use annual data since 1972 to estimate the inflation
process in India. Annual data—that is, what is available—is not very useful
for the authorities interested in inflation. This is even more true of a developing economy—the structure has changed so much that to pretend that the
data set represents the same "model" is far-fetched. Also the strict distinction
between a demand-side and a supply-side variable becomes blurred as the
collection of data becomes more infrequent.[22]

Chand and Singh's preferred model (D3) of (a backward-looking)
Phillips curve has a term representing excess demand, and various terms
denoting cost push effects, apart from the lagged endogenous variable. The
supply-side variables are wage increases of public sector employees, inflation in world oil prices and the domestic market price of oil, world inflation,
and changes in rainfall and foreign exchange reserves. Statistical fit notwithstanding, if this is all we can say about the inflationary process in India,
then it is not very much.

Aggregate demand is captured by the lagged fiscal deficit and the nominal
interest rate. Now, fiscal deficit is a very poor indicator of the fiscal stance of

19. Chand and Singh discuss monetary targeting and exchange rate targeting. Hence I
do not repeat these points.
20. Svensson (1997).
21. Fraga, Goldfajn, and Minella (2004).
22. See their lagged fiscal deficit entering aggregate demand. Even in India, a road can
be constructed in a year's time—is the expenditure on the road demand-side or supply-
side?

the government, and the determinants of nominal interest rates have undergone substantial liberalization. Thus from the viewpoint of conduct of monetary policy, these indicators do not add much. Chand and Singh also claim that changes in foreign exchange reserves can be viewed as a supply-side phenomenon! It might have been better to write out a parsimonious model and test the price implications of it, rather than the kitchen-sink approach in the paper.

General Discussion

T. N. Srinivasan expressed frustration that much of the discussion of macroeconomic policy lacked the framework that a strong theoretical model anchored in general equilibrium would provide. At the same time, he agreed that many of the more coherent models, such as real business cycle, appeared to have little to do with reality. But the lack of a clear underlying model made it difficult to evaluate the policy, he said. Others argued that the inflation-targeting framework incorporated many elements of the Keynesian model, something that was thought to be out of fashion. Some participants questioned whether India's nontraditional labor markets precluded a Phillips-curve type analysis.

Participants noted a very large decline in inflation since the 1980s in numerous countries in all parts of the globe. To what extent was that the result of a greater emphasis by policymakers on reducing inflation, or could it be traced to other factors, such as depressed commodity markets and, until recently, low energy prices? Countries that experienced significant declines in inflation relied on a wide range of different monetary policies.

Several participants were concerned about the focus on the interest rate as the primary tool for implementing the inflation-targeting framework. In India the two most important interest rates were the bank loan and deposit rates, neither of which was directly influenced by the Reserve Bank. India did not yet have large financial markets with market-determined rates. There were doubts that financial asset markets in Indian had sufficient depth to absorb large changes in interest rates without the risk of a meltdown.

An additional concern was the adequacy of the price index that would be used. The wholesale price index had the broadest commodity coverage, but it excluded a lot of services. It also lacked adjustments for technological innovations and quality improvements.

Others questioned how the policy would affect the ability to respond to other concerns, such as price bubbles in asset markets or large exchange rate movements. Conversely, it was pointed out that bubbles in equity markets were very hard to define, particularly in India where some firms had experienced very high rates of earnings growth. One participant noted that the uncertainty over India's future growth potential meant nominal income targeting was unlikely to be a viable alternative for setting monetary policy.

Some participants were struck by the weak influence of aggregate demand on inflation and questioned whether monetary policy had sufficient impact on the economy to be effective in controlling inflation. They thought that India in its current stage would be better served by a coordination of fiscal and monetary actions.

References

Aghenor, Pierre-Richard. 2002. "Exchange Rate: An Introduction to Inflation Targeting." In *Inflation Targeting: Design, Performance, Challenges;* edited by Norman Loyaza and Raimundo Soto. Santiago: Central Bank of Chile.

Arif, R. R. 1996. "Money Demand Stability: Myth or Reality—An Econometric Analysis." DRG Study 13. Reserve Bank of India, Mumbai.

Balakrishnan, Pulapre. 1991. *Pricing and Inflation in India.* New Delhi: Oxford University Press.

———. 1992. "Industrial Price Behaviour in India." *Journal of Development Economics* 37: 309–26.

———. 1994. "How Best to Model Inflation in India." *Journal of Policy Modeling* 16: 677–83.

Ball, Lawrence, and Niamh Sheridan. 2003. "Does Inflation Targeting Matter?" Paper preapred for a National Bureau of Economic Research conference on Inflation Targeting, January 23–25, Bal Harbor, Fla.

Bhattacharya, B. B., and Madhumita Lodh. 1990. "Inflation in India: An Analytical Survey." *Artha Vijnana* 32 (1): 25–68.

Bernanke, Ben, and Mark Gertler. 1999. "Monetary Policy and Asset Volatility." *Economic Review* 84 (4): 17–52.

Bernanke, Ben, S. Thomas Laubach, Adam S. Posen, and Frederic S. Mishkin. 2001. *Inflation Targeting.* Princeton: Princeton University Press.

Broner, Fernando A., and Roberto Rigobon. 2004. "Why are Capital Flows so Much More Volatile in Emerging than in Developed Countries?" Economics Working Papers 862, University of Pompeu Fabra.

Buiter, Willem H. 2004. "The Elusive Welfare Aspects of Price Stability as a Monetary Policy Objective: Should New-Keynesian Central Bankers Pursue Price Stability?" NBER Working Paper No. 10848.

Chand, Sheetal K. 1997. "Nominal Income and the Inflation-Growth Divide." IMF Working Paper WP/97/147. International Monetary Fund, Washington. October.

Callen, Tim, and Dongkoo Chang. 1999. "Modeling and Forecasting Inflation in India." IMF Working Paper WP/99/119. International Monetary Fund, Washington.

Fraga, Arminio, Ilan Goldfajn, and Andre Minella. 2003, "Inflation Targeting in Emerging Market Economies." In *NBER Macroeconomics Annual,* edited by M. Gertler and K. Rogoff. Cambridge: National Bureau of Economic Research.

Friedman, Milton. 1968. "The Role of Monetary Policy." *American Economic Review* 58: 1–17.

Gordon, David Robert. 1981. "Output Fluctuation and Gradual Price Adjustment." *Journal of Economic Literature* 19: 493–530.

Government of India. 1994. *Economic Survey 1993–94.* New Delhi: Government of India Press (PLU).

———. 1996. *Economic Survey 1995–96.* New Delhi: PLU.

Harvey, Andrew C., and Albert Jaeger. 1993. "Detrending, Stylised Facts and Business Cycle." *Journal of Applied Econometrics*, pp. 231–47.

International Monetary Fund (IMF). 2005. *International Financial Statistics.* Washington.

Joshi, Vijay, and Ian M. D. Little. 1994. *India: Macroeconomics and Political Economy, 1964–1991.* New Delhi and Oxford: Oxford University Press.

Kydland, Finn E., and Edward C. Prescott. 1977. "Rules rather than Discretion: The Inconsistency of Optimal Plans." *Journal of Political Economy* 85 (3): 473–92.

Lucas, R. E. 1976. "Econometric Policy Evaluation: A Critique." *Carnegie-Rochester Conference Series on Public Policy* 1: 19–46.

McCallum, Bennet T. 1994. "A Semi-Classical Model of Price Level Adjustment." *Carnegie-Rochester Conference Series on Public Policy* 41 (December): 251–84.

McKibbin, Warwick J., and Kanhaiya Singh. 2003. "Issues in the choice of a Monetary Regime for India." Brookings Discussion Papers in International Economics 154.

Mishkin, Frederic S. 2000. "Inflation Targeting in Emerging Market Countries." *American Economic Review* 60 (May): 105–9.

———. 2004. "Can Inflation Targeting Work in Emerging Market Economies?" Working Paper 10646. National Bureau for Economic Research, Cambridge, Mass.

Mishkin, Frederic S., and Klaus Schmid-Hebbel. 2005. "Does Inflation Targeting Make a Difference?" Paper presented at the Annual Conference of Central Bank of Chile.

Phelps, Edmund S. 1968. "Money-Wage Dynamics and Labor-Market Equilibrium." *Journal of Political Economy* 76 (4): 678–711.

Pradhan, Basanta K., and Arjunan Subramanian. 1998. "Money and Prices: Some Evidence from India." *Applied Economics* 30: 821–27.

Rangarajan, C. 1998. *Indian Economy: Essays on Money and Finance.* New Delhi.

Reserve Bank of India (RBI). 2004. "Report on Currency and Finance 2003–04." Mumbai.

Singh, Kanhaiya. 2002. "Inflation, Economic Growth and Monetary Policy in India: A Macroeconomic Analysis." Research School of Pacific and Asian Studies, Australian National University, Canberra.

Singh, Kanhaiya, and Kaliappa Kalirajan. 2003. "The Inflation Growth-Nexus in India: An Empirical Analysis." *Journal of Policy Modeling* 25: 377–96.

Svensson, Lars E. O. 1997. "Inflation Forecast Targeting: Implementing and Monitoring Inflation Targets." *European Economic Review* 41: 1111–46.

———. 1999. Inflation Targeting as a Monetary Rule." *Journal of Monetary Economics* 43: 6607–54.

———. 2003. "What Is Wrong with Taylor Rules? Using Judgment in Monetary Policy through Targeting Rules." *Journal of Economic Literature* 41: 426–77.

Svensson, Lars E. O., and Michael Woodford. 2004. "Implementing Optimal Policy through Inflation-Forecast Targeting." In *The Inflation-Targeting Debate*, edited by Ben S. Bernanke and Michael Woodford, pp. 19–83. Chicago: University of Chicago Press.

Taylor, John. B. 1993. "Discretion versus Policy Rules in Practice." *Carnegie-Rochester Conference Series on Public Policy* 39: 195–214.

SURJIT S. BHALLA
O(x)us Research and Investments, New Delhi

TIRTHATANMOY DAS
O(x)us Research and Investments, New Delhi

Pre- and Post-Reform India: A Revised Look at Employment, Wages, and Inequality

Major economic reforms were introduced in India in 1991–93. Before then India was, by most accounts and most definitions, a relatively closed economy. Both the domestic and external opening up of the economy have continued since June 1991. However, the reforms have been accompanied by an intense intellectual and political debate about their success. Detractors contend that the economic reforms have not benefited the poor to a desirable extent, that inequality has increased significantly, that growth has been of the "jobless" variety, and that unemployment has emerged as a major social and political problem.

This paper attempts to document in as thorough a manner as possible the development of the Indian economy over the last thirty-odd years. The issues are inherently contentious. For example, much has been written about the constancy of annual gross domestic product (and per capita GDP) growth rates both before and after 1991–92—about 5.6 percent (3.5 percent). But this constancy is based on a loose identification of the pre-reform period as 1980 to 1990 and the post-reform period as 1991 to 2000. July 1991 marks the beginning of the economic reform period, and a correct definition of the pre-reform period would put its end point as June1991, followed by a transition cusp year (1991–92), which also marks the beginning of the post-reform period. If this simple and mandatory correction to the definition of pre- and post-reform periods is made, then per capita GDP grew at an average annual

We would like to thank Barry Bosworth for detailed comments and Suman Bery for extremely helpful discussions. We would also like to thank Esther Duflo and Devesh Kapur for comments on an earlier draft.

183

rate of 3.1 percent before the reforms and at an annual average of 4.1 percent afterward (1991 through 2004); in other words, the growth rate of per capita GDP rose an average of 1 percentage point in the post-reform period.

While macroeconomic statistics indicate a significant acceleration in per capita GDP growth, some commentators perceive that the post-reform growth process has been inequitable. And equity, no matter what the defin-ition, has always been of paramount importance to Indian intellectuals, politicians, and policymakers.

The concerns about equitable growth are highlighted with references to employment growth and the rate of unemployment. For example, in the 1980s, the employment-unemployment surveys produced by the National Sample Survey Organization (NSSO) indicated that jobs had increased at an annual rate of 2.3 percent (1980 to 1991); in the 1990s (1991 to 2003), annual job growth increased by only 1.9 percent. It has also been contended that wage growth of agricultural workers was halved in the 1990s, increasing at a rate of only 2.5 percent, compared with a 4–5 percent annual increase in the 1980s.[1] Critics claim that unemployment rates increased between 1993–94 and 1999–2000. Critics also argue that if the NSSO consumer expenditure (CE) survey for 1999–2000 is made "comparable" to 1993–94, it shows not only that inequality has increased since reforms but that the pace of poverty decline has slowed.[2] Thus, the critics allege that all the statistics point to the same conclusion—the post-reform period is charac-terized by inequitable, jobless growth, higher unemployment rates, and increased inequality. In a country where nearly 40 percent of the population was absolutely poor in the early 1980s, a legitimate question arises: if eco-nomic reforms were so good, how come they produced so little?

This paper wades into this political and ideological minefield by examining the nature of employment, unemployment, wages, and inequality in India between 1972 and 2003. The exercise, in a large part, is one of accounting; that is, looking at what the data show and at what the scholars say happened and determining whether the scholars' conclusions derive from the data.

A large part of the argument about inequitable growth after the reforms were initiated is based exclusively on NSSO *consumption* surveys, and

---

1. These data are from the Agricultural Wages in India (AWI) series, not the NSSO. These calculations exclude the crisis year 1991–92 from the pre-reform period and include it in the post-reform period. Our method is to consider the crisis year as belonging to both periods.

2. Deaton and Dreze (2002) and selected papers in Deaton and Kozel (2005).

then only on the large sample years: 1993–94 and 1999–2000.[3] This method is incorrect. The employment and wage surveys conducted almost annually by NSSO for the last decade are a rich source of information on trends in wage income and therefore in consumption and poverty. The sample sizes in the other sample years are large enough for conclusions about these trends, and most experts advocate their use.[4] In addition, non-NSSO wage (and therefore incomes) data are available on an annual basis, so time trends can be calculated for the "true" pre-reform period, 1991 and earlier, and the "true" post-reform period, 1991 and later. In other words, the artificial constraint of using 1993–94 as a pre-reform year is not operative with annual data.

Use of this additional NSSO data (and inclusion of survey years after 1999–2000) changes the post-reform employment growth picture considerably. Job growth is no longer anemic; it accelerates to a high 2.9 percent rate for the 2000–03 period. The weekly unemployment rate in 2003 declined to 3.1 percent, 1.3 percentage points lower than in 1999–2000. This is also among the lowest observed jobless rate since the mid-1970s and is considerably lower than the average of 4.5 percent that prevailed in the 1970s and 1980s.

In addition, examination of census and NSSO data reveals that the 1990s were characterized by a decline not just in the rate of growth of employment (as noted by most observers) but also a decline in the rate of growth of the *potential labor supply*, that is, people of age fifteen to fifty-nine. This decline had major "intended" consequences for the labor market: if the labor market was characterized by underemployment in the 1980s, and per capita GDP growth accelerated, then the labor market would reveal, through the extra induced demand for labor, much less underemployment in the 1990s. The flip side of this tightening labor market should be an increase in the rate of growth of real wages. Contrary to the "halving" of wage growth for agricultural workers after reform found by many experts, we find that wage growth accelerated for most classes of workers and remained at least constant for agricultural workers.

The plan of this paper is as follows. The next section documents the data, definitions, methods, and various methodological issues associated with the NSSO data on employment. Then we provide background information on the structure of the Indian labor market and how it has changed

3. The Indian fiscal year is from April 1 to March 31; hence, the nomenclature 1993–94, for example, which means data from April 1, 1993, to March 31, 1994. The agricultural year (and most NSSO surveys) are for the agricultural year July 1 to June 30.
4. See, for example, Deaton and Dreze (2002); and Sen and Himanshu (2004a, 2004b).

since the 1970s. Data on employment are examined to verify whether the post-reform period has been characterized by jobless growth, and the trend in unemployment in India from 1972 to 2003 is explored. Next we take a detailed look at the different estimates of wage growth, derived from several different sources of data, and follow with an examination of the trends in wage income and consumption inequality since the mid-1970s, dealing particularly with the proposition that inequality worsened pervasively in the post-reform period. We conclude with the reasons why the results in this paper differ somewhat from the conventional wisdom on employment growth, unemployment, and wage growth, among other subjects.

Data, Definitions, and Methods

One of the primary data sources used by analysts to evaluate socio-economic developments in India is the various surveys conducted by the NSSO. Official data on poverty come from the consumer expenditure surveys conducted every five years by the NSSO. The last such large sample survey was conducted in the agricultural year July 1999–June 2000; the previous three such surveys were undertaken in 1993–94, 1987–88, and the calendar year 1983.

Much of our analysis focuses on a different set of NSSO surveys, the employment and unemployment (E&U) surveys. These surveys contain a wealth of information; indeed, they form the "official" source of information for the government on this important issue.[5]

Records on earnings, wages, activity status, occupation, education, and the like are recorded at the individual level in the E&U surveys. For each member of the household (upward of 120,000 households in the large sample surveys and 30,000–60,000 households in the annual surveys), detailed data are tabulated relating to activity in the preceding seven days. The survey asks about the nature of work (self-employment, unpaid family labor, paid labor, paid labor in government works programs), the number of days of work (measured in half-day units) in each activity, and total earnings received. For self-employment and unpaid family labor, no earnings are reported, either actual or imputed. From these data, the NSSO authorities assign three classifications for each individual: a usual status of employment, a weekly status, and a current daily status (CDS).

5. See, for example, Kapila and Kapila (2002), who reproduce in a single volume three reports by the Indian government on unemployment.

The E&U surveys have not been much used for trends on household *incomes and welfare* for three important reasons. First, a parallel consumer expenditure survey has always been available to derive information on poverty, and this parallel survey is also the official, hence definitive, source for trends on poverty. Second, household income is generally believed to be more difficult to measure accurately than household expenditure. Third, the NSSO household income data are incomplete in that they only have information on labor income.

But the NSSO consumption expenditure data are not without their share of problems. The urgency for an alternative source of information on poverty therefore arose sometime *before* the publication of the NSSO 1999–2000 CE survey, which was doomed from the outset to be controversial. A major reason was the recognition that the national accounts data were revealing consumption information that the NSSO surveys were not fully capturing. Some have argued that this gap was to be expected since the consumption of the rich is difficult to capture in household surveys. But this argument stretches the imagination because a small percentage of households at the tip of the distribution could not possibly account for half of national consumption, as a comparison of the survey results to the national accounts for 2001–02 appeared to show.

Definitions of Unemployment

In 1970 an expert group published a report, referred to here as the Dantwala report, on the unemployment situation in India. This report made the point that it was inappropriate to measure unemployment rates according to the conventional method used in developed countries, which asked whether a person was employed during the previous week, and if not, whether she was looking for work. The expert group concluded that unemployment in the Indian economy could not be accurately measured by weekly status, especially because so many workers were engaged in agriculture, so much of the work was seasonal, and so much underemployment was visible. The report therefore advocated the construction of a daily unemployment rate based on a person-day concept. This concept estimates the fraction of days that persons are unemployed out of the total labor force days.

The three states of activity are employed, unemployed, and not looking for a job. *Usual status* uses the previous year as the reference base. Under this classification, the state of activity on which a person spent a plurality of time in the preceding 365 days is defined as the *principal status*. If the

most common occurrence for an individual during the year was unemployment, then the individual was considered unemployed according to usual
status.

For persons classified according to *current weekly status*, the reference
period is the previous week. A priority order of employed, unemployed,
and not in the labor force is established; individuals are assumed to be
employed if they were employed for at least one hour in the survey week.
Absent employment, individuals were unemployed if they were available
or looking for work at any time during the week; otherwise they were not
in the labor force.

The *current daily status* definition of unemployment is meant to focus
on person-days. For each of the previous seven days, individuals are asked
to report their work and labor force status for each half-day unit. If they
worked less than four hours in the day, they are counted as employed for
half the day and unemployed for the remainder if they were available for or
seeking work. The aggregate of seven days yields an estimate of person-
days of employment and unemployment (daily status) in the economy.

Data on Wages

The NSSO data on daily wages were easily computed as total earnings from
wage employment in the preceding week divided by the number of days
associated with wage employment. In addition, we used three other sources
to estimate rural and agricultural wages: Agricultural Wages in India (AWI),
Cost of Cultivation (CoC) surveys, and a new series (since 1998–99) published by the Ministry of Agriculture in the *Indian Labour Journal*.[6]

In rural areas, and especially among small cultivators, wage income is
an incomplete indicator of family income because it excludes the contribution of family labor as well as income from any form of self-employment,
including cultivation. But there is no problem in interpreting trends in per-
day wages as indicators of what is happening to the growth in incomes of
those whose major asset is labor, especially the poor.[7]

6. Data for the AWI series for the 1980s are taken from Dreze and Sen (2002) and ILO
(1996); for the 1990s, data came from the *Economic Survey*, Indian Ministry of Finance.
These data are in nominal terms; the consumer price index for agricultural laborers (CPIAL)
is used as the price deflator to obtain wages in real terms (with CPIAL in 1993 equal to 100).
7. As Sen and Himanshu (2004a, 2004b) point out, there is a "problem" with the wage
surveys before 1999–2000 in that they did not include data on overtime payments. The
definition of overtime payments that were excluded is unclear, however. In any event, the
impact of this omission in measuring wage growth of the poor is likely to be minimal, if not
inconsequential.

A simple calculation of the NSSO trend in real wage growth can help to resolve some of the various debates on what happened to poverty and inequality in India in the 1980s and 1990s. No definitional changes are involved in the NSSO wage data, so there should be little controversy over what it says. The derived growth in real wages for the 1980s and 1990s can help shed light on the respective pace of poverty decline in the two periods— a higher rate of wage growth in the 1980s, for example, would indicate that the growth process was more pro-poor in the pre-reform period. A faster growth rate for urban wages (relative to rural) in the 1990s may be indicative of increasing inequality.

NSSO Population Adjustments

The population projections based on NSSO household weights do not match the population as revealed by census data. These individual weights (computed from household weights) were adjusted, for rural and urban areas separately, for each of the survey years to keep the aggregate population equal to the census population at the time of the survey. For example, in 1983, India had an estimated population of 734 million and an urbanization rate of 23.8 percent. Hence, the rural and urban populations that year were 559.3 million and 174.7 million, respectively. The NSSO survey weights yield a rural population of 519.4 million and an urban population of 162.2 million. A "matching" was achieved by multiplying the weight for the rural areas of the economy by 559.3/519.4, and multiplying the weights for the urban areas by 174.7/162.2.

Definition of Pre- and Post-Reform Periods

The start of the economic reform period is not controversial; in June 1991: a new government came into power, with Dr. Manmohan Singh as the finance minister (Singh became the prime minister of India in May 2004). To confront a severe balance of payments crisis, a series of policy initiatives were introduced starting in early July 1991. Among other things, the rupee was devalued by 20 percent, peak tariffs were reduced from 300 percent to 110 percent, and a structural adjustment loan from the International Monetary Fund (IMF) was obtained in 1991.[8]

The end of the pre-reform period *is* controversial. The pre-reform period is often defined as the years 1980–91, bolstered by a considerable literature

8. See Virmani (2005) for a comprehensive listing, with dates, of the various reforms initiated in India since 1970.

suggesting that GDP growth in India actually took off in the early 1980s and that for much of the post-reform period, GDP per capita growth was the same as in the 1980s.[9] However, it is unclear why the 1970s should not be part of the pre-reform period, since several of the policy initiatives undertaken then continued into the 1980s and were overturned as part of the reform package adopted in 1991–93. Thus, the 1972–73 NSSO employment survey forms a convenient starting point for the pre-reform period.[10]

Although the literature on GDP growth identifies 1991 as the break point between the pre- and post-reform periods, such is not the case with the literature on wages, poverty, and inequality. The reason: the lack of a large sample NSSO survey in 1991, or 1990, or even 1992. The first large NSSO survey *after* the initiation of reforms is the 1993–94 survey, conducted from July 1993 to June 1994. The earliest pre-reform large sample survey year is 1972–73; the earliest pre-reform year for which NSSO unit-level data are available is 1983. Either can be used as the beginning of the pre-reform period. The last pre-reform large sample NSSO year is 1987–88, but given that this was a drought year, it is not a good choice for the end of the pre-reform period. Data convenience has dictated the choice of 1993–94 as the cusp year between the pre- and post-reform years. NSSO large sample surveys are extremely useful, but they are not necessarily coincident with the history or timing of economic reforms. The reality is that the end of the 1993–94 survey year (June 1994) is a full three years *after* the institution of reforms in July 1991 and thus cannot be construed as the beginning. That even this simple conclusion is controversial is indicated by an alternative view expressed by Duflo. In commenting on an earlier draft of this paper, Duflo stated that "using 1993–94 as a pre-reform year may be inappropriate, but using it as a post-reform year certainly is as well."

If reforms were initiated in July 1991, then to what period does the financial year April 1991 to March 1992 belong? There are strong arguments for defining1991–92 as a pre-reform year. This was a crisis year (GDP growth of only 1 percent), in large part because of the unsustainable nature of economic policies of the 1980s. Part of the process of economic reforms is that such policies bring about a structural readjustment that often results in a short-term decline. Hence, a "worst case" calculation is to consider the

9. See Bhalla (2000, 2002a), Panagariya (2004), Rodrik and Subramaniam (2004), and Virmani (2004a, 2004b) for discussions and comparison of the growth rates in the 1980s and 1990s.
10. The text reports calculations, whenever possible, for both definitions of the pre-reform period: 1972–91 and 1980–91.

cusp year 1991–92 as belonging to *both* the pre-reform and the post-reform era. Thus, the data are presented for three periods: two pre-reform periods, 1972–91, and the high-growth years 1980–91; and a post-reform period, 1991–2003, the last year for which most data are available.

A Broad Overview of the Labor Force

While the conclusions of the Dantwala unemployment report were relevant in the 1960s, the view of India as a traditional low-income country does not have much applicability today. In the 1960s India was one of the poorest countries in the world; today it is on the verge of being classified as middle income, albeit at the lower end of the range. In the 1950s agricultural output accounted for more than half of GDP; today it is less than 20 percent. At the end of the 1970s nonfarm income was 21 percent of rural incomes; by 1999–2000 this fraction had doubled to 42 percent.[11]

NSSO E&U surveys provide several details about the large transformation of the Indian economy. Some basic data for the Indian workforce since 1983 are reported in table 1. Overall, the agricultural workforce increased at a robust annual rate of 2.4 percent in the 1980s; in the 1990s, the rate of growth was minus 0.2 percent per year.[12]

The number of young, illiterate workers (illiteracy is defined as less than two years of education; young workers fall in the fifteen- to twenty-four age group) is rapidly declining. In 1983 about half of all young workers were illiterate; by 1999–2000, this fraction had declined to less than a third (table 2). Illiterate workers in the entire workforce constituted 55 percent in the early 1980s; by the end of the 1990s, this fraction had declined to 44 percent (table 3).

The loss in agricultural jobs in the Indian economy has been made up by increases in employment in services and production. In fact, for the 1983–2000 period, job growth in production-related activities has outpaced job growth in services (2.8 versus 2.3 percent a year), a somewhat surprising result given the common belief that production-related employment has stagnated because of labor laws and other limitations.

11. Foster and Rosenzweig (2003).
12. The 1980s is the period 1980–89, the 1990s the period 1990–99; however, when the discussion pertains to NSSO large sample data, then "the 1980s" refers to the ten-and-a-half-year period 1983 to 1993–94, and "the 1990s" refers to the six-year period, 1993–94 to 1999–2000.

TABLE 1. Structural Changes in Employment According to Weekly Status

	Millions of workers			(log) Annualized growth (%)		
Workforce	1983	1993–94	1999–2000	1983 to 1993–94	1993–94 to 1999–2000	1983 to 1999–2000
Official (all ages)	263	346	368	2.6	1.0	2.0
15–59 years	229	311	334	2.9	1.2	2.3
15–59 years[a]	228	304	322	2.7	0.9	2.1
Agriculture (15–59 years)	142	183	181	2.4	–0.2	1.5
Cultivators[a]	79	96	90	1.8	–1.0	0.8
Farmers other than cultivators[a]	8	14	14	5.3	0.2	3.4
Agricultural laborer[a]	49	65	69	2.7	1.1	2.1
Nonagriculture (15–59 years)	86	122	141	3.3	2.4	3.0
Production[a]	43	59	68	3.1	2.3	2.8
Service[a]	10	11	14	1.5	3.6	2.3
Unpaid, self-employed	122	160	166	2.6	0.6	1.9

Source: NSSO Employment and Unemployment surveys conducted in 1983, 1993–94, and 1999–2000.
a. The computation of aggregates includes only those observations where occupation codes are not missing.

TABLE 2. Illiteracy in the Young Workforce, 15–24 Years

Workforce	1983	1993	1999
Total (millions)	61.3	75.7	74.4
Illiterate (millions)	31.1	30.1	24.2
Illiterate as percent of workforce	50.7	39.8	32.5

Source: NSSO Employment and Unemployment surveys conducted in 1983,1993–94, and 1999–2000.

A perspective on the rate of change of the skill levels (human capital) of the Indian work force can be seen in table 3. Two structural aspects are apparent. First, the skill levels are advancing rapidly. Second, females are catching up to men, with the share of women attaining more than a primary school education (six years) growing much faster than the share of men.

Table 4 provides data on this changing occupational structure. Growth in "good" jobs (defined as wage-earning rather than self-employment or family work, higher-valued and more-skilled occupations rather than un-skilled workers, and the like) is far outpacing the growth in "bad" jobs. The highest rate of job growth is for professional and technical workers, and within this workforce, the female job rate is growing faster than the male job rate (6.4 versus 5 percent). It should be emphasized, however, that

TABLE 3. **Changing Levels of Education in the Labor Force**

Years of education	Millions of workers			(log) Annualized growth (%)		
	1983	1993–94	1999–2000	1983 to 1993–94	1993–94 to 1999–2000	1983 to 1999–2000
Male						
0	74	79	75	0.6	−0.7	0.1
2 or fewer	78	82	79	0.4	−0.6	0.0
2–6	47	60	59	2.4	−0.2	1.5
6 or fewer	125	142	138	1.2	−0.4	0.6
More than 6	48	73	95	4.0	4.3	4.1
6–11	41	59	75	3.3	4.1	3.6
More than 11	7	15	20	7.1	4.9	6.3
Total	173	215	233	2.1	1.3	1.8
Female						
0	52	67	66	2.4	−0.2	1.5
2 or fewer	53	68	67	2.4	−0.2	1.5
2–6	7	14	15	6.6	1.7	4.8
6 or fewer	60	82	82	3.0	0.1	2.0
More than 6	5	11	15	7.9	5.8	7.2
6–11	4	8	12	7.5	6.1	7.0
More than 11	1	3	4	9.5	5.1	7.9
Total	64	92	98	3.5	0.9	2.5
All workers						
0	126	146	142	1.4	−0.5	0.7
2 or fewer	131	150	146	1.3	−0.4	0.6
2–6	53	74	74	3.1	0.2	2.0
6 or fewer	184	223	220	1.8	−0.2	1.1
More than 6	53	84	110	4.4	4.5	4.4
6–11	45	67	87	3.7	4.3	3.9
More than 11	8	17	23	7.4	4.9	6.5
Total	238	307	330	2.5	1.2	2.0

Source: NSSO Employment and Unemployment surveys conducted in 1983, 1993–94, and 1999–2000.

the share of professionals in the total workforce is still very small (only 23.5 million workers in 1999–2000, although that was more than double the number in 1983).

Table 5 provides details on the composition of the workforce according to the "paid" status of the worker. The Dantwala report underlined the fact that most workers in India were casual workers, entering and exiting the labor force according to season, and that family workers were a large fraction. In the 1990s (1993–94 to 1999–2000), self-employed workers and family workers in rural areas showed no growth. Overall, wage and nonwage jobs expanded at the same rate in 1983–93, but during the next six years wage employment outpaced nonwage employment, indicating both the

TABLE 4. Occupational Composition of the Work Force in India

	Millions of workers			(log) Annualized growth (%)		
Occupation	1983	1993–94	1999–2000	1983 to 1993–94	1993–94 to 1999–2000	1983 to 1999–2000
Male						
Professional, administrative, technical, manager	8.0	13.8	18.3	5.1	4.7	5.0
Clerical	6.6	9.4	10.3	3.3	1.4	2.6
Sales	11.7	19.8	21.0	5.0	1.0	3.6
Production	32.1	48.2	56.8	3.9	2.7	3.5
Service	5.9	7.7	9.4	2.5	3.3	2.8
Agriculture, fishery	92.6	118.9	118.0	2.4	–0.1	1.5
Total	157.0	217.9	233.7	3.1	1.2	2.4
Female						
Professional, administration, technical, manager	1.8	4.0	5.2	7.5	4.3	6.4
Clerical	0.5	1.3	1.5	8.8	2.4	6.5
Sales	2.1	2.9	2.7	3.3	–1.4	1.6
Production	7.4	11.0	11.3	3.8	0.4	2.6
Service	2.7	3.5	4.5	2.6	4.2	3.2
Agriculture, fishery	44.4	67.0	68.4	3.9	0.3	2.6
Total	58.8	89.6	93.5	4.0	0.7	2.8
All						
Professional, administrative, technical, manager	9.9	17.8	23.5	5.6	4.6	5.3
Clerical	7.1	10.7	11.7	3.9	1.5	3.0
Sales	13.8	22.7	23.7	4.8	0.7	3.3
Production	39.5	59.2	68.1	3.9	2.3	3.3
Service	8.6	11.2	13.9	2.6	3.6	2.9
Agriculture, fishery	137.1	185.9	186.4	2.9	0.0	1.9
Total	215.8	307.6	327.2	3.4	1.0	2.5

Source: NSSO Employment and Unemployment surveys conducted in 1983, 1993–94, and 1999–2000.

growth of good jobs and the move toward less casual, and more modern employment, in the post-reform 1990s.

In sum, the Indian workforce is increasingly better educated, with female education expanding at a faster pace than male education; the share of unskilled workers in the labor force is declining, growth in agricultural jobs has halted, and paid jobs are taking up this slack.

Decline in the Rate of Growth of the Potential Labor Force

Some perspective on "jobless" growth can be obtained by observing the rate of growth of *potential* labor supply, where potential signifies the *physical*

TABLE 5.   Wage and Nonwage Jobs

Category	Millions of workers			(log) Annualized growth (%)		
	1983	1993–94	1999–2000	1983 to 1993–94	1993–94 to 1999–2000	1983 to 1999–2000
Wage earners						
Rural	72.7	97.5	110.3	2.8	2.0	2.5
Urban	30.8	42.8	49.0	3.1	2.3	2.8
Total	103.5	140.3	159.3	2.9	2.1	2.6
Male	75.7	102.1	116.5	2.9	2.2	2.6
Female	27.8	38.1	42.7	3.0	1.9	2.6
Total	103.5	140.3	159.3	2.9	2.1	2.6
Self-employed, family workers (no wage data)						
Rural	106	140	140	2.6	0.0	1.7
Urban	20	31	35	4.3	2.3	3.5
Total	126	171	175	2.9	0.4	2.0
Male	91	117	121	2.4	0.6	1.7
Female	34	53	54	4.2	0.2	2.7
Total	126	171	175	2.9	0.4	2.0
Family workers						
Rural	35.1	58.6	59.6	4.9	0.3	3.2
Urban	4.1	7.2	8.0	5.4	1.8	4.1
All India	39.2	65.8	67.6	4.9	0.4	3.3

Source: NSSO Employment and Unemployment surveys conducted in 1983, 1993–94, and 1999–2000. Family workers are a subset of the self-employed individuals and hence no wage data are available for them.

availability of individuals ages fifteen to fifty-nine. If inward and outward migration is not significant, then employment cannot exceed this rate of growth. It can and does exceed this ceiling if the labor force participation rate (LFPR) increases, especially the LFPR of women. Otherwise, just demographics alone (in the absence of migration) constrains the rate of growth of employment. Some of the decline in job growth in India apparently results from this phenomenon, that is, a decline in growth of the potential labor force growth is partly responsible for the so-called jobless growth of the 1990s.

Population growth in India has been declining—from an annual average of 2.1 percent in the 1980s to 1.9 percent in the 1990s.[13] At the end of the decade, the annual population growth rate had further declined to only

13. Census years are 1981, 1991, 2001, and so on. Thus the census years for the 1980s are 1981–91; for the 1990s, 1991–2001, and so on.

1.6 percent a year. Table 6 documents a little-known and therefore less-appreciated fact—the rate of growth of India's potential labor force (those in the fifteen to fifty-nine age group) also declined in the 1990s, from 2.6 percent a year to 2.3 percent. NSSO figures reflect the same decline in population growth—from 1.9 percent a year in the 1983 to 1993–94 period to 1.7 percent a year in the 1993–94 to 1999–2000 period. The NSSO rate of growth is lower in both time periods because the NSSO surveys were conducted two years after the 1981 and 1991 censuses. The NSSO figure for the rate of growth of the potential labor force, however, declines much more rapidly—from a 2.6 percent annual average in the 1980s (the same as the census) to only 1.7 percent in the 1990s, for an average decline of 0.9 percent, compared with a 0.3 percent decline in the census data.

TABLE 6. Potential Labor Force in India, 1981–2001

Category	Millions of people			(log) Annualized growth (%)		
	1981[a]	1991	2001	1981–91	1991–2001	1981–2001
Population						
Census	683	846	1,027	2.1	1.9	2.0
NSSO	734	899	999	1.9	1.7	1.9
Population, 15–59 years						
Census	358.8	465.5	585.7	2.6	2.3	2.5
NSSO[a]	393.6	515.5	572.4	2.6	1.7	2.3

Source: Census of India 1981, 1991, and 2001; NSSO Employment and Unemployment surveys conducted in 1983, 1993–94, and 1999–2000.

a. NSSO population estimate and corresponding growth rates are computed for years 1983, 1993–94, and 1999–2000.

Given that the change in the NSSO and census population growth rates are of similar magnitude, the reasons for the difference in the two potential labor force growth rates are unclear. One possible explanation could be the differences in the beginning and end years of the data in the two samples. The nature of the bias, however, is unclear and deserves further investigation.

The fact remains, however, that at least a partial explanation for the much-discussed jobless growth phenomenon of the 1990s lies in the data sources, which show a decline in the rate of growth of the potential labor force. This is *not* a decline in supply induced by a weakening job market, but rather a structural decline that is not insignificant. This finding implies that one should expect to find a decline in the rate of employment growth in the 1990s, everything being equal. In other words, less employment growth was needed in the 1990s to keep unemployment rates constant.

Decline in Labor Force Participation Rate

An additional factor explaining the low growth rate of employment in the post-reform 1990s is a decline in the labor force participation rate itself.[14] The LFPR in 1993–94 was a high 58.3 percent. By 1999–2000 it had declined to 56.4 percent, a level even lower than the LFPR observed sixteen years earlier in 1983 (57.7 percent). See table 7 (and related discussion about labor force and daily unemployment rates) for details. This decline in the LFPR in the 1990s averaged 0.55 percent a year, indicating that job growth in the 1990s would have declined by the same percentage. It is coincidental, and interesting, that an advanced economy like the United States has also experienced this phenomenon in recent years. A common explanation for both societies is that there are increasing numbers of individuals in the potential labor force who are staying out of the labor force for longer periods than in the past; some of these individuals are increasing their education. As shown earlier in table 3, in India, individuals with more than eleven years of education increased at a 4.9 percent pace in the 1990s, considerably higher than the growth rate of the labor force.

TABLE 7. Derivation of Person-Day Labor Force Participation Rates

	1983		1993–94		1999–2000	
Category	All persons	Age 15–59	All persons	Age 15–59	All persons	Age 15–59
Person (millions)	734	394	899	515	999	572
Person days (millions)	5,138	2,758	6,293	3,605	6,993	4,004
Persons days in labor force (millions)	1,820	1,590	2,330	2,100	2,490	2,260
Labor force participation rate (percent)	35.4	57.7	37.0	58.3	35.6	56.4

Source: NSSO Employment and Unemployment surveys conducted in 1983, 1993–94, and 1999–2000.

A direct estimate of the role played by increasing education enrollments on the decline in labor force growth is provided in table 8. The labor force grew at a 1.3 percent rate in the 1990s; if education enrollment had stayed the same as it was in 1993–94, the labor force would have grown at an annual pace of 1.5 percent. Hence, the education-induced decline in the LFPR, and therefore in the labor force, was at the rate of 0.2 percent a year.

14. The computation of LFPR is not on the basis of person but on the basis of person days, that is, the ratio of total number of person days in labor force to the total number of person days in the reference week for the age group ages fifteen to fifty-nine.

TABLE 8. **Is Education Responsible for the Decline in LFPR**

	Millions of people			(log) Annualized growth (%)	
Category	1983	1993	1999	1983 to 1993–94	1993–94 to 1999–2000
Population	394	515	572	2.6	1.7
Enrollment	22	40	48	5.5	3.1
Enrollment rate	5.7	7.7	8.4	2.9	1.4
Labor force	238	321	348	2.9	1.3
Adjusted labor force[a]	238	321	352	2.9	1.5

Source: NSSO Employment and Unemployment surveys conducted in 1983, 1993–94, and 1999–2000.
a. Available labor force (ages 15–59) in 1999–2000 with the enrollment rate of 1993–94.

These two phenomena—a decline in the rate of growth of the potential labor force induced by demographics and a decline in the rate of growth of the actual labor force induced by increasing education—explain *all* the decline in employment growth. For the period 1991–2001, the census data indicate potential labor force growth of 2.3 percent a year. The decline in LFPR is 0.55 percent a year, so jobs should have grown at 1.75 percent a year in the 1990s. Actual job growth (1991–2003) was at the rate of 1.7 percent a year.

The Pre- and Post-Reform Periods: What Should One Expect?

Table 9 documents the trends in some of the major macroeconomic variables for the pre- and post-reform periods. In keeping with the discussion in the previous section, data are presented for two pre-reform periods: 1972–91 and 1980–91. Given that the longer period is more unfavorable to the pre-reform period, the comparison between 1980–91 and 1991–2003 is emphasized in the discussion.

Per capita GDP accelerated after the reforms, from an average of 3.1 percent a year to 4.1 percent. This should have normally been associated with higher employment growth, but that is possible only when both the LFPR and productivity growth remain constant. Given the sharp acceleration in skill levels (and therefore productivity), however, some decline in the rate of job growth was to be expected. And the rate of job growth did decline, from 2.4 percent a year to 1.7 percent, mirroring the decline in the potential labor force growth noted earlier.

Growth in private income per worker mirrored productivity growth, almost tripling from 1.6 percent a year to 4.2 percent. [15] Agricultural wage

15. Growth in private income per worker is computed as the ratio of private income (national accounts) and the workforce (NSSO data).

TABLE 9. Average Annual Growth in Selected Indicators
Percent

Indicator	Before reform		After reform
	1972–91	*1980–91*	*1991–2003*
Employment	2.0	2.4	1.7
GDP, per capita	2.3	3.1	4.1
Wage, agricultural laborer (AWI, real)	2.0	3.1	3.3
Wage, agricultural laborer (CoC, real)	2.0	3.0	3.7
Private income per worker	1.8	1.6	4.2
Population	2.2	2.1	1.9
Population (age 15–59)		2.6	2.3

Source: NSSO Employment and Unemployment surveys conducted in 1983, 1993–94, and 1999–2000; *Handbook of Statistics on Indian Economy* (2004) by the Reserve Bank of India; Agricultural Wages in India (AWI), and Cost of Cultivation (CoC) Survey of Principal Crops, published by the Ministry of Agriculture, Government of India; National accounts database developed by *Economic and Political Weekly*; Census of India 1981, 1991, and 2001. Population data are from Census of India 1981, 1991, and 2001, for the period 1981–91 and 1991–2001.

growth—growth in wages of the poorest workers—showed a *sharp* acceleration from the pre-reform period 1972–91 and a mild acceleration from the shorter pre-reform period, 1980–91. This acceleration is noted for both sources of agricultural wage data, the AWI and CoC surveys. The AWI series indicates a mild acceleration, from 3.1 to 3.3 percent, while the CoC data indicate a sharper uptrend, from 3.0 to 3.7 percent a year. It should be emphasized that, paradoxically, the AWI series has been used by several authors to argue that agricultural wage growth collapsed in the post-reform period.[16] These contradictory conclusions pertaining to the AWI data are evaluated in greater detail later in this paper.

Employment

This section uses the weekly activity status definition to interpret trends in employment. Two major questions are asked. First, what has been the trend rate of growth of employment? Second, how has this trend varied between the pre- and post-reform periods? This analysis responds in part to policy concerns that employment growth stagnated in the post-reform period—the jobless growth phenomenon.

Employment Growth, 1972–2003

There were eighteen NSSO employment surveys conducted between 1972 and 2003, six of which were large sample surveys (1972–73, 1977–78,

16. See Deaton and Kozel (2005) for a sampling.

1983, 1987–88, 1993–94, and 1999–2000) and twelve of which used smaller samples. Not all the surveys were conducted for the agricultural year, which extends from July through June. The center of this "benchmark" year is December. Table 10 adjusts the "raw" weekly employment figures for those surveys that have a non-December center (see also box 1). For example, the 2002 survey was conducted from July to December and the 2003 survey from January to December. Employment between these two surveys grew at a rate of 4.1 percent a year; so the adjusted level for December 2003 (the center of the 2003–04 agricultural year) is 400 million. In other words, if the 4.1 percent growth rate had extended for another six months, the level of employment would have been 400 million rather than 393 million.

TABLE 10. Employment, Unemployment, and Labor Force
Millions unless otherwise indicated

Survey round	Year	Labor force	Unemployed	Rate (%)	Employment	Employment[a]
27 (1972–73)	1972	231	10	4.3	221	221
32 (1977–78)	1977	245	11	4.5	234	234
38 (Jan–Dec83)	1983	275	12	4.5	263	266[a]
43 (July87–June88)	1987	296	14	4.8	282	282
45 (July89–June90)	1989	317	11	3.5	306	306
46 (July90–June91)	1990	328	13	4.0	315	315
47 (July–Dec91)	1991	338	15	4.4	323	326[a]
48 Jan–Dec92)	1992	349	18	5.2	331	337[a]
50 (July93–June94)	1993	359	13	3.6	346	346
51 (July94–June95)	1994	352	7	2.0	345	345
52 (July95–June96)	1995	355	8	2.3	347	347
53 (Jan–Dec97)	1997	363	9	2.5	354	356[a]
54 (Jan–June98)	1998	358	13	3.6	345	337[a]
55 (July99–June2000)	1999	385	17	4.4	368	368
56 (July2000–June01)	2000	377	10	2.7	367	367
57 (July01–June02)	2001	396	13	3.3	383	383
58 (July02–Dec02)	2002	394	13	3.3	381	380[a]
59 (Jan03–Dec03)	2003	405	12	3.0	393	400[a]

Source: NSSO Reports on Employment and Unemployment available at (mospi.nic.in/stat_act_t14.htm).
a. Indicates adjustment to original data to make the employment estimate conform to a July–June year.

Employment Trends

A long-term trend line is fitted to all employment surveys since 1972 (figure 1). The large sample surveys for 1972–73 and 1999–2000 sit on the trend line (annual rate of growth of 1.9 percent), while 1993–94 survey has the largest positive residual (5 percent). In contrast the residual for 1983 is

---

BOX 1.   Employment: Small and Large Sample Surveys

A semi-log regression of employment on time, with a dummy for the years in which there was a large sample survey, yields the following:

Ln(*Employment*) = −31.7 + 0.019*year −0.0116*large sample dummy
            (−15.5)   (18.4)   (−0.64)

Number of observations = 18; adjusted R^2 = 0.971; t statistics in parentheses.

The lack of significance of the large sample year dummy suggests that one can pool the data for the two sets of surveys. A larger sample was not expected to make much difference to the aggregate trend, given that even the small samples surveyed more than 40,000 households. It is encouraging to see that the coefficient is significant at only the 50 percent level of confidence (t statistic of −0.64).

FIGURE 1.   Employment in India by Weekly Status, 1972–2003

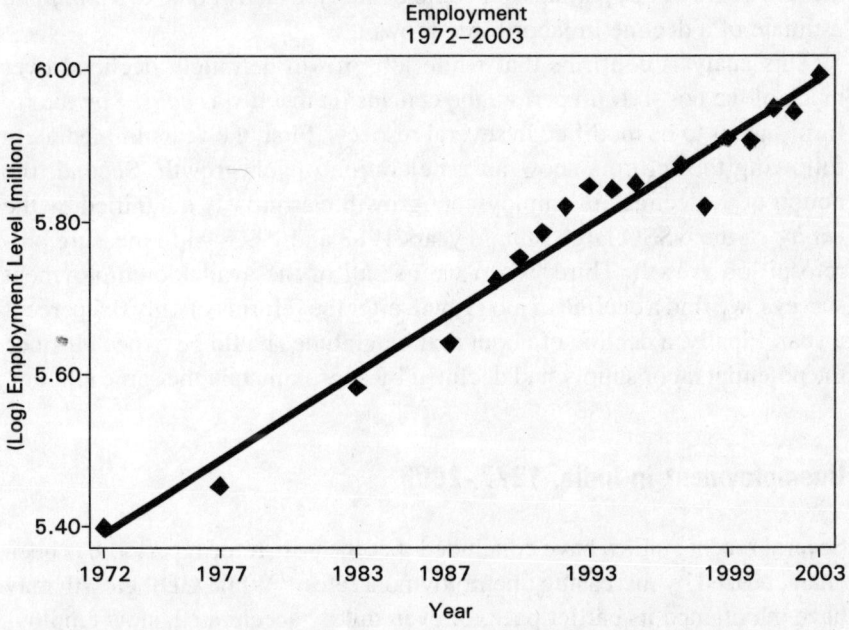

2 percent *below* trend. Most analysts have used the NSSO survey years of 1983, 1993–94, and 1999–2000 to derive implications about what happened not only between these survey years but also in the pre- and post-reform periods. The uneven pattern of residuals is suggestive of the problems that can arise if just three data points are used to derive conclusions about

employment growth. If 1983 is below trend and 1993–94 is above trend, then this means that growth is overstated for the pre-reform period by 0.7 percent a year (7 percent divided by ten years). Analogously, growth is understated for the 1993–94 to 1999–2000 period by 5 percent over six years, or 0.8 percent a year. The average annual growth rate (based on all the surveys available rather than just the large sample surveys) is 2.3 percent for the pre-reform period and 1.8 percent for the post-reform period.

Thus, the headline *decline* in employment growth rates between the two periods is not 1.6 (2.6 percent a year pre-reform versus 1 percent a year post-reform), but only 0.5 percent (from 2.3 percent to 1.8 percent). The much-talked about jobless growth in the post-reform period is actually job growth of 1.8 percent a year, a rate not much different than the thirty-year average of 1.9 percent. As noted earlier, the 0.5 percent annual decline in the rate of growth is, perhaps not coincidentally, exactly equal to a *minimum* estimate of a decline in labor force growth.

This analysis confirms that while job growth definitely declined over much of the post-reform period, the conclusion that it was *caused* by the reforms needs to be modified in several respects. First, the years immediately following the reforms show an acceleration of job growth. Second, the notion of a "decline" in employment growth was grossly magnified by the *choice* of the NSSO large sample years 1983 and 1993–94 to measure pre-reform job growth. Third, when we use all of the available employment surveys, we find a decline in job growth after the reforms of only 0.5 percent a year. Finally, a decline of about that magnitude should be expected since the potential labor supply had declined by approximately the same amount.

Unemployment in India, 1977–2003

Several recent studies have concluded that the post-reform period has been characterized by increasing unemployment rates.[17] While GDP growth may have maintained its earlier pace, or even mildly accelerated, slow employment growth was more the reality of the post-reform period, and given India's high population and labor force growth, increasing unemployment rates were to be expected. The increasing unemployment problem was also viewed as serious enough to warrant a serious policy response. Hence, at the end of 2004,

17. In particular, three Planning Commission studies, two authored by Gupta (2002a, 2002b), and the third the recently released "Mid-Term Appraisal of the Tenth Five-Year Plan" (2005).

the government introduced a job program that is expected eventually to guarantee a job to every person in rural India who wants a job.[18] To begin with, this Employment Guarantee Act promises to provide 100 days of work a year to at least one person in each rural household. This policy initiative follows directly from the strong belief that unemployment rates in India are disturbingly high. Whether this view is supported by any evidence is examined below.

As mentioned earlier, there are *three* different definitions of unemployment in India: unemployment according to usual status, weekly status, and daily status. These different definitions allow for a *variety* of interpretations about what happened to unemployment in India after the institution of economic reforms in 1991. Table 11 reports the official data according to the usual, weekly, and daily status of unemployment for the period 1972–2003.

Unemployment Rates: Usual and Weekly Status

The usual status of unemployment measures structural or long-term unemployment. If a person was in the labor force (working or seeking work) and unemployed for the major part of the year, her usual status would be unemployed. Under this definition unemployment has hovered between 2 and 4 percent for the last thirty years, and in 2003 was at the lower end of the range: 2.2 percent.

Since it is a long-term measure, the usual status may not be the most useful indicator of unemployment. Weekly status may be a more meaningful measure of unemployment. A person is considered unemployed on a weekly status if she was unemployed for all seven days in the preceding week. A major advantage of using the weekly status is that it is the definition of choice for most countries of the world.

For urban areas, weekly unemployment rates were between 6.6 and 7.9 percent in the pre-reform period and declined to 5 percent by 2003. In rural areas, the magnitude is considerably lower for both periods—between 3.7 and 4.2 percent in the pre-reform period, and 2.4–3.9 percent in the 1990s (2.4 percent in 2003). On an all-India basis, the unemployment rates ranged between 4.3 and 4.8 percent before1991, and between 3.1 and 4.4 percent after the reforms (in 2003, the level was a low 3.1 percent). The ostensibly high unemployment rate observed in 1999–2000, 4.4 percent, is near the low end of the range for the pre-reform years.

---

18. "The proposed Act gives a legal guarantee of employment to anyone who is willing to do casual manual labor at the statutory minimum wage"; see Dey and Dreze (2004).

TABLE 11. Official Unemployment Rates (Usual, Weekly, and Daily), 1972–2003

Percent

Category	1972	1977	1983	1987	1993	1994	1995	1997	1998	1999	2000	2001	2002	2003
Rural														
Daily	8.2	7.7	7.9	5.3	5.6	n.a.	n.a.	n.a.	n.a.	7.2	n.a.	n.a.	n.a.	n.a.
Weekly	3.9	3.7	3.9	4.2	3.0	1.6	1.5	1.9	2.8	3.9	2.1	2.7	2.5	2.4
Usual (principal)	n.a.	3.3	1.9	3.1	1.8	1.0	1.3	1.4	2.3	2.0	1.3	1.5	1.6	1.5
Urban														
Daily	9.0	10.3	9.5	9.4	7.4	n.a.	n.a.	n.a.	n.a.	7.7	n.a.	n.a.	n.a.	n.a.
Weekly	6.6	7.9	6.8	7.1	5.8	4.0	4.0	4.5	5.8	5.9	4.7	4.7	5.6	5.0
Usual (principal)	n.a.	8.8	6.0	6.6	5.2	3.8	4.0	4.1	5.7	5.2	4.2	4.4	5.0	4.2
All India														
Daily	8.3	8.2	8.3	6.1	6.0	n.a.	n.a.	n.a.	n.a.	7.3	n.a.	n.a.	n.a.	9.1
Weekly	4.3	4.5	4.5	4.8	3.6	2.2	2.1	2.6	3.5	4.4	2.8	3.2	3.3	3.1
Usual (principal)	n.a.	4.2	2.8	3.8	2.6	1.7	1.9	2.1	3.1	2.8	2.0	2.3	2.5	2.2

Source: NSSO reports on Employment and Unemployment situation.

n.a. Not available.

Unemployment: Daily Status Definition

Both the usual and weekly status definitions of unemployment may be inappropriate for a developing economy like India. The 1970 Dantwala committee offered a new definition of employment to reflect the peculiarities of unemployment in a large agrarian economy. For such an economy, it was felt that a *time rate*, rather than a *person rate*, of unemployment would be more useful. Hence, a definition of unemployment was needed that would incorporate the fraction of time in a week that a person was unemployed. Alternatively, data on daily employment and unemployment can be used to generate a *person* rate of unemployment according to the definition that a person is considered unemployed if on any half day she did not work and was looking for work, and this calculation is repeated for each of the fourteen half days of the week.[19]

For the daily status definition of unemployment, NSSO codes two separate categories—code 81, the traditional unemployment definition (looking for work and not employed); and code 82, a nontraditional definition (not working, not seeking to work, but available for work). Code 82 accounted for 2.3 percent of the labor force in 1983 and for 1.5 percent in 1999–2000. The code 81 rate decreased marginally over the same period, from 6 percent to 5.7 percent (table 12). The results are similar for the fifteen to fifty-nine age group.

That unemployment has been declining is also indicated by the calculation of the *duration* of unemployment for the daily unemployed. This shows a steady decline from 1983 onward—2.4 days in 1983, 2.3 days in 1993–94, and 2.2 days in 1999–2000 (table 13). A large fraction, almost a third, of the daily unemployed are those who are unemployed for one, two, or three days a week. These short-duration daily unemployed were 3.1 percent of the labor force in 1983, 2 percent in 1993–94, and 2.6 percent in 1999–2000. In rural India, where most of the measurement problems referred to by the Dantwala report occur, a very small percentage of the rural workforce is unemployed for all seven days of the week: 2.6 percent in 1983, 2.2 percent in 1993–94, and 3 percent in 1999–2000.

A clear trend that emerges from our analysis of different definitions of unemployment (and a trend consistent with the data on employment) is that unemployment rates in the post-reform period were about 1.5–2 percentage points below those in the pre-reform years (1977–78, 1983, and 1987–88),

---

19. The actual definition has fourteen units, with each day comprising of two half-day units.

TABLE 12. Unemployment Rates According to Daily Status Definition
Percent unless otherwise indicated

Definition	All persons			Age 15–59 years		
	1983	1993–94	1999–2000	1983	1993–94	1999–2000
Person (millions)	734	899	999	394	515	572
Person days (millions)	5,138	6,293	6,993	2,758	3,605	4,004
Person days in labor force (millions)	1,860	2,370	2,520	1,620	2,130	2,290
Labor force participation rate	36.2	37.7	36.0	58.7	59.1	57.2
Total days of employment (millions)	1,710	2,220	2,340	1,480	1,990	2,120
Total days of unemployment (code 81) (millions)	111	111	144	102	106	137
Total days of unemployment (code 82) (millions)	43	32.4	39	38.1	29.5	35.5
Person-day unemployment rate (7 day workweek, code 81)	6	4.7	5.7	6.3	5	6
Person-day unemployment rate (7 day workweek, code 82)	2.3	1.4	1.5	2.4	1.4	1.6
Person-day unemployment rate (7 day workweek, code 81+82)	8.3	6.1	7.3	8.6	6.4	7.5
Official unemployment rate (NSSO, person days concept)*	8.3	6.0	7.3	*	*	*

Source: NSSO Employment and Unemployment surveys conducted in 1983, 1993–94, and 1999–2000.
*The NSSO does not compute daily unemployment rates for those aged 15–59 years, so data for this classification category are not available.

a significant amount. Thus, the big picture, according to the employment, labor force, and unemployment data, is that after reforms, the rate of growth of the potential labor force fell to less than 2 percent a year; the rate of growth of employment declined to an annual rate of 2 percent, and unemployment rates declined significantly. These are long-term trends; looking ahead, it appears that employment growth will match expected growth in the labor force (8 million people annually). It is encouraging to note that for 2000–03, employment growth far exceeded this minimum level.

Poverty, Education, and Frictional Unemployment

The relationship between poverty and unemployment is a controversial one. Some argue that the poor remain poor because they cannot find employment. Others argue that the poor are poor because they lack human and physical capital, not because they lack job opportunities or jobs.

TABLE 13.   Unemployment, 1983 to 1999–2000, by Daily Status
Percent

Status	Unemployment rates		
	1983	*1993–94*	*1999–2000*
All India			
7 days unemployed	3.3	2.8	3.6
4 or more days unemployed	5.3	4.1	4.8
More than 1 but fewer than 4 days	3.1	2.0	2.6
Total	8.4	6.1	7.4
Total (official)	8.3	6.0	7.3
Average duration of unemployment of those who are unemployed for more than 1 but fewer than 7 days a week	2.4	2.3	2.2
Rural India			
7 days unemployed	2.6	2.2	3.0
4 or more days unemployed	4.8	3.6	4.4
More than 1 but fewer than 4 days	3.4	2.2	2.9
Total	8.1	5.8	7.3
Total (official)	7.9	5.6	7.2
Average duration of unemployment of those who are unemployed for more than 1 but fewer than 7 days a week	2.4	2.3	2.2
Urban India			
7 days unemployed	5.8	5.1	5.5
4 or more days unemployed	7.1	5.9	6.3
More than 1 but fewer than 4 days	2.2	1.4	1.7
Total	9.3	7.3	8.0
Total (official)	9.5	7.4	7.7
Average duration of unemployment of those who are unemployed for more than 1 but fewer than 7 days a week	2.3	2.3	2.2

Source: NSSO Employment and Unemployment surveys conducted in 1983, 1993–94, and 1999–2000.
Note: Duration of unemployment is obtained by multiplying the weighted average of the days unemployed in a week (as a proportion of the days in labor force) by 5.

There is an additional dimension—the relationship between education and unemployment. It has been argued that the jobless growth of the 1990s provided employment only for the educated rich; the uneducated poor were left behind. If so, then one should observe a strong negative relationship between education and unemployment, that is, the less educated you are, the more likely you are to be unemployed. There is an alternative hypothesis about this particular relationship, which yields the opposite sign. With economic development, and especially with globalization, one should expect the more educated members of the labor force to search longer for "better" jobs. This hypothesis would imply that unemployment rates and education are positively related, that is, the rich have a much higher probability of unemployment than the poor.

The NSSO data strongly support the latter explanation. Table 14 reports the unemployment rates and education levels for various classifications of households. The different patterns yield one very firm conclusion: the mean education level of the unemployed is very high and has been increasing over years. For the weekly status definition, the mean education attainment of the unemployed in 1983 was six years, almost two-and-a-half times the mean education level of an average Indian. The story in 1999–2000 is no different: the mean education level of the unemployed increased to 7.2 years. Such individuals, in terms of education, are in the top 10 percent of society.

TABLE 14.   Education and Unemployment, Weekly Status

Category	1983	1993	1999
Unemployment (%)			
Rural	3.5	2.7	3.4
Urban	7.3	5.9	6.1
All India	4.3	3.4	4.1
Poor[a]	4.5	3.2	4.5
Agricultural laborer household	5.0	3.2	4.3
Mean education years of labor force			
Rural	2.2	2.8	3.3
Urban	5.8	6.3	6.9
All India	3.0	3.6	4.2
Poor[a]	1.9	2.2	2.5
Agricultural laborer household	1.1	1.6	1.9
Mean years of education of unemployed			
Rural	4.9	6.3	6.1
Urban	7.9	9.0	9.1
All India	6.0	7.3	7.2
Poor[a]	4.3	5.3	4.5
Agricultural laborer household	2.2	3.1	3.3

Source: Employment and Unemployment surveys conducted by NSSO for 1983, 1993–94, and 1999–2000.
a. The poor are defined as those with monthly per capita consumption less than the official poverty line.

Wages and Income

This section examines whether wage growth provides corroborative evidence for the assumed deleterious effects of slower job growth. For example, a slower rate of wage growth in the post-reform years would be strong evidence

that job growth in the 1990s was of a lackluster variety. Indeed, one important reason why the finding of slow job growth was generally accepted was
because some analysts pointed to a sharp decline in the rate of growth of
wages (particularly the wages of unskilled agricultural workers) as evidence
of "bad" reforms. [20] This evidence was deemed to be consistent with the associated "findings" that reform-led growth was lopsided, that poverty had not
declined as fast as it had in the 1980s, and that reforms had caused an increase
in inequality. The important issue of trends in inequality is taken up in the
next section; the discussion here centers on the question of wage growth.

There is only one source of data on wages of *all* workers: the NSSO E&U
large sample surveys conducted in 1983, 1993–94, and 1999–2000. [21] Annual
wage data are necessary for a meaningful analysis of the pre- and post-reform
years, but these data are available only for agricultural workers. As a result,
researchers have attempted to "match" the annual agricultural wage data with
the periodic NSSO wage data to derive implications for overall wage growth
in the pre- and post-reform period. These analyses are evaluated in detail
below.

Rural and Urban Wage Growth

If the focus of interest is in economywide wage growth, and or rural-urban
wage growth, then the only source for such information is the NSSO large
sample E&U surveys. These surveys are of limited use for interpreting
trends in the pre- and post-reform periods. If NSSO period II (1993–94 to
1999–2000) real wage growth rates are observed to be higher than NSSO
period I (1983 to 1993–94), then one can reach the "safe" conclusion that
wage growth was better in the post-reform period. If the wage growth rate
shows a decline in NSSO period II, then unless one knows what happened
in the intervening five years (1988–89 to 1992–93), years which overlap
both the pre-reform and the post-reform periods, there is little that can be
said about pre- and post-reform growth. [22]

With these caveats, it is the case that the time profile of real wage growth,
as revealed by the NSSO data, shows an unambiguous acceleration. Wage

20. Agricultural workers constitute a large fraction of the poor in the country and live
in households whose primary, and almost exclusive, source of income is from labor.

21. The NSSO survey year 1987–88 seems to yield a highly inaccurate division of the
labor force by sex; hence, analysis of wage data from this source is ignored.

22. Some indication about what happened to wages in this intervening period is yielded
by the data on agricultural wages; the AWI and CoC wage series reveal an annual growth
rate of 0.7 and 3.1 percent, respectively.

growth figures for all workers in India accelerated from an annual average of 2.5 percent to 4.5 percent (table 15). This wage growth pattern is consistent with annual GDP per capita growth, which rose from 3 percent to 4.3 percent over the same years. Per worker income growth also showed a sharp acceleration, from 1.6 to 4.7 percent annually.

TABLE 15. (Log) Annualized Growth of Wages, per Capita GDP and Private Income per Worker

Category	1983 to 1993–94	1993–94 to 1999–2000
NSSO data		
Agricultural workers	2.6	2.6
Rural India	2.5	4.1
Urban India	2.4	4.9
All India	2.5	4.5
National accounts data		
GDP, per capita	3.0	4.3
Private income	1.6	4.7

Source: NSSO Employment and Unemployment surveys conducted in 1983, 1993–94, and 1999–2000, *Handbook of Statistics on Indian Economy, 2004–05*.

Thus, both the national accounts and NSSO survey figures are in close agreement that wage and income growth nearly doubled after reforms. For agricultural workers, NSSO data suggest a constancy in the rate of growth of about 2.6 percent a year both before and after reforms. These twin findings—a large increase in the overall wage growth of workers and constancy in wage growth of the poorest agricultural workers—are at variance with the general belief that wage growth, especially of agricultural workers, collapsed in the post-reform period.

Wage Growth of Agricultural Workers before Reforms

This general belief holds that the rate of growth of wages of agricultural workers fell back from a high of about 5 percent a year in the 1980s to a low of about 2.5 percent a year after the reforms. These results are based on the AWI (a non-NSSO series that was discontinued after 2000). Despite this result being contradicted by the NSSO data showing a constancy in the rate of growth of agricultural wages, the finding gained currency both because of the sharp "unexplained" fall, and because it was endorsed by authoritative experts.

Gupta was the first to "discover" a large decline in the growth rate of agricultural wages postreforms: "Change in real wages in pre-reforms (1981–91)

period was 4.7 percent and in the post reform period (1991–99) 2 percent."[23] Using a semi-log regression, Dreze and Sen conclude: "The growth rate of real agricultural wages fell from over 5 percent per year in the 1980s to 2.5 percent or so in the 1990s.[24] Deaton and Dreze use these earlier studies to conclude: "According to recent estimates based on AWI data, real agricultural wages were growing at about 5 percent per year in the eighties and 2.5 percent per year in the nineties."[25] Sen and Himanshu echo the same conclusion: "The different time-series available agree that, *although less than during the 1980s*, 1990s growth of real agricultural wage rates averaged 2–3 per cent per annum at the national level" (emphasis added).[26]

As row 1 of table 16 illustrates, NSSO data show growth in agricultural wages between 1993 and 2000 of 2.6 percent a year, a number very close to the much-cited AWI figure of 2.5 percent for the 1990s. Indeed, this correspondence was taken as "proof" that wage growth had collapsed after the reforms. Apparently, it was assumed that since the 1990s figures from the two data sources matched, the 1980s wage figures would also match. In other words, it was assumed that the average annual NSSO wage growth figure for the 1980s would be close to 4.5 or 5 percent that the AWI data showed.

TABLE 16. Growth in Agricultural Wages, by Various Data Sources, Selected Periods
Percent

Survey	1972–91	1980–91	1991–2003	1983 to 1993–94	1993–94 to 1999–2000
NSSO	n.a.	n.a.	n.a.	n.a.	n.a.
Average growth	n.a.	n.a.	n.a.	2.6	2.6
AWI					
Average growth	2.0	3.1	3.3	4.2	2.2
Semi-log	3.0	4.4	3.1	3.0	2.8
CoC					
Average growth	2.0	3.0	3.7	5.0	2.5
Semi-log	2.8	3.8	3.5	4.0	2.5

Source: Agricultural Wages in India (AWI); Cost of Cultivation (CoC) of principal crops survey; NSSO Employment and Unemployment surveys conducted in 1983, 1993–94, and 1999–2000.
n.a. Not available.

23. Gupta (2002b, p. 468). We obtain somewhat different estimates: 3.1 percent a year in the 1981–91 period, and 1.9 percent a year in the 1991–99 period.
24. Dreze and Sen (2002, p. 348).
25. Deaton and Dreze (2002, p. 3737).
26. Sen and Himanshu (2004a, p. 4238).

But as we have just observed, the NSSO wage growth for the 1980s was much less than the AWI estimate of 2.6 percent a year—the same as in the 1990s.

Sundaram challenged the collapse in wage growth hypothesis by laboriously documenting the pattern of NSSO wage growth for the 1980s and 1990s.[27] He documented wage growth for twenty groups of agricultural workers (ten occupational groups sorted by gender). For twelve of these groups, he reported an acceleration in wage growth, for four groups a deceleration, and for four groups a constancy. The overall average growth in both periods: 2.8 percent a year. "The evidence from the NSSO Employment Unemployment Surveys offers *no* support at all for the hypothesis of a slowdown in the rate of growth of average daily wage earnings of adult casual labourers during the 1990s relative to that between 1983 and 1994," Sundaram concluded.[28]

Sundaram's estimates for wage growth were also supported by Ahluwalia, who used NSSO data to document the large wage acceleration that occurred in the two six-year periods immediately surrounding the reforms (1987–93 and 1993–99).[29] The Ahluwalia report showed a 0.8 percent growth in real wages for casual male workers in the NSSO pre-reform period, and an acceleration to 3.6 percent growth in the post-reform period. Thus, it appears that *no* aspect of the NSSO data shows any decline in the rate of growth agricultural wages in the post-reform period, let alone a collapse.

Evaluation of Data on Agricultural Wages

Neither Sundaram's extensive evaluation nor Ahluwalia's supporting evidence appeared to have any impact on the "conventional wisdom" holding that agricultural wage growth collapsed after reforms. Different authors have used different methods and data series to make their claims. Table A-1 presents the nominal and real data on agricultural wages for every year since 1970. The reader can choose her own pre- and post-reform periods for estimations, and conclusions.

There are three major non-NSSO sources of data, and all of these data are for the agricultural year July to June. The most widely used wage series is the AWI series, which is available for the years 1960–2000. A new wage series (most likely a replacement for the AWI) started in 1997–98 and is available through 2002–03; this series is published in the *Indian Labour*

27. Sundaram (2001a, 2001b).
28. Sundaram (2001a).
29. Ahluwalia (2002).

Journal (ILJ). The third wage series is less widely used but more comprehensive. It is derived from various issues of *Cost of Cultivation* (CoC) in India. This series, which has details on the principal crops cultivated, the wage bill, and the quantity of labor used, began in 1970.[30] All three surveys are conducted by the Ministry of Agriculture. Table A-1 to this paper reports both the original and "filled" data for missing observations since 1999–2000; these have been filled in by grafting the *growth* rate as observed in the "parallel" ILJ agricultural wage series for the period 1999–2003. Real wages, in 1993 prices, are obtained by using a common deflator, the national average of the consumer price index for agricultural laborers (CPIAL). By using this common deflator, issues of divergence due to the use of different price series do not arise.

What Do the Wage Data Show?

This comprehensive tabulation of agricultural wages in India yields several insights into the evolution of wages in India. The AWI and CoC series show almost the same nominal wage for 1971 and 1980; and both show a large, 5 percent increase in 1984.[31] However, the close correspondence in the two series begins to diverge just before the reforms of 1991. In 1990 the AWI series reveals a wage that is 6.5 percent higher than the average wage shown by the CoC; in 1999–2000 (the last year of the AWI data), the AWI wage level is 3 percent *lower*. In between, in 1993–94, the two wage series show an equal nominal wage. Looking at just these end-point differences (in 1990 and 1999), the AWI series shows an average annual growth rate in the 1990s that is 1 percent lower than the rate shown by the CoC series.

There are two methods for deriving an estimate of growth for any period of time: average growth (given by the difference in the values in the end years); or a semi-log regression. The latter disproportionately weights the outlier years. A simple semi-log regression of the AWI series for the period 1980–91 yields a growth coefficient of 4.4 percent; for the period 1991–2003, the coefficient is 3.1 percent (table 16). The CoC data (same time periods, same semi-log method) show a constancy in the rate of growth: 3.8 and 3.5 percent a year in the two periods. But the figures for the more

30. We are grateful to Mr. Praduman Kumar, Ministry of Agriculture, for kindly providing the data on cost of cultivation for different crops in India, 1970–2000.

31. No easy explanation is available for such a large jump in just one year. What is suggestive is the fact that 1982 was one of the lowest rainfall years and 1983 one of the best. So the 1984 wage increase might have involved some "catching up" in the agricultural sector.

reliable estimate of annual average growth tell a very different story—*both* sources point to an acceleration in the rate of growth of agricultural wages, from 3.1 to 3.3 percent a year in the AWI data; and from 3.0 to 3.7 percent a year in the CoC data.

The conclusion that agricultural wage growth collapsed is now explained. If a *semi-log regression estimate* of the AWI series for the 1980s is inappropriately juxtaposed with NSSO agricultural wage growth between 1993–94 and 1999–2000 (2.6 percent), and if, inappropriately again, the earlier period is believed to be pre-reform and the latter post-reform, then it does appear that wages of agricultural workers collapsed to half their pre-reform level.

Pre- and Post-Reform Economic Performance: A Review of the Evidence

As discussed earlier, it is incorrect to define the pre- and post-reform periods according to the availability of NSSO large-sample data. Table17 documents the growth rates according to NSSO survey dates, and according to dates corresponding to reform periods. Growth results are presented for the two pre-reform periods: 1972–73 to 1991–92 and 1980–81 to 1991–1992. The post-reform period is defined as 1991–92 to 2003–04. Note that the cusp year, 1991–92, is considered as being part of both the pre-reform and the post-reform periods. There are arguments that it should belong to both periods

TABLE 17.   Pre- and Post-Reform Wage Growth

	Including crisis year (1991–92)			Excluding crisis year (1991–92)		
	Pre-reform		Post-reform	Pre-reform		Post-reform
Category	1972–91	1980–91	1991–2003	1972–90	1980–90	1992–2003
Employment (in millions), NSSO	2.0	2.4	1.7	2.0	2.4	1.6
GDP, per capita (A) (NA)	2.3	3.1	4.0	2.5	3.5	4.3
Wage, farm laborer (AWI, real)	2.0	3.1	3.3	2.5	4.1	3.1
Wage, farm laborer (CoC, real)	2.0	3.0	3.7	2.3	3.5	3.7
Private income, per worker (NA and NSSO)	1.8	1.6	4.4	2.2	2.3	4.7
Population	2.2	2.1	1.6	2.2	2.1	1.6
Population (age 15–59)		2.6	2.3		2.6	2.3

Source: NSSO Employment and Unemployment surveys conducted in 1983, 1993–94, and 1999–2000; *Handbook of Statistics on Indian Economy* (2004) published by Reserve Bank of India; Agricultural Wages in India and Cost of Cultivation survey of principal crops published by Ministry of Agriculture, Government of India; National Accounts (NA) database developed by *Economic and Political Weekly*; population data are from Census of India 1981, 1991, and 2001 and for period 1981–91 and 1991–2001.

or to neither period. If the crisis year is excluded, the reform period shows a greater acceleration in growth. Consequently, to present a "worst case" picture of the reform period, the discussion below pertains to only the comparison that includes the cusp year in both periods.

Employment growth slowed in the post-reform period, as discussed earlier. No matter what the income indicator used (GDP per capita, private income per worker, agricultural wages), the post-reform period shows an acceleration. There is thus little evidence that the reform period was bad for the average, or the agricultural, worker.

Figure 2 documents the data on agricultural wage growth. Figure 2a shows the correspondence in the real wage *levels* of the AWI and CoC wage series; the two are near identical for several end-points: 1970, 1980, 1990, and 1999, but there is great divergence for the years 1985–89. In these years, the AWI wage levels are considerably higher than the CoC wage levels; hence, it is no surprise that the wage *growth* figures for the AWI series are higher for the 1980s. Figure 2b illustrates the differences as revealed by semi-log regressions; a decline in the slope for the AWI is observed for the 1990s (from a 4.4 percent annual trend to a 3.1 percent annual trend), while the CoC series shows a constancy.

FIGURE 2.   Agricultural Wages

a. Wage Growth, 1970–2003

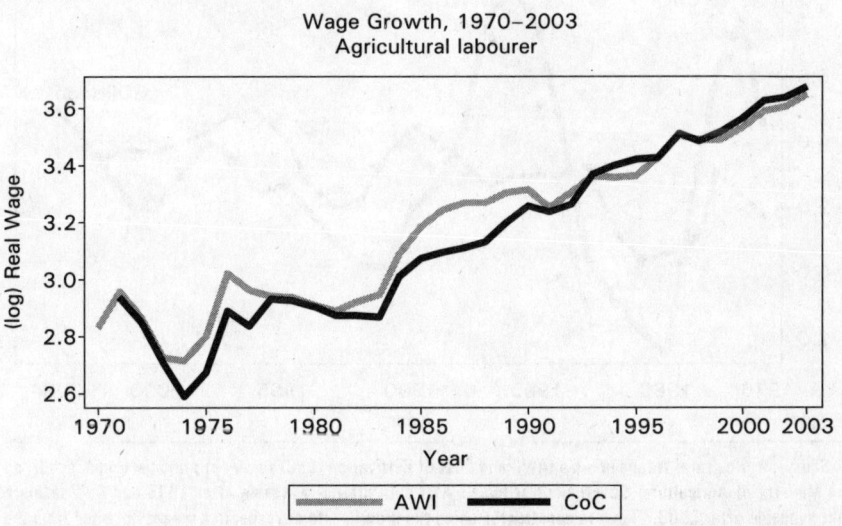

(Figure 2 continued)

(Figure 2 continued)

b. Wage Growth Trends, 1980–2003

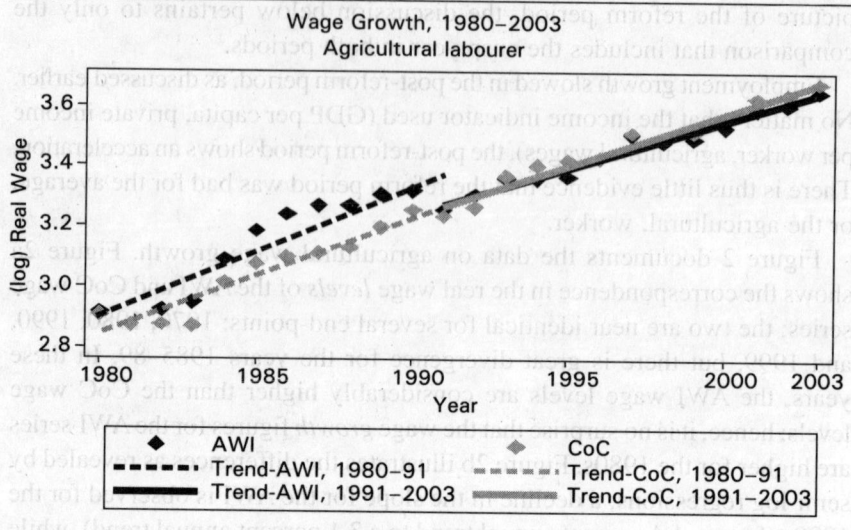

c. Rolling Regression Results for Agricultural Wages and GDP per capita, 1971–2004

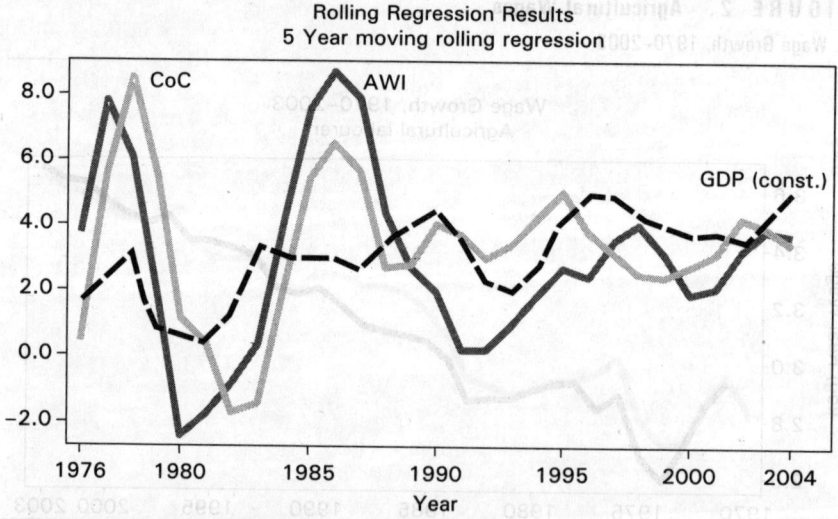

Source: Agricultural Wages in India (AWI) and Cost of Cultivation (CoC) survey of principal crops, published by Ministry of Agriculture, Government of India. AWI data are not available after 1998 and CoC data are not available after 2000. They are constructed using the growth rate of respective wages obtained from the *Indian Labour Journal*.

Figure 2c reports the results for a rolling regression for the two wage series and GDP per capita growth; the estimates are for a ten (and five) year initial window period 1970–79, and then for subsequent ten-year periods obtained by adding and subtracting one year; for example, the first estimate is for the period 1971–76, the next for the period 1972–77, and so on. This figure clearly shows that GDP per capita has steadily accelerated to a growth rate of 4 percent a year. Both the AWI and CoC wage series accelerate to over 8 percent a year in the mid-1970s, only to collapse to 2 percent a year in the years ending 1980 (AWI) and 1982 (CoC). Both wage series then reach a local peak in 1986 (a growth rate between 6 and 8 percent a year) and then fall to a low in 1991 or 1992. By 2003–04, both wage series reveal a growth rate close to 4 percent.

This section has presented all the data available for the period 1970–2003. Regardless of the definition of wages used, or whether the crisis year should or should not be included in both periods, there is no evidence to support the conventional wisdom of a precipitous decline in the rate of growth of wages of the poor. [32] Indeed, the evidence points to a small acceleration. The other *derived* conjecture of the reform critics is that given the "reality" of a wage growth decline, it would be consistent to expect that inequality increased with economic reforms. But as we have just documented, there was no decline in wage growth of agricultural workers. Inequality outcomes are a function of several factors, and as the next section shows, the net effect of the various factors on inequality trends has been close to zero.

What Happened to Inequality after the Reforms?

The controversy over what happened to employment, unemployment, and agricultural wages is underpinned by one common belief: economic reforms initiated in 1991 and continued by every government since then, led to an increase in inequality. The primary basis for this conclusion is the 1999–2000 NSSO consumer expenditure survey. Consumption inequality for this fiscal year is alleged to have been significantly higher than inequality in 1993–94. (As discussed earlier, this comparison is inappropriate since reforms were initiated two to three years before 1993–94.)

32. Only one data source (AWI) shows a decline in the rate of growth of agricultural wages, which is observed if the crisis year 1991–92 is excluded from the analysis. However, even in this specification, the alternative CoC wage series actually shows an acceleration in wage growth, from 3.5 percent a year from 1980 to 1990 and 3.7 perent a year from 1992 to 2003.

Besides, and to make the inference about a pervasive inequality change even more problematic, the definition of some major items of consumption underwent a major change in the 1999–2000 survey. So a strict, noncontroversial comparison of consumption inequality between the two fiscal years is just not possible.[33] Even if a comparison is made, as attempted by various authors, the nominal change in inequality observed between the two years is less than 8 percent, and the higher level of inequality in 1999–2000 is slightly less than that observed in the pre-reform years 1983 and 1987–88. In other words, even the worst case estimates of inequality change in the 1990s still reveal a level of inequality less than that observed in the years preceding the reforms.

This conclusion diverges considerably from the findings that consumption inequality worsened sharply after the economic reforms in 1991. Several articles in Deaton and Kozel attempt to document this worsening "trend."[34] In another prominent study, Deaton and Dreze conclude: "Except for the absence of clear evidence of rising intra-rural inequality within states, we find strong indications of a *pervasive* increase in economic inequality in the nineties. This is a new development in the Indian economy: until 1993–94, the all-India Gini coefficients of per capita consumer expenditure in rural and urban areas were fairly stable. Further, it is worth noting that the rate of increase of economic inequality in the nineties is far from negligible" (emphasis added). [35] Sen and Himanshu wrote: "It is now *certain that economic inequality increased sharply during the 1990s in all its aspects* and, as a result, poverty reduction deteriorated markedly despite higher growth" (emphasis added).[36]

It bears emphasis that Sen and Himanshu do not offer any direct evidence of increased inequality in the 1990s; their indirect evidence consists of a mixing of data on different definitions of consumption in the different survey years. Deaton and Dreze arrive at their conclusion on the basis of a *synthetic* estimate of the old definition of consumption in 1999–2000, a variable for

33. The changing definitions are as follows: all goods are one of three types: food, durables, and nondurables, nonfood (NDNF). Before and including 1993–94, data on food consumption was collected on a thirty-day recall basis; in 1999–2000 food information was collected on both a thirty- and a seven-day basis. Data on durables were gathered on a thirty-day and annual basis through 1993–94, and then only annually in 1999–2000. Data on NDNF were collected on a thirty-day basis throughout. How these changing definitions affect both the mean and the distribution is a subject explored in considerable detail in Bhalla and Das (2004).

34. Deaton and Kosel (2005).

35. Deaton and Dreze (2002, p. 3740).

36. Sen and Himanshu (2004b, p. 4361).

which information was not gathered in the 1999–2000 survey. This they do on the basis of some very plausible assumptions.

Trends in Consumption Inequality

There are two possible adjustments that can be made to the 1999–2000 survey to make the consumption definition compatible with the 1993–94 survey (and earlier surveys). One method is to adjust the 1999–2000 new consumption data to conform to the 1993–94 old consumption definition.[37] The second method is to make 1993–94 compatible with the 1999–2000 definition.[38] Both adjustments are imprecise but nevertheless meaningful.

Figure 3 presents data for real consumption inequality from 1951 to 1999–2000. Data for 1951–82 are from the WIDER income distribution database, and those from 1983 to 1999–2000 are derived from our own calculations. The Planning Commission price deflator for each state and the rural-urban categories is used to deflate nominal expenditures. For 1951–63, a sharp decline in consumption inequality is observed; for the next forty years, the Gini varied in a very narrow range, 0.30 to 0.32. Real consumption

FIGURE 3.   Consumption Inequality (Gini) in India, 1951–99

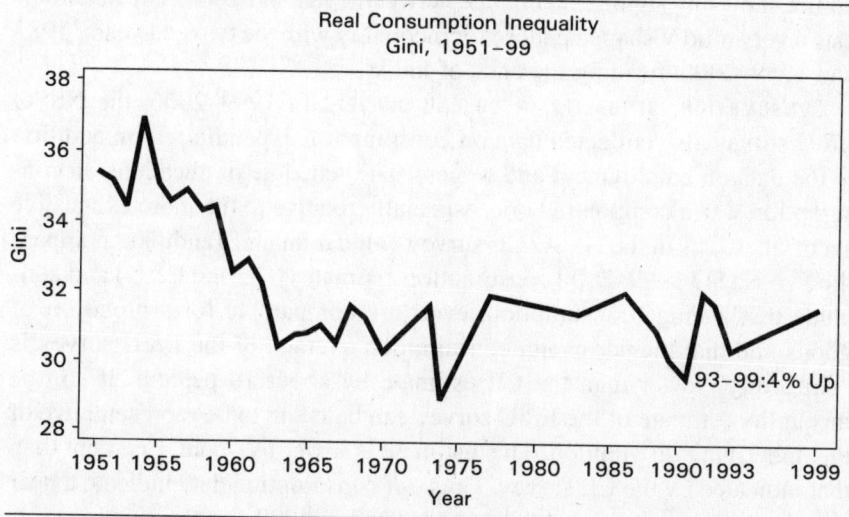

Real Consumption Inequality
Gini, 1951–99

Note: Data from 1951 to 1982 from WIDER income distribution database; from 1983 onward, authors' computations. Nominal expenditures deflated by the state, urban/rural price indices.

37. Deaton and Tarozzi (2000) advocate this approach.
38. This method is put forth by Sundaram and Tendulkar (2003).

inequality in the much discussed 1993–94 to 1999–2000 period went up a paltry 4 percent.

This inequality result is at sharp variance with the conventional wisdom of a "pervasive" increase in inequality in the 1990s. The largest such increase is reported by Deaton and Dreze, a 7.8 percent increase in nominal inequality between 1993–94 and 1999–2000 (variance of logs measure of inequality).[39] Using Sundaram and Tendulkar's new definition, the real inequality increase during that period was only 4.2 percent.

No matter what the definition of consumption (old or new, nominal or real), the conventional result that inequality worsened sharply in the 1990s is just not obtained. All series indicate an increase in inequality in the 1990s; the magnitude of this change, however, is very small (less than 8 percent). Further, real inequality seems not to have worsened as much as nominal inequality; the magnitude of change is about half that of change in nominal inequality (around 4 percent). Finally, for all the definitions of real inequality change in the 1990s relative to the 1980s, there is an improvement in inequality; for all the nominal changes, the net change in inequality is mildly positive.

NSSO consumption data, like the wages and income data reported later, do not show any significant change between 1983 and 2000. The data indicate a very mild V shaped pattern for inequality with the two end years, 1983 and 1999–2000, forming the ends of the V.

CONSUMPTION INEQUALITY: NSSO E&U SURVEY. In 1999–2000, the NSSO E&U survey also collected data on consumption expenditures (in addition to the data on employment and wages). The schedule of questions on consumption was a compressed one, especially relative to the more exhaustive set of questions in the NSSO CE survey. Sundaram and Tendulkar compare the two NSSO 1999–2000 consumption estimates (CE and E&U) and conclude that average consumption levels are comparable for a broad set of goods and that the per capita consumption average of the E&U survey is "uniformly" lower than the CE estimate by about 10 percent. If so, the inequality estimate of the E&U survey can be taken to be representative of the underlying distribution. This estimate is lower by about 4 percent than that indicated by the CE survey. Thus, *all* consumption data indicate a near constancy in inequality for the period, 1983 to 1999–2000.

CONSUMPTION INEQUALITY: RATIO OF URBAN TO RURAL CONSUMPTION. Both Deaton and Dreze and Sen and Himanshu use an additional indicator of inequality trends: the change in the ratio of average urban to average rural

39. Deaton and Dreze (2002).

consumption. Though there is no theoretical linkage, both sets of authors assume that a rise in the ratio implies an increase in inequality. An increase in the ratio is indeed observed in both real and nominal terms. But change in this ratio does not correspond with change in inequality. The ratio increases by about 11 percent between 1983 and 1993–94 and by 8 percent between 1993–94 and 1999–2000. However, this increase is consistent with inequality improving during the first period and inequality mildly worsening in the second period. This suggests that the urban-rural ratio of average consumption is *not* a reliable indicator of inequality change.

CONSUMPTION INEQUALITY: ADJUSTED NSSO CONSUMPTION. One additional estimate of consumption inequality is presented in table 18.[40] The estimates showing a decline in poverty for India (and several other developing countries) are suspect because in the 1990s, the growth in mean consumption as measured by surveys was considerably lower than the growth in mean consumption shown in national accounts.[41] This is one bias that would tend to indicate that poverty levels in the 1990s were overstated. A bias in the opposite direction stems from the likelihood that consumption by the rich is underestimated in the surveys; hence, survey averages would tend to overstate the consumption of the poor. What is needed is an *adjusted* estimate of the survey mean; one such estimate is provided by "correcting" the NSSO data for the systematic measurement error that is introduced because the NSSO survey captures a reduced amount of total consumption (as revealed by the national accounts). The NSSO survey and national accounts estimates are "matched" for nineteen items, and the matched estimate is taken to be the true level of aggregate consumption. For example, in 1999–2000, cereal consumption in the survey was 17.5 percent below the national accounts estimate, so each survey household's per capita cereal consumption is increased by 17.5 percent. If a poor household did not consume any "motorcycle," the "motorcycle error" would not be transmitted to its adjusted consumption. This method does not suffer from definitional or measurement problems, but it does assume that the national accounts per capita consumption estimates of different goods are correct.

The inequality levels of the marked-up *adjusted* consumption are higher than the NSSO survey consumption, by about 10 percent. In other words, once the data are adjusted for all of the "missing" consumption, inequality,

---

40. This estimate was first presented in Bhalla (2002a, 2002b), reproduced in Deaton and Kozel (2005).

41. This point is discussed extensively in Bhalla (2002a, 2002b).

TABLE 18. Consumption Inequality, per Capita Expenditure, NSSO Data, 1983 to 1999–2000

| | | | | | (log) Change, % | | |
Consumption category	1983	1987	1993–94	1999–2000	Period I	Period II	1999–2000 over 1983
Nominal expenditures							
Old definition of consumption (Gini)[a]	0.33	0.33	0.33	n.a.	n.a.	n.a.	n.a.
New definition of consumption (Gini)[a]	0.30	0.30	0.30	0.32	−0.7	6.0	5.3
National accounts–adjusted consumption (Gini)[b]	0.36	n.a.	0.35	0.37	−2.8	5.6	2.7
Urban/rural ratio of mean consumption							
Old definition of consumption[a]	146.2	155.8	162.8	n.a.	10.8	n.a.	n.a.
New definition of consumption[a]	n.a.	n.a.	162.8	175.9	n.a.	7.7	n.a.
Real expenditures[c]							
Old definition of consumption (Gini)[a]	0.32	0.31	0.30	n.a.	−5.2	n.a.	n.a.
New definition of consumption (Gini)[a]	0.29	0.28	0.28	0.29	−6.2	3.9	−2.3
National accounts–adjusted consumption (Gini)[b]	0.35	n.a.	0.33	0.35	−5.9	5.9	0.0
Urban/rural ratio of mean consumption							
Old definition of consumption[a]	110.0	107.8	116.8	n.a.	6.0	n.a.	n.a.
New definition of consumption[a]	n.a.	n.a.	116.9	124.8	n.a.	6.5	n.a.

Source: NSSO Consumer Expenditure survey for years 1983, 1993–94, and 1999–2000, National Accounts data from CSO and EPW CD-ROM.

n.a. Not available.

a. For old and new definitions of consumption, see text.

b. National accounts–adjusted refers to the adjusted per capita consumption, with adjustments made at the household and item level, that is, by "matching" of item expenditures, in survey and national accounts. See text for details.

c. The rural-urban state poverty line is used as the price deflator.

at any point in time, is higher by 10 percent. This is consistent with the belief that the rich understate their consumption by a greater degree than do poor people. However, the inequality trend according to marked-up consumption is exactly the same as the unadjusted consumption. For the adjusted data, the real Gini in 1983 was 0.35, which declined to 0.33 in 1993–94 and returned to 0.35 in 1999–2000. In other words, the adjusted data show a

mild V and no change between the pre- and post-reform periods—the same
result shown by unadjusted consumption data.

Collecting all the available data, the overwhelming conclusion is that
there has been no trend in per capita consumption inequality between 1983
and 1999–00. For the two post-reform years 1993–94 and 1999–2000, inequality increased mildly, with the most extreme estimate of the change
being only 7.8 percent.[42]

Trends in Wage and Income Inequality

Unlike the NSSO consumption surveys, the NSSO E&U data do not have
any definitional problems and the wage data can be used to assess changes
in wage and income inequality. These surveys are a rich source of data on
those individuals who report wage and salary income; and for this population, the trend in wage inequality is easily estimated. By use of a simple
human capital model, wage incomes can be derived for those workers (self-
employed and family workers) for whom wage data are not reported. This
allows for an approximation to trends in overall income inequality.

INCOME INEQUALITY CHANGE, 1975–76 TO 1994–95. Figures 4 and 5 document the results on all the income inequality surveys conducted in India.
The only organization to collect complete data on income distribution in
India is the NCAER. Two of its surveys, in 1975–76 and in 1994–95, were
national in coverage. These NCAER surveys indicate an increase in inequality of only 10 percent for the twenty-year period (Gini values of 0.39 and
0.43 in the two years).

The NSSO per capita income data is incomplete; it contains information
on wages but has no data on earnings from self-employment or capital. The
data can be made "complete" by estimating an earnings function model. This
model uses information on years of education, experience, and experience
squared to separately estimate an income function for urban and rural areas
and for males and females. From an imputed wage for each worker, total and
per capita wage income for each household is derived.

A cross-check on this imputed NSSO income distribution is provided
by comparing it to the distribution obtained from the complete NCAER data
(complete in the sense that the organization collected information on all
sources of income from all members of the family). The 1975–76 NCAER
distribution has a Gini of 0.39, not much different from the adjusted NSSO

---

42. Deaton and Dreze (2002).

FIGURE 4.   Income Inequality in India, 1955–99

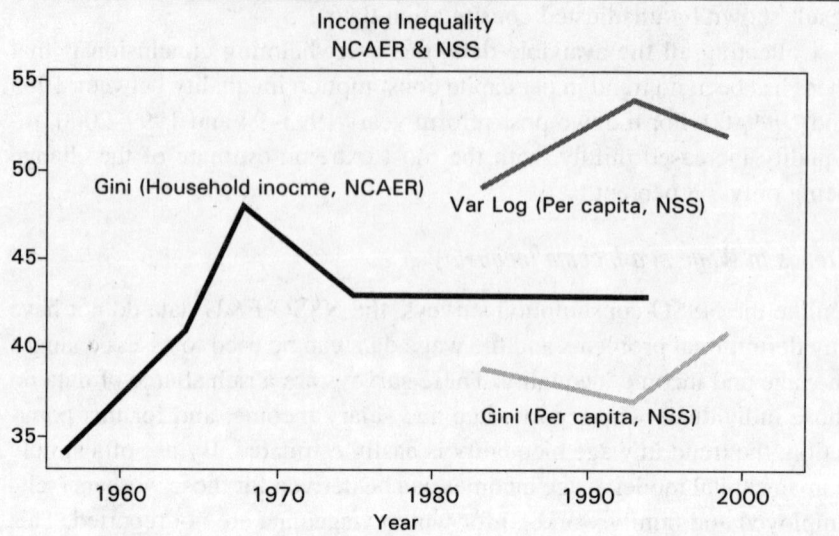

FIGURE 5.   Income Inequality, by Percentiles, NSSO Data, 1983–99

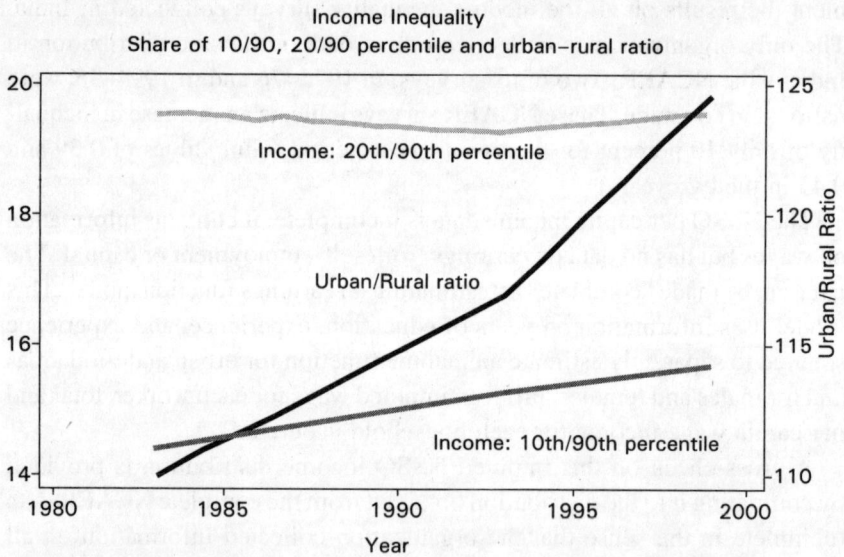

Gini of 0.42 for 1983; the 1994–95 NCAER distribution has a Gini of 0.43, a level very similar to the NSSO adjusted Gini of 0.41 for 1993–94.

The Gini for NSSO real wage inequality declines from 0.39 in 1983 to 0.37 in 1993–94 and then rises to 0.41 in 1999–2000—the same pattern as that obtained for nominal wages.[43] A different inequality measure, the variance of logs, shows a reverse pattern, that is, a peak in inequality in 1993–94 and a large decline (about 25 percent) thereafter. In other words, depending on the measure of inequality, wage inequality either increased in the 1990s by a small amount (Gini) or decreased by a large amount (variance of logs). But in all cases, the 1999–2000 level is little different than the 1983 level. This difference in the Gini and variance of log measures results most likely occurs because the Gini is more sensitive to changes near the *middle* of a distribution.

That this is indeed the case is indicated by the NSSO percentile data on wages and wage growth. Figure 5 plots these data for the period 1983 to 1999–2000. The poorest tenth and twentieth percentiles gain relative to the ninetieth percentile, between 1993–94 and 1999–2000.

INCOME INEQUALITY WORSENING: YET ANOTHER ESTIMATE. This constant inequality pattern for the 1990s (relative to the 1980s) is far removed from the conventional wisdom, where it is more or less assumed that not only did inequality worsen after the reforms, but that it did so by a large amount. One study by Banerjee and Piketty uses data on *income taxes* (paid by less than 3 percent of the population) to derive conclusions about changes in overall income distribution.[44] This heroic study has been much cited as corroborative "proof" that inequality worsened in India since the economic reforms. Banerjee and Piketty conclude that the top 0.01 percent of Indians had faster growth than the average ("the rich got richer") and that this phenomenon had "a non-trivial impact on the overall income distribution." In their 2005 update, Banerjee and Piketty warn that "if the same pattern of divergence between the rich and the rest that we saw over the past decade is repeated over the next decade, the income distribution consequences will be much more drastic than what we have so far seen."[45]

But this conclusion does not follow from the data and analysis that they present. The change in status of the top 0.01 percent will have precious little bearing on inequality unless the same change is enjoyed by, say, the top 1 or 2 percent or perhaps even the top 10 percent. For example, inequality is likely to *improve* if the top 0.01 percent gains (relative to the average) and the top 1 percent loses (again, relative to the average). The net effect is an

---

43. Real wage income figures are obtained by deflating nominal wage incomes by a price deflator which varies across states and regions (urban and rural).

44. Banerjee and Piketty (2003). See also Banerjee and Piketty (2005).

45. Banerjee and Piketty (2005, p. 528).

improvement in overall inequality since the top 1 percent has 100 times the weight of the top 0.01 percent.[46]

But even if the top 1 percent of taxpayers had faster-than-average growth, it is still questionable whether inequality would worsen. The Banerjee and Piketty conclusion rests on the assumption that rates of tax compliance remain unchanged. Whether they have or not is an empirical matter, and there is strong evidence suggesting that income tax compliance rates have increased markedly, and in a nonlinear fashion.[47] In other words, there is a "missing middle" in India's tax returns. Both the richest and the poorest of the 20 percent of India's population that is tax eligible have much higher compliance ratios (about 30–50 percent) than the less than 10 percent tax compliance ratios of those in the middle of the tax distribution.

Even worse for the Banerjee and Piketty analysis and conclusion is the fact that their own Pareto-constructed income data show that inequality *improved* in the 1990s. Table 19 reports the Banerjee and Piketty synthetic estimates (Pareto distribution derived from tax data) of income (in 1999–2000 prices) for the top 0.01 percent of the population, the top 1 percent, the 99th percentile, and so on for 1992–93, 1993–94, and 1999–2000. NSSO worker distribution for 1993–94 is used as a benchmark and the Banerjee and Piketty growth rates are imposed on this distribution, along with the growth in average per worker incomes for the bottom 98 percent of the worker population.

What Happened to Poverty in the 1990s?

The pace of poverty reduction is a function of two important variables (in addition to the shape of the distribution close to the poverty line): the rate of income growth, and the change in inequality.[48] If inequality stayed approximately the same in the 1980s and 1990s, then the pace of poverty reduction

46. One discussant, Kaushik Basu, claimed in his comments on our paper that the Banerjee–Piketty study *does* lead to the logical inference that there was an unambiguous *increase* in income inequality: "The [Banerjee-Piketty] claim is that inequalities have gone up, because 0.01 percent have a high growth, so the top end of income is pulling up very rapidly.... [W]hat you get is Lorenz curve pulling down. If the Lorenz curve is pulling down, then by virtually any measure of inequality, inequality has gone up." Both theoretically and empirically, we disagree. If the top 0.01 percent has a higher rate of growth than the average, and the top 1 percent a lower than average rate of growth, then, all else being equal, inequality has improved. This is indeed what occurs with the Banerjee–Piketty data (see table 19).

47. For evidence on increasing tax compliance, see Bhalla (2002b, 2004c); and Kelkar (2002).

48. On the shape of the distribution close to the poverty line, see Bhalla (2002a, 2002b).

T A B L E   1 9 .   **Banerjee–Piketty Data Indicating Income Inequality Improvements in the 1990s**

Income class	Level (in Rs. 000)			Cumulative growth (%)	
	1992–93	1993–94	1999–2000	1992–99	1993–99
Above 99.99 percentile	1,161	2,428	4,034	247.6	66.2
Above 99 but below 99.99	126	157	191	51.6	21.7
Top 1 percent	136	180	230	68.3	27.7
99th percentile	73	90	88	20.0	–3.0
Top 2 percentiles	105	135	159	51.4	17.4
Average worker income	20	21	29	43.9	39.9
Gini	0.4203	0.4203	n.a.	0.4198[a]	0.4079[a]
Variation of logs	0.7240	0.7240	n.a.	0.7206[a]	0.7053[a]

Source: Banerjee and Piketty (2003) for growth in wages of the top 2 percent of the population; average worker income is the ratio of private income (national accounts) and number of workers in the economy (NSSO surveys); the distribution of per worker income is obtained from NSSO E&U survey, 1993–94.

a. Derived indexes with the NSSO income distribution data for the base year (1992–93 or 1993–94) and Banerjee–Piketty percentile growth rate for the intervening years.

n.a. Not available.

can only slow in the 1990s if the rate of consumption growth declines. But as we have just seen, all indicators of income change show an acceleration in per capita growth in the post-reform period. So the pace of poverty reduction should have been faster in the 1990s, but it is observed to be lower. Why? The answer is that the NSSO consumer expenditure surveys have been capturing less and less of the consumption as indicated by the national accounts, with the consequent result that the growth of per capita consumption, according to the NSSO consumption surveys, has only been a cumulative 8 percent between 1993–94 and 1999–2000; some authors argue that the *cumulative* six-year growth in expenditures of the poor was no more than 3 percent![49] According to the national accounts data, per capita consumption grew at an annual rate of 3.2 percent in the 1990s; the NSSO-based growth rate was only 1.3 percent a year.

Table 20 provides a comprehensive listing of all the different growth rates in the two NSSO periods. Only the NSSO consumption growth shows a constancy; all other estimates (including the NSSO E&U surveys) show a sharp acceleration. The magnitude of average growth in the 1990s by all NSSO nonconsumption survey sources is also considerably higher—by at least 1.5 percentage points a year, or 9 percent over six years. This puts into

49. See Sen and Himanshu (2004a, 2004b).

TABLE 20. Per Capita Annual Growth in the 1980s and 1990s: Alternative Estimates

Indicator	1983 to 1993–94	1993–94 to 1999–2000	1983 to 1999–2000
GDP (National Accounts)	5.1	6.5	5.6
GDP per capita (National Accounts)	3.0	4.5	3.6
Per worker income (National Accounts)	1.6	5.6	3.1
Rural wages (NSSO)	2.5	4.1	3.1
Urban wages (NSSO)	2.4	4.9	3.3
Agricultural worker wages (NSSO)	2.6	2.6	2.6
Per capita consumption (National Accounts)	1.5	3.2	2.2
Per capita consumption (NSSO), old definition	0.8	1.8[a]	1.2
Per capita consumption (NSSO), new definition	1.2	1.3	1.2
Poor rural workers (Sen and Himanshu)	n.a.	0.5	n.a.

Source: NSSO Employment and Unemployment surveys conducted in 1983, 1993–94, and 1999–2000; *Handbook of Statistics on Indian Economy* (2004) published by Reserve Bank of India; Government of India; National Accounts (NA) database developed by *Economic and Political Weekly*; Census of India 1981, 1991, and 2001; Sen and Himanshu (2004a).

a. Obtained from Deaton and Dreze (2002).

n.a. Not available.

perspective the needless debate in the poverty literature in India on the likely percentage by which the NSSO consumer expenditure survey data for 1999–2000 overstated mean expenditures. The maximum possible over-statement in total 1999–2000 expenditures is considerably less than 2 per-cent, a magnitude close to the difference in annual growth between the NSSO consumption survey and other data!

The different NSSO survey estimates of cumulative growth between 1993–94 and 1999–2000 (the difference that is relevant for poverty calcu-lations) diverge by about 20 percentage points—8 percent for consumption growth compared with 28 percent for growth in rural incomes. An adjust-ment of 1 or 2 percentage points in consumption due to overreporting of food expenditures in 1999–2000 is therefore very, very minor. Thus, the sig-nificant "growth gap" between average wage growth and average per capita rural consumption growth during the 1990s dwarfs any calculations of the over- or underestimate of mean per capita expenditures in 1999–2000. The NSSO average consumption growth for six years in the 1990s is equal to the NSSO rural income growth for one year and four months; and Sen and Himanshu's cumulative consumption growth of only 3 percent in the 1990s is achieved by an average NSSO agricultural wage worker in little over a year, and by a rural wage worker in only three months.

A worst case estimate of *average* consumption growth is obtained by taking the wage growth achieved by the *poorest of the poor*, agricultural workers. And the poorest workers achieved annual growth of 2.6 percent for sixteen-and-a-half years. If this wage growth is imposed on the consumption distribution of 1983 (the most unequal distribution for all the NSSO large sample survey years), then poverty levels for different years can be generated. These poverty levels will be different from the official levels because of differences in growth; the distribution remains relatively most unequal for the 1983 distribution. If the growth rates are worst-case estimates, so are the derived poverty levels, and changes. The predicted poverty level in 1999–2000, on the basis of *average* per capita consumption growth being equal to the growth in incomes of the *poorest* workers (2.6 percent a year), is only 13 percent, fully *half* the official head count ratio of 26 percent. Note that average annual rural wage growth in the 1990s was much higher than 2.6 percent, and imposition of this larger growth would obviously imply an even lower poverty level in 1999–2000. This simulation vividly illustrates the magnitude of the upward bias in poverty calculations that results from assuming that the average per capita NSSO consumption growth reflects reality.

Conclusions

The accepted view about the behavior of the Indian economy before and after the reforms is as follows. In the 1980s economic growth averaged around 5.5 percent a year. Population growth was around 2 percent, so per capita growth averaged 3.5 percent. Employment growth was more than 2.5 percent, and unemployment rates were low. Rural India, where most of the poor reside, benefited enormously as wages of agricultural workers expanded at a rate of about 4–5 percent each year.

At the end of the 1980s, the Indian economy ran into a balance of payments crisis, and, in response, the Government of India instituted major economic reforms in the short space of two years, 1991–93. The nature of these reforms was not controversial, and every government since then has continued with them. According to the conventional view, however, these reforms did not materially benefit the economy. The GDP growth rate stayed the same, and employment growth collapsed to about 1 percent a year. Following this apparent slackening in demand, unemployment rates skyrocketed, and agricultural wage growth fell to half its pre-reform rate. Because the reforms were oriented toward the rich, urban parts of the economy, this sector benefited disproportionately more. Aggregate inequality worsened, and worsened significantly.

There are debates within this overall story, but the broad parameters are accepted by most economists, sociologists, policymakers, and politicians. The objective of this paper was to take a second look at the conventional conclusions; by doing so, we find that virtually every conclusion noted above is either unsupported or reversed. In the last few years, annual GDP growth of around 7 percent now makes the post-reform GDP (and GDP per capita) growth significantly *higher* than it was before the reforms. Regarding employment, evaluation of census and NSSO data indicates that the rate of growth in the supply of working-age people *declined* by 0.3–0.7 percent a year in the post-reform period. This demographic shift has been ignored by most analysts who have examined the slow job growth of the 1990s. If the size of the potential labor force has declined, it means that employment growth has to be less (and wages higher) to keep the labor market in equilibrium, all else being equal. Further, NSSO employment data for the period 2000–03 (also considered a period of jobless growth) shows healthy growth of 2.9 percent a year, a pace well above growth of potential labor supply (around 2 percent a year).

On deeper examination, the conclusion that the growth rate of agricultural wages collapsed is also shown to be wrong. Although Sundaram and Ahluwalia had pointed out that the NSSO data indicated *no* decline in wage growth in the post-reform 1990s, this finding was ignored by most analysts.[50] Examination of all the non-NSSO data on agricultural wages also indicates no support for the view that wages collapsed; instead, overwhelming support is obtained for the conclusion that wage growth of poor agricultural workers at least stayed constant. NSSO data reveal that wage growth of rural and urban workers accelerated sharply in the post-reform period. Unemployment rates, while higher in 1999–2000 than in 1993–94, were still lower than the levels prevailing in much of the pre-reform period. By 2003 unemployment rates had declined to a near thirty-year low (and were much lower than that they had been just four years earlier in 1999–2000).

Data on both consumption and income inequality were examined in detail. Both consumption and income data reflect the mildest of inverted V's, with the pre-reform period being one end and 1999–2000 being the other, and 1993–94 being the low point of inequality. However, the improvement between 1983 and 1993–94 is less than 9 percent, and the subsequent

50. Sundaram (2001a, 2001b); Ahluwalia (2002).

worsening was only about 4 percent or so. Thus, the post-reform year 1999–2000 is observed to have marginally *lower* inequality than either of the two pre-reform years, 1983 or 1987–88.

Thus, one consistent view of the economy has been replaced by another consistently opposite view. Previously, it was thought that reforms were not effective in raising aggregate growth, employment, and wages. Because the reforms involved some macroeconomic policies, such as devaluing the rupee, reducing tariffs, making the economy more open, and making exports competitive, critics of the reforms did not ask why these seemingly sensible policies were not having a positive effect. However, no one, not even the critics, has questioned the basic thrust of economic reforms: the necessity of opening up the economy, the reduction in import tariff rates to international levels, the goal of making the rupee more competitive, and the abolition of the industrial licensing system.

The new picture we show here is also consistent: the reforms were remarkably successful in generating jobs and reducing unemployment rates, and the data used are the *same* as those arguing the opposite. For some of the revised conclusions, there is the advantage of having additional data, but most previous findings were questionable even based on old data. One explanation for the (faulty) previous set of findings is that like news, research occurs in waves. Researchers "build" on prior research, sometimes with an ideological filter. So a wave of opinion becomes a new "reality." And this reality can become policy, as has recently occurred in India. Unemployment rates are at historic lows, the unemployed are found to be the educated nonpoor, and yet the government, perhaps aided by the previous jobless growth "findings," decides to embark on an employment guarantee scheme for the rural unemployed—a category of workers showing the least amount of unemployment.

TABLE A-1. Agricultural Wages from Different Sources[a]

	Nominal						Real					
Year	AWI	CoC	NSSO	Plowman AWI	Unskilled ILJ	Plowman ILJ	AWI	CoC	NSSO	Plowman AWI	Unskilled ILJ	Plowman ILJ
1970	3.0						16.9					
1971	3.4	3.3					19.2	18.9				
1972	3.4	3.4					17.6	17.3				
1973	3.3	3.5					15.3	15.0				
1974	4.8	4.2					15.1	13.3				
1975	5.0	4.4					16.5	14.5				
1976	5.4	4.7					20.5	18.0				
1977	5.6	5.0					19.4	17.1				
1978	5.4	5.4					18.9	18.8				
1979	5.8	5.8					18.8	18.7				
1980	6.5	6.5					18.4	18.3				
1981	7.2	7.1					18.0	17.7				
1982	7.8	7.4		6.7			18.6	17.7		16.8		
1983	8.9	8.2	6.6				19.1	17.6	14.9			
1984	10.3	9.5					22.0	20.3				
1985	11.8	10.6					24.2	21.7				
1986	13.1	11.4					25.5	22.1				
1987	14.8	12.7					26.3	22.4				
1988	16.7	14.6					26.3	22.9				

Year											
1989	18.3	16.4				27.3	24.5				
1990	19.9	18.7				27.6	25.9				
1991	22.3	21.9	21.5			25.9	25.4	25.0			
1992	26.3	25.3				27.3	26.2				
1993	28.9	29.0		19.6		28.9	29.0	19.6			
1994	32.2	33.6				28.7	30.0				
1995	35.9	37.9				28.9	30.6				
1996	41.7	41.8	37.7			30.8	30.9	27.9			
1997	46.5	46.8	43.5			33.3	33.5	31.2			
1998	50.8	50.4		42.6	53.7	32.8	32.6		22.9	27.5	34.7
1999	53.2	54.4		46.7	59.8	32.9	33.6		23.8	28.9	37.0
2000	55.0[b]	57.0		48.9	61.9	34.1	35.4		25.3	30.3	38.4
2001	59.3[b]	61.5[b]		51.2	66.7	36.3	37.6		25.6	31.3	40.8
2002	62.0[b]	64.2		53.0	69.7	36.7	38.1		28.1	31.4	41.3
2003						38.4	39.5				46.8
2004	71.5[b]	73.1[b]		54.4[b]	93.3[b]	40.0	41.0		30.5		52.3

Source: Agricultural Wages in India (AWI), Cost of Cultivation (CoC) of principal crops survey, and *Indian Labour Journal* (ILJ) are all published by the Ministry of Agriculture, Government of India. The AWI series appears to have been discontinued from 2000–01 onward and been replaced by the ILJ series. Updating of the series for the years 2000–01 to 2002–03 was done by grafting on the growth rate as observed in the ILJ series onto the other series; the 2004–05 data has been updated via the growth rate for 1999–2000 to 2004–05 observed for agricultural workers in the NSSO survey for 1999–2000 and the Indian Retirement, Earnings and Savings (IRES) (survey for 2004–05) conducted by Ministry of Finance, Government of India. NSSO refers to data collected by the Employment-Unemployment surveys conducted in years 1983, 1993–94, and 1999–2000.

a. Data on agricultural wages are collected for various categories of agricultural workers, the most common of which is a plowman. Blank spaces indicate data not available.
b. Indicates that the number has been derived using other wage data series.

Comments and Discussion

Kaushik Basu: How successful have the Indian reforms of the early 1990s been? This question has been the source of much controversy, heartburn, and debate. The aim of the paper by Surjit Bhalla and Tirthatanmoy Das is to contribute to this debate by looking at three broad parameters of performance: job creation, poverty, and inequality. Toward this objective the authors marshal an extremely impressive range of data sources—various rounds of the National Sample Survey—including Employment-Unemployment and Consumer Expenditure surveys, data from Agricultural Wages in India and Cost of Crop Cultivation surveys, and more. This empirical reach is commendable, and learning how the numbers are collected and collated makes for interesting reading.

Nevertheless, the paper fails to persuade because it attempts to slay too many dragons. The paper begins by outlining a long list of "accepted views" about what has happened to growth, employment, poverty, and inequality, with the aim of taking a "second look" at all these conventional wisdoms, and "by doing so," Bhalla and Das find that "virtually every conclusion ... is either not supported or reversed." Now, whenever an author finds that "virtually every" conventional wisdom is wrong, clearly the sensible strategy is to question one's own analysis, instead of *everybody* else's. And if the authors of this paper had done so, they would have themselves discovered most of the flaws that I discuss below.

The main problem of the paper is—over-zealousness. In evaluating the reforms, the authors refuse to give an inch. *Everything*, it seems, has turned out for the better. The subtext is that no government intervention is needed. All is hunky dory. The paper ends up, effectively, as an endorsement of the BJP-government slogan "India shining."

Conventional Wisdom

Let us look into their argument in some detail. First of all, what Bhalla and Das describe as conventional wisdom, held by virtually all Indian economists, is not so. For instance, they say "the conventional view" is that the "GDP growth rate remained the same" before and after the reforms and that poverty did not decline. On the contrary, there is widespread agreement

234

that the post-reform GDP growth rate is higher—somewhat, compared with the 1980s, and, significantly, compared with earlier times. Likewise, there is increasing agreement that poverty, as defined by the percentage of the population below the poverty line, had gone down by the end of the 1990s. It is true that the fifty-fifth round of the NSSO, because of its effort to collect data on consumption for both the last seven days and the last thirty days, creates comparability problems with previous NSSO surveys. But, thanks to two excellent papers, by Deaton and by Sen and Himanshu, we have as good insights into poverty changes as can be gleaned from the data.[1] And it is evident that, although the decline is not as sharp as had been claimed by the then-BJP government, poverty has gone down.

The other two conventional wisdoms are rightly described in the paper. It is widely believed that the higher growth of the 1990s has not been accompanied by a commensurate growth in jobs and that inequality—regional and personal—has gone up.

As a consequence, the paper has little to add on GDP growth and poverty. What is therefore of potential interest is what it has to say on "jobless growth" and inequality. The paper's conclusions on inequality—namely, that everybody else is wrong—turns out, on inspection, to be invalid. The discussion on jobless growth is more interesting. The numbers here are messy enough that one cannot reach an easy conclusion. But the data collated and organized in this paper is, in itself, deserving of attention.

Jobless Growth

The authors' basic contention is that the number of new jobs created each year since the reforms may be low, but that does not translate into a high unemployment rate because the increase in labor force has itself been low. They construct this finding by using a variety of interesting data sources. While their final conclusion does not stand up to scrutiny, the process of building up to that conclusion makes for absorbing reading.

The final conclusion is marred by some small flaws and one conceptual omission. Take, for instance, the authors' observation, "If inward and outward migration is not significant, then employment growth cannot exceed [the] rate of growth [of potential labor supply]." "Potential labor supply," it is worth reminding the reader, is the total working age population, unmindful of whether a particular person wishes to work or not. This definition contrasts with the "labor force," which consists of the population working or

1. Deaton (2001); Sen and Himanshu (2004a).

looking for work. It is now easy to see that the quoted sentence is invalid and occurs because of an elementary confusion between "level" and "growth." It is indeed true that the level or size of the labor force or the size of the working population cannot exceed the level of potential labor force. But that is not so for the growth rates. Consider two years in which there is no change in the potential labor force. But suppose in the first year half the people in the potential labor force worked and in the second year everybody worked. In that case growth in the potential labor force is zero, and growth in jobs is 100 percent, thereby demonstrating the invalidity of the quoted sentence.

It is not as if the authors are unaware of this, as later remarks by them demonstrate. The source of their mistake is overzealousness. So keen are they to keep the labor force growth rate low (since that tends to make the unemployment rate low) that they end up making this error. Not surprisingly, the unemployment rate that they calculate for the year 2003—namely, 2.2 percent—would put Japan to shame.

The handling of dates also raises questions. The paper goes through a rather convoluted argument to explain why 1990–91 should be treated as belonging to both the pre-reform and the post-reform periods. Since 1990–91 was one of the worst years for the Indian economy, treating it in both periods immediately ensures that the post-reform changes will look better than the changes in the pre-reform period.

The more serious mistake is that of not making room for what is known in the literature as the "discouraged worker effect."[2] It is well known that when the job scenario gets bad and work becomes consistently hard to find, people often withdraw from the labor market, that is, they become too discouraged to continue searching for work. When this happens, the size of the unemployed pool (those without work *and looking for work*) goes down, and so the unemployment rate goes down. This of course is no reason for celebration since the improvement in the unemployment rate in cases like this is simply a statistical artifact.

Inequality

Turn now to inequality. Bhalla and Das dismiss out of hand Deaton and Dreze's findings on "the pervasive increase in economic inequality in the nineties," as based on "a synthetic estimate." They also dismiss Sen and Himanshu's claims on worsening inequality as a consequence of their "mixing of data on different definitions of consumption." But there are many

2. See discussion in Basu, Genicot, and Stiglitz (2003).

other writers who subscribe to the view of deteriorating inequality in India. In fact, on this the authors are right that there is near-consensus. And this is so for the good reason that inequality has been getting worse for several decades and particularly in the 1990s.[3]

The increase in inequality is true whether one looks at overall measures, such as the Gini coefficient or the variance of logs, or at segments of the population, such as the class of income-tax payers. By most overall measures applied to NSSO data, inequality in 1999 was worse than it was in 1993. One can quibble over whether these are good years to compare and whether these are the best numbers to look at, but the fact remains that the large NSSO surveys show a worsening in the 1990s.

Bhalla's disagreement with Banerjee and Piketty is based on a simple misunderstanding. Banerjee and Piketty show a sharp worsening of income distribution at the top—namely, that the richest 0.01 percent of the population grew sharply richer between 1992 and 1999.[4] Their income rose by an astonishing 348 percent. Banerjee and Piketty do not claim that *therefore* inequality increased overall. So Bhalla and Das's claim that during the same period the top 2 percent of the population had a decrease in its income share, and that this amounts to evidence of "anomalies" in the Banerjee–Piketty study, is not meaningful.

On this they also misquote me. My comment was in the context of the claim made in an earlier version of their paper that Banerjee and Piketty's findings are compatible with unchanged inequality "since *it very well might be the case that the super-rich are taking from the very rich*, leaving the aggregate inequality unchanged" (my italics). I had merely pointed out that, if the italicized part of the quote were true, then anybody with familiarity with Lorenz curve analysis would be able to see that inequality would have to get worse. So Bhalla and Das's claim was untenable.

Spurious Causality

One widespread weakness is the presumption that whatever happened after the reforms was *caused* by the reforms. Throughout the paper the language used is that of causality between the reforms and changes in the economy. "The new... picture shows that the reforms were remarkably successful in generating jobs," it is pointed out. But no effort is made to link the greater

3. See, for example, Ahluwalia (2000); Rao, Kalirajan, and Shand (1999); Banerjee and Piketty (2003); and Basu (2004).
4. Banerjee and Piketty (2003).

jobs (to the extent that that was so) to the reforms, excepting that the reforms preceded the jobs.

What this analysis misses is that hundreds of changes are taking place at any time. And especially in this age of globalization, when a change in Brazil or South Africa or the United States can affect outcomes in India, it is not clear that all changes in the late 1990s can be attributed to the Indian reforms of the early 1990s. The increasing economic inequality is a case in point. I think this inequality is intimately connected to globalization and technological changes and would occur in individual countries whether or not economic reforms had occurred. It may not be a matter of coincidence that inequality is on the rise in so many nations—the United States, China, and India. As the globe shrinks the lower end of the U.S. labor market faces increasing competition from China and India, and so the wages of lower-end jobs in the U.S. get pulled down, relatively. Equally, as the labor market for skilled workers and professional managers becomes more integrated globally, the top-end incomes in India and China increase sharply. This causes inequality in India and China to rise. This is nicely compatible with Banerjee and Piketty's findings regarding Indian inequality.

Moreover, while Indian inequality is huge in absolute terms, it is not particularly bad in relation to what is happening to other nations. Take the simple measure of the ratio of the income of a nation's richest 10 percent divided by the income of the poorest 10 percent. According to the World Bank's *Human Development Report*, this ratio for Brazil is 85, for China 18.4, for the United States 15.8, and for India 7. So the Indian problem is big in absolute terms but not in relative terms.

My belief is that while these large inequalities are embarrassing, there is little that any individual country, especially one that is poor and a relatively small player in the global marketplace, can do about it without driving away capital and skilled labor. So if inequality is to be tackled, coordinated global action will be needed. That is something that has to be entrusted to an international organization. And given that the world does not have an appropriate organization for this task, it may need to create one.[5]

Government Interventions

Turning to the subtext of government interventions, that old debate of "whether markets or governments" is dead, and mercifully so. Most contemporary economists recognize that it is not a matter of which but of how

5. I have argued this in Basu (2006).

much of which and where. I have personally taken the view that in a variety of market matters, India needs to rely much more on free contracts, instead of terms and conditions laid down by the government. One area in urgent need of reform on this score is labor market policy, where much more market-based flexibility is needed. At the same time, when it comes to poverty and matters concerning basic standard of living parameters, there is need for purposive government intervention. And for that it is immaterial whether poverty has gone down or risen and whether inequality today is more or less. What needs to be agreed is whether there is too much poverty and inequality is too high. And on this question, anybody who is aware of India's surging economy and also sees the roadside dwellers in big cities and reads about the conditions of farmers in the semi-arid areas of the country can easily agree that the huge deprivations suffered by some segments of the population are wrong.

I am aware that not every wrong can be corrected. As I have already argued, a single nation can only do a limited amount to reduce inequality in today's globalized world. On poverty and unemployment, there is a lot that government needs to and can do, and the government should not wait until we economists have sorted out whether the first-derivative of the trends of these indicators over the last decades were positive or negative.[6]

Devesh Kapur: The paper addresses two politically salient issues in India—employment and inequality—that are critical not just to debates on the effects of reforms but also to the evolution of India's political economy. It challenges the prevailing consensus that reforms have not delivered on employment. The paper subsequently extends the analysis to the other two legs of the holy trinity of the critiques of reforms—poverty and inequality—and finds a much happier story there as well. According to the paper's analysis, the reforms have delivered on all three fronts—employment, poverty, and inequality—and critics are head-in-the-sand Cassandras.

The paper is empirically rich and in its key messages serves an important gadfly function. Its analysis and discussions on employment are more persuasive, however, than those on inequality. Even if the claims of jobless growth are exaggerated, how is one to understand the decline in employment growth rates? The paper argues that fewer numbers are entering the labor force because a larger number of the age cohort is enrolled in higher education.

6. Ferro, Rosenblatt, and Stern (2004).

Nonetheless, there is no denying that given the robustness of India's economic growth, the expectations of higher employment growth have not been met. What could be the reasons for anemic employment growth?

One, it might reflect noise in the data. How meaningful are employment and wage data in a country where more than half the population is self-employed? India does not collect income data in any systematic way. And as for consumption expenditures, the growing discrepancy between the NSSO and the national accounts data puts that into question as well. Comparing wages over time is sensitive to the choice of deflators—but in India the deflators have themselves become more error prone because of a failure to incorporate quality improvements. In addition, studies on changes resulting from reforms are particularly sensitive to the choice of year when the reforms began and whether 1991 should be included or excluded in the pre- or post-reform era. Studies are also sensitive to the choice of the terminal year. For instance, initial studies showed a large payoff from reforms as growth accelerated; however, as growth moderated in the late 1990s, studies suggested that the growth in the post-reform decade differed little from that in the 1980s. However, a renewed burst of growth over the last few years has again shifted the tenor of the debate.

Two, it could simply be that as education and household incomes rise, people can now "afford" to be unemployed because they are no longer as poor as in the past. However, while unemployment increased with education between 1983 and 1993, it dropped (albeit slightly) in the more recent period (1993–2000).

Three, lower employment growth could reflect differential sectoral growth rates, especially if India's economic growth is being driven by sectors with low employment elasticities (human-capital-intensive services and capital-intensive manufacturing), even as growth in sectors with high employment elasticities (agriculture) has dropped. There has been a modest decline in employment within public and private registered enterprises (which are concentrated in manufacturing and services), in the post-reform period. In the public sector, total employment (including central government, state government, local government, and quasi-government) increased rapidly in the 1970s and 1980s from 10.7 million in 1971 to 16.0 million in 1981 and 19.1 million in 1991. It barely changed over the next decade rising to 19.1 million in 2001 before declining to 18.6 million in 2003.[7] The growing dominance of the service sector in GDP, with its greater prevalence of

7. "Employment Statistics in India," *Economic and Political Weekly*, May 3, 2003, for 1971–2001 and Ministry of Labor, Government of India, "Annual Report 2004," for 2003.

contract and informal labor, has meant that even though this has been the fastest-growing sector, employment within the registered portion has not grown commensurately. Among large firms in this sector, the largest growth in employment has been in the information technology sector, while modest growth in private banks has been offset by the pruning of jobs in public sector banks.[8]

The stagnation of employment in the formal manufacturing sector, despite robust growth (averaging more than 7 percent since the reforms began), poses another puzzle. One explanation is that productivity growth in the 1990s put a damper on labor demand. However, strong total factor productivity growth should increase profits and reinvestment, and the resulting capital accumulation should drive employment demand. A second explanation is that there has been a change in the "intensity" of employment as distinct from the "extensity" of employment. For instance, Bhalotra found that between 1979 and 1987, the manufacturing sector saw a significant increase in working hours (resulting in the equivalent of changing from a five- to a six-day shift). As a result earnings rose rapidly, employment and wage rates much less so.[9] A third explanation is that labor law rigidities have made firms wary of increasing employment lest they be saddled with extra labor in lean times. If so, one should observe faster growth in firms with fewer than a hundred employees (since the rigid labor laws apply only to larger firms), and an increase in capital intensity as firms substitute capital for labor.

Just how critical are rigid labor regulations to employment growth? Clearly they cannot explain the slowdown in employment growth since the same regulations were valid earlier. Indeed, as with much else in India, it is not the existence of regulations per se but their enforcement that matters more. And the declining bargaining strength of labor over the past two decades (evident for instance in the decline in strikes and a relative increase in lockouts) reflects the diminishing political clout of organized labor in India. Moreover, the Supreme Court has taken a tougher stance on labor indiscipline, in contrast to the 1970s and 1980s. Consequently, firms have been able to deploy a variety of strategies to get around labor laws from voluntary retirement schemes to outsourcing to technological upgrading to employing contract labor.

Other evidence also supports an implication of the paper that labor flexibility is not perhaps as critical an issue as it is made out to be. Labor regulations are cited by just 16.7 percent of respondents in firm-level surveys in

8. See Shirsat (2005) for a recent analysis of service sector employment gains and losses.
9. Bhalotra (1998).

India as a critical impediment facing India's manufacturing sector. Other factors ranging from corruption among public officials, courts, regulation, taxes, lack of financing, poor infrastructure, and policy uncertainty are all cited by firms as more important in deterring investment than labor regulations. Nonetheless, it is the case that India does worse than many countries on the rigidity of employment index (that is, policies related to hiring and firing of workers). While India does better than the average for low-income countries, it does worse than middle-income countries and substantially worse than China. However, it would seem that if India could bring its bankruptcy procedures in line with Chinese standards, that might give an even larger fillip to the manufacturing sector than changing labor laws (table 21).

TABLE 21. **Comparative Business Climate in India**

Measure	India	China	Lower-middle income	Upper-middle income
Time required to start a business (days)	89	41	53	46
Time required to enforce contracts (days)	425	241	398	408
Time to resolve insolvency (years)	10.0	2.4	3.4	3.4
Index of ease of hiring and firing workers (0 = least rigid, 100 = most rigid)	48	30	40	34

Source: World Bank, *World Development Indicators, 2005*, table 5-3.

The principal reason for the decline in employment growth rates would appear to be the anemic growth of agriculture, the country's largest employer. Agriculture growth rates in India sharply declined from 3.4 percent between 1985–86 and 1994–95 to 1.8 percent between 1995–96 and 2002–03. It is not surprising that the growth rate of agricultural employment declined from an annual average of 2.6 percent between 1983 and 1993 to 0 percent between 1993 and 1999. While the occupational category "farmers and fisherman" increased by nearly 49 million in the former period, it increased by just 0.5 million in the latter period. In a sector that has high employment elasticities, such a large relative decline in growth rates in the post-reform era is bound to have adverse affects on national employment figures.

The paper makes a brave attempt to undermine studies that appear to show increases in inequality. I am skeptical of the analysis that inequality in India has not increased. At the upper tail both consumption and wage data are very inadequate in their ability to capture changes in income. Nonwage sources of income, particularly income from financial and property assets, have become much more important for the upper deciles of the population.

Moreover, the rates of return to education have increased. The educational premium has widened in India in the 1990s paralleling the experience elsewhere.[10] Given the very high degree of educational inequality in India, a widening education premium cannot but have an adverse affect on income inequality. Additionally there is substantial evidence that interstate inequality is increasing because of diverging growth rates, largely due to the failure of some northern states (especially Uttar Pradesh and Bihar) to enact reforms.

Given their political salience and welfare implications, employment and inequality will continue to attract analytical attention. Among the many questions that need addressing, I highlight a few.

—There is a need to move beyond comparing outcomes pre- and post-reforms to counterfactual analysis—what would have happened if reforms had not occurred?

—A shift in the analytical focus from the national to the state level might allow a better scrutiny of the data. For instance interstate variation in employment growth coupled to interstate growth rates would be a good cross-check of possible inconsistencies in the data as well as the causal mechanisms.

—Export growth rates since liberalization have been almost double GDP growth rates. Consequently one would expect growing employment in export-oriented sectors, especially since export intensity in an industry appears to have a positive impact on employment.[11] How much of a difference is this likely to make if export growth continues at its recent robust clip?

—As distinct from the level of wages and employment, have reforms resulted in greater wage and employment volatility? If this is the case, are there implications for creating or enhancing insurance mechanisms that might also make labor more amenable to reforms in labor regulations?[12]

—Given changes in labor demand, the supply of skills is an important issue that needs better understanding. To the extent that economic reforms change the structure of the economy, they also result in changes in the demand for skills. For instance a growing urban economy needs a large number of skilled technicians—be it plumbers or electricians or auto

10. See, for example, Duraiswamy (2000); and Desai, Kapur, and McHale (2003).
11. Banga (2005).
12. Hasan, Mitra, and Ramaswamy (2003).

244 INDIA POLICY FORUM, 2005–06

mechanics. An educational system geared to producing people with degrees but no skills will result in a sharp supply-demand mismatch. Consequently one can have both higher levels of unemployment coexisting with sharp increases in wage rates for a range of other occupations and skills. For policy purposes, it is imperative to identify skill supply-demand mismatches.

From an analytical and policy perspective, it might be fruitful to examine changes in inequality among different social groups in India and its causes. For instance, intercaste earnings inequality appears to have fallen in the last two decades while interreligion earnings differences have risen.[13] And while unequal distribution of observed skills explained inequality among urban male workers in the 1980s, unequal returns on observed skills became a more important determinant in the 1990s.[14] The reasons may have to do with the evolution of Indian politics and society, but the precise mechanisms need careful analytical attention.

Esther Duflo: The last few years have been marked with lively debate on the trends in poverty, inequality, wages, and employment in India. Some of the best Indian and international scholars have contributed to the debate, approaching it from a variety of angles and using a variety of data sources. This literature is both rich and of high quality. The paper by Bhalla and Das adds to this literature by presenting new evidence on each of these aspects.

The paper revisits some known arguments and brings some original data to bear. It is a very rich piece of work that leaves almost no stone unturned. Clearly, substantial work went into this piece, and the end-product is impressive both in its scope and ambition.

The main merit of this paper is the lesson that looking at the multiplicity of data with a unique viewpoint is dangerous. By trying to show that reforms in the 1990s have been bad for the poor, some authors may have overlooked certain pieces of data that went against their own opinions. In fact, according to Bhalla and Das, it is not just one or two authors who have overlooked isolated pieces of data that did not fit with their theories; essentially everyone who has ever worked on the subject has gotten *all* the pieces of data systematically wrong. In contrast to the misleadingly coherent picture that emerges from this body of work (poverty has dropped, but not as fast as one may have

---

13. Bhaumik and Chakrabarty (2006).
14. Kijima (forthcoming).

hoped; formal employment and wages have stagnated; inequality has increased), Bhalla and Das present a new picture of the 1990s and early 2000s, equally coherent, but with the exact opposite message: unemployment was stable in the 1990s and decreased in the 2000s; wages increased faster in the 1990s than before; and therefore inequality must have remained stable and poverty must have decreased. According to the authors, indeed it did: they say the "poverty rate, correctly calculated, is only 13 percent today." To reach these conclusions, the paper needs to revisit what the authors present as common, if erroneous, knowledge.

Strangely enough, given how aware the authors are that strong priors can lead one to make choices and assumptions that are at best contentious, Bhalla and Das seem to repeatedly fall into this trap themselves, always picking the pieces of data that best fit their argument. The paper covers impressive ground and makes many forceful claims. It is outside the scope of these comments to scrutinize every single one of these claims, so I will highlight just some of these issues, picked somewhat at random.

In the discussion on employment, the authors argue that the small sample can be used because on average it gives the same answer as a large round: later on, however, we are told that 1993–94 is "above trend" relative to the other years (small sample), and that the treatment of this particular year is at the center of the "re-visit" of the data (since the authors do not contest the fact that employment growth was low between 1993–94 and 1999, relative to previous years). With a small number of employment-unemployment surveys, can one really claim that there is nothing special about the large survey in one paragraph, and in the next say that the 1993–94 period seems above trend? How do we know that this is not a data issue, with the small sample giving different answers than the large sample? Another way to interpret the same results would be to say that the growth in employment was high before the reforms and low afterward. If 1993–94 is a post-reform year, using this year actually underestimates the difference in the pre-reform trend. Incidentally, as figure 1 shows, the growth of employment seems to have been fast in the years 1987–93 and to have slowed a bit afterward. The authors seem to assume that the problem is solved, since they draw a unique trend for the entire period, and this of course implies that the 1987 data was "below" trend and the 1993 data "above" trend. This implication rules out the hypothesis that there may have been a trend break in employment growth from the outset. I also do not understand where the observation that there was an "acceleration" of job growth in the year immediately following the reform comes from (the rate of growth is exactly the same after 1990 as it was just before, according to figure 1).

More fundamentally, the discussion on employment and unemployment somehow misses the main point. The worry is not that people are declaring themselves to be unemployed, but that despite economic growth, they are employed in a variety of unskilled, unproductive, low-paying informal jobs. In surveys Abhijit Banerjee and I have conducted in Udaipur district, Rajasthan, and Hyderabad, India, we show people to be remarkably active: they have a small plot of land in a rural area, or a small business in the city; they are working a day job whenever labor is available; and they somehow get by in this way, through a combination of multiple occupations and temporary migration.[15] A very small minority have a stable employment source, including their land, which does not provide enough resources for a family to live on. Their land is too small, their businesses are undercapitalized, and they have essentially no assets to speak of. These poor people would presumably be better off if they had salaried jobs and could be matched with some capital, and yet they are not. With its focus on whether someone was working or not in the past week, this paper ignores the issue that has really troubled researchers and policymakers: most of the poor remain small-scale entrepreneurs, in the sense that they bear most of the risk associated with their businesses, and this has apparently not changed with liberalization.

The section arguing that inequality has not increased between 1993 and 1999 is particularly disappointing. To start, it presents a misleading impression of the work both by Banerjee and Piketty and by Deaton and Dreze. Beginning with Deaton and Dreze, this paper states that they (as well as Sen and Himanshu) claim that rural-urban inequality is an indicator of overall inequality. They do not. Instead, their argument is that inequality in rural areas has been more or less constant, but that it has risen within urban areas, between urban and rural areas, and between states that are doing well economically and states that are not. The argument presented in this paper (table 19 and associated discussion) that the Banerjee–Piketty data in fact show a decline in inequality does not make any sense. They show an increase of income in *all* the top shares (0.1 percent, 1 percent, and so on), which is clearly an indication of an increase in inequality at the top. They do point out that the top 1 percent grows similarly to the rest of the population for the 1990s. There is simply no way this data indicates a "decrease" in inequality, and the paragraph trying to show the opposite gives the impression of trying to defy gravity. The only substantial comment on Banerjee–Piketty is that the increase in the top share is an artifact of higher reporting due to the decline in the top marginal rate. Banerjee and Piketty discuss the matter at length in

15. Banerjee and Duflo (2006).

the paper, and they make two observations: First, the trend in the increase in the top share started well before this episode and is quite continuous, suggesting it cannot be explained by this decline. Second, the magnitudes are not right: explaining a tripling of the top share with a decline of the top rate of 40–60 percent would seem to be really difficult.

One could quibble with the construction of some of the numbers in the "consumption inequality section" as well. For example, the section on "real inequality" uses the Planning Commission price indexes to deflate consumption. As Deaton and Tarozzi have shown, these indexes grossly overstate urban relative to rural prices. Using the indexes will therefore "reduce" inequality (since they make the richest group appear poorer than it is), and one can hypothesize (though not having done it, I will not present this as a foregone conclusion) that this will also reduce the trend in inequality, because the urban areas are getting rich faster than the rural areas. Bhalla and Das could have avoided this problem by using the Deaton–Tarozzi index. The construction of the data in some sections of this paper is unclear. In particular, I was not sure whether the "adjusted consumption" data is now calculated using Deaton's initial suggestion, or with the adjustments that Bhalla had subsequently proposed (and that turned out to be incorrect, as demonstrated by Deaton and Dreze). Since there is no reference to this debate, it is not entirely clear what was done.

What is, however, the most surprising in this section of the paper is the treatment of the numbers in the text. Why is an increase in the Gini coefficient of 8 percent (or 4 percent for that matter) "small"? Given that this indicator was stable for long periods of time before, we are talking about a very large percentage increase. What is the statistical test that allows the authors to conclude that this increase is "insignificant"? This tendency to use the word "significant" or "insignificant" throughout the paper without any specific meaning (except to refer to what these authors consider significant or not) is somewhat disconcerting. Finally, how is it that in the conclusion we are left with the thought that consumption inequality decreased between 1983 and 1999, when most numbers in the authors' own tables suggest just the opposite (it is just the "real" number, which has the problem we discussed above, that shows a decline).

The arguments on why the NSSO overstates poverty and understates consumption by the poor have been extensively discussed elsewhere, and this is probably not the place to discuss them once again. The widening discrepancy between the NSSO data and the national accounts is troubling, however, and is likely to reflect problems with both data sources. Additionally, it is true that the level and the increase of this "missing consumption" is of an order of magnitude larger than what turned out to be the effect of the change in the NSSO reference period. Yet, we did not know this until Deaton and others did the exercise, so there is really little point in criticizing the exercise just because the answer turned out to be that the problem was not that bad. Here, the authors propose applying the growth in agricultural wages calculated *from the NSSO* to the income distribution in 1983; the conclusion is that the rate of poverty thus calculated is 13 percent, rather than 26 percent as the NSSO consumption data suggest. It is not very clear why the wage data is a better variable for evaluating the growth in the consumption of the poor than the measures of their consumption calculated from the NSS. Many of the poor are not working for wages, or not working for wages for most of the year. The fact that the wages, when paid, have increased, does not tell us what the rate of increase of income is for this population, and even less what the rate of consumption increase is. It is precisely because labor income is hard to calculate that the NSSO (like most surveys around the world) tries to evaluate economic welfare by measuring consumption. This is fraught with difficulties, but if one wants to say something on measuring consumption-based poverty, there seems to be no escape.

Bhalla and Das teach us, in part by their criticisms of others, but perhaps even more by their own practices, that using aggregate time-series data to try to say something about the impact of liberalization on poverty is a somewhat doomed effort. The NSSO data is available only for key years, including the 1993 year that is difficult to categorize as "before" or "after" liberalization, depending on how long one thinks economic processes take. The paper explicitly ridicules me for ignoring (in my discussion of a previous version of the paper) that 1993 comes after 1991. It is true that I am an economist, rather than a historian, but I can still manage this level of sophistication with the chronology. The point was that we have no idea when the reforms started to have an impact, since we do not know (and are not given a model for) the time-series process that generates this data. Given that phenomena like employment and unemployment are in large part "medium-run" phenomena, one should be forgiven for thinking that placing 1993 squarely in the "after" period, and therefore attributing the outcomes in that year to the reforms, is in large part wishful thinking. We discussed this in the context of the employment data. The same importance regarding how to treat the year 1993 is true for inequality, where the conclusion that inequality increased in the 1990s is based on the comparison 1993–99. The point is that we do not know whether to "attribute" events in 1991, 1992, or 1993 to the reforms or not. And there is no reason to think we should know. Given how much else has happened in the world over time, attributing any change in the time series to the reforms is very hazardous.

A serious effort to document the patterns in the data, without trying at all costs to establish causal links (in either direction) between them and the reforms, is definitely very valuable. But to investigate the causal effect of liberalization on poverty and inequality, one needs more than a time series with, in the worst case, three points including an ambiguous one. It will be necessary to be somewhat more creative in the use of the available data, perhaps exploiting differences across regions on the effect of liberalization. For example, Topalova uses a district-level panel of inequality and poverty measures to trace the impact of trade liberalization on poverty at the district level, exploiting the fact that the initial industrial composition of a district predicts how much a particular district is affected by liberalization.[16] Foster and Rosenzweig study the impact of countryside industrialization on welfare, and show that India's entry into the global economy has reduced the gender gap by increasing incentives to provide girls with an English education.[17] These papers all tell us something precise about a specific causal mechanism. They can be evaluated on the merit of their assumptions without having to make guesses about when the right date to start counting a year as being "post-globalization" is. The desperate effort to read a consistent pattern into the disparate pieces of data has led these authors to tarnish their commendable effort in accumulating so much data with avoidable mistakes and exaggerations.

General Discussion

T. N. Srinivasan pointed to the difficulties of interpreting the aggregate data in the absence of some underlying structural model of the labor market. However, it is difficult to know how to characterize labor markets in India. Certainly there is no unified national market, and even at the regional level it is heavily segmented between rural and urban; within the rural sector there is significant movement in and out of agriculture on a seasonal basis. Similarly, it is difficult to evaluate the impact of the reforms without thinking through the process of how their effects might be transmitted to the various labor markets. He concluded that the construction of a structural model is a challenging task but crucial to answering the questions asked in the paper.

16. Topalova (2005).
17. Foster and Rosenzweig (2003); Munshi and Rosenzweig (forthcoming).

In addition, he thought that a full understanding of the design of the NSSO surveys was important to interpreting the results. He argued, for example, that the surveys were meant to be interpreted as percentages of the relevant populations and that it was potentially misleading to present estimates in levels form, as is done in the paper. Similarly, he believed that the price indexes used to construct measures of real wages needed to be interpreted with caution.

Pranab Bardhan was surprised by the large deceleration of growth in the population of labor force age that is reported in the paper for the post-1993 period. He was puzzled about how the census and NSSO estimates could be so different, and he would like to have some corroborative evidence. He also expressed concern that the overall unemployment rate is under-reported by an increasing amount. He traced it to the growing role of women, who were more likely interpret the survey question about seeking employment as implying work outside of the family.

Several participants questioned the meaning of unemployment within the context of the current Indian economy, particularly as it applied to the rural sector. Many Indians are too poor to be unemployed. Their poverty emerged as underemployment and low productivity, not unemployment. Similarly, several participants argued that the trade liberalization and similar measures should be expected to affect productivity, not unemployment. Robert Lawrence also suggested that it may be necessary to adjust the data for cyclical factors and to differentiate between the immediate effects of reform and the longer-term impact.

Arvind Panagariya raised a concern about the importance of labor market regulations. He thought that simply asking firms about hindrances to expansion of employment would not elicit meaningful responses if they did not believe the regulations were under consideration for change. Thus, it would be necessary to inquire in greater depth to obtain useful responses. Others noted that large-scale manufacturing did not grow more rapidly after the trade liberalization and believed that suggested an influence of the restrictive labor market regulations. Apparel in particular was an area in which India should have been an appealing location for large-scale firms serving the export market. At the same time, it was pointed out that several empirical research studies directly examined the impact of the labor market regulations and found it to be small. The issue remains quite unsettled.

References

Ahluwalia, Montek. 2000. "Economic Performance of States in the Post-Reforms Period." *Economic and Political Weekly* (May 6): 1637–48.

———. 2002. "Report of the Task Force on Employment Opportunities." In *Planning Commission Reports on Labour and Employment*, edited by R. Kapila and U. Kapila. New Delhi: Academic Foundation.

Banerjee, Abhijit, and Esther Duflo. 2006. "The Economic Lives of the Poor." *Journal of Economic Perspectives.*

Banerjee, Abhijit, and Thomas Piketty. 2003. "Top Indian Incomes, 1956–2000." BREAD Working Paper 46, September (www.cid.harvard.edu/bread/papers/working/046.pdf).

———. 2005. "Are the Rich Growing Richer: Evidence from Indian Tax Data?" In *The Great Indian Poverty Debate*, edited by Angus Deaton and Valerie Kozel. New Delhi: Macmillan India Ltd.

Banga, Rashmi. 2005. "Impact of Liberalisation on Wages and Employment in Indian Manufacturing Industries." Working Paper 153. Indian Council for Research on International Economic Relations, New Delhi.

Basu, Kaushik. 2004. "The Indian Economy: Up to 1991 and Beyond.'" In *India's Emerging Economy: Performance and Prospects in the 1990s and Beyond*, edited by Kaushik Basu. Cambridge, MA: MIT Press.

———. 2006. "Labor Laws and Labor Welfare in the Context of the Indian Economy," in *Poverty, Inequality and Development,* edited by R. Kanbur and A. de Janvry. New York: Springer.

———. Forthcoming. "Globalization, Poverty and Inequality: What is the Relationship? What can be Done?" *World Development.*

Basu, K., G. Genicot, and J. Stiglitz. 2003. "Minimum Wage Laws and Unemployment Benefits When Labor Supply is a Household Decision." In *Markets and Governments*, edited by K. Basu, P. B. Nayak, and R. Ray. New Delhi: Oxford University Press.

Bhalla, Surjit S. 2000. "This Is India's Decade." *Developing Trends*. O(x)us Research & Investments, New Delhi, February.

———. 2002a. "Imagine There's No Country: Poverty, Inequality and Growth in the Era of Globalization." Institute of International Economics, Washington.

———. 2002b. "Tax Compliance in India." Background paper for the Indian Ministry of Finance, New Delhi, February 12.

———. 2003. "Recounting the Poor: 1983–99." *Economic and Political Weekly* 38, no. 4 (January 25–31): 338–49.

———. 2004a. "Not as Poor, Nor as Unequal, as You Think: India, 1950–2000." Report on research project entitled *The Myth and Reality of Poverty in India*, Planning Commission, Government of India, May.

———. 2004b. "The Occam's Razor Model of Growth: India 1950–2004." Paper presented at a National Bureau of Economic Research conference, Boston, September 17.

Bhalla, Surjit S. 2004c. "Reform of Personal Income Tax in India." www.oxus.in, July 2; background paper for the Kelkar Task Force report.

Bhalla, Surjit S., with Tirthatanmoy Das. 2004. "Why Be Afraid of the Truth? Poverty, Inequality and Growth in India, 1983–2000." www.oxus.in, December.

Bhalotra, Sonia. 1998. "The Puzzle of Jobless Growth in Indian Manufacturing." *Oxford Bulletin of Economics and Statistics* 60 (1): 5–32.

————. 2002. "The Impact of Economic Liberalization on Employment and Wages in India." (www.ecn.bris.ac.uk/ecsrb/papers/indialib.pdf).

Bhaumik, Sumon, and Manisha Chakrabarty. 2006. "Earnings Inequality in India: Has the Rise of Caste and Religion-Based Politics in India Had an Impact." IZA Discussion Paper 2008 (ftp://repec.iza.org/RePEc/Discussionpaper/dp2008. pdf), March.

Dantwala, M. L., chairman, Planning Commission. 1970. "Report of the Committee of Experts on Unemployment Estimates." Government of India, New Delhi.

Datt, Gaurav, and Martin Ravallion. 2002. "Is India's Economic Growth Leaving the Poor Behind?" *Journal of Economic Perspectives* 16 (Summer): 89–108.

Deaton, A. 2001. "Adjusted Indian Poverty Estimates for 1999–2000." Working Paper, Princeton University.

Deaton, Angus, and Alessandro Tarozzi. 2000. "Prices and Poverty In India." Princeton Research Program in Development Studies (www.wws.princeton.edu/~rpds).

Deaton, Angus, and Jean Dreze. 2002. "Poverty and Inequality in India: A Re-examination." *Economic and Political Weekly* 37 (September 7): 3729–48.

Deaton, Angus, and Valerie Kozel, eds. 2005. *The Great Indian Poverty Debate.* New Delhi: Macmillan India Ltd.

Desai, Mihir, Devesh Kapur, and John McHale. 2003. "The Fiscal Impact of High Skilled Emigration." WCFIA Working Paper 03-01. Harvard.

Dey, Nikhil, and Jean Dreze. 2004. "Employment Guarantee Act: Made Simple." Paper prepared for a convention on Employment Guarantee and the Right to Work, Constitution Club, New Delhi, October 19.

Dreze, Jean, and Amartya Sen. 2002. *India: Development and Participation.* New Delhi: Oxford University Press.

Duraiswamy, P. 2000. "Changes in Returns to Education in India: 1983–94: By Gender, Age-Cohort, and Location." Economic Growth Center, Yale University.

Ferro, M., D. Rosenblatt, and N. Stern. 2004. "Policies for Pro-poor Growth in India.' In *India's Emerging Economy: Performance and Prospects in the 1990s and Beyond*, edited by K. Basu. Cambridge, MA: MIT Press.

Foster, Andrew D., and Mark R. Rosenzweig. 2003. "Agricultural Productivity Growth, Rural Economic Diversity, and Economic Reforms: India, 1970–2000." Paper prepared for the D. Gale Johnson Memorial Conference, October 25 (adfdell.pstc.brown.edu/papers/johnson.pdf).

Gupta, S. P., chairman, Planning Commision. 2002a. "Report of the Special Group on Targeting Ten Million Employment Opportunities per Year over the 10th Plan Period." Reproduced in Kapila and Kapila (2002).

Gupta, S. P., chairman, Planning Commision.2002b "Report of the Steering Committee on Labour & Employment for the 10th Five Year Plan (2002–2007)." Reproduced in Kapila and Kapila (2002).

Hasan, Rana, Devashish Mitra, and K. V. Ramaswamy. 2003. "Trade Reforms, Labor Regulations and Labor-Demand Elasticities: Empirical Evidence from India." NBER Paper 9879. National Bureau of Economics and Research, Cambridge, Mass.

International Labor Organization (ILO). 1996. "Economic Reforms and Labour Policies in India (1996)." Report prepared for a UN Development Program project (www.ilo.org/public/english/region/asro/newdelhi/papers/1996/tss1/) .

Kapila, Raj, and Uma Kapila. 2002. *Planning Commission Reports on Labour and Employment.* New Delhi: Academic Foundation.

Kelkar, Vijay, Ministry of Finance, Government of India. 2002. *Report of the Task Force on Direct Taxes.* New Delhi, December.

Kijima, Y. Forthcoming. "Why Did Wage Inequality Increase? Evidence from Urban India." *Journal of Development Economics.*

Munshi, Kaivan, and Mark Rosenzweig. Forthcoming. "Traditional Institutions Meet the Modern World: Caste, Gender, and Schooling Choice in a Globalizing Economy." *American Economic Review.*

Panagariya, Arvind. 2004. "India in the 1980s and 1990s: A Triumph of Reforms." IMF Working Paper WP/04/43. International Monetary Fund, Washington, March.

Planning Commission. 2002. "Mid Term Appraisal of the Ninth Five Year Plan (1997–2002)." Chapter 21. Government of India, New Delhi.

———. 2005. "Mid-Term Appraisal of Tenth Five Year Plan (2002–2007)." Government of India, New Delhi. June.

Rao, M. G., K. P. Kalirajan, and R. Shand. 1999. "Convergence of Incomes in Indian States—A Divergent View." *Economic and Political Weekly* (March 27): 769–78.

Rodrik, Dani and Arvind Subramanian. 2004. "Why India Can Grow At 7 Per Cent a Year or More: Projection and Reflection." *Economic and Political Weekly* 39 (April 17): 1591–96.

Sen, Abhijit, and Himanshu. 2004a. "Poverty and Inequality in India— I." *Economic and Political Weekly* 39 (September 18): 4247–63.

———. 2004b. "Poverty and Inequality in India—II: Widening Disparities during the 1990s." *Economic and Political Weekly* 39 (September 25): 4361–75.

Shirsat, B. G. 2005. "Jobs Are Passe in Manufacturing Sector." *Business Standard,* August 25.

Sivasubramanian, S. 2004. *The Sources of Economic Growth in India, 1950–1 to 1999–2000.* New Delhi: Oxford University Press.

Sundaram, K. 2001a. "Employment and Poverty in the 1990s: Further Results from NSSO 55th Round Employment-Unemployment Survey 1990–2000." *Economic and Political Weekly* (August 11–17): 3039–49.

Sundaram, K. 2001b. "Employment-Unemployment Situation in the Nineties: Some Results from NSSO 55th Round Survey." *Economic and Political Weekly* (March 17): 931–40.

Sundaram, K., and Suresh Tendulkar. 2003. "Poverty Has Declined in the 1990s: A Resolution of Comparability Problems in NSS Consumer Expenditure Data." *Economic and Political Weekly* (January 25–31): 327–37.

Topalova, Petia. 2005. "Trade Liberalization, Poverty, and Inequality: Evidence from Indian Districts." NBER Working Paper 11614. National Bureau of Economic Research, Cambridge, Mass.

Virmani, Arvind. 2004a. "India's Economic Growth: From Socialist Rate of Growth to Bhartiya Rate of Growth." Working Paper 122, Indian Council for Research on International Economic Relations, New Delhi, February.

———. 2004b. "Sources of India's Economic Growth: Trends in Total Factor Productivity." Working Paper 131, Indian Council for Research on International Economic Relations, New Delhi, May.

———. 2005. "Policy Regimes, Growth and Poverty In India: Lessons of Government Failure And Entrepreneurial Success." Working Paper 170, Indian Council for Research on International Economic Relations, New Delhi, October.

World Institute for Development Economic Research (WIDER). 2004. Income Distribution database, Helsinki (www.wider.unu.edu/wiid/wiid.htm).

World Bank. 1997. *India: Achievements and Challenges in Reducing Poverty*. Washington.

ROGER G. NOLL
Stanford University

SCOTT J. WALLSTEN
AEI-Brookings Joint Center for Regulatory Studies

Universal Telecommunications Service in India

Telecommunications reform in India began in the 1980s, but a struggle to find reforms that would substantially improve industry performance lasted for more than a decade. Beginning in the new millennium, technological change and new government policies encouraged competition, primarily from mobile telephony, and performance improved dramatically (figure 1). Not surprisingly, telecommunications access has increased far more quickly for wealthy and urban consumers than for poor and rural consumers. To address this gap, India has adopted so-called universal service policies, especially targeting rural villages. These policies rely primarily on subsidizing the incumbent state-owned carrier, despite its unimpressive historical performance.

An innovative part of India's universal service policy is a series of auctions in which providers bid the subsidy they seek for building village public telephone (VPT) networks and rural household phones. In the first auction, the only bidder and hence the recipient of the subsidy was Bharat Sanchar Nigam Limited (BSNL), the incumbent state-owned carrier for nearly all of India. Subsequent auctions drew some private sector participation and helped reduce the subsidy that was provided. Nonetheless, the auction process has generally favored BSNL and is probably not the most effective mechanism for either minimizing the state subsidy or identifying the most efficient provider. Meanwhile, the taxes that finance the access subsidy are highly distortionary. Moreover, private mobile operators are expanding service rapidly, which calls into question the presumption that a subsidy scheme targeted at VPTs is cost-effective.

The funds for implementing the universal service policy come from two sources. One is a tax on the revenues of all telecommunications carriers. The other is "access deficit charges" on subscribers of systems owned by private carriers. These fees are paid directly to BSNL. In theory, these fees

FIGURE 1. Fixed and Mobile Phones in India

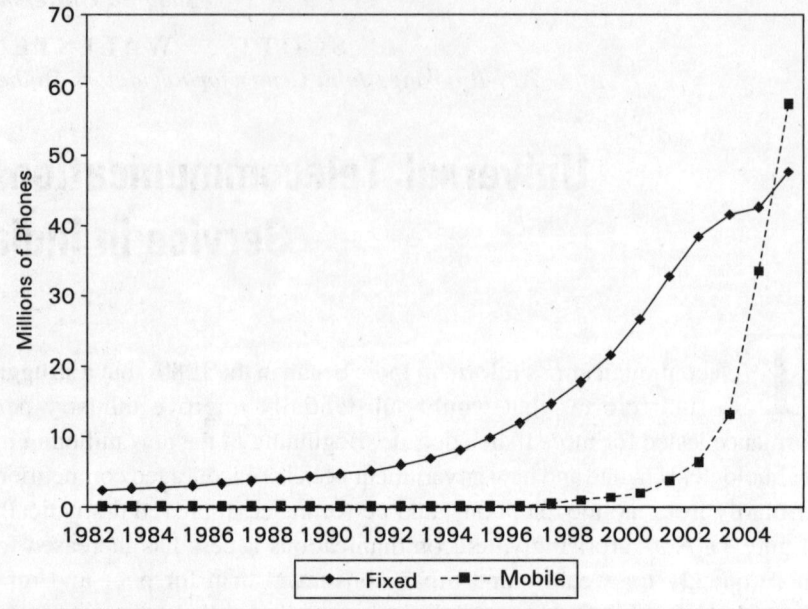

Source: Telecom Regulatory Authority of India. *The Indian Telecom Services Performance Indicators.* Various years.

reimburse the incumbent for its (mostly unmet) obligation to provide service in places where revenues cannot cover costs. In reality, the incumbent does not disaggregate its costs in any way that makes it possible to determine whether revenues exceed costs in any particular geographic area or other market segment.

This paper evaluates India's universal service policies. The next sections provide a brief introduction to Indian telecommunications and analyze universal service explicitly. The final section draws conclusions.

A Brief History of Indian Telecommunications Reform

Since 2000 the telecommunications sector in India has improved dramatically.[1] In 1982–85, before structural reform began, the annual growth rate of telephone penetration was about 7 percent. In 1986 telecommunications services were separated from postal services and divided into three

1. This section is based on Noll and Wallsten (2005). For a thorough and fascinating analysis of the history of Indian telecommunications, see Desai (2004).

parts. Local service in Delhi and Mumbai was given to a corporatized state-owned enterprise, Mahanagar Telephone Nigam Limited (MTNL), and the rest of local service plus domestic long-distance service was given to BSNL, which remained a part of the Department of Telecommunications. Minority interests in MTNL subsequently have been sold to private corporations, and today the government owns 56 percent. BSNL eventually was corporatized on October 1, 2000, and may be partially privatized in the next few years. Finally, Videsh Sanchar Nigam Limited (VSNL) was created as a government-owned corporation to operate international telephone service. This reorganization increased the growth in telephone lines to slightly less than 10 percent a year.

The next major reform began in 1991 with the commitment to allow the private sector to provide some services, including both fixed and mobile wireless telephony. Procedures for granting private licenses were developed and implemented over several years, so private operators began to enter only at the end of 1995. During this period the state-owned enterprises (SOEs) continued to be monopolies but expected entry in the future. Performance improved, with the number of lines in service more than doubling in five years.

Between 1996 and 2001, private wireless carriers offering both fixed and mobile service entered the industry, and the SOEs faced competition for the first time. Wireless services grew slowly during this period. By 2001 fixed wireless accounted for only 3 percent of lines, and mobile telephony accounted for about 10 percent, while the SOEs roughly tripled their number of lines in service and thus accounted for about 80 percent of the growth in penetration.

From 2001 to mid-2005 total telephone lines grew from about 30–104 million, tripling again in only four years. An important change from the 1990s is that wireless telephony accounted for nearly all of this growth, and private carriers accounted for most of the growth in wireless telephony. Between March 2002 and June 2005 the number of fixed lines grew from 38.4 to 46.9 million, a gain of 8.5 million, while the number of mobile lines grew from 6.4 to 57.4 million, or by more than 50 million.[2] Moreover, as of June 2005, the SOEs served 40.75 million fixed-service lines, compared to 37.85 million in March of 2002—an increase of less than 3 million. Most of this increase occurred early in the period. Fixed-line penetration by the SOEs has been essentially constant since late 2003. Meanwhile, private fixed-wireless carriers provided 0.6 million lines in March 2002 and 6.1 million

2. TRAI (2004, 2005b).

lines in June 2005, an increase of 5.5 million.[3] In mobile wireless, the SOEs, which were allowed to enter only at the beginning of the recent reform period, grew from 0.2 million to 12.0 million subscribers between March 2002 and June 2005, whereas the private carriers increased their penetration from 6.2 million to 45.4 million. Thus, an important part of the recent success of Indian telecommunications is the growth of wireless services provided by private companies. As of mid-2005 private companies provided 51.5 million lines, or nearly half of the total, compared with 15 percent of all lines in March 2002. In June 2005 wireless telephony accounted for 63.5 million telephones, or 61 percent of telephone penetration, compared with 16 percent in March 2002.

Universal Service: Theory and Practice

Universal service refers to the idea that an infrastructure public utility, such as electricity, transportation, water, or telephony, should be available to everyone. Universal service policies are typically rationalized in three ways.[4] First, externalities related to the consumption of infrastructure services might make it economically efficient to subsidize prices for those who cannot afford the service at cost. Positive externalities imply that the total benefits from providing service to an individual exceed the benefits to an individual subscriber. If the private marginal cost of service exceeds the private marginal benefit by less than the amount of the external benefit, then some individuals will not subscribe even though the social benefit of serving them exceeds their cost of service.

Second, some services might be "merit goods"—goods and services that society believes everyone should have, regardless of whether they are willing to pay for them. A policy decision that certain goods and services ought to be subsidized may come from a belief that everyone should achieve a certain minimum standard of living or a concern that individuals are unable to accurately assess the private benefits of consuming these services.[5] If society

3. Penetration data are from the TRAI website at http://www.trai.gov.in/pr11jul05.htm. These data differ somewhat from estimates by the Cellular Operators Association of India http://coai.in/archives_statistics_2005_q2.htm.
4. Cremer and others (1998a, 1998b).
5. For example, it is sometimes argued that people might not fully appreciate the benefits of consuming clean water if they are unaware of the costs associated with consuming polluted water or unable to fully assess the risks associated with doing so (Shirley and Ménard 2002).

is more concerned about consumption of merit goods than the overall welfare of poor people, subsidies for these goods might be preferable to direct monetary transfers because people may choose to spend cash transfers on something other than the service society wants to encourage.

Finally, political factors or regional development goals may induce government to transfer resources to rural or low-income constituents. In countries with large rural populations, like India, politicians may face a political incentive to ensure that their rural constituents have access to the same services as do urbanites.

Rationale for Universal Service in Telecom

Universal access to some types of infrastructure is easier to justify than to others. Water and sewerage, for example, involve large health externalities, and bringing these services to everyone can yield large social benefits. But it is not at all obvious why universality is legally mandated in some sectors but not others. Nearly every country in the world has laws mandating some type of universal access to telecommunications services, but the economic rationale behind these laws is weak.

The typical economics argument defending policies regarding universal service in telecommunications is that service is underprovided because of network externalities. Network externalities in telecommunications mean that the benefits a new consumer accrues from connecting (the private benefits) are less than the total benefits to society, because when an additional person connects to the network all other subscribers benefit by being able to communicate with the new subscriber. Therefore, individuals may not face a strong enough incentive to subscribe, thus requiring subsidies to induce socially optimal subscription. This argument is incomplete and therefore misleading.[6] Even if the benefits to the new subscriber are less than the total benefits, the private benefit may still exceed the cost for nearly all subscribers, in which case a general subsidy of service is mostly wasted. Second, because services become more valuable when more people are connected, the firm providing access captures some of the benefits from network externalities. Consequently, although network externalities are external to the individual, they are not necessarily external to firms providing the service, potentially removing the need for subsidies. In other words, network externalities by themselves do not necessarily imply telecommunications undersubscription and a need for subsidies. Third, all

---

6. See Cremer and others (1998a, 1998b) for a more complete discussion of this issue.

subscribers receive an external benefit from subscriptions by others, implying that each person should subsidize the service of the other. Consequently, on average the subsidy a subscriber receives to take service ought to be roughly equal to the amount of subsidy that subscriber should be willing to pay to induce others to subscribe.

In developing countries, the case for subsidizing access service by the incumbent wire-line carrier is further undermined because the incumbent wire-line monopoly, whether privatized or state-owned, generally has not offered service in poor urban areas. Indeed, in the era of state-owned enterprises, telecom providers had little incentive to invest in any telecommunications services, as witnessed by the appallingly long waiting period to obtain connections and the poor quality of service following installation. As a result, telephone penetration and use were low, even considering developing countries' low incomes, and service to poor and rural areas was horrible (figure 2).

Economics research provides convincing empirical evidence that the case for extensive cross-subsidization in telecommunications is weak.[7] Among the conclusions are the following:

—Cross-subsidization systems are inefficient because the amount transferred among services and households is much greater than the net subsidy to low-income consumers;

—the cross-subsidy system has little effect on the penetration of telephone service because it taxes usage services, which have relatively high price elasticities of demand, in order to subsidize access, which has a very low price elasticity of demand;

—low-income households, if given the choice, would generally prefer cash to a subsidy for telephone service; and

—in developing countries, almost no low-income households subscribe to access service while many make calls from pay telephones or call centers, so taxing usage to subsidize access transfers income from the poor to the middle class.

That the alleged market failures in telecommunications do not provide a convincing rationale for universal service policies should not come as a surprise considering the origins of universal service in telecommunications. Universal service policy in telecommunications does not have its roots in the desire to ensure telephone access to all people. Instead, early in the twentieth

7. See, for example, Clarke and Wallsten (2002); Crandall and Waverman (2000); and Rosston and Wimmer (2000).

FIGURE 2.   **Telephone Penetration in Low- and Middle-Income Nations**[a]

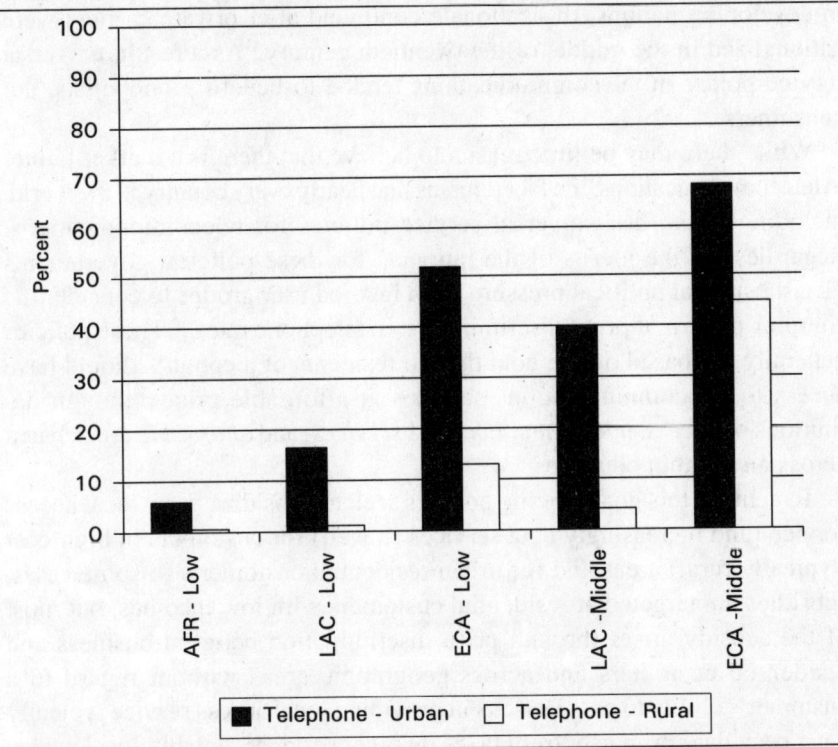

Source: Clarke and Wallsten (2002). Data from MEASURE DHS+ Demographic and Health Surveys.
a. AFR is Sub-Saharan Africa; LAC is Latin America and Caribbean; ECA is Europe and Central Asia. Low is low-income countries; Middle is middle-income countries. Regional averages are computed as simple averages (no weighting). Classifications of urban and rural households are based on original classifications in the DHS+ datasets. Coverage implies that the household has a connection to that service in its house. Data are for all countries in these regions for which data were available for various years between 1994 and 2000.

century universal service policy arose from the desire by the Bell Telephone Company, which constructed the first telephone network in many nations throughout the world, to stifle competition. Universal service did not mean that everyone should have a telephone. Instead, it meant that everyone who had telephone service should be allowed to have only a Bell telephone.[8] Universal service was to be achieved through price discrimination within a single monopoly provider; competition would undermine this process by attracting entrants who would "cream-skim" customers who were charged the highest prices. In other words, universal telephone service was a rationale

8. Mueller (1997).

for granting and preserving monopoly, not for ensuring service to everyone. In developing nations, this rationale continued after private carriers were nationalized in the middle of the twentieth century.[9] As a result, universal service policy in telecommunications tended to benefit monopolists, not consumers.

While there may be little reason to believe that there is a market failure in telecommunications, the fact remains that nearly every country in the world, including India, has universal service policies for telecommunications. Regardless of the merits of the rationale for these policies, governments face substantial political pressure from favored user groups to consider the complex pattern of price-discrimination in telephone rates.[10] These policies generally are based on the goal that all residents of a country should have access to telecommunications services at affordable prices, though definitions of *access*, *telecommunications services*, and *affordable* are debated across and within countries.

To achieve this goal, pricing policies seek to subsidize basic local access service (and increasingly data services as well) for customers in high-cost (typically rural) areas and for urban residential customers. In some cases, subsidies are targeted at residential customers with low incomes, but most of the subsidy arises through price discrimination between business and residential customers and across geographic areas without regard to a customer's ability to pay. Deficits in providing local access service typically have been paid primarily from taxes on other services, notably local usage, long-distance, international calls and, more recently, mobile telephone service.

India has been no exception to any of these trends. Telephone service stagnated under state ownership. Despite the Department of Telecommunications' (later BSNL's) mandate to provide service in rural areas, relatively few villages had even a public telephone, let alone were offered private telephone access, during the era of state-owned monopoly. In 1995 approximately 185,000 villages out of more than 600,000 had a public telephone, and in 1998 only 2.6 percent of rural households had telephone service (figure 3).[11] And, as Das and Srinivasan note, those numbers exaggerate the true state of telecommunications in rural areas because village surveys "revealed that more than 60 percent of ...VPTs were faulty. Of the remaining, a high percentage were disconnected due to non-payment of dues, so

9. Noll (2000).
10. Estache, Foster, and Wodon (2001).
11. Jain and Das (2001).

F I G U R E 3 .   Share of Indian Households that Own a Telephone, 1999

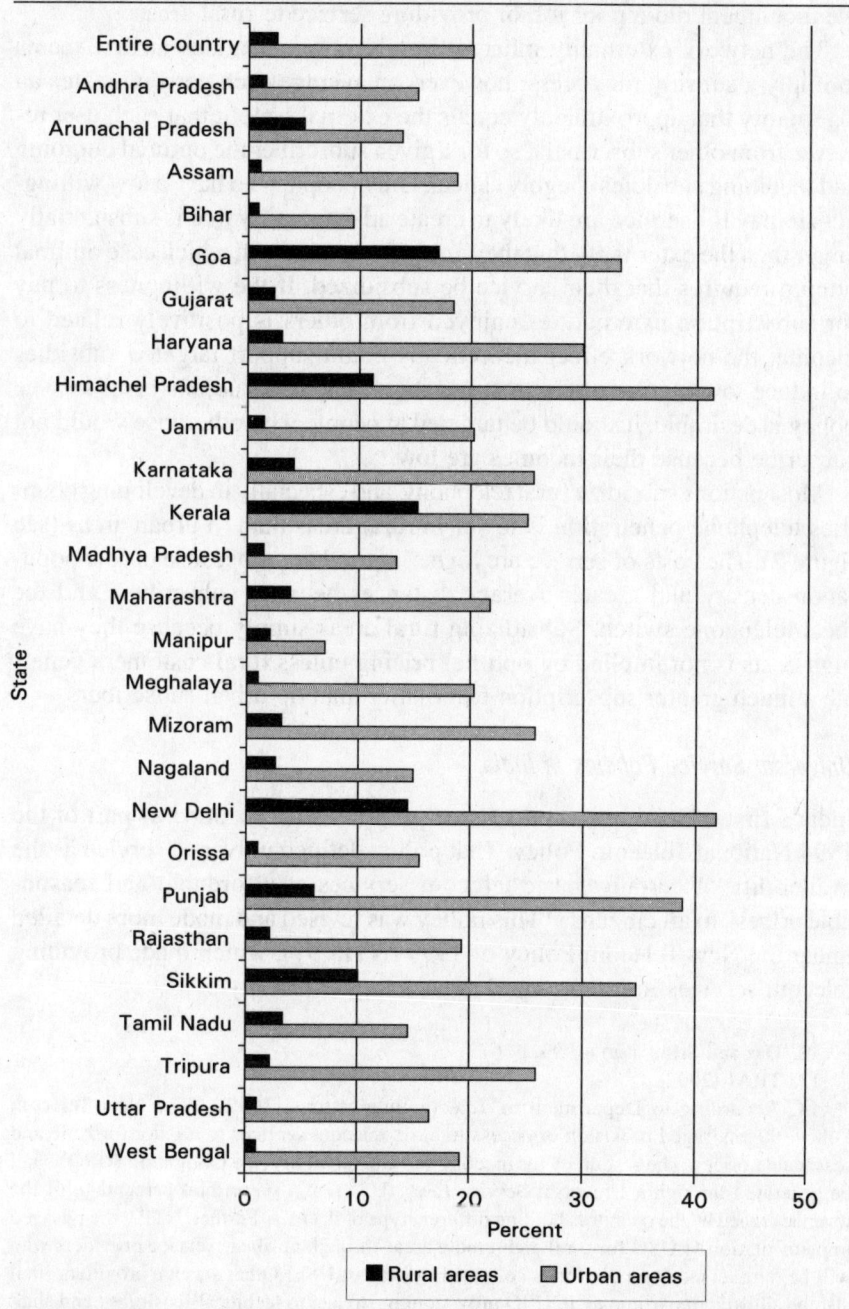

Source: Derived from MEASURE DHS+ Demographic and Health Surveys, Survey of India, 1998–99.

that in effect, very few are in actual use."[12] Clearly, before recent reforms, the incumbent did a poor job of providing service to rural areas.

The network externality inherent in telecommunications at first seems to imply a subsidy for access; however, on average each person creates an externality that approximately equals the external benefit that each user receives from other subscribers, so for a given subscriber the optimal outgoing and incoming subsidies roughly cancel. Only people who have a low willingness to pay for service are likely to create an externality that is substantially larger than the externality that they enjoy from others, in which case optimal pricing requires that their service be subsidized. If the willingness to pay for subscription externalities enjoyed from others is positively related to income, the network effect theoretically could support targeted subsidies to induce low-income users to subscribe. Thus, if a true universal service policy is desirable, it should be targeted at people who otherwise would not subscribe because their incomes are low.

Most nations subsidize rural telephony, and especially in developing countries telephone penetration is lower in rural areas than in urban areas (see figure 2). The costs of service are higher in rural areas because of low population density and greater average distances between subscribers and the local telephone switch. Subsidizing rural areas simply because they have high costs is not implied by optimal pricing unless rural customers generate a much greater subscription externality than do urban subscribers.

Universal Service Policies in India

India's first official universal service program was included as part of the 1994 National Telecom Policy. That policy defined universal service as the availability of certain "basic telecom services at affordable and reasonable prices" to all citizens.[13] This policy was revised and made more detailed under the New Telecom Policy of 1999 (NTP '99), which made providing telecom services in remote rural areas a higher priority.[14]

12. Das and Srinivasan (1999, p. 673).
13. TRAI (2002).
14. According to Department of Telecommunications (2002), "The New Telecom Policy '99 envisaged provision of access to basic telecom services to all at affordable and reasonable prices. The resources for meeting the Universal Service Obligation (USO) shall be generated through a Universal Service Levy (USL), at a prescribed percentage of the revenue earned by the operators holding different type of licenses. Further, NTP '99 envisaged implementation of USO for rural and remote areas through all Basic service providers who will be reimbursed from the funds collected by way of USL. Other service providers shall also be allowed to participate in USO provisioning subject to technical feasibility and shall be similarly reimbursed out of the funds of USL."

Among other goals, the NTP '99 aimed to:

—Provide voice and low-speed data services to the 290,000 villages with no service by 2002.

—Provide Internet access to all district headquarters by the year 2000.

—Achieve telephone on demand in urban and rural areas by 2002.[15]

In addition, policymakers hoped to increase rural teledensity from 0.4 telephones per hundred people in 2000 to 4 by 2010.[16] The NTP states that universal service objectives will be funded through a universal service levy. When the 2002 goals were not met, the Department of Telecommunications (DoT) issued clarifying guidelines on how universal service activities should proceed.[17] DoT adopted two objectives: providing public telephones in villages and providing household telephones in rural areas. The first objective was given higher priority.

The universal service fund is based on an implicit assumption that competition among private providers will not generate service in rural areas and that the magnitude of the subsidy can be minimized by allowing only one firm to receive a subsidy in each area. The cost of the subsidies is raised through two taxes. The first, the universal service levy, is a tax of 5 percent of adjusted gross revenues on all telecommunications providers except "pure value added service providers" such as Internet Service Providers (ISPs). These universal service funds (USF) go to the DoT, which distributes them as discussed below. The second includes access deficit charges (ADCs), which are incorporated into interconnection charges and are paid directly to the incumbent state-owned enterprise (BSNL) to compensate it for providing below-cost service in rural areas. While collecting the universal sevice levy is relatively simple, distributing the funds so that they actually help meet universal service objectives is far more difficult. The ADC, meanwhile, is intensely controversial. We discuss these two issues below.

Allocating the USF: Auctioning Subsidies

The USF is intended to reimburse the net cost (cost minus revenues) of providing rural telecom service. Because costs may differ across different types of service and different service segments, separate auctions determine

---

15. Government of India (1999).
16. TRAI (2000).
17. Department of Telecommunications (2002).

the actual reimbursement to be awarded for each.[18] Previously, in awarding licenses for cellular telephone service, DoT had divided the country into twenty telecom "circles" (which loosely follow state boundaries). These circles were used as the basis for geographic reference in the rural subsidy auctions. The magnitude of the subsidy for each area is determined through an auction mechanism that was proposed by Dr. Rakesh Mohan, then a member of Telecom Regulatory Authority of India (TRAI), in his dissent from a recommendation by the commission on how to implement universal service. In this process, telecommunications firms submit bids for providing service. The firm bidding the lowest subsidy, subject to the bid being no higher than a set benchmark, is eligible to be reimbursed that amount from the fund. Benchmarks were set using information primarily from the incumbent, BSNL. Any firm with a license to provide basic or cellular service in the relevant service area was eligible to bid.[19] The winner received a subsidy for seven years, subject to review after three years.

Subsidy auctions have been used elsewhere in the world with some success. In a fair bidding process with multiple bidders, firms should bid the smallest subsidy necessary for them to provide service. Chile and Peru were among the first to implement this method, giving licenses to operators that agreed to serve areas for the smallest subsidy.[20] In Chile, the average winning subsidy from 1995 to 1999 was about half the maximum benchmark, while in Peru the subsidy was only about one-quarter of the benchmark.[21] These experiences reveal that auctions are feasible and that the subsidies required were far less than the incumbents had previously led policymakers to believe were necessary.

The first two Indian subsidy auctions, relating to Primary VPTs and the replacement of Multi Access Radio Relay-based VPTs, yielded a different result. In nineteen of the twenty circles only one firm bid for the subsidies,

---

18. According to commentators at the National Council for Applied Economic Research, six auctions have taken place, covering the following six services and service segments: Operation and Maintenance of Village Public Telephones in certain villages (Finalized January 2003); Replacement of Multi Access Radio Relay-based VPTs installed before January 4, 2002 and technology upgrading of existing VPTs (finalized September 2003); Provision of additional rural community phones in larger villages with at least one VPT (finalized September 2004); Provision of VPTs in villages that remained uncovered (finalized October 2004); Installation of High Speed Public Telecom Information Centers (HPTICs) (not finalized as of this writing); and provision of household telephones in rural and remote areas identified for subsidy support (finalized March 2005).

19. Department of Telecommunications (2002).

20. Cannock (2001).

21. Intven and Tetrault (2000).

the incumbent BSNL.[22] Not surprisingly, given the thin market, BSNL bid exactly the benchmark amount, which was the maximum subsidy DoT was prepared to provide. Additional firms bid in the following three auctions, yielding a more positive outcome. While the incumbent won one of those three auctions and parts of the other two, private providers did win parts of two auctions, and in two of the three auctions winning bids were substantially lower than the benchmark.

The failure of the first two auctions to create genuine competition for rural public service arose from at least three problems. First, the calculations for the benchmark subsidy plausibly were not based on accurate information or on the appropriate standard, which is the incremental cost of public telephone service. The cost data used for calculating these benchmarks were provided primarily by BSNL. While there were rigorous independent attempts to verify the information, BSNL's accounts are aggregated in a way that makes it impossible to separate costs for different operations, which in turn makes incremental cost calculations extremely difficult.[23]

Second, BSNL receives nearly all of the access deficit charge cross-subsidies (discussed in detail below). The incumbent has potential gains from manipulating how cost information is aggregated across service categories and across high-cost and low-cost areas, because these data determine not only the benchmark subsidy for public telephones, but also the magnitude of the net deficit for all local access service. If some ambiguous cost elements are allocated to subsidized areas, the effect will be to increase both the public telephone subsidy and the ADC subsidy.

Third, bidding was open only to basic service operators already providing rural service in the area. BSNL, even though it historically had not served many villages, owned some facilities in these areas; however, few other firms had entered these markets, in part because they were opened only recently and in part because disputes about the terms and conditions of interconnection with BSNL remained unresolved. The fact that the first two auctions covered VPTs already provided almost entirely by the incumbent operator thus gave a distinct advantage to the incumbent and limited the ability of private operators to compete. Firms not yet operating could bid for the public telephone subsidy only if no other bids were received or if the bids by others exceeded the benchmark.[24] By precluding firms that were not

22. Ghosh (2004).
23. See, for example, Ramachandran (2003).
24. Intelecon Research and Consultancy Ltd. (2002).

already present, the subsidy scheme did not encourage either entry or innovation in rural services.

The auction procedure that was set up advantaged the incumbent while providing no incentive to improve efficiency. In particular, if only a single firm can qualify for the subsidy and if that firm is then reimbursed the difference between its own estimates of its revenues and costs, the subsidized firm has no incentive to reduce costs unless it can do so in ways that can be hidden from the DoT. Moreover, with only one subsidized firm in the entire nation, even benchmark competition (whereby differences between monopolies in different areas are used to evaluate performance and adjust the subsidy) is impossible, while the subsidies themselves make it impossible for nonsubsidized firms to enter the market.

By 2005 the USF had disbursed Rs. 17 billion (about $375 million).[25] About 520,000 VPTs had been installed, nearly all by BSNL.[26] In 2005–06, an additional Rs. 12 billion (about $250 million) was to be distributed from universal service funds with the hope of serving the remaining 66,000 villages by 2009.[27] Evaluating the effectiveness of this spending is virtually impossible. No estimates have been made of the number of VPTs that would have been installed without the program by either BSNL or others, especially if the interconnection dispute between them had been resolved. The sole metric available seems to be the gross number of VPTs installed. No data are yet available about the share of VPTs in working order, the price of phone calls in rural areas before and after the program began, or actual usage.[28]

The subsidy scheme for encouraging investment in VPTs is only the first part of a two-part policy. An auction for subsidies for rural household phones was concluded in 2004 as a first step toward distributing funds for connecting individual households. This step is potentially far more important than the first. Many more telephone lines are at stake in devising a plan for implementing extensive residential access than for providing more public telephones. While even in the best of circumstances firms might not have found subsidies for a relatively small number of public telephones an attractive basis for entering rural areas, subsidies for a much larger number of residential lines clearly are more attractive. Indeed, this auction generated relatively substantial interest among private operators, and the winning

---

25. US $1 = Rs. 45 or Re. 1 = US $0.022 cents in October 2005.
26. Chidambaram (2005).
27. Chidambaram (2005); Press Information Bureau (2005).
28. As of the time of this writing, a mid-term review of the outcomes of the first two auctions was in progress and not yet available.

subsidy bid was about 40 percent lower than the benchmark. BSNL won subsidies for 1,267 Short Distance Charging Areas (SDCAs, the basic service unit identified for subsidies), while two private operators won subsidies for 418 SDCAs.[29] While the auction was a relative success, policymakers should be careful to ensure that the subsidies do not perpetuate an inefficient rural telephone monopoly.

Access Deficit Charges

Access deficit charges (ADCs) are essentially fees paid by private entrants to the incumbent based on the premise that basic access providers face unprofitable social service obligations and should therefore be compensated for them by entrants who are free to seek out profitable customers. These deficits arise from the assumption that price ceilings on basic monthly access service charges, set by TRAI, are below the cost of service for a large number of customers. As one DoT official put it, "private operators started services from creamy areas, so they have a clear advantage over BSNL. The state-owned operator has to provide services in rural areas at a subsidised rate, which reduces its ability to compete with private operators in the creamy areas."[30]

The magnitude of the funds transferred through the ADC is not trivial. TRAI originally estimated the annual "access deficit" at Rs. 130 billion (about $2.85 billion), but recently cut its estimate by more than half to Rs. 53.4 billion (approximately $1.2 billion).[31]

ADCs are imposed only on some calls. The top panel of table 1 shows the original system of ADCs, and the bottom panel shows the charges that were adopted in 2005. The differences between the two systems are that the old system, but not the new, imposed higher charges on long-distance calls over 50 kilometers between calling areas (circles) and that the new system has lower charges for international calling but introduces higher prices for incoming calls. No ADCs are imposed on local calls or long-distance calls under 50 kilometers that originate and terminate in fixed-access networks. Likewise, no charge is imposed on these calls if they originate and terminate on wireless networks. All calls between fixed and wireless networks now pay Rs. 0.3 per minute (about 0.7 of a U.S. cent),

29. According to comments received from NCAER, December 2005.
30. Intelecon Research and Consultancy (2004).
31. TRAI (2003).

TABLE 1. Access Deficit Charges

Rupees per minute

Access deficit charges	Local calls	Intracircle calls		Intercircle calls			
		0–50 kms	>50 kms	0–50 kms	50–200 kms	>200 kms	ILD[a]
Before January 2005							
Fixed—Fixed	0.0	0.0	0.3	0.3	0.5	0.8	
Fixed—WLL(M)[b]	0.3	0.3	0.3	0.3	0.5	0.8	
Fixed—Cellular	0.3	0.3	0.3	0.3	0.5	0.8	4.25
WLL(M)—Fixed	0.3	0.3	0.3	0.3	0.5	0.8	
WLL(M)—WLL(M)	0.0	0.0	0.0	0.3	0.5	0.8	
WLL(M)—Cellular	0.0	0.0	0.0	0.3	0.5	0.8	4.25
Cellular—Fixed	0.3	0.3	0.3	0.3	0.5	0.8	
Cellular—WLL(M)	0.0	0.0	0.0	0.3	0.5	0.8	
Cellular—Cellular	0.0	0.0	0.0	0.3	0.5	0.8	4.25

				Intercircle calls	ILD calls	
				All distances	Outgoing	Incoming
After January 2005						
Fixed—Fixed	0.00	0.00	0.30	0.30		
Fixed—WLL(M)	0.30	0.30	0.30	0.30		
Fixed—Cellular	0.30	0.30	0.30	0.30	2.50	3.25
WLL(M)—Fixed	0.30	0.30	0.30	0.30		
WLL(M)—WLL(M)	0.00	0.00	0.00	0.30		
WLL(M)—Cellular	0.00	0.00	0.00	0.30	2.50	3.25
Cellular—Fixed	0.30	0.30	0.30	0.30		
Cellular—WLL(M)	0.00	0.00	0.00	0.30		
Cellular—Cellular	0.00	0.00	0.00	0.30	2.50	3.25

Source: TRAI (2003, 2005b).

a. ILD means international long-distance.

b. WLL(M) means literally, Wireless Local Loop (Mobile). This refers to a type of wireless service that was originally intended for only limited mobility.

whereas before 2005 they could pay as much as Rs. 0.8 (about 1.8 cents). The incoming foreign charge has been cut from Rs. 4.25 (about 9 cents) to Rs. 3.25 (about 7 cents), with a further cut to Rs. 2.5 (5.5 cents) for outgoing calls. The net impact of the ADC system is that private entrants, Indians who make international calls, and foreigners subsidize the state-owned incumbent.

The ADC fee structure is highly inefficient for two reasons. First, the price elasticity of demand is much greater for usage than for access. Hence, taxing usage to finance access substantially distorts the former to obtain very little gain in the latter. The significance of this distortion is growing as the usage of the telecommunications network for wireless data services grows. Access to data service providers is usually over fixed lines, and third-generation mobile telephones make extensive use of wireless data services. Thus, the ADC taxes a service of growing importance to consumers.

Second, the application of the tax to only some calls creates another distortion. An individual user who calls mostly people on one type of network has a financial incentive to acquire access service using the same technology as the parties being called. This incentive is not trivial: users who place five three-minute local calls a day can save Rs. 135 per month (about $3) by using the same technology for access as the people they are most likely to call.

Eliminating the difference in prices according to distance and whether the calls were between circles eliminated a third distortion. A call over a distance of 225 kilometers between adjacent states was taxed nearly three times as much as a call of the same distance within a state. Again, the difference was not trivial—Re. 0.5 (about 1 cent) a minute. This particular form of price discrimination had no plausible basis in efficiency, vertical equity (by income), or horizontal equity (within income groups), and the government made the correct decision to eliminate it.

The distribution of payments from the ADCs also varies according to the type of call. For local calls between fixed and mobile networks, the fixed network gets the fee regardless of whether it originates or terminates the calls. For long-distance charges between fixed-line carriers or other long-distance calls originating in a fixed line carrier, "bill and keep" applies—that is, the originating network keeps all of the revenue. For intracircle calls (whether local or long-distance) from mobile to fixed networks, the former pays the latter directly, but for intercircle calls, the long-distance carrier collects the tax and pays it to the terminating carrier. For international calls originating or terminating in a mobile carrier, the ADC goes to BSNL, the state-owned company that is the only wire-line access provider in most of India.

The magnitude of the ADC fee is the same for all fixed carriers, regardless of their actual cost of service. Thus, carriers for which usage is especially high receive a greater total subsidy than carriers for which usage is low. Local telephone networks typically have declining average costs per call as the number of calls increase, but the reimbursement formula gives greater subsidies to system with more calls per subscriber—and hence less of a need for a subsidy. Moreover, like most goods, telephone usage has a positive income elasticity of demand; hence, the reimbursement scheme provides a greater cross-subsidy from usage to access service in richer parts of India. Because rural areas generally have lower average incomes but higher costs per user, the magnitude of the subsidy is likely to be inversely proportional to a community's ability to pay for service. In short, the highest per capita subsidies will flow primarily to fixed carriers in the highest-income urban areas. Fixed carriers in low-income rural areas with no mobile service will receive the smallest subsidy. Even within BSNL, which receives most of the ADC payments, the incentive created by this system is to extend access service in rich urban areas before service is provided to low-income and rural areas.

The mobile companies have complained vociferously about the ADCs. The Cellular Operators' Association of India (COAI) noted that the case for subsidizing BSNL in this way is weak considering BSNL's profitability and the fact that "there is no legal, structural or financial accounting separation for BSNL's various product lines," making it impossible to know which of BSNL's activities are provided below cost.[32] In effect, the ADC amounts to little more than a government mandate that private firms subsidize the incumbent state-owned enterprise.

International long-distance carriers, notably the dominant firm VSNL, also object to the ADC. VSNL argues that the ADC has encouraged a grey market in international calls that are able to avoid the ADC.[33] The presence of ways for some users to evade the charge raises more fundamental issues than simply the adverse economic impact on VSNL. First, the fact that the ADC applies to only some international service providers creates a wedge in prices and gives rise to the possibility that a more costly provider will capture customers from more efficient firms. The ADC fee of more than 7 cents a minute is a significant fraction of the marginal cost of international calls and so drives a huge cost gap between the carriers that must pay the fees and those that do not.[34] Second, if the ADC charge is set to recover the total net loss from basic service, bypass of this sort will cause the ADC charge to increase for users who do not have access to the bypass alternative. Thus, the gap in prices created by the charge will widen, causing ever-widening distortions in patterns of use among services and providers.

TRAI had intended to impose ADC fees for five years and has recently reduced the fee so that it now represents about 10 percent of the sector's

32. Ramachandran (2003).
33. "ILD Operators Want Access deficit Charge Scrapped," *The Financial Express*, May 7, 2004.
34. Even between the U.S. and India, many calling cards offer prices below 10 cents a minute from the United States to India, which is especially noteworthy given that the ADC alone is about 9 cents a minute (http://www.nobelcom.com/nobelcom/jsp/productselection/productselection.jsp?from_country=1&to_country=130).

revenue rather than 30 percent when it was first introduced.[35] Because of the rapid growth in telecommunications infrastructure now under way and because much of the investment in the network is so durable, a five-year period will have an enduring effect on the structure and efficiency of telecommunications in India. Thus, a subsidy system that encourages inefficiency and entrenches the state-owned monopoly provider can create lasting costs; the methods for subsidizing basic service should be re-examined to minimize these costs.

OTHER PITFALLS. While not explicitly part of India's universal service plans, competition in mobile telecommunications arguably has done more to bring service to the poor than any policy to date. With the successful introduction of competition, mobile service has expanded dramatically. As figure 1 demonstrated, the number of mobile telephones substantially exceeds the number of fixed lines. While wealthy urban people are the first to adopt mobile telecommunications, the rapid growth in the share of the population with mobile phones reflects new access to telecommunications by people who were too poor or without the necessary political connections to get a telephone in the old state-owned monopoly regime.

Mobile telephony is predominantly available in urban areas but is rapidly expanding into rural areas as well. TRAI predicts that by 2006 more than half of all rural villages, representing 70 percent of the rural population, will have mobile service.[36] This rapid expansion of mobile service into rural areas without subsidies suggests that the current universal service plan may be misdirected. Indeed, India's policies to promote rural access may actually inhibit universal service. The ADC fees fall heavily on mobile users, including the poor. In other words, to the extent that the poor use mobile telephones, they subsidize the incumbent's fixed-line network, which serves mainly the middle class and businesses.

Subsidies and tariff regulations also discourage private investment. If a favored firm is subsidized for providing service in an area, other firms will be less likely to invest there. That is, a subsidized firm has artificially lower costs, making it more difficult for any other firm to compete. In addition, Singh notes that rural tariffs are lower than in other areas.[37] Artificially low tariffs discourage investments and competition in high-cost areas by making it even more difficult for an investor to compete with an inefficient incumbent.

35. TRAI (2004).
36. TRAI (2004).
37. Singh (2005).

Conclusion

While slow starts with reform in the 1990s leave India still lagging behind other developing countries, like China, telecommunications has largely become a huge success story in India. After years of quite nominal growth and extremely poor service, competition has emerged largely from wireless providers, resulting in explosive growth in the availability of telecommunications services. Like nearly every country in the world, India's telecom reforms have included policies intended to provide universal access to telecommunications services for all citizens.

India's universal service policies have focused primarily on rural areas and are funded through two primary mechanisms: a universal service levy and an access deficit charge. The universal service levy is a fee charged to all telecommunications providers, and the funds raised are distributed through an auction process. The auction design initially discouraged competition, and the incumbent state-owned provider, BSNL, has been the main recipient of these funds, though subsequent auctions had more robust participation, reducing the subsidies. The access deficit charge is a complex set of usage charges paid from entrants to the incumbent to compensate it, in theory, for its historical provision of service in high-cost areas.

India's universal service policies may unfortunately have the unintended consequences of deterring investment in precisely the areas it hopes to target. The subsidies discourage competition, and the most efficient operators are taxed to support the least efficient operator. Fortunately, most of the telecommunications market in India is so competitive that growth may not be hampered by these inefficient policies. Nonetheless, because telecommunications is such an important industry, it is crucial to minimize inefficiencies. India's best approach for achieving universal service is to ensure that its policies promote competition and do not favor any single firm over another.

Comment and General Discussion

Harsha V. Singh: The paper by Noll and Wallsten focuses on Universal Telecommunication Service, which is also referred to as Universal Service Obligation (USO) in common parlance. The paper's main conclusions are:

—Like nearly every country in the world, India's telecom reforms have included policies on universal access for all citizens.

—India's USO policies have focused primarily on rural areas.

—They are funded through two primary mechanisms: a universal service levy and access deficit charges.

—The auction design initially discouraged competition and the incumbent state provider, BSNL has been the main recipient of the funds.

—Access deficit charges are a complex set of usage charges paid from entrants to the incumbent to compensate, in theory, for its historical provision of services in high cost areas.

—India's USO policies may have unintended consequences of deterring investment in precisely those areas that it wishes to target.

—With subsidies, most efficient operators are taxed to support the least efficient operator.

—India's best approach to ensure achieving universal service is to ensure that its policies promote competition and do not favor any single firm over another.

The paper is a good attempt to understand and analyze the universal telecommunications service operations in India, but it remains subject to a number of shortcomings. I focus on these shortcomings in my comments, but that should not be seen as reducing in any way the positive contribution of the paper.

The shortcomings in the paper can be described, in parts, as

—being inaccurate or incomplete

—being out of date

The views are strictly those of the author and should not be ascribed to any other person, organization, or institution.

—overlooking the fact that the policy may have been implemented in a particular manner for reasons that may have been specifically mentioned or discussed by the Telecom Regulatory Authority of India

—not fully accounting for the changes that have taken place with respect to both USO and the access deficit charge policy.

ADC Policy

The authors are correct in characterizing USO policy in India as being mainly, though not exclusively, focused on the rural sector. They are, however, not entirely correct when they identify two separate initiatives, the USO Fund and the ADC payments, as funding the USO. The USO program is not funded by the ADC program. The focus of the ADC regime is to help the fixed-line operators to phase in their adjustment during a period when they are not in a position to carry out requisite tariff rebalancing and face a sharp decline in long-distance tariffs and competition from services such as mobile, which have tariffs with surplus for monthly rental and shorter-distance call tariffs (that is, their tariffs are more rebalanced). This aspect can be seen, for example, in paragraph 2 of TRAI's Interconnect Usage Charges (IUC) Regulation of October 2003, which states, among other things, that:

> Prior to the opening up of the telecom sector, the loss due to access deficit for basic service operators [BSOs] was being taken care of through a cross-subsidy from profits to BSOs from a share of the domestic and international long distance tariffs. With competition in the domestic and international long distance segments as well as among the fixed line/WLL(M) [wireless in local loop with limited mobility] and cellular mobile, leading to a sharp decline in the prevailing tariffs, the extent of cross subsidy has decreased in a major way. The competition in long distance markets continues and this will mean that the tariffs are likely to decline further. In such a scenario, since the access deficit for fixed line arises due to tariffs being specified for social reasons, there is a case for providing the access deficit amounts to these service providers. In contrast to the fixed line service providers, the other access providers have tariff forbearance for call charges, and are allowed to charge higher average amounts for local calls than those charged by fixed line operators.

This thought is reiterated in paragraph 42 of the TRAI's IUC Regulation of January 6, 2005, which states, among other things, that:

> ADC funds have been provided to fixed line service providers to cover the short-fall in revenues for access (i.e. the deficit), and in a situation of incomplete tariff re-balancing, sustain the service even with intense competition in the long distance market. The Authority recalled in this context that either due to the Regulator or the Government, an upper limit was imposed on the fixed line

rental charged by BSNL, and the other fixed line service providers were also constrained since BSNL has been the market leader in this regard. Consequently an access deficit arises because the revenues from rental charged are much below the cost based rental, with the latter being calculated based on the capital cost for the local call portion of the network (please see the Regulations of 24th January and 29th October, 2003 for more detail). A major portion, i.e. about three-fifths of the cost base for estimating the cost based rental is accounted for by the capital expenditure in the last mile portion of the network.

There is, of course, an overlap between the USO and the ADC regime in the sense that when the ADC amount is calculated, the extent of USO support already provided (which is part of the revenue of the operator) is deducted to estimate the ADC net base. As the USO amount keeps increasing, the net cost base for the ADC is reduced. Also, one of the criteria for distinguishing the main beneficiary of the ADC is rural coverage. However, it is not the only criterion for this purpose, nor is the focus of ADC policy the USO regime. This is shown, for example, by the fact that the ADC is provided also to fixed-line operators that have a virtually negligible presence in the rural areas.

Thus, the discussion on the ADC does not pertain to USO policy as such. However, it is given major importance in the paper and is subject to some of the shortcomings that are relevant to the paper, so I address it here.

The paper is not correct in stating that the amount of ADC is collected mainly from the private operators. It is collected from all operators, including the incumbent, BSNL. This is shown, for example, by table 6 in the TRAI's IUC Regulation of January 6, 2005 (reproduced here as table 2). A noteworthy feature of the group of other operators to which the last column of the table refers is that it includes BSNL mobile operations. Of course, the amount transferred from private operators—that is, other than from Bharat Sanchar Nigam Limited (BSNL) mobile and Mahanagar Telephone Nigam Limited (MTNL) mobile—to BSNL fixed is a net subsidy from the private sector operators to the public sector incumbent.[1] However, the relevant amounts are much lower than the total amounts of ADC mentioned in the paper. It is noteworthy that in February 2006 the TRAI further amended the ADC regime and reduced the overall amount of ADC funding by one-third, in comparison to the amount calculated for 2005.

Further, the paper mentions that the ADC regime should apply equally to all service providers. The TRAI did consider such a regime, which would be based, for example, on share of revenue, but was unable to implement

1. MTNL is a public sector telecom operator providing services to Mumbai and Delhi.

TABLE 2.   ADC Collections
Rupees in crores

IUC regime applicable	Total amount of ADC	Amount of ADC funding to BSNL	Amount of self-funding by BSNL fixed	Net amount of ADC to BSNL fixed funded by others
As per January 24, 2003 regulation calculations	13,518	12,381	10,084	2,298
As per October 29, 2003 regulation calculations	5,340	4,792	2,264	2,528

such a regime because it conflicted with some of TRAI's other important objectives, such as keeping the local charges for fixed calls low, not increasing the monthly rentals (as the amount of rental increase for collecting the same revenue for ADC would be very large), and keeping the tariff burden on domestic calls low. Thus, even though the TRAI wanted to switch to a revenue share regime for ADC (thus treating all service providers in the same way), it could not do so in view of its other objectives. Some of these points are discussed by the TRAI, for example, in paragraphs 49 to 60 of the Explanatory Memorandum of TRAI's IUC Regulation of January 6, 2005. The discussion in the Explanatory Memorandum specifically addresses a number of criticisms in the paper. As the situation has changed and the other objectives could be met together with imposition of a percentage revenue share regime, the TRAI has implemented such a regime for ADC. In the most recent amendment in the regime, dated February 23, 2006, the TRAI has changed the per minute ADC charge to a revenue share percentage (with revenues not including rural revenues for fixed-line service). It has kept the per minute ADC charge for international calls, while reducing the amounts per minute.

Another criticism in the paper is that the ADC regime does not cover all the calls in a similar manner. This too was considered by the TRAI and was not put in place for a combination of reasons, including the aforesaid objectives and the feasibility of implementing such a regime. The Explanatory Memorandum to the TRAI's regulations provides an indication of, and the reasoning for, the policy choices adopted by the regulator after weighing various objectives and taking into account the possibility of technically implementing various policy options.

Thus, in my view, an important weakness of the paper is that it has not adequately considered the issue of feasibility of implementation of policies. This is also valid, for instance, with regard to the criticism that the TRAI stipulated the same charges for ADC without taking into account the difference in costs among operators. This point completely overlooks the problems that one faces with implementing a regime within the technical constraints prevailing in India. Problems relating to implementation are discussed by the TRAI in its regulations as well as the consultation paper.

Likewise, the paper raises the issue of grey area traffic arising from the ADC regime as if it is an issue that has not been addressed or discussed by the TRAI. The effect of the regime on grey traffic has been addressed by the TRAI in several contexts, including for example, in paragraphs 61 to 69 of the Explanatory Memorandum of the January 26, 2005, IUC regulation. There, the TRAI recognizes the choice that it has to make between two conflicting objectives (one of them being addressing grey markets), the choice that it does make, and the reasons for doing so. It would have been appropriate for the authors to examine and discuss these aspects rather than just note that the regime gives rise to grey traffic and its associated problems.

In the context of grey traffic too, the evolving market situation has allowed the TRAI to achieve more of its composite objectives. For example, in its revision of the ADC regime in 2006, the TRAI has reduced the difference arising due to the ADC from 7 to 1.8 cents for outgoing calls and to 3.5 cents for incoming calls. This is to be seen together with the supplementary monitoring regime in place, within a mechanism involving the ministry, the vigilance agencies, and service providers (TRAI discusses this in its January 6, 2005 regulation). However, even with the changes there is still a significant arbitrage margin, but with the rapid growth that is taking place, it is likely that this part of the ADC regime too may be converted to a revenue share next year, before the whole ADC regime is phased out in 2008.

Another criticism is that the ADC charges are imposed on usage and not on the access price, and that such a policy does not favor the poor users because the price elasticity of usage is much higher than that for access. This argument overlooks several points, starting with the reason for instituting the ADC regime itself.[2] The ADC was put in place to help the fixed operators adjust in a situation where tariff rebalancing could not take place through policy or the market. In this situation, imposing a charge on access would be akin to undertaking tariff rebalancing, which was not possible in the first

2. There are a number of other points also, including the fact that in India one of the reasons for the increase in the subscriber base has been a reduction in the prepaid card amount, which is similar to an access price. This would suggest a very high elasticity for a reduction in access price and would also suggest that increasing access price does not benefit the poor. For another work arguing that raising access prices is not pro-poor, see Asian Development Bank and others (2006).

place. Second, any charge on access price would have to be relatively large charge, making it impossible to implement. In fact, one major constraint for the policymaker, after doing the tariff rebalancing that it implemented from 1999 to 2001, was the inability to make large changes in the price for monthly access and local calls. In fact, when the TRAI increased somewhat the local call price in 2003, the public sector operator, under pressure from the Parliament and the government, continued to charge the previous low local call price in its general tariff package. Ignoring this fact would have meant relinquishing to some extent the objective of allowing a phasing in of adjustment for the fixed operator, especially for BSNL which had a countrywide network and was the backbone for the telecom services in the country. (Even now, mobile network covers only about 35 percent of the country's population; in contrast, BSNL covers virtually the entire population: it has about 37,000 exchanges in the country, of which about 30,000 are rural exchanges. All of these exchanges are linked to reliable media; 90 percent are linked to fiber.)

One also needs to remember that the ADC regime is time bound and will expire in 2008 (in contrast, the USO policy will continue). Moreover, the regime involves a reduced amount of ADC each year, and as the implementation issues get tackled, the regime is changed to achieve the additional objectives that were not possible earlier.

A major point arising from the discussion on ADC in the paper is that the distortions introduced by the regime would lead to an adverse enduring effect on the structure and efficiency of telecommunications service in India. While the point regarding distortions is correct, the conclusion on the enduring adverse effects appears to be an exaggeration. Since 2003 (the year when the ADC regime was implemented), the additional subscriber base in India, mainly mobile, has been increasing at unprecedented rates, achieving each year more than what the country had achieved in the first fifty years of its independence (table 3). The monthly additional subscriber base in March 2006 was over 5 million. With such growth, the point regarding lasting adverse effect needs to be seriously reconsidered.

USO Policy

I will not address the details of the discussion on whether USO in telecom is a valid public policy objective. It is a policy followed by most countries that emphasize timely roll-out of telecom services in areas that are otherwise commercially unviable or unattractive, given the large investments required to meet the small demand reflected in the market. A case can be made that

TABLE 3.   Number of Fixed and Mobile Telephones and Telephone Density

Year ended March 31	Fixed (Million)	Mobile (Million)	Total number of phones per 100 population
1948	0.08	–	0.02
1951	0.10	–	0.03
1961	0.33	–	0.08
1971	0.98	–	0.18
1981	2.15	–	0.31
1991	5.07	–	0.60
1992	5.81	–	0.67
1993	6.80	–	0.77
1994	8.03	–	0.89
1995	9.80	–	1.07
1996	11.98	–	1.28
1997	14.54	0.34	1.56
1998	17.80	0.88	1.94
1999	21.59	1.20	2.33
2000	26.51	1.88	2.86
2001	32.44	3.58	3.53
2002	37.94	6.43	4.29
2003	40.62	12.69	5.11
2004	42.84	33.69	7.17
2005	45.90	52.21	9.08
2006	49.75	89.92	12.73

universal service is socially important, but as the policy is in place (as it is in most countries), and will remain, it is more important to discuss the policies used to achieve the USO objective.

The paper has correctly identified the limitation of the Indian auctioning scheme for USO, in the sense that the first round of bids is allowed only for those operators that have a license for the relevant service area. However, the paper overlooks an important point regarding implementation. Since there are existing licensees for the relevant license area, if they are not allowed a first option in the USO bid, there could be legal challenges from them and the process could be delayed.

Further, the USO policy has evolved over time, taking account of the operational difficulties and implementing changes to address them. Thus the effectiveness of these policies has increased with the changes implemented in the scheme.[3] While this is acknowledged in the paper, the bulk of the

3. See for example, Singh (2005).

analysis focuses on the initial phase when the existing fixed operators were not fully functional and their networks still have relatively narrow coverage.

Likewise, the paper mentions that a mid-term review of the outcomes of the first two auctions is in progress, but criticizes the USO scheme for not having adequate information on the number of village public telephones in working order. While this criticism was once valid, the USO scheme now has a built-in review process that will produce such information (and has already begun doing so).

Further, the government has been considering extending the coverage of USO policy to certain rural infrastructure for mobile service (such as towers and cable for part of the network).[4] That would further enhance the effectiveness of the USO assistance. Moreover, once a national-level license is put in place by the government, as suggested by the TRAI in its recommendations on unified licenses, the legal issue restricting the number of operators in each license area would be largely addressed as each license area would have significant competition from the most extensive service providers.

In addition, within a few years, the mobile telephony is likely to cover most of the rural population (it presently covers about 35 percent of the population), and the need for supporting the present form of USO policy would be substantially diminished. The TRAI has recognized this likelihood in a number of its public statements and in some of its papers.[5] Thus, the policy thrust with respect to telephony under USO will shift toward greater reliance on the market, and the focus of the future USO policy in India is likely to emphasize Internet and broadband over time.

Over time, there is quickly going to be greater reliance on the market and on mobile services, and thus the policy is following the lines suggested in the paper. However, the paper does not discuss the ongoing shift of the USO support policy toward Internet and broadband. In this regard, it is noteworthy that the public sector operator, BSNL, has linked about 30,000 rural exchanges with fiber and has installed about 500,000 route kilometers of fiber in the country under the New Telecom Policy 1999. This provides a very good basis for extending Internet and broadband to most parts of India.

Conclusion

The paper is a good attempt to assess the USO policy of India. It has a number of shortcomings, however, including the fact that it overlooks the nature

4. The ministry is in the process of moving a proposal for the cabinet to change the relevant Act of Parliament for this purpose.

5. See for example, TRAI (2004).

of policies that it mentions as being used in India to support USO, implementation constraints faced by the policymakers, attempts by the policymakers to balance different objectives (which include some of the objectives emphasized in the paper), the reasons given for the choice of specific policies, and ongoing policy developments that address to a greater extent the objectives which earlier could not be fully addressed due to implementation constraints. It is noteworthy, however, that the general direction of policies followed by the Indian government and the telecommunications regulator are akin to those emphasized by this paper. Because of this and the rapid growth in the sector, the concerns outlined in the paper are perhaps not as serious as the authors project.

General Discussion

Abhijit Banerjee commented that the theory under which everybody ought to have a telephone and, therefore, the maximization of the number of telephones was a social objective seemed completely bizarre and somewhat distant from the economic objective. He then went on to ask how the scheme for village public telephones worked. What was the incentive to maintain the telephone? The problem in some villages is that the village public telephone has not been repaired for many years. So, how do you build incentives for the telephone to be repaired, even if you offer a subsidy for it?

Harsha V. Singh responded that the latest USO scheme actually incorporated an implementation mechanism. If the telephone was out of service from seven to forty-seven days, the quarterly subsidy due to the provider was adjusted on a pro rata basis. If it was out of order for longer than forty-five days, the provider got no subsidy. Monitoring was done in various ways, including sample surveys and the examination of consistency in the billing data.

Another participant stated that if India wanted to use wireless service to increase teledensity in the rural areas, which is probably the way to go, it needed to price the spectrum appropriately. For many rural areas the spectrum should be given free, at least for some period of time, because at the moment the shadow price of the spectrum is zero. In response, Harsha Singh advised everyone to read the recommendations of the Telecom Regulatory Authority of India, where the thoughts expressed by the participant had been reflected.

Suman Bery addressed the issue of private versus public sector as the provider of the universal service in telecommunication. India has a situation where a public-sector incumbent exists and is here to stay, where the incumbent is powerful compared with the regulator, where the incumbent has most of the existing data and can manipulate them. This offers an interesting case study. If one tries to put an auction scheme in place on the basis of the data from the existing provider, a whole range of both institutional and public finance issues arises. The public finance issue is, of course, what determines the merit good and should this be a merit good? Once this set of issues has been sorted out, one must think of a clever auctioning mechanism—with ways of revealing willingness to supply, willingness to demand, and clear ways of designing the contract—that gets around some of these information problems. Bery suggested that the participants who thought analytically about these issues could give the authors a sense of the direction in which the paper could be extended.

Esther Duflo commented that there was no clear economic case for subsidizing use of the phone service. Arvind Panagariya concurred with Duflo, arguing that at best one could make a case for a subsidy to cover the fixed cost of laying down the line and putting up the phone booth. Beyond that, assuming a constant per-unit cost of making a call including the maintenance cost, the user should be charged for the service. Another participant stated that the marginal cost argument is important as a form of test as to whether the demand is sufficient to cover the maintenance cost.

Another participant responded to some of the issues raised. It had been mentioned that the price of the spectrum in the rural areas should be zero or heavily discounted. The TRAI is considering ways to introduce the spectrum pricing incentive to increase rural coverage in areas where the existing teledensity is very low. The participant also said that some participants appeared to have confused interconnectivity with roaming. For example, he said, if you are carrying, say, an Airtel mobile phone and you are going to some rural areas with BSNL coverage, but your telephone does not work, that is not an interconnection issue. The issue is whether BSNL has a roaming agreement with Airtel. The roaming agreement is a commercial agreement between two operators.

In the case of a new operator, the regulator intervenes to have the incumbent grant him a roaming agreement for a limited period, say, two years, during which the entrant must roll out his own network. After the end of that period, roaming agreements must be made by mutual consent on purely commercial grounds. It must be remembered that the BSNL entered the mobile market seven years after the mobile operators had been in business. For seven years these mobile operators could not significantly expand their mobile coverage in the rural areas. Now seven years after the BSNL has expanded the mobile coverage, it would be wrong to expect the regulator to force the BSNL to offer roaming agreements to other operators. The same problem has arisen in other countries such as Italy.

Pradeep Baijal of the TRAI said that he was an outsider to the telecom sector and looked at the USO issue dispassionately. He went on to provide the contrary perspective. He said he did not understand why we talked of a universal service obligation. A couple of years back we had 1 percent teledensity. Then we said, my goodness, we will have universal service obligation, which really meant that this 1 percent of the population would subsidize the remaining 99 percent in the waiting list, or the government will come in and look after them. That is our present policy. We are very bothered about the 99 percent. We say, let the 1 percent existing subscribers bear the burden of service for the rest.

Baijal noted that despite all the big statements, teledensity rose to barely 1.92 per 100 people from 1948 to 1998, a fifty-year post-independence period. After the government and TRAI made some regulatory changes in 2003, we added about 2 percent teledensity both in 2003–04 and 2004–05 and would add 3 percent in 2005–06. At the current rate of monthly growth, we should add 5 percent teledensity in 2006–07. Despite a high rate of taxation in India, intense competition in the sector, brought in by regulation, against the earlier cost plus regulation, tariffs are three-fourths of the lowest tariff anywhere else in the world, including China. Returning to the universal service obligation, Baijal said that 70 percent of the potential consumers are in the rural areas. They have access to extremely low tariff and as a result, there is a huge demand in the rural areas. It may be recalled that the urban mobile growth in India was catalyzed by the introduction of the new cellular technology and introduction of intense competition in the sector. It can be replicated in rural areas if mobile towers cover such areas. Last year the geographical coverage of our population was 20 percent. This year the geographical coverage has expanded to 30–35 percent. We are looking for the coverage to go to 70–80 percent because the demand is huge, but the dispersal of population presents a slightly suboptimal business case for operators. The policy should therefore aim at coverage of a large part of the population by mobile towers.

The second element of the policy should be to make the sharing of infrastructure mandatory if a subsidy is used to put in the towers. The incumbent has 30,000 exchanges with optical fiber through public subsidy, which it is not prepared to share. It has the support of international precedents. The incumbent has the right to interconnect to anywhere in the world but it says you cannot roam on my network.

Baijal said teledensity in rural areas could be expanded by bringing down the entry costs. Let anyone put in towers. We know the number of towers that should be there, he said. Give capital subsidy to anyone who would put up towers. That capital subsidy can come from the USO fund, which has high annual accruals and huge balances. The fund is statutorily meant for giving rural connectivity.

The session concluded with Wallsten making three points. First, the argument that India is mostly rural and that there is a huge gap between urban and rural penetration is not by itself an argument in favor of universal service. One needs more than that to defend universal service obligation and there is not a clear economic justification for it. The poor people in rural areas have more pressing needs than telecommunication services.

Wallsten's second point related to the issue of whether mobile telephony should be subsidized in rural areas. Subsidies available to some providers reduce the incentives of others to invest, since their competitors will be subsidized. Reduced incentives to invest can delay competition, which is the best method of improving telecommunications services.

Finally, spectrum is an important but complicated question. The answer is not automatic that it should be given free in rural areas. Auctions have been used successfully for spectrum and there is no reason why it cannot be auctioned in rural areas. But one of the problems of auction is that government must understand that its purpose is not to raise money for the treasury, but to allocate spectrum efficiently.

References

Asian Development Bank, Japan Bank for International Co-operation, and the World Bank. 2006. *Connecting East Asia: A New Framework for Infrastructure.* Washington.

Cannock, Geoffrey. 2001. "Telecom Subsidies: Output-Based Contracts for Rural Services in Peru." Washington: World Bank.

Chidambaram, P. 2005. "Budget 2005–2006: Budget Speech." New Delhi: Ministry of Finance.

Clarke, George, and Scott Wallsten. 2002. "Universal(ly Bad) Service: Providing Infrastructure Services to Rural and Poor Urban Consumers." *World Bank Policy Research Working Paper Series.* Washington.

Crandall, Robert, and Leonard Waverman. 2000. *Who Pays for Universal Service? When Telephone Subsidies Become Transparent.* Washington, DC: Brookings.

Cremer, Helmuth, Farid Gasmi, Andre Grimaud, and Jean-Jacque Laffont. 1998a. "The Economics of Universal Service: Practice." Economic Development Institute Discussion Paper. World Bank, Washington.

———. 1998b. "The Economics of Universal Service: Theory." Economic Development Institute Discussion Paper. World Bank, Washington.

Das, Pinaki, and P. V. Srinivasan. 1999. "Welfare Implications of Telecom Tariff Reform." *Economic and Political Weekly* 34: 672–75.

Department of Telecommunications. 2002. "Guidelines for Implementation of Universal Service Support." Government of India, Ministry of Communications and Information Technology, Delhi.

Desai, Ashok. 2004. "Indian Telecommunications: Trends and Portents." Working paper. National Council of Applied Economic Research, New Delhi.

Estache, Antonio, Vivien Foster, and Quentin Wodon. 2001. "Making Infrastructure Reform Work for the Poor: Policy Options Based on the Latin American Experience." World Bank, LAC Regional Studies Program, Washington.

Ghosh, Shyamal. 2004. Personal Communication.

Government of India. 1999. *New Telecom Policy 1999.* New Delhi.

Intelecon Research and Consultancy Ltd. 2002. "India: Universal Service Fund may fail to lift off." *regulateonline.org.*

———. 2004. "India: Continued Strife over Access Deficit Charge." *regulateonline. org.*

Intven, Hank, and McCarthy Tetrault. 2000. *Telecommunications Regulation Handbook.* Washington: World Bank.

Jain, Rekha, and Pinaki Das. 2001. "A Framework for Assessing Universal Service Obligations: A Developing Country Perspective." TPRC Research Conference on Communication, Information and Internet Policy, Washington.

Mueller, Milton Lawrence. 1997. *Universal Service: Competition, Interconnection, and Monopoly in the Making of the American Telephone System.* Cambridge, MA: MIT Press.

Noll, Roger G. 2000. "Telecommunications Reform in Developing Countries." In *Economic Policy Reform: The Second Stage*, edited by Aune O. Krueger, pp. 183–242. Chicago: University of Chicago Press.

Noll, Roger G., and Scott Wallsten. 2005. "Telecommunications Policy in India." Working paper. Stanford Institute for Economic Policy Research, Stanford, Calif.

Press Information Bureau, Government of India. 2005. "One Year of UPA Government: Major Decisions and Initiatives—Communications and IT." Ministry of Communications and Information Technology, New Delhi.

Ramachandran, T. V. 2003. "TRAI Consultation Paper on IUC Issues: Concerns on the Calculation of Access Deficit." Cellular Operator's Association of India, New Delhi.

Rosston, Gregory, and Bradley Wimmer. 2000. "The 'State' of Universal Service." *Information Economics and Policy* 12 (3): 261–83.

Shirley, Mary M., and Claude Ménard. 2002. "Cities Awash: A Synthesis of the Country Cases." In *Thirsting for Efficiency: The Economics and Politics of Urban Water System Reform,* edited by Mary M. Shirley, pp. 1–42. Oxford: Pergamon Press.

Singh, Harsha Vardhana. 2005. "USO Experience in India." Paper prepared for the Fifth Services Expert Meeting of the Organization for Economic Cooperation and Development and the World Bank, February 3–4, Paris.

Telecommunications Regulatory Authority of India (TRAI). 2000. "Consultation Paper on Universal Service Obligations." New Delhi.

————. 2002. "Recommendations of the TRAI on Universal Service Obligations." New Delhi.

————. 2003. "TRAI Finalises the Results of the IUC Review." Telecommunications Regulatory Authority of India, New Delhi.

————. 2004. "Growth of Telecom Services in Rural India: The Way Forward." New Delhi.

————. 2005a. *The Indian Telecom Services Performance Indicators April–June 2005*. New Delhi.

————. 2005b. "TRAI Announces a New Access Deficit Charge (ADC) Regime." New Delhi.